Reporting Vietnam

Reporting Vietnam
Media and Military at War

William M. Hammond

 University Press of Kansas

Published by the University Press of Kansas (Lawrence, Kansas 66049), which was organized by the Kansas Board of Regents and is operated and funded by Emporia State University, Fort Hays State University, Kansas State University, Pittsburg State University, the University of Kansas, and Wichita State University.

Library of Congress Cataloging-in-Publication Data

Hammond, William M.
    Reporting Vietnam ; media and military at war / William M. Hammond.
        p.   cm. — (Modern war studies)
    Includes index.
    ISBN 0-7006-0911-3 (cloth : alk. paper) ISBN 0-7006-0995-4 (pbk.)
    1. Vietnamese Conflict, 1961–1975—Press coverage—United States.
2. Armed Forces and mass media—United States—History.   I. Title.
II. Series.
DS559.46.H38   1998
959.704′38—dc21   98–23810

British Library Cataloguing in Publication Data is available.

Printed in the United States of America

10 9 8 7 6 5 4 3

For those who served

Contents

Preface

What went wrong between the military and the news media in Vietnam? No one could have anticipated, when the war began, the corrosive animosity that would develop between the two as the conflict evolved. Neither could anyone have predicted that the controversies the war sparked would continue to fester for more than a generation following its end, souring relations between the military and the news media into the foreseeable future.

There were, indeed, no precedents for what happened. The military and the news media had often been at odds in earlier conflicts, but both sides had decided during World War II that cooperation held more benefits than confrontation. The mood had continued through the Korean conflict. Although tensions increased, relative harmony had still prevailed.* The two began the Vietnam War in the same spirit. Before 1965, journalists questioned assertions of progress that flowed continually from the U.S. mission in Saigon, but they showed great sympathy for the American fighting man. The military reciprocated. Confidently rejecting censorship when the question arose, it set up a system of voluntary guidelines for the press that promised to maintain security without infringing on the rights of reporters. Over the years that followed, nonetheless, the attitudes of both groups turned. By 1971, the two sides were such angry antagonists that the president of the United States, Richard M. Nixon, would himself declare that, Communist depredations notwithstanding, "our worst enemy seems to be the press."

This book is an account of how it all came to be. A description of official efforts to manage the U.S. government's relations with the news media during the war, it is a synthesis and refinement of my two earlier volumes on that subject.

---

*See William M. Hammond, "The News Media and the Military," in *Encyclopedia of the American Military,* ed. John E. Jessup and Louise B. Ketz (New York: Scribner, 1994), pp. 2085–14.

The first of those studies, *Public Affairs: The Military and the Media, 1962–1968,* was published by the U.S. Army's Center of Military History in 1989. The second, covering the years between 1968 and 1973, appeared in 1996. Heavy with foot-notes, those works continue to be of use to the academic community in its research and teaching, and to the army in its leadership training. At more than a thousand pages when combined, however, they are too massive for all but the most dedicated general readers. This smaller work is for that broader audience. It contains all of the substance of its predecessors, less the dense background detail.

Like the works from which it is drawn, this book focuses on the interactions that developed between official agencies and the news media as the Vietnam War progressed. Although it is not primarily a history of the press itself, it has had to pay close attention to what the media said. To that end, my associates Ann David, James Broussard, and Douglas Shoemaker and I spent thousands of hours re-viewing the vast collection of news reports that the Defense Department gath-ered during the war. Beyond that, I also used the various works of Peter Braestrup, Lawrence Lichty, George Bailey, Daniel Hallin, and other historians who have researched the news media's war coverage.

On the whole, my selection of topics to treat and of news stories to cover took its direction from the materials contained in government files. If a news report or commentary generated enough attention on the part of officials to earn mention in their records, it gained much more prominence in my eyes than those stories and editorials, however well or ill conceived, that never attracted much formal official censure or approval. The presence of that report in official files meant, as well, that I had some chance of divining the role it played in official thinking, the stresses it created, and the reactions it sparked.

Straight news reports, particularly those appearing in the so-called elite press— the *Washington Post,* the *New York Times, U.S. News & World Report, Time, Life, Newsweek,* other periodicals of the sort, and the increasingly influential Ameri-can television networks—drew the attention of officials in the United States and South Vietnam, especially when they conflicted with the official line on an event. They thus often constitute the points of departure for my case studies. Editorials and commentaries by syndicated columnists also figure in, however, because they sometimes sustained the issues far longer than the news itself would have and provided the spur that prompted some action or reaction on the part of officials. Overall, I have attempted to balance the two kinds of reporting in order to create an effect that might approximate what an intelligent reader or viewer of the day would have experienced as he or she encountered the news and commentaries surrounding an event.

Many people contributed to the study. In addition to those mentioned in the prefaces to the two books from which this one is drawn, this book is heavily in-debted to a number of individuals. Stephen Ambrose of the University of New Orleans; Theodore Wilson of the University of Kansas; George Herring of the University of Kentucky; Colonel James Fetig (U.S.A. Ret.), formerly a chief spokesman for the National Security Council; and author Neil Sheehan backed the idea of an abridged work and offered helpful suggestions on ways to proceed. Brig. Gen. John W. Mountcastle, Jeffrey Clarke, Graham Cosmas, George MacGarrigle, Joel Meyerson, John Elsberg, and Arthur Hardyman of the U.S. Army's Center of Military History were also generous in their support. A number of these individuals read the work in whole or in part and made many important suggestions and corrections. Peter Braestrup of the Library of Congress was particularly helpful, always ready to drop what he was doing to give advice and to offer encouragement. His recent passing leaves a true void for all of us who knew him.

My editors at the University Press of Kansas deserve special thanks. Mike Briggs supported the project from the beginning and was always ready with a word of encouragement. Meanwhile, Rebecca Knight Giusti and her copy editors seemed always to have just the right word at hand.

My wife, Lilla, and my son and daughter, Michael and Elizabeth, deserve my special thanks for putting up with me over the two years it took to pull this book together. Their encouragement was constant and their patience exemplary. I could not have done it without them.

INDOCHINA
1969

0 _____ 150
Miles

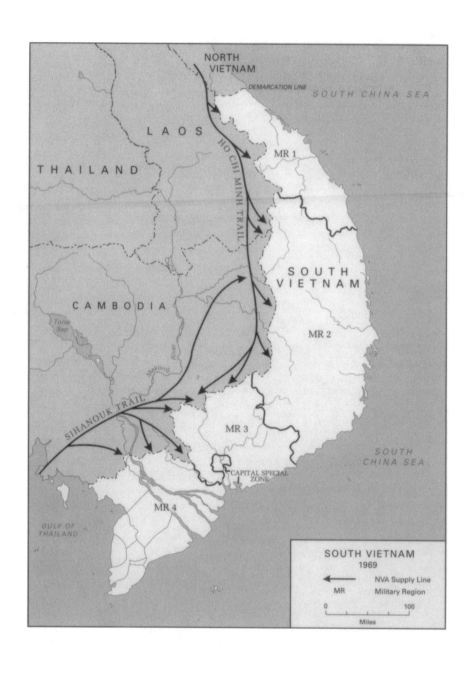

NORTH VIETNAM

DEMARCATION LINE

SOUTH CHINA SEA

LAOS

THAILAND

HO CHI MINH TRAIL

MR 1

SOUTH VIETNAM

CAMBODIA

Tonle Sap

MR 2

Mekong River

SIHANOUK TRAIL

MR 3

CAPITAL SPECIAL ZONE

SOUTH CHINA SEA

GULF OF THAILAND

MR 4

SOUTH VIETNAM
1969

NVA Supply Line

MR   Military Region

0   100

Miles

1

Taking Sides

No grasp on the war

In the beginning, during the 1940s and 1950s, the American news media had little interest in either Southeast Asia or Vietnam. Preoccupied with Europe and the cold war, they followed events in the region only fitfully, when breaking news occurred. The reporters who covered the emerging war in Vietnam—Robert Shaplen and Harold Isaacs of *Newsweek,* for example, scholar and sometime *Nation* correspondent Bernard Fall, Jim Lucas of the Scripps-Howard syndicate, and Australian freelancer Denis Warner—thus chronicled the rise of the Communist insurgency that racked South Vietnam but usually visited the country on short-term assignments. Only a few such as Fall stayed long enough to gain much expertise.[1]

The official agencies that handled the press in Vietnam during the early years had little control over what those reporters wrote. The French colonial government set up a system of censorship, but correspondents had only to travel to Singapore or Hong Kong to say what they wanted. As for the American news media, much of what they published on the subject reflected their nation's preoccupation with Communism and the cold war. When the *New York Times* issued its first editorial on Vietnam in January 1955, it thus warned its readers to be wary of Communist-controlled North Vietnam, which had just won its independence from France under the Geneva Agreement of 1954. In the same way, after the United States threw its weight behind Ngo Dinh Diem, who became South Vietnam's president in 1955, journals in the United States ignored the new leader's despotic tendencies and instead highlighted his anti-Communism.[2]

All that changed, however, toward the end of 1960, when the deaths of four hundred civilians in an abortive coup against Diem prompted the *New York Times* to dispatch Homer Bigart to South Vietnam's capital city, Saigon. Joining a small band of resident correspondents—Malcolm Browne of the Associated Press (AP), Ray Herndon of United Press International (UPI), Nicholas Turner

1

of Reuters, Pierre Chauvet of Agence France Presse, and stringers James Wilde of *Time* and François Sully of *Newsweek*—Bigart became the first of a flood of journalists who began to arrive as the war in Vietnam grew.[3]

The basic policy governing how the U.S. mission in Saigon handled these reporters reflected the way the administration of President John F. Kennedy conceived of the American role in the war. Claiming that the United States was in South Vietnam only to render advice and support in that nation's war against the Communists, U.S. spokesmen informed the press of American activities but followed the Diem regime's guidance on all other matters. The approach seemed right at the time. Preoccupied with the cold war in Europe, the United States hoped to strengthen the confidence and self-reliance of the South Vietnamese leaders so that they could shoulder their own burdens. It could hardly do so by usurping their prerogatives.[4]

The policy was bound, nonetheless, to cause trouble. When an insecure Diem ordered news of a failed military operation suppressed, U.S. spokesmen had no choice but to respond to queries from the press with "I have been ordered by the Vietnamese Joint General Staff not to talk to you about this subject." The news stories that followed inevitably made more of the no comment than of the defeat. One headline in the *New York Times* blared, "Americans Under Orders to Withhold News."[5]

Kennedy's secretary of defense, Robert S. McNamara, understood the problem, but he found it difficult to sidestep the definitions the United States had laid out for itself in South Vietnam. He ordered the officers advising Diem's troops to declassify information on the war "within their judgment," but since those individuals were under orders to defer to South Vietnamese instructions, little changed.[6]

The effort to close off information had, indeed, many attractions for American policy makers. To begin with, the enemy operated from within a society where every word was controlled, so his periodicals contained little more than propaganda for American intelligence analysts to read. By contrast, the free press of the United States gave the enemy important details on almost every aspect of U.S. policy. It was only natural, in that light, for American officials to seek to even the score by holding the press in check. In the same way, the good image of the United States seemed at risk in South Vietnam. Not only would the enemy make propaganda of any official American acknowledgment that the United States was assuming a more aggressive role in the war, there were also the American people to consider. Although well disposed to South Vietnam, they were preoccupied with the good life and little disposed to foreign adventures. If their lukewarm commitment to Diem faded because of negative news reporting, the effort to curb Communist ambitions in Southeast Asia might sink. The less said, so the reasoning went, the better.[7]

All of these concerns coalesced in a February 1962 directive designed to codify and stabilize handling of the press in Vietnam. Known as Cable 1006, it stressed all media outlets seem the same. (country) to country)

TAKING SIDES   3

that while newsmen would always concentrate on the activities of Americans, "it is not . . . in our interest . . . to have stories indicating that Americans are leading and directing combat missions." To remedy the problem, public affairs officers were to impress upon the Saigon correspondents that "frivolous, thoughtless criticism" of the South Vietnamese made cooperation with Diem difficult to achieve. They were also to keep reporters from accompanying military operations that might generate unfavorable news reports.[8]

The cable's authors justified it as an effort to achieve "maximum cooperation" with the press and instructed the U.S. ambassador to keep reporters informed as far as security allowed. While the directive recognized the right of the press to cover the war, however, it also stressed the need for officials to operate without the interference of newsmen. Far from opening information, it prompted the U.S. mission in Saigon to retain rules for the withholding of information that had long poisoned the ability of public affairs officers to deal effectively with the press.

Official spokesmen, for example, had never acknowledged that armed U.S. helicopters were taking offensive action against the enemy, or that American pilots were flying combat missions for the South Vietnamese air force. In the same way, they had never confirmed in public that those aircraft dropped flaming napalm (a form of jellied gasoline) on the enemy because the Communists might use the admission in their propaganda. It made no difference that reporters knew everything, or that a photograph of a napalm canister exploding in a great bloom had appeared on the cover of *Life* magazine in early 1962. Compounding the problems those policies created, high-level officials in both Saigon and Washington insisted on maintaining in public that South Vietnamese forces were succeeding in the war when the personal experiences of reporters suggested the opposite.[9]

both got work together

Correspondents dismissed the U.S. mission's optimism as one more attempt to placate Diem. They were correct, but only to an extent. The U.S. ambassador to South Vietnam, Frederick E. Nolting, Jr., and the commander of the U.S. Military Assistance Command, Vietnam (MACV), Gen. Paul D. Harkins, truly believed that South Vietnam's fortunes were improving, and they could cite impressive evidence to that effect. Following a decision in 1961 to reinforce Diem's armed forces, an augmented corps of American advisers had strengthened the South Vietnamese army's supply systems, improved its communications, and restructured the training of its troops. By early 1963, as a result, government forces riding armored personnel carriers and American helicopters were entering formerly inviolate enemy strongholds. Unfamiliar with the new tactics Diem's troops had learned and terrified of the helicopters, the Communists, for a time, suffered defeat after defeat.[10]

Progress also seemed to be occurring in the effort to win South Vietnam's peasantry to the side of the government, the so-called pacification program. Officials could cite statistics showing an impressive increase in the number of enemy-dominated areas subdued and declines in the frequency of enemy-initiated incidents. A program to regroup the people of the countryside into so-called strategic hamlets away from enemy influence also seemed to be succeeding. As a result, official spokesmen avowed, South Vietnam's people were for the first time learning basic democratic practices through the election of village leaders by secret ballot.[11]

Aware that the enemy was indeed off balance, many correspondents were at first upbeat themselves. Although Bigart and Sully both had doubts, *New York Times* reporters Robert Trumbull and David Halberstam were impressed. "Vietnamese Rout Red Unit," rang the headline on one Trumbull story. Halberstam's work was so favorable that the State Department commended the reporter to his employers for his accuracy and fairness. The trend, however, lasted only long enough for the Viet Cong to learn to cope with the new tactics their opponents had learned. When they had done so and once more began to win battles, questions inevitably arose in the press, and the answers reporters received were often less than forthcoming.[12]

One of the most detailed criticisms came from *New York Times* reporter Jacques Nevard. Writing in July 1962, Nevard drew upon well-placed sources within the U.S. mission to assert that the government's statistics were suspect. Since many occupants of strategic hamlets had been rounded up and forcibly resettled, he said, the walls around the villages seemed to have been designed as much to keep the residents in as to keep the Viet Cong out. Although nine thousand American servicemen had boosted the efficiency of South Vietnam's armed forces, the enemy also seemed to be growing stronger by the day.[13]

Halberstam likewise began to have doubts. "This is a war fought in the presence of a largely uncommitted . . . peasantry," he wrote on 21 October, "by a government that has yet to demonstrate much appeal to large elements of its own people. . . . The closer one gets to the actual contact level of this war, the further one gets from official optimism."[14]

Under normal circumstances, the U.S. mission ought to have been able to put the misgivings of the press to rest without great difficulty. An organization with a well-defined, coherent program and a measure of internal agreement among the members of its staff can often settle the doubts of outsiders by turning a unified face to the world. But unity of that sort was unattainable in the South Vietnam of 1962. Relying on statistics supplied by South Vietnamese officials—who well knew that the Americans wanted high enemy body counts and generous estimates of the percentage of the population loyal to the government—the ambassador and his top military aides asserted that the war was going well. Their subordinates, junior officers with extensive experience in the field, believed the opposite. Over time, as the situation in South Vietnam deteriorated, pressure between the two groups grew. Denied a hearing by their superiors, the dissenters turned to the press in hopes of putting their views within reach of agency heads in Washington. Inclined to place more reliance in government than in upstart reporters, editors viewed the reports that followed with distaste and edited away many of their most alarming conclusions, but enough got through to set the governments of both the United States and South Vietnam on edge. Concerned that the leaks would alienate Diem, officials at the U.S. mission threatened the reporters' sources but took no action against the Saigon correspondents themselves. Instead, on the theory that censorship of the news could only stimulate opposition to the war within the American public, they told Diem that success on the battlefield was the best antidote to criticism.[15]

Diem shared none of the Americans' inhibitions. He censored his own press and could not understand why the United States was unable to do the same. Believing that the Saigon correspondents were in sympathy with the Viet Cong, he decided to move against them on his own. Bigart and Sully were his first targets. An old war correspondent with vast experience, Bigart had been blunt in saying that Diem's disorganized government could never overcome an enemy as resourceful as the Viet Cong. A freelancer who lacked Bigart's experience, Sully had been just as direct. Worse, he wrote for *Newsweek,* whose editors had never made any secret of their dislike for Diem and his regime.

The president made his move in March 1962 by ordering the two reporters deported. Since the expulsion of correspondents representing periodicals as influential as the *Times* and *Newsweek* could only complicate efforts to maintain public and congressional support for the war, the State Department instructed Nolting to back the reporters. The ambassador complied, warning Diem that news stories praising the success of recent helicopter operations might cease if the two reporters were expelled. Diem understood and relented, but he nonetheless cut off Sully's access to official interviews and to government-sponsored trips into the field.[16]

The situation held until July, when it began to come apart. Just before leaving for home at the end of his tour of duty, Bigart took a parting shot at Diem by blaming the war's lack of progress on the president's failure to win the loyalty of his people. He then predicted astutely that if Diem failed to reform his autocratic regime, the United States would have to either replace him with a military junta or commit troops to the war. Shortly thereafter, Sully followed with a story of his own. Arguing that American pilots could fly helicopters for the South Vietnamese but could never give them an ideology worth dying for, he quoted an unidentified South Vietnamese general who attributed most of the country's ills to Diem. Adding a twist of its own, *Newsweek* accompanied the story with a picture of South Vietnamese militia women commanded by Diem's sister-in-law, Madame Ngo Dinh Nhu. The caption read: "Female militia in Saigon: the enemy has more drive and enthusiasm."[17]

Bigart left the country before Diem could react, but Sully remained well within the regime's reach. Shortly after Sully's story appeared, Madam Nhu issued an open letter expressing her "profound indignation" at his disrespect for South Vietnam's women. Government-controlled newspapers then opened

President Ngo Dinh Diem entertains Ambassador Frederick E. Nolting. (Naval Photographic Center)

up, accusing the reporter of opium smuggling, sexual perversion, and spying for the Viet Cong. The police put him under surveillance, and Diem once more ordered him to leave.[18]

The rest of the Saigon correspondents interpreted Diem's move as a threat to themselves but were divided on what to do. Reporters on temporary duty in Vietnam favored a moderate protest, while the regulars wanted something more. Suspicion of Sully grew. At one point, newsmen at a meeting convened to decide on an approach turned on the reporter to ask pointedly whether he had ever been a Communist or a French spy. In the end, only six of the journalists agreed to sign a strongly worded protest to Diem. The remainder issued a more cautious statement the next day.[19]

Emboldened by the affair and convinced that the United States would do little to deter him, Diem next moved to permanently ban *Newsweek* from South

Vietnam. Nolting again protested. Any attempt to banish such an important magazine, he said, would convince the world that South Vietnam was too weak to stand criticism and that Diem was attempting to hide his failures. If that happened, the American people would begin to question their government and would throw further support for the regime into doubt.[20]

Diem backed off, but the respite proved temporary. On 25 October, he moved against another reporter, James Robinson of NBC News. Robinson had offended Diem by remarking in private that his family was a "clique" and that a long interview with him had been a waste of time. The U.S. mission made the usual round of appeals, but this time its arguments failed. Within days, Robinson was on his way to Hong Kong. A short while later, Diem's brother Ngo Dinh Nhu asserted that the regime intended to expel any reporter who belittled his family or questioned his country's ability to win the war.[21]

The moment called for an American response. If the U.S. mission continued to tolerate obvious provocations, Diem might decide he had a free hand to do what he wanted to the press. For a time, Nolting considered a public repudiation of Diem's actions, and the Kennedy administration gave some thought to threatening a cutoff of U.S. support for cultural programs, but in the end no one did anything, and even the news media failed to protest. As one State Department officer explained, neither Sully nor Robinson was among the "outstanding" members of his profession, and NBC was unsure whether Robinson deserved all-out support. The result was predictable. Diem made no effort to change his ways, and the Saigon correspondents once more concluded that Nolting and his staff were against them.[22]

Over the days that followed, the Diem regime added to the effect by fanning the flames. Long annoyed by critical news stories based on interviews with American advisers and members of South Vietnam's military, government officials ordered all correspondents visiting units in the field to submit their questions to commanders in advance. Those officers were then to clear their responses with higher headquarters. Taking the process one step further, the commander of the South Vietnamese Seventh Division issued instructions requiring reporters to seek special permission before covering his units in the field. Since the Seventh was fighting in South Vietnam's Mekong delta, a region south of Saigon easily accessible to reporters, the ruling hit correspondents hard.[23]

The State Department instructed Nolting to seek suspension of the bans, and the South Vietnamese complied, but only after a month's delay. In the interim, on 9 November, the AP outlined the Saigon correspondents' complaints in a dispatch that went around the world. David Halberstam followed on 21 November with an angry denunciation in the *Times* that all but blamed the U.S. mission for what had happened. In an even more emphatic memorandum to his editors, the reporter asserted that the South Vietnamese armed forces were attempting to "veto" adverse stories in the press by keeping reporters from getting the news. The *Times* passed the memo to the State Department. Officials there responded that they were trying to have the restrictions rescinded. They nevertheless demolished whatever good their revelation might have caused by asserting that the United States was only a guest of the South Vietnamese and had to be circumspect when commenting on their war.[24]

Considering themselves under threat, reporters retained their informal military sources but pulled away even more from the U.S. embassy and the viewpoint its spokesmen represented. Depending on the word of angry South Vietnamese officials, indignant U.S. advisers, and bitter American pilots who risked their lives daily without recognition, they began to seek the evidence they needed to prove that Diem was losing the war.

They found it in January 1963, shortly after the South Vietnamese lifted their restrictions on access to the delta. Learning that a Viet Cong company was operating near the village of Ap Bac in the delta province of Dinh Tuong, the Seventh Division launched a heavy attack in hopes of an easy victory. When the force reached its objective, however, it encountered not a company but the 514th Viet Cong Battalion, a well-trained and highly motivated regular unit of nearly four hundred men. Although the South Vietnamese force was almost three times the size of its quarry and had the benefit of fifty-one U.S. advisers, it let the enemy escape.[25]

During the fighting, in just five minutes, five U.S. helicopters went down: two to enemy fire, one to a mechanical failure, and two because their pilots flew gallantly into the enemy's guns to rescue comrades who were already safe. The advisers called for an airborne drop to the east to plug the enemy's one route of escape. The paratroopers dropped to the west, where friendly fire killed some. Toward dusk, an inaccurate air strike caused more casualties. The next morning, long after the enemy had gone, artillerymen shelled their own troops for more than ten minutes.[26]

Bad luck and inexperience were to blame for some of what happened, but Diem's own policies contributed. Concerned that a victorious officer might attract enough popular support to challenge his rule, the president had long before stifled the initiative of his commanders by reprimanding those who took too many casualties. The officers on the scene at Ap Bac—none above the rank of captain—knew the game. Allowing air strikes to do the work, they delayed and made purposeful mistakes.[27]

The Saigon correspondents learned of the battle following the first day's fighting, but they made up for lost time by traveling to the scene to interview the advisers who had been present. Since those officers were angry and willing to talk, the reporters learned a great deal. Several also overheard a classified briefing convened in an unsecured area for General Harkins. In the end, their dispatches read like the official report of the operation but with many lurid details. One quoted an adviser who had exclaimed that the battle had been "a miserable damn performance." Others mistakenly told of how one of three dead Americans had gone down while begging reluctant Vietnamese infantrymen to advance.[28]

The editorials and commentaries that followed were biting. The *Washington Daily News,* for example, termed Ap Bac a "humiliation." The *Baltimore Sun* described the enemy "slipping away . . . ahead of a half-hearted Vietnamese pursuit." The *Detroit Free Press* wondered how Diem's harsh dictatorship could give peasant soldiers any motive to fight at all.[29]

In response, the U.S. mission backpedaled. Concerned that the uproar could only harm relations with Diem (and despite classified cables to Washington affirming that the whole affair had been a fiasco), official spokesmen attempted to put a good face on what had happened. Confessing to occasional setbacks, Harkins, in particular, declared that the South Vietnamese were gaining nonetheless. "Anyone who criticizes the fighting of the Armed Forces of the Republic of Vietnam," he said, "is doing a disservice to the thousands of gallant and courageous men who are fighting in the defense of their country."[30]

Harkins's allegation to the contrary, the Saigon correspondents had exercised considerable restraint in what they had written about Ap Bac. Refusing to repeat many of the truly extravagant remarks advisers had made, they had caught the essence of what had happened. Neither had they meant any disservice to the United States. Instead, disagreeing with tactics, they had argued that the U.S. government should push Diem aside, take control of the war itself, and allow American efficiency and know-how to do the job.[31]

The battle nonetheless marked a divide in the history of the war. Before it, American reporters had criticized Diem and badgered embassy officials but had still viewed themselves as making common cause with their nation's government. After it, they decided their government was lying and withdrew. Believing the press was out of control, Ambassador Nolting, General Harkins, and other high U.S. officials did the same. Enmity began to grow. "I'll get you, Paul Harkins," an angry Halberstam is reported to have shouted while driving past the general's quarters in Saigon. High officers felt the same about the press. One of Harkins's principal subordinates, Air Force Maj. Gen. Milton B. Adams, for example, avowed bitterly in private that official tolerance for the press was the only real frustration he had experienced during his tour of duty in Vietnam.[32]

The situation in South Vietnam worsened dramatically on 8 May 1963, when a crowd of Buddhists assembled at a radio station in Hue, the nation's second-largest city, to protest an order by the Diem regime banning the display of religious flags on the birthday of the Buddha. The group's spokesmen pointed out that Roman Catholics had been permitted to display their flags just a few days before to celebrate the birthday of Hue's archbishop, Diem's brother Ngo Dinh Thuc. When the crowd refused to disperse, an army unit fired on the demonstrators, killing nine.[33]

Seeking support, Buddhist leaders contacted the U.S. embassy in Saigon but found that the Americans were intent on stabilizing Diem. Recognizing that the Saigon correspondents had access to a worldwide audience, the Buddhists then decided to cultivate the press. From then on, reporters had easy access to the

movement's leaders, who gave them the dates, times, and locations of future protest demonstrations. They kept it all to themselves.[34]

Over the next several months, as the Buddhists marched and Diem's police
retaliated, sensation followed sensation in the press. Perhaps the high point came
on 11 June 1963, when AP reporter Malcolm Browne photographed a Buddhist
monk as the man splashed himself with gasoline and set himself ablaze to protest
Diem's policies. The picture went around the world.

Diem blamed everything on the Communists, but the Buddhists had, in fact,
spurned offers of aid from North Vietnam. Diem's refusal to open up his government was at the root of the disturbances. Lacking any outlet for their discontent,
South Vietnam's middle classes had come to sympathize with the demonstrators,
and officials at all levels of the nation's bureaucracy were feeding inside information on the government's intentions to Buddhist leaders.[35]

Meanwhile, rather than deal directly with the press as the Buddhists did, Diem
took the opposite approach. Besides censoring news dispatches, he allowed his
police to shadow reporters and to assault them when they covered Buddhist demonstrations. U.S. embassy officials expressed concern at these tactics, particularly Diem's use of American-armed and American-trained police to harass reporters and to beat Buddhists while television cameras recorded everything. Yet
for the most part they again compromised. Making vehement representations
in private and on one occasion even warning Halberstam to move to a hotel because he made too easy a target at his rented house, they did nothing in public
that might alienate Diem. General Harkins's command even stopped flying reporters to Hue lest members of the regime come to suspect that MACV agreed
with the reporters.[36]

Willing to believe the worst of Diem, the Saigon correspondents, for their part,
sometimes made mistakes. On one occasion, they became convinced that Diem's
forces had used blister gas on Buddhist demonstrators. Aware that the United
States had never supplied South Vietnamese forces with such agents, Harkins's
spokesmen requested a delay in publication until they could investigate. Most reporters complied, but one pushed ahead. In the end, degenerated tear gas manu-
factured during World War II proved to be to blame, but by then the damage had
been done. In the same way, reporters time and again referred to South Vietnam
as a predominantly Buddhist nation. In fact, the bulk of the country's people
were ancestor worshipers, and the Buddhist protest itself was mainly an urban,
politically oriented phenomenon.[37]

If distorted news stories posed problems, however, the effects of information
leaked to the press by American officials critical of Diem were far worse. On one
occasion in June, for example, the U.S. mission's chargé d'affaires, William Trueheart, flailed Diem with strong language during a meeting and threatened that
the United States might dissociate itself from his activities if they continued. Almost a direct command from the United States, the episode was certain to hu-
miliate Diem if it became public. Yet Trueheart had hardly finished speaking be-

General Paul D. Harkins. (Indochina Archives)

fore a high-level official in Washington informed Max Frankel of the *New York Times* of the encounter. The newspaper put the story on page 1, destroying Trueheart's ability to deal with Diem from then on.[38]

The Defense Department could do little about leaks from the State Department, but it resolved to put the Saigon correspondents' main sources, the advisers, under leash. At about the time of the Trueheart affair, McNamara thus instructed the agency responsible for training the army, the U.S. Continental Army Command (CONARC), to instruct U.S. Army personnel in South Vietnam to confine their conversations with reporters to "areas of personal responsibility and knowledge" and to avoid generalizations. Broad estimates of progress were to be the province of higher-ups.[39]

It was all common sense and should have gained little attention, but CONARC could not leave well enough alone. After stating its basic policy, it went on to explain in detail how the advisers should deal with reporters. "Your approach . . . should emphasize the positive aspects of your activities and avoid gratuitous criticism. Emphasize the feelings of achievement, the hopes for the future, instances of outstanding individual or unit performance and optimism in general. But don't destroy your personal credibility by gilding the lily. As songwriter Johnny Mercer put it, 'You've got to accentuate the positive and eliminate the negative.'"[40]

US
censoring
Saigon
reporters?

Although the memorandum was for internal use only, the frictions separating the top of the U.S. mission from its lower levels ensured that the document would fall into the hands of the press. Indeed, shortly after it appeared, David Halberstam acquired a copy and made it the subject of a dispatch to the *Times.* Avoiding the phrase *news management,* he subtly implied the same thing by quoting a cover letter accompanying the memorandum that said, "Indoctrination of military personnel in the importance of suppressing irresponsible and indiscreet statements is necessary." Since *indoctrination* connoted *brainwashing* in the minds of many Americans, the reporter's meaning leaped out at his readers. Halberstam strengthened the suggestion by noting that CONARC had used excerpts from his stories in the *Times* out of context in making its point that the press was guilty of distorted reporting.[41]

In itself, the dispute over the CONARC memorandum was minor. A far more damaging article ran in August, when the *New York Times* published a major story by Halberstam dealing with conditions in the Mekong delta. For some time, Halberstam, Neil Sheehan of the AP, and *Time* stringer Merton Perry had been researching stories on the fighting in the region to establish once and for all whether the war was going well or poorly. Sheehan's account was never published, and *Time* refused to carry Perry's because it contradicted the magazine's pro-Diem line, but the *New York Times* put Halberstam's on page 1 of its 15 August edition. Drawn from knowledgeable sources in the field, the report challenged the U.S. government's cautious optimism by asserting that the Viet Cong had become so "cocky" in their self-assurance that they were even picking fights.[42]

Statistics, Halberstam said, showed what was happening. South Vietnamese casualties had increased by 33 percent, while those of the enemy had fallen. Government weapons losses, a major source of armaments for the Viet Cong, had risen by 20 percent, while those of the enemy had declined by 25 percent. Meanwhile, many South Vietnamese administrators tended to believe that the strategic hamlets, by drawing people out of sparsely settled regions, had enhanced the enemy's ability to move at will through remote sections of the delta. As a result, the Communists had established more than thirty fortified villages in the center of Vinh Long Province, an area the government had once hoped to secure with ease. The story concluded with a quotation from an anonymous American official who seemed baffled. "Frankly," the man said, "we civilians don't have the answer yet and the military doesn't either. I'm just not sure what it is."[43]

The report drew vehement responses from within both the government and the news media. Secretary of State Dean Rusk took up the issue personally, commenting pointedly at a Washington news conference that Halberstam was wrong. Incidents of Communist sabotage and propaganda had decreased in the delta, he said, and the strategic hamlet program was drawing new areas of the region under government control. Marguerite Higgins of the *New York Herald-Tribune* also spoke out. Avowing that she had just returned from a four-week visit to South

Vietnam in which she had received briefings from the highest officials, she said she could not understand how the Viet Cong could conduct the "mobile warfare" Halberstam had alluded to when they had "no vehicles and no airplanes." The furor became so vehement, for a time, that it prompted the *Times* to suggest that Halberstam tone down his dispatches. The reporter threatened to resign, and nothing more was said.[44]

Over the days that followed, the U.S. mission in Saigon conducted a lengthy review of the article. The report it produced asserted that roads were open in the delta, that rice deliveries were reaching Saigon, and that the percentage of the population under government control continued to rise. As for Halberstam's statistics on weapons losses and improvements in Communist equipment, they made little difference. The enemy could never find every rifle dropped on a battlefield nor ever surmount the enormous tactical advantage the arrival of the helicopter had given the South Vietnamese. The reporter's remarks about the strategic hamlets were also wide of the mark. The program would have a material effect on the enemy's mobility once it had developed enough to free militia units for duty in the field.[45]

The rebuttal corrected a few of Halberstam's statistics but otherwise fell short, as some of MACV'S own internal assessments showed. Nine months earlier, Col. F. P. Serong, an Australian adviser on counterinsurgency on Harkins's staff, had submitted a report that could have been an outline for Halberstam's analysis. The enemy captured many high-quality weapons, Serong said, while Diem's forces took mainly inferior ones. As for the strategic hamlets, the regime had built most near important roads and had neglected inaccessible regions. The government thus controlled the country's communications arteries but allowed the enemy to dominate the intervening spaces.[46]

One month later, Col. Daniel B. Porter, the U.S. Army's senior adviser in the Mekong delta region, told General Harkins that leadership within the South Vietnamese armed forces continued to lag. As long as that was so, he said, the nation's soldiers would falter in combat. Harkins was unreceptive. When South Vietnam's troops faced the enemy "man to man," he said, they won. Good training and equipment could only stimulate their self-confidence. The United States should allow them to do the work and should refrain from assuming the burden itself.[47]

Although Harkins had a point, major segments of the news media in the United States had by then begun to turn against the long-term solution he favored. Diem's oppression of the Buddhists was the reason. When Madame Nhu referred callously to a Buddhist suicide as "another monk barbeque-show," the *Chicago Tribune*—no bastion of liberalism—remarked that if the decision to extend massive U.S. support to South Vietnam had been sound, the decision to support Diem's dictatorship had been unsound, and there was "no diplomatic or humanitarian reason" for it to continue. Anti-Communist *U.S. News & World Report,* meanwhile, denied that the Buddhists had ever been subject to religious

What could have been done differently?

persecution but still asserted that Diem's repressive tactics were counterproductive. The choices that remained were few and difficult. The United States could withdraw from South Vietnam, assume command by injecting its own troops into the fighting, or take the hard line with Diem that would be needed if further progress were to occur.[48]

U.S. News chose the third alternative, but that required time, and time was running out. On 16 August, the day after Halberstam's report appeared, Henry Cabot Lodge replaced Nolting as U.S. ambassador to South Vietnam. The scion of an old political family and an aristocrat of sorts, he was just the kind of American who might have achieved rapport with Diem. Despite his pleasing demeanor, however, Lodge possessed an instinct for action that verged on the ruthless, and the situation he found in Saigon left little room for the pleasantries that might have prevailed under other circumstances. For Diem and his brother Nhu had chosen the interval between Nolting's departure and the new ambassador's arrival to settle with the Buddhists once and for all.

They made their move early on 21 August, after South Vietnam's military chiefs complained that the disturbances were harming the morale of their troops and sought permission to declare martial law and to send monks from outlying areas home. Diem and Nhu acceded to the request, but Nhu added a twist of his own that night. Suspecting military plots against the regime and seeking to discredit the officer corps, he disguised elite, U.S.-trained police and special forces units as regular army soldiers and sent them crashing into pagodas all across South Vietnam. They beat and arrested more than fourteen hundred monks. On the day after the raid, Nhu cut the telephone lines to the U.S. embassy and the homes of American diplomats to ensure that the Americans' first knowledge of what had happened came from him. He then blamed everything on the army, avowing that a declaration of martial law had never even crossed his mind.[49]

With little reason to suspect Nhu's story, the U.S. mission allowed the Voice of America to broadcast news that the attack had been entirely an army operation. Later in the day, following the arrival of better information, the State Department abandoned the approach. But even then, unsure of the full dimensions of what had occurred and in hopes of chastising Diem without breaking with him, it issued only a lukewarm rebuke.[50]

If the U.S. government wavered, the Saigon correspondents had no doubts. Days before the raids, disaffected South Vietnamese officials close to Diem had informed them that an attack was imminent. With ample time to prepare, they watched what happened firsthand.[51]

Nhu tried to stop them by closing Saigon's telephone and telegraph office and installing rigid censorship. He also sanctioned the arrest and interrogation of reporters. At one point, harassment became so intense that policemen confiscated an automobile hired by CBS correspondent Marvin Kalb containing eight thousand dollars' worth of camera equipment while it was parked directly in front of General Harkins's headquarters. Only Joseph Fried of the *New York Daily News*

Malcolm Browne's photo of a monk immolating himself. (AP/Wide World Photos)

got anything through. Gaining an interview with Madame Nhu by allowing her to censor his story personally, he saw his dispatch waved through censorship unscathed, with only the adjectives *despicable* and *miserable* added to each mention he had made of the Buddhists.[52]

In the end, nevertheless, Nhu's efforts had little effect. Rather than risk damaging speculation in the United States, the U.S. embassy opened its own cable facilities to the press. After the State Department ended the practice because it threatened to jeopardize American communications in countries more hostile to U.S. ends than South Vietnam, reporters turned to "pigeons"—travelers, military aircraft crews, anyone leaving the country—to smuggle their reports to Hong Kong and Singapore for transmission to home offices. When the U.S. command threatened military aircraft crews with courts-martial if they participated, the reporters switched to employees of civilian airlines.[53]

Aware all along that Nhu was involved in the attacks, the correspondents checked among their sources, confirmed the facts, and put the news on the wire. When the U.S. mission insisted on blaming the South Vietnamese army, the contrast between the two approaches seemed so striking that the editors of the *New York Times* placed the reports side by side on page 1 of the paper's 23 August edition.[54]

The situation remained fluid until embassy officers interviewed a number of

very disorganized.

prominent generals and members of their staffs. Maj. Gen. Tran Van Don, the commander of the South Vietnamese army for the duration of martial law, told them that the Voice of America's announcement blaming the army had hurt the service's standing with the people. He added ominously that things could not revert to what they had been and that certain government ministers "had to be changed." When other officers seconded the general, the Voice of America quickly corrected its error.[55]

By that time, the news media in the United States had begun to speculate that the Kennedy administration was reassessing its relationship with Diem. Official sources denied the stories, but within two days the State Department revised its instructions to Ambassador Lodge. "The U.S. government cannot tolerate a situation in which power lies in Nhu's hands," it said. "Diem must be given a chance to rid himself of Nhu. . . . If he remains obdurate . . . we must face the possibility that Diem himself cannot be preserved."[56]

Although U.S. officials contacted some of Diem's generals to investigate the possibility of a coup, those officers were as yet unprepared to overthrow the regime. The U.S. mission was itself divided. Lodge believed that the situation was deteriorating rapidly, but Harkins declared emphatically that nothing of the sort was happening.[57]

The new ambassador listed his misgivings in a long cable to President Kennedy. Summarizing a "very private" conversation he had held with Maj. Gen. Duong Van Minh, one of South Vietnam's most influential officers, he reported that the general believed the enemy was gaining because Diem was alienating South Vietnam's people. Meanwhile, corruption was rampant within the government, the theft of American aid was common, and the heart of the army was not in the war. By then, the Saigon correspondents had made many of Lodge's points in their dispatches, and editorials to the effect that Diem had "outmaneuvered" the United States were beginning to appear. Criticism was also rising in Congress, where Senator Frank Church of Idaho introduced a resolution calling for an end to U.S. aid to South Vietnam if Diem continued his inept policies.[58]

President Kennedy dispatched Secretary of Defense McNamara and Gen. Maxwell D. Taylor to Saigon on a fact-finding mission. By that time, the Saigon correspondents had become so prominent in the debate over the war that the Defense Department devoted one-quarter of a 135-page trip book for McNamara to a refutation of their arguments. Included was a 24-page attack on Halberstam's Mekong delta report and a slashing commentary on the Saigon correspondents that had appeared in the 20 September edition of *Time*. The reporters were so opinionated, *Time* had avowed, that they dismissed any version of events other than their own, particularly any that suggested South Vietnam might be winning the war.[59]

In the end, McNamara chose a middle course. Asserting that enough progress was occurring to allow the withdrawal of most U.S. personnel by 1965 if Diem took hold of his problems, he recommended a suspension of long-term development aid to prod the president toward reform. Kennedy followed that advice, suspending some aid programs and terminating support for the special units that had carried out the pagoda raids. In the end, however, his moves had little effect. Repression of the Buddhists continued, leading a monk to burn himself to death in protest on 5 October while three American correspondents watched. Police smashed the reporters' cameras.[60]

A short while later, interpreting Kennedy's stronger line toward Diem as a signal that a coup might be welcome, a group of generals contacted U.S. officials to see what the American position would be if they took action. The Kennedy administration again chose a middle course, responding through Lodge that it would neither participate in a coup nor thwart one. Instead, the United States would support any regime in South Vietnam that could attract the allegiance of the nation's people while fighting the Communists effectively. Taking that assurance at face value, the generals struck, assassinating Diem and Nhu on 1 November and installing a junta headed by Minh.[61]

Diem's death ended the debate over the war's progress. As the populations of South Vietnam's cities took to the streets in wild celebration, the country's jails emptied, and former prisoners told tales of torture and mutilation. Meanwhile, the Viet Cong went on the attack to cut off and destroy as many of Diem's poorly positioned strategic hamlets as possible. By December, Kennedy himself had fallen to an assassin's bullet, and McNamara had changed his estimate of the situation. Circumstances were bleak, he told Kennedy's successor, President Lyndon Baines Johnson. South Vietnam had been deteriorating for some time.[62]

The affirmation could be seen as vindication for the Saigon correspondents, but it was, in fact, more a commentary on the failure of the U.S. government to assess the situation properly. For months, relying on sources close to the action, reporters had insisted that the war was going poorly. Caught between that avowal and a sincere desire to instill confidence in the South Vietnamese, Ambassador Nolting and General Harkins had responded by concentrating on the reporters' errors of detail while dismissing their more broadly based estimates of the situation. In the end, while hardly without defects, the reporters' impressions proved far closer to the truth than the supposedly hard statistics of the U.S. mission.

Marguerite Higgins would later assert that sensations in the news media emanating from Saigon infected deliberations on the war in Washington. Yet whatever the role of the press in what happened, that of the Kennedy administration appears to have been far more important. A government with a clear idea of where it was going and why could have marshaled enough unanimity within official circles to drown out the dissenters in its ranks. President Kennedy, however, was preoccupied with events in Europe and Cuba, and he attempted time and again to postpone hard decisions on Vietnam by adopting compromise positions that promised to leave his options open. In the vacuum that resulted, dissenting midlevel officials at the U.S. embassy and disgruntled officers advising Diem's army could speak their minds to the press with little risk. And they received a ready ear not only from the Saigon correspondents but also from those officials in Washington who were themselves still pondering what to do. Over the next ten years, as the war waxed and waned, the press would never again have more influence over the shape of U.S. policy than it did at that moment.[63]

Another dimension to what happened, however, also requires telling. As an incident related by Peter Arnett shows, the American news media in Vietnam were caught in a dilemma. One hot noonday, Arnett stood outside the Saigon market watching a Buddhist monk squat on the pavement, squirt himself with gasoline, and flick a cigarette lighter. "I could have prevented that immolation by . . . kicking the gasoline away," Arnett said later. "As a human being I wanted to. As a reporter I couldn't. . . . I would have propelled myself directly into Vietnamese politics. My role as a reporter would have been destroyed along with my credibility." Instead he photographed the man burning in the street, dashed back to his office to file his pictures, and, by giving the Buddhists the means they needed to publicize their cause to the world, assumed the very role he had sought to avoid.[64]

To say that, however, is hardly to blame the messenger for the message he carried. For if Arnett had done the opposite and avoided the story, his decision would have been just as much of an intervention into South Vietnamese politics, but this time on behalf of Diem. There was no middle ground for him or for the rest of the Saigon correspondents. Since whatever they said or wrote could be made to serve one agenda or another, they had altered the war by their very presence, becoming as much a part of it as any soldier in the field.

President Kennedy might have avoided the problem by allowing Diem to censor the news or to evict offending correspondents from his country, but the allegations that would have arisen in Congress and the press that he was squandering American lives and treasure on a *clandestine* war in Southeast Asia were unthinkable to an American politician. Lyndon Johnson would confront the same limitation. Unable to censor the news, he and his advisers would begin almost immediately to cast about for some way to keep the press in check without incurring the massive political liabilities the process might entail.

2
Maximum Candor

The overthrow of Diem inaugurated a brief period of optimism in South Vietnam, but the mood changed within days. With the advent of a triumvirate headed by Maj. Gen. Duong Van "Big" Minh, power struggles ensued as politically acceptable men supplanted those identified with the old regime. Then, on 30 January, just as the situation seemed to be settling down, Maj. Gen. Nguyen Khanh overthrew Minh, inaugurating another period of chaos. By March, thirty-five of forty-one province chiefs had been replaced, and security against the Viet Cong was lagging throughout the country. Meanwhile, Khanh had no wide political following, and even his standing with the army seemed doubtful.[1]

American public opinion reflected the downward trend in Vietnam. The Harris poll reported that whereas 57 percent of Americans had earlier approved of their government's handling of the war, no more than 43 percent could say the same at the end of March 1964. As for solutions to the problem, 35 percent of those questioned favored the establishment of a neutral government in South Vietnam, while only 28 percent opposed it, but a staunch 56 percent continued to favor a policy of supporting an anti-Communist regime in Saigon.[2]

Although well aware that some 63 percent of Americans paid little or no attention to the war, President Johnson and his advisers were concerned about the public's ambivalence. They considered American involvement in South Vietnam important to the preservation of their nation's place in the world, but they were uncertain that the American people would accept the increase in casualties that a decision to stay might entail. As a result, they set about preparing the strongest possible political and military case for future action against North Vietnam while attempting to draw no more attention to the subject than necessary.[3]

For a time, the president thought that a few speeches by administration stalwarts would prepare the way for a hard and realistic public viewpoint on the war without playing the issue on too large a scale. As chaos widened in South

Vietnam, however, the Saigon correspondents plied their readers with news of defeats and disunion, ensuring that the opposite occurred. As early as 3 January 1964, for example, a headline in the *Washington Post* praised the Viet Cong soldier as "Probably Best Vietnam Fighter." On 6 January, the *Baltimore Sun* capped an article titled "Anti-Red Move Fails in Vietnam" with an anonymous comment from a U.S. adviser to the effect that the Viet Cong had become so defiant in their attacks that they seemed to be laughing at their South Vietnamese enemy. Meanwhile, the *New York Times* pointed out that during a recent operation a numerically superior government force backed by heavy air support had allowed a surrounded Viet Cong battalion to escape. Adding insult to injury, it noted that the enemy unit involved had been the 514th Viet Cong Battalion, the same one that had escaped almost exactly a year before at Ap Bac.[4]

Ambassador Lodge was disturbed by the stories. So was the State Department, which instructed him to put an end to unrestrained comment by U.S. advisers. On that occasion, General Harkins stood by his officers, protesting that outbursts of feeling were a normal reaction to stress and that official measures to control them would be more damaging to the effort in South Vietnam than the news stories that resulted. Despite his misgivings, however, he issued a memorandum to his officers calling for restraint. It quickly found its way into the hands of the Saigon correspondents. "Harkins Curbs Yank Beefs on S. Viet Regime," a headline in the *New York Daily News* shortly declared. "South Vietnam Gag," echoed the *Chicago Sun-Times*.[5]

Despite these stories and others like them, much of the venom that had characterized press reporting during the final year of the Diem regime was gone. Diem and Nhu were no longer present; Buddhist suicides had stopped; and official optimism had faded before a recognition that the war was going poorly. In addition, Ambassador Lodge had taken personal control of press relations at the U.S. embassy and by so doing had healed many of the animosities that had characterized official relations with the press during the Nolting years. His approach was simply stated. "I have . . . had it in mind to background the U.S. press," he told the State Department, "but from long experience I have learned that it is much better to wait for them to come to you instead of you sending for them. If I were to send for them to tell them how well the war was going they would not believe it, and I would suffer the same fate as so many others." As it was, he added, his approach was paying dividends. Reporters such as Neil Sheehan of UPI and Hedrick Smith of the *New York Times* who in the past had criticized the mission were in line to see him, and "I hope to be able to get some ideas across."[6]

Although successful, Lodge's approach was too personal to have much effect on the ability of the U.S. mission to deal effectively with the news media over the long term. Since the ambassador had total control of press relations, the U.S. Information Agency's representative at the embassy, Barry Zorthian, could do little on his own to assist reporters and was mainly responsible only for propaganda operations. As a result, misinformation in news dispatches often went uncorrected, and since the ambassador had only limited time for the press, overall direction of the mission's public affairs drifted. Complicating matters, the corps of correspondents in South Vietnam had grown from an initial body of about eight resident reporters to one that numbered more than forty. Although some were new, a number were by then veterans—Peter Arnett of the AP; Frank McCullough of *Time;* Merton Perry and François Sully of *Newsweek;* Neil Sheehan, now of the *New York Times;* Dean Rusk's brother-in-law Jack Foisie of the *Los Angeles Times;* and Beverly Deepe of the *Christian Science Monitor,* to name just a few. All could ask difficult questions.[7]

With the war expanding and problems ever-present in Saigon, pressure began to build in Washington for an examination of public affairs policy in Vietnam. In an official study on all aspects of U.S. operations in South Vietnam, Brig. Gen. John M. Finn recommended expansion of the MACV's public affairs office, the assignment of well-experienced public affairs officers to positions in the field, and the appointment of a civilian to head the agency. A group of that sort, Finn's analysts explained, would be more likely to win the confidence of the press than a strictly military team. Finn's recommendations were seconded by Lt. Col. Lee Baker, USAF, the chief of MACV public affairs. Baker added that the rules obscuring the U.S. Air Force's role in the war, the use of napalm, the employment of army and marine helicopters, and the presence of jet aircraft in the country also had to go because the press knew everything and they caused more trouble than they were worth.[8]

Officials in Washington set the recommendations aside, but procrastination became more difficult as 1964 lengthened. On 28 March, the *Indianapolis News* published the letters home of Capt. Edward "Jerry" Shank, a U.S. Air Force pilot who had been killed while flying combat missions in South Vietnam. By mid-April the story was running in almost every important newspaper in the United States, and on 4 May, *U.S. News & World Report* printed the letters in full, titling the story "A Captain's Last Letters from Vietnam, 'We Are Losing. Morale Is Bad. . . . If They'd Just Give Us Good Planes. . . . ' " The letters outlined the air force's supposedly secret activities in South Vietnam and delivered a scathing indictment of U.S. public affairs policy on the war. "What gets me the most is that they won't tell you people what we do over here," Shank had declared. "We—me and my buddies—do everything. The Vietnamese 'students' we have on board are airmen basics. The only reason they are on board is in case we crash there is one American 'adviser' and one Vietnamese 'student.' " Senator Margaret Chase Smith of Maine placed the letters into the *Congressional Record* with the comment that there was "a desperate need" for the American people to hear the truth about Vietnam. Further congressional comment occurred on 8 May, when *Life* reprinted the letters.[9]

The assistant secretary of defense for public affairs, Arthur Sylvester, was able to demonstrate that *Life* had edited Shank's letters to make them more critical than they actually were, but the rejoinder had little effect. Instead, the families of

Captain Edwin Gerald Shank, USAF. (Connie Shank)

some of the Americans killed in Vietnam bought a full-page advertisement in the *Washington Star* to list the names of the 127 Americans killed since January 1961. They commented that they believed the list was incomplete and that many more Americans had died than had been reported.[10]

While the controversy was at its height, Carl Rowan, the director of the U.S. Information Agency, returned from a fact-finding mission to South Vietnam with a recommendation that Barry Zorthian receive control of the entire information program. Zorthian would never be able to stop critical news stories, Rowan said, but he could at least end the confusion and promote "the stories we want told." Meanwhile, Arthur Sylvester moved to bring Col. Rodger Bankson, one of the army's most experienced public affairs officers and a veteran of the censorship program during the Korean War, to Washington. He instructed Bankson to establish a Southeast Asia Division within the Office of the Assistant Secretary of Defense for Public Affairs. The organization was to know everything it could about the war so that it could deal intelligently with the press corps in Washington while developing sound policy guidance for the field.[11]

On 2 June, a high-level conference convened in Honolulu to consider the situation in South Vietnam. A subcommittee composed of Sylvester, Rowan, Zorthian, and a number of other experienced information officers evaluated the public affairs program. The group reported that conditions in South Vietnam were unsatisfactory on many counts and that the public affairs program had yet to be devised that could turn defeats into victory or South Vietnamese lassitude into enthusiasm. Insisting that public affairs had to become an integral part of every activity undertaken to meet the crisis, the group went on to draft suggestions to correct what was wrong. Central to the effort that emerged was a realization that one man had to have overall authority for dealing with the Saigon correspondents. Although reporting to the ambassador, that individual would have to be a "czar" with the authority to marshal whatever resources he needed, particularly transportation, to move reporters to the positive side of the story.[12]

Colonel Rodger Bankson. (Peter Bankson)

With that principle in place, the group turned its attention to operations in the field. Besides recommending the elimination of all directives that forced official spokesmen to dissemble, it concluded that the military had to assign better information officers to South Vietnam. As it was, highly qualified men seemed to consider service in Southeast Asia a drag on their careers, and several had even resigned rather than accept a posting to Saigon. The group also insisted that the army and the air force would have to spend more time training their men in how to deal with reporters if they wanted to reduce the number of incidents in which their personnel sounded off to the press.[13]

President Johnson acted on the recommendations shortly after the conference ended, appointing Barry Zorthian the U.S. mission's chief public affairs officer. Subject only to the ambassador, Zorthian was to set policy; promote good relations between the embassy, MACV, and the Saigon correspondents; correct erroneous news reports; and assist the press in covering the positive side of the war.[14]

Zorthian assumed his duties on 6 June and began to work with Harkins's deputy, the officer who would become U.S. military commander in South Vietnam on 20 June, Gen. William C. Westmoreland. The two moved quickly to make the MACV Office of Information (MACOI) the sole release point in South Vietnam for news of military operations. Reorganizing the agency, they gave it three new divisions: Troop Information, responsible for the command newspaper and all activities involved with the orientation and indoctrination of military personnel;

Press Relations, which would handle queries from reporters, daily briefings, and news releases; and Special Projects, which would find positive stories and take correspondents to them. Besides handling field trips for the press, the division was also to supervise public affairs officers stationed in each of South Vietnam's corps tactical zone headquarters and to advise the South Vietnamese military on matters that might create public affairs problems.[15]

Over the weeks that followed, MACV and the U.S. Information Service in Saigon set up a division of labor. Zorthian supervised overall contact with the press, set policy in concert with Westmoreland and the ambassador, and oversaw South Vietnamese relations with the news media. MACV and the Special Projects Division, meanwhile, established a press center, organized press trips into the field, tipped reporters to overlooked stories, and cultivated particularly influential correspondents. Coordinating interviews with the ambassador and other important American and South Vietnamese officials, MACOI also laid plans to provide reporters with specially prepared news stories, radio tapes, and film clips.[16]

To further the program, Westmoreland began to include reporters on his trips into the field, made appearances at weekly MACV press briefings, and traveled to locations where his presence might attract the press to favorable stories. Zorthian, meanwhile, began a series of weekly, off-the-record briefings dealing with the subtleties of the situation in South Vietnam. Together, the two pressured the Defense and State Departments to ensure that the information released by officials in Washington coincided with the word from Saigon. They also began to push for a program to bring editors, businessmen, and other American opinion leaders to Saigon, where they could be exposed to the importance of what the United States was accomplishing. Returning home, those dignitaries and celebrities could then make special appearances to talk about what they had seen.[17]

Coinciding with these efforts, on 7 July the State Department framed a new public affairs policy for the war. Since public and congressional support were essential for the success of U.S. policy and would never survive in a climate of hostility and suspicion, the agency stipulated that MACV and the U.S. mission were to promote "maximum candor and disclosure consistent with the requirements of security." Keeping Washington agencies fully informed so that all concerned could speak with a common voice, members of the American mission were to refrain from any activity that would mislead the press or damage relations with the news media.[18]

Following that line and aware that the press had a long memory, Westmoreland and Zorthian pressed the army and the State Department to remove those individuals at the U.S. mission who had been identified with the problems of the past. Westmoreland, in particular, wanted an army officer with training and experience in ground warfare to take charge at MACOI. Arguing that such an individual would be well suited to tell the story of the war, he suggested Bankson, who had just visited Saigon on an information-gathering tour.[19]

Sylvester declined to release Bankson, and the air force objected to the replacement of Baker with an army officer on grounds that Westmoreland was clearly attempting to build up the army's role in the war at the expense of the air force. Sylvester sided with the air force on grounds that the two services were already feuding over the use of helicopters in Vietnam and that another confrontation might prove embarrassing. Westmoreland went along but quietly continued to press for the change. When the U.S. commander in chief, Pacific, Adm. Harry D. Felt, sided with him in December, the chief of staff of the air force, Gen. E. B. LeBailly, regrouped by proposing a compromise. Westmoreland could have an army chief of information in Saigon if he allowed the deputy chief to be an air force officer. In addition, since MACOI's Press Relations section was an ideal place to provide perspective on the air war, an air force officer would also take charge of that division. The Defense Department accepted the proposal, giving MACOI the army orientation Westmoreland wanted.[20]

At that point, Sylvester and Westmoreland agreed on a plan to prepare future MACV chiefs of information for the job they would face. Leaving Bankson in Washington for the next year to serve as special assistant for Southeast Asia, Sylvester appointed the chief of information, U.S. Army, Europe, Col. Benjamin W. Legare, to head MACOI. At the end of one year, Bankson would succeed Legare in Saigon, while Col. Winant Sidle, a former deputy chief of U.S. Army information, became special assistant for Southeast Asia. Upon Bankson's departure from Saigon, Sidle would take his place, and some other officer would move into the Washington post for a year. The system held until 1970, when the position of the special assistant for Southeast Asia—much to the grief of the public affairs program in Vietnam—perished in an unthinking Defense Department reorganization.[21]

Replacing Lodge as ambassador in June 1964, Gen. Maxwell D. Taylor embraced the new policy by instructing Zorthian to ensure that the U.S. mission's dealings with the press were "effective and responsible." Those wishes notwithstanding, the new ambassador shortly found that U.S. credibility in South Vietnam depended on more than good intentions. The needs of international diplomacy, the political agenda of the Johnson administration, and South Vietnamese instability all played a part, and each, in its own way, conflicted with the policy of maximum candor.[22]

A case in point was Laos. The United States considered that country essential to American success in South Vietnam and viewed its neutrality, as stipulated by the Geneva Agreements of 1962, as essential to any long-term settlement of the Indochina question. During April 1964, however, that policy came under threat when a group of right-wing generals deposed Neutralist premier Souvanna Phouma, and Communist insurgents, the Pathet Lao, launched an offensive on the Laotian Plaine des Jars. The United States sent Assistant Secretary of State William P. Bundy to Vientiane to settle the crisis. He succeeded in winning the restoration of Souvanna's government but could do little about the offensive. Instead, President Johnson inaugurated low-level jet reconnaissance of Pathet Lao positions on the Plaine and authorized U.S. civilian pilots to fly air strikes for the Laotian air force.[23]

The Johnson administration said nothing in public about the evolving American role in combat, affirming on 21 May only that Souvanna had granted permission for reconnaissance flights. The line held for slightly more than two weeks but began to give way on 6 June, when Pathet Lao gunners downed a reconnaissance aircraft. The State Department immediately confirmed the loss but nothing more. Within hours, without any announcement, the president authorized armed escorts to accompany reconnaissance flights over Communist territory.[24] When one went down the next day while actively engaging enemy antiaircraft batteries, the State Department attempted to deny the Communists any propaganda advantage by confirming in a confidential backgrounder for the press that the aircraft had been armed, but it said nothing about whether the pilot had fired his guns.[25]

The approach only postponed the inevitable. On 9 July, President Johnson ordered a retaliatory strike in Laos to demonstrate U.S. resolve. When a Communist Chinese news service denounced the attack, newspapers around the world took up the story, and reporters in the United States began to clamor for an explanation. The State Department pushed for a change in policy, arguing that further dissembling could only open the way for critics in Congress and the press to charge that the president was irresponsibly attempting to hide the American role in the war. Souvanna, however, refused to go along lest he lose his Neutralist stance. As a result, the only explanation reporters received was a restatement of the earlier announcement and an avowal that "it is not in the interest of the government of Laos or of those who undertake these hazardous missions that any operational part of their work should be discussed." The press, in turn, responded much as the State Department had predicted. The *New York Herald-Tribune* attributed the blackout to election-year politics. The *Washington Post* declared that it was indeed sad when the people of the United States had to rely on China's news agency for word of covert operations in Vietnam. Widely respected *Aviation Week* avowed that events so regularly contradicted the Defense Department's reports on the war that some reporters refused to believe a story "until it had been officially denied."[26]

In the end, the affair damaged U.S. credibility, but it was only the beginning of the problem. For if the need for cordial relations with Souvanna dictated how far the United States could go in talking about the war in Laos, similar circumspection prevailed where South Vietnam was concerned. Whatever the dictates of "maximum candor," no member of the U.S. mission in Saigon was ever to offend his hosts by commenting publicly on their internal affairs.[27]

If South Vietnamese sensitivities were involved, however, the wishes of the Johnson administration also came into play. Besides seeking to preserve a free hand in Southeast Asia by keeping the war in low profile, the president sometimes used leaks to the press to send signals to Hanoi, and he disliked having the effects of those messages diluted by derogatory news stories. On one occasion, to his chagrin, after quoting articles in the *New York Times* by columnist Walter Lippmann to show that South Vietnam was falling apart, North Vietnam's prime minister, Pham Van Dong, had even commented disparagingly that there was "no light at the end of the tunnel" for the United States.[28]

As far as the South Vietnamese were concerned, no American in Saigon believed it was possible to exclude all mention of their operations from American briefings, if only because local administrators declined to deal candidly with the press.[29] As a result, MACV held daily briefings on both U.S. and South Vietnamese topics, and Zorthian convened weekly backgrounders on any subject reporters wanted to raise.[30]

The approach had reason on its side, but it rapidly ran afoul of the Johnson administration's tendency to question every news story that threatened its stance on the war. A case in point occurred during June 1964, when Col. Wilbur Wilson, a U.S. Army senior adviser, held a frank background briefing for the Saigon correspondents in which he contended that if the South Vietnamese had improved 100 percent, they still had to do better to win the war. Many of the nation's generals had won their ranks through political maneuvering and were no match for the enemy's commanders. Meanwhile, the country itself was seven hundred years behind the times in political maturity and incapable, unless it changed, of matching the nineteenth-century techniques for seizing power that the Communists employed. The AP carried an account of the session the next day, prompting a cable from the Defense Department to Westmoreland. The agency wanted details of the interview because, in combination with the Laotian imbroglio, it might shake public and congressional confidence in the president's policies. Westmoreland could only respond that Wilson had said nothing the assembled reporters had not already known.[31]

In the end, the briefing caused no problems, but officials in Washington continued to become agitated every time unfavorable news appeared. For example, when reporters revealed during July that a series of costly enemy ambushes had seriously disrupted the movement of South Vietnamese convoys, the State Department and the Central Intelligence Agency (CIA) began to complain that such stories could only destroy the American public's confidence in the military capabilities of the South Vietnamese. For a time, the Defense Department debated whether MACV might establish an in-house news service of its own to counter fast-breaking stories in the press by alerting Washington agencies to embarrassing developments. Official communications circuits were already overloaded, however, and even if adequate resources had existed, government officials could never have gathered and transmitted correct information quickly enough to refute news stories compiled from partial impressions by reporters working against deadlines.[32]

In the end, whether the United States could succeed in creating a good image for the war depended on the South Vietnamese government and army. If they could take hold of their problems, create a regime honest enough and efficient enough to win their people's trust, and do what was necessary to make genuine inroads against the Viet Cong, all would be well. Reporters would see what was happening and write about it—much as they had earlier when the helicopter had temporarily thrown the enemy off balance. The opposite, however, was also true. The most brilliant public affairs program could never hide the fact that the situation in South Vietnam was continuing its downward slide.

Nguyen Khanh's bid for power provides a case in point. The Johnson administration had worked assiduously to depict itself as a resolute but nonbelligerent protector that intended "no rashness" and sought "no wider war," but Khanh decided that his political needs took precedence. Seeking to rally the nation to his side by advocating an aggressive, all-out assault on North Vietnam, he informed *New York Herald-Tribune* correspondent Beverly Deepe on 14 July that the North Vietnamese had recently begun an "overt invasion" of his country by moving three full battalions, eighteen hundred men, into South Vietnam. With North Vietnam's aggression established, he then declared at a Saigon rally on 20 July that U.S. tactics were too slow and that the allies had to carry the war to the enemy's heartland. "To the North!" he led the crowd in shouting. "To the North!" Two days later, the commander of South Vietnam's air force, Air Vice Marshal Nguyen Cao Ky, added momentum to the campaign by telling reporters that South Vietnam had been sending sabotage teams into North Vietnam for three years and that his pilots were even then training for possible air attacks.[33]

As soon as Khanh made his first charges, MACOI moved to underscore the president's nonbelligerent stance by holding a background briefing on enemy infiltration. Acknowledging that North Vietnamese soldiers had been entering the country as individuals, official spokesmen asserted that no evidence existed to imply that those soldiers were operating as organized units. The distinction struck a chord with the press. From then on, the American news media paid little attention to Khanh's assertion that the North Vietnamese were "invading" his country.[34]

The U.S. embassy's efforts to pull Khanh into line were less successful. When Ambassador Taylor requested that he repudiate Ky's remarks, the premier declined and permitted members of his regime to leak what had happened to the press. Later Khanh nodded to American pressure by avowing in public that he had never envisioned a massive military assault on North Vietnam, but even then he left the issue open by adding enigmatically that his army would continue its energetic efforts to remove the Communist scourge. As one South Vietnamese official told Zorthian, Khanh and Ky were in no position to back down. If they did, they would appear to their countrymen to be puppets who reversed their public comments at every American whim.[35]

If American policy makers could do little to curb Khanh, they did manage to turn the uncertainty his comments caused to good purpose. During August, when North Vietnamese gunboats were alleged to have attacked the U.S. destroyers *Maddox* and *Turner Joy* in the Gulf of Tonkin, the United States not only retaliated by launching air attacks against North Vietnamese naval bases but also sent a veiled threat to Hanoi that echoed Khanh's themes. When reporters asked at a news conference whether the United States would tolerate South Vietnamese attacks against the North, official spokesmen responded that since the North was the aggressor, South Vietnamese attacks would count as "retaliation" for years of cruel and vicious attacks.[36]

For a time following Johnson's reprisal raids, there seemed some hope that the president might gain the free hand in Southeast Asia that he sought. Although the press would later question the circumstances under which the Gulf of Tonkin attacks had occurred and

Major General Nguyen Khanh.
(Department of Defense)

whether the second had even happened, neither the news media nor the Johnson administration appears to have doubted at the time that both were real. The incident gave the president an opportunity to push a resolution supporting his policies in South Vietnam through Congress, and his subsequent reprisal raids against North Vietnam galvanized American public opinion. Indeed, prior to the raids, 58 percent of those polled by Louis Harris disagreed with the president's handling of the war. Afterward, 85 percent approved.[37]

Khanh, however, was not to be denied. On 7 August, he took advantage of the confusion to declare a state of emergency in South Vietnam. Shortly afterward, he promulgated a new constitution and had himself declared president. The moves did not sit well with many of the South Vietnamese people. By 17 August, Buddhist and student unrest were spreading, and violent riots were occurring in some areas. Abashed, Khanh annulled his constitution, resigned the presidency, and withdrew to the resort town of Da Lat to sulk, but when no new leader emerged to take his place, the chaos only deepened. At Taylor's behest, Khanh resumed the premiership on 3 September, but then he almost fell to a coup that was aborted only at the last moment.[38]

The picture of South Vietnamese demoralization that emerged during those days magnified doubts already circulating within the American news media. *Newsweek* observed that over the preceding six months Khanh had managed to maintain his own power but little else. Peter Grose of the *New York Times* questioned whether there was any hope for a stable government in Saigon. Peter

Kalischer of CBS News compared South Vietnam to Humpty Dumpty. And Stanley Karnow of the *Saturday Evening Post* quoted an angry U.S. Army adviser who had said, "We've thrown in helicopters, aircraft, artillery, and with each new machine the ante goes up. Nobody wants to fight because some new gadget is supposed to be coming along to win the war painlessly."[39]

As the crisis continued, it began to taint the "maximum candor" program. Malcolm Browne of the AP and other correspondents asserted that the "free junkets" for stateside celebrities and journalists put the recipients under a psychological obligation to follow the official line. In the same way, many reporters were convinced that the dedication of only a single helicopter for the use of the press served mainly to limit and channel reporting of South Vietnam's problems.[40]

Whatever their protestations, however, newsmen had little difficulty getting the facts or telling the story, and the picture they drew was one of spreading decay and impending impasse for the American effort. "Each day, the situation assumes a new dimension of chaos," the *Washington Star* avowed. "Each day, the chance of restoring a minimum of effective government becomes dimmer." The U.S. mission was saying almost the same thing. "The month . . . was characterized by political turbulence, uncertainty . . . , and confusion as to the future," its monthly assessment for September asserted. "Viet Cong incidents increased. Government military operations decreased in all categories excepting small unit operations. . . . The manpower picture continued to be unsatisfactory. . . . [And] there is little or no evidence of overall progress."[41]

By November, many members of the American public had reached the same conclusions. They swept Johnson into office with 61 percent of the vote, but polls showed that no more than 42 percent of them gave the president high marks for his handling of the war. By December, that support had dwindled to 38 percent. "Maximum candor" may have improved the U.S. mission's relations with the news media, but it had failed to achieve its primary objective: the creation of a climate of opinion favorable to the president's ends in South Vietnam.[42]

3

Keeping the Options Open

The final months of 1964 brought no end to the chaos in South Vietnam. Buddhist unrest continued, an abortive coup occurred, and the enemy strengthened his areas of control throughout the country. As the extent of the nation's demoralization became apparent, Defense and State Department analysts began to consider the possibility that the Saigon regime might lose all ability to rule. They concluded that a program of gradually increasing air attacks against North Vietnam had the best chance of improving the situation. Besides boosting South Vietnamese morale, it would strengthen the American negotiating position and show the world that the United States stood by its allies.[1]

Concerned with the upcoming presidential election, President Johnson temporized. He had no wish to close out his options by choosing war, particularly when his political opponent, Barry Goldwater, was already calling for escalation. In addition, one out of four Americans was still oblivious to the war in Southeast Asia, and many more were unprepared for the hard choices it might entail. There was no telling what those individuals would do if pushed too hard. They might reject his candidacy, ending his political future, or they might press so fervently for all-out war that few choices would remain for him to make. In either case, the prospects would dim for his domestic agenda, the program of reforms and improvements labeled the "Great Society" that he hoped to establish after his reelection. In the end, caught between the two extremes, he accepted the idea of attacks in principle but made no firm commitment to action.[2]

While Johnson hesitated, Barry Zorthian received few guidelines for dealing with the press. Aware that the news media needed authoritative sources to give their reports weight and that officials could use that requirement to get their message across, he followed his own instincts. If reporters asked questions about undesirable or embarrassing subjects, he told his associates, the information was to be forthcoming unless military security was at risk. Only in that way would official spokesmen establish the cooperation they needed with the press to open reporters to subjects they wanted told. The military might experience some inconvenience, and news stories unflattering to the South Vietnamese might appear, Zorthian reasoned. Nevertheless, the truth was seldom as bad as hearsay, and once it was out in the open it might awaken the American public.[3]

Zorthian was as good as his word. Early in November 1964, when *Life* magazine requested an on-the-record interview with top mission officials, he supported the idea. Such an interview was a rare opportunity, he said, to publish extended official quotations that avoided the paraphrasing of reporters and the misreadings it sometimes involved.[4]

The panel met on 14 November, with four *Life* correspondents interviewing Taylor, Westmoreland, Zorthian, and several other representatives of the U.S. mission. All concerned mentioned areas of progress, but Westmoreland was by far the most optimistic. Paying no heed to a memorandum he had recently sent to the ambassador that underscored the "inefficiency, corruption, disinterest and lack of motivation" of South Vietnam's government, he praised the nation's military and avowed that it was inconceivable to him that the Viet Cong could ever win the war. Ambassador Taylor kept the meeting in focus by observing pointedly that the outcome of the conflict was still in doubt and that it would ultimately hang on which of the opponents had the strongest will to win. Even so, he likewise emphasized that it was no time for Americans to take counsel in fear or to sell either their own nation or South Vietnam short.[5]

The interview had the desired effect. *Life* published it on 27 November along with a series of articles covering important aspects of the war. Most of the pieces followed the approach laid down by Taylor, balancing descriptions of the difficulties accompanying American involvement with portrayals of men who believed in what they were doing. Although problems dominated, so did Taylor's plea for patience. President Johnson could have asked for nothing better.[6]

The interview never directly addressed whether the United States should bomb the North, but one official did suggest in passing that North Vietnamese infiltration into the South was on the rise. In that way, it fitted into a series of ongoing revelations by the U.S. mission designed to suggest that the enemy was becoming more aggressive and that the United States might have to escalate the war. The Johnson administration played the effort in low key because of the coming presidential election. Even so, by mid-November, those disclosures, an enemy attack at Bien Hoa that claimed four American lives and six B-57 jet bombers, the appearance of the *Life* interview, and an announcement that Ambassador Taylor would shortly visit Washington to confer on the war combined to surround the issue of the war with a sense of urgency. Speculation began to rise in the press that the administration was preparing to move the conflict off dead center, editors began to call for an end to procrastination, and public opinion polls put the war at the top of the problems the American public wanted solved. Congress caught the mood. "We either have to get out or take some action to help the

Vietnamese," Senator Richard Russell of Georgia intoned in the *National Observer.* "They won't help themselves."[7]

Although the news media were hardly as prepared for war as it appeared—the *New York Times,* for one, considered escalation foolish without a stable South Vietnam—Johnson was probably as close to having a nation prepared for strong action as he would ever be. The president, however, also had doubts. He intensified air strikes in Laos and increased covert naval attacks against the North Vietnamese coastline, but he also instructed Taylor to tell Khanh that nothing more would be done until a government existed in Saigon that could exploit the openings further attacks on North Vietnam would create.[8]

The attacks in Laos that followed Johnson's decision were so cautious that the North Vietnamese apparently failed to distinguish them from the earlier armed reconnaissance. Indecision also hobbled the administration's efforts to prepare American and world public opinion for the attacks on North Vietnam that clearly loomed. The revelation of North Vietnamese infiltration seemed the best approach, but the president wanted to preserve his flexibility and continued to temporize.[9]

Left to themselves, reporters began to speculate on the next direction the war would take. A few came uncomfortably close. Well connected with individuals high in the Defense Department, Hanson Baldwin assumed that any U.S. escalation would involve air attacks and suggested that targets in Laos would be involved. The *New York Daily News,* meanwhile, combined items on the public record with shrewd deductions to conclude that Taylor already had some sort of authority for attacks in Laos and North Vietnam. When other reporters built speculative stories on those leads, Zorthian did not try to correct them. They served, he said, to confuse the enemy.[10]

Taylor considered Zorthian's approach too unstructured and continued to push for a planned and deliberate process of revelation in order to keep control over the information involved and to achieve maximum impact. Aware that State Department analyst Chester L. Cooper had just completed a white paper on enemy infiltration, he suggested that the administration release its findings in a series of background briefings. While preparing the American public for whatever action the United States decided to take, the step would help to persuade uncommitted nations that North Vietnam was indeed an aggressor.[11]

The State and Defense Departments considered Taylor's suggestions but on 19 December once more concluded that caution should prevail. Since the Saigon correspondents had pressed for several weeks for some sort of disclosure, however, they did authorize Zorthian to brief reporters on the general nature of Cooper's evidence and what it showed. No numbers were to be released. If anyone asked why, official spokesmen were to say that the picture of enemy infiltration was always changing.[12]

In deciding to withhold the Cooper report, the Johnson administration assumed it still had the public relations initiative, but time was running out. On the

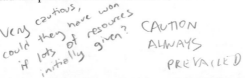

Very cautious, could they have won if lots of resources given initially? CAUTION ALWAYS PREVAILED

evening of 19 December, Khanh and a group of young generals that included Air Vice Marshal Ky and Lt. Gen. Nguyen Van Thieu dismissed South Vietnam's legislative body, the High National Council, and the country's civilian premier, Tran Van Huong. A coup d'état in retaliation for the council's refusal to compel the retirement of senior generals who blocked the advancement of younger officers, the act destroyed any semblance of South Vietnamese stability.[13]

At a meeting following the coup, Taylor confronted the plotters. "Now you have made a real mess," he lectured them. "We cannot carry you forever if you do things like this." He then informed Khanh that the United States could never cooperate with two governments in South Vietnam, one civilian with responsibility and the other military with power. Khanh responded on 22 December with an Order of the Day to his armed forces. In it he declared that it was better to live poor but free than as slaves of foreigners and Communists. Turning to the press, he then told Beverly Deepe in an interview that Taylor's activities had been "beyond imagination as far as an ambassador is concerned."[14]

Taylor responded to the article that followed with an off-the-record background briefing for the Saigon correspondents that pointedly excluded Deepe. Holding little back, he ascribed the South Vietnamese army's most recent failures to the unprofessionalism of the nation's generals, who stayed in Saigon while mere captains fought the war. If some commanders were "first class," he added, others bordered on being "nuts." Learning of what had transpired from other reporters and believing she was under no obligation to observe rules she had never agreed to, Deepe retaliated for the slight she had received with an article that told everything Taylor had said. The *Herald-Tribune* gave the piece a lurid title: "Taylor Rips Mask off Khanh."[15]

Although the South Vietnamese came close to declaring Taylor persona non grata, nothing happened in the end. Instead, on 25 December, enemy sappers blew up the Brink Hotel, a U.S. billet in Saigon, killing two Americans and wounding fifty-one. Responding to the emergency, the U.S. mission moved immediately to defuse the issues underlying the dispute with Khanh. Taylor had never intended to disparage anyone, its spokesmen told the generals. Indeed, had the coup against Huong not occurred, the United States might have retaliated against North Vietnam.[16]

The generals sought to save face with a hostile response, but by 30 December Khanh had repudiated his interview with Deepe and was calling for compromise on all sides. On 6 January, the generals announced a formula for ending the crisis. There would be no High National Council, but the army would restore full control to a civilian government under Huong. That done, Huong would begin planning for the election of a truly representative national assembly.[17]

The calm that followed lasted for only ten days. Buddhist leaders had already announced that they opposed any government headed by Huong. When he returned to power, they seized on one of the government's first decrees, an enlargement of the army's draft calls, as an excuse to riot. With disorders spreading from

Helping someone who is so disorganized.

city to city and the Buddhists calling for armed resistance to the United States and its lackeys, the generals finally gave in, ousting Huong one final time on 27 January 1965.[18]

The turmoil sparked a debate in Congress over further American aid to South Vietnam. Antiwar senators such as Frank Church of Idaho called for American disengagement, but even such pro-administration stalwarts as Richard Russell of Georgia began to express doubts. A poll of congressional opinion by the AP found the Senate deeply divided. Of sixty-three senators queried, three wanted immediate withdrawal, eight favored commitment of U.S. forces against North Vietnam, thirty-one recommended a negotiated settlement when South Vietnamese prospects improved, and ten favored prompt negotiations.[19]

Editorial writers were as perplexed as Congress, but they were unified in condemning the Johnson administration's lack of leadership. The editors of *Life*, for example, lamented that the enemy's intentions were becoming more credible while those of the United States remained clouded, and Keyes Beech of the *Chicago Daily News* scored the administration for suppressing the story of North Vietnamese infiltration. Arthur Dommen of UPI, meanwhile, revealed for the first time the full extent of American air operations in Laos.[20]

The American public, for its part, was deeply ambivalent. Four out of five of those who said they followed the war closely agreed in a January Gallup Poll that South Vietnam was losing the war, two out of three believed the country would never form a stable government, and eight out of ten asserted that they would support a peace conference even if it included the leaders of mainland China. Even so, few advocated unilateral American withdrawal. Instead, 50 percent thought that the United States should defend independent nations from Communist aggression, and four out of seven asserted that the nation should commit American forces if a military crisis loomed.[21]

Equating any negotiated U.S. withdrawal with "surrender on the installment plan," Gen. Harold K. Johnson, the chief of staff of the army, rebuffed those advocating immediate negotiations by calling in public for "patience, persistence and determination." Former ambassador Lodge said the same thing in an article in the *New York Times Magazine*, and both Rusk and McNamara began quiet efforts to inform congressional leaders of the facts contained in the Cooper study. They also authorized Zorthian to hold a backgrounder on the subject for the Saigon correspondents.[22]

By that time, American policy makers were virtually convinced that they could no longer avoid a decision on widening the war. During the last week in December 1964, as the dispute between Khanh and Taylor had reached its height, the enemy had launched an unprecedented multiregiment operation to seize the village of Binh Gia in Phuoc Thuy Province. Concentrating on the power struggle in Saigon, South Vietnamese commanders had allowed 177 of their men to be killed and 181 more to be wounded; 104 were listed as missing. American casualties came to 6 killed, 9 wounded, and 3 missing. Shortly after the battle ended, the

Secretary of Defense Robert McNamara with Ambassadors Maxwell Taylor and Henry Cabot Lodge. (Don North)

Chinese Communist *People's Daily* crowed that the engagement had been "a smartly conducted . . . battle of annihilation" in which the Viet Cong had shown that they had grown into "a formidable liberation army." Convinced that action was imperative, William Bundy responded to the development by telling Secretary Rusk that many nations appeared to believe the United States was seeking a more competent administration in Saigon than anyone could reasonably expect. He advocated reprisal raids against North Vietnam as soon as the enemy provided an excuse. Ambassador Taylor agreed. The United States, he said, had to risk a change.[23]

President Johnson again wavered. Although he said he favored reprisals, he declined once more to do anything that might later limit his options. How, he asked, could he embark on a major escalation without first clearing the decks by evacuating American dependents from South Vietnam? And how could he communicate the return of those dependents to the press without appearing to be running away in the eyes of the world? Rather than take any action, at Taylor's suggestion, he dispatched White House adviser McGeorge Bundy to South Vietnam to evaluate the situation.[24]

Arriving on 3 February, Bundy rapidly determined that conditions were about as bad as everyone had said. If he had any doubts, they vanished on the morning of 7 February, Saigon time, when enemy mortarmen and sappers killed 9 Americans and wounded 108 in an attack on the U.S. airstrip at Pleiku. Retaliating with air strikes against targets in North Vietnam, President Johnson seized upon the event as the excuse he needed to order all American dependents in the South to leave and to declare his determination to ensure the independence of South Vietnam.[25]

The American news media generally backed the move, but they also followed the lead of conservative columnist David Lawrence in warning against an un-thinking slide into all-out war. Columnist Max Lerner, meanwhile, observed that those who said the war was "a futile folly" would go unchallenged until President Johnson clarified what he was doing in South Vietnam.[26]

Well aware that justifications were necessary, the Johnson administration was already hard at work preparing them. While analysts from the State and Defense Departments worked on updating the Cooper report for release to the press, unidentified sources began leaking analyses to the news media suggesting that North Vietnam could avoid further destruction by terminating its support of the Viet Cong. On 12 February, President Johnson attempted to endow American in-volvement in the war with high moral purpose by avowing at a Lincoln's birthday luncheon that the United States was "a city on the hill" and responsible "for the protection of freedom on earth."[27]

On 27 February, the State Department finally released the Cooper report. Contending that 75 percent of the forty-four hundred Viet Cong known to have entered South Vietnam during the first eight months of 1964 were ethnic North Vietnamese, the document cited twenty-five interviews with captured infiltrators as proof. It went on to list captured enemy weapons and ammunition manufac-tured outside of South Vietnam in order to establish that North Vietnam was the Viet Cong's main supplier, and then detailed the organization the Hanoi regime had established to control the war in the South.[28]

Presented with great fanfare, the white paper fell flat. Although journals such as the *Baltimore Sun* and the *Washington Daily News* asserted that the document contained "overwhelming evidence" of North Vietnam's culpability, many more picked at the study. Long an opponent of the war, the *St. Louis Post-Dispatch* termed the work a weak attempt to justify further attacks on the North. The *New Republic* avowed that of the twenty-five infiltrators named in the study, only eight had been positively identified as North Vietnamese, and the *Providence Journal* observed that if the Communists had broken the Geneva Agreements of 1954, so had the United States.[29]

Chester Cooper would later complain that his study was doomed from the start because its most important sources were too highly classified to cite, but in fact, the report was mainly the victim of months of procrastination during which the United States had squandered whatever initiative it had on a vain hope that the South Vietnamese government might stabilize. As a result, when President Johnson finally authorized his long-awaited bombing campaign on 2 March, 83 percent of Americans may have rallied to his side, but three out of four also no longer believed victory was possible. The reaction of the press to Cooper's paper reflected the trend. The study was, in the eyes of many reporters, not a justification for a new and victorious initiative but, as the *New York Times* observed, "a tacit admission of failure."[30]

Despite the criticism, Barry Zorthian was convinced that the U.S. mission's relations with the news media in Vietnam were as good as could be expected, and that the bad feelings of earlier years between reporters and officials had all but disappeared. President Johnson, however, was less certain. As the new year lengthened and he moved deeper into war, his sensitivity to every news story that called his policies into question grew.[31]

Johnson's decision during November to begin outright bombing attacks in Laos (Operation Barrel Roll) provides a case in point. At first, the program was so understated that the Communists failed to take much notice. Public relations problems were few. That changed on 12 January 1965, when Johnson authorized a heavy attack on an important bridge in northern Laos, and Radio Hanoi began to claim that Communist gunners had shot down several fighter bombers. In the past, public affairs officers had passed off such announcements by affirming that an incident had indeed occurred but that the planes had been on a legitimate reconnaissance mission. This time, that was not enough. The Communists had announced a major attack. If the United States stayed with the old formula, reporters would inevitably conclude that official spokesmen were lying. Steering a middle course between the president's desire for a low profile and the need to preserve official credibility, official spokesmen admitted the loss of two aircraft but avoided saying anything about a reconnaissance mission. Pressed on the point, they then fell back on the rejoinder that "this is an operational matter upon which we cannot comment."[32]

The comment did nothing to reduce conjecture in the press. Instead, reporters deduced that an important change of policy had occurred and began to speculate. At first they concentrated on whether the attack had been an escalation and whether such strikes could be either effective or moral. Then their remarks broadened. While Laurence Barrett argued in the *New York Herald-Tribune* that the American public's need to know the nature of the war overrode political reasons for keeping quiet about the raid, UPI alleged that U.S. aircraft had been attacking in Laos for seven months. Meanwhile, Reuters noted that the aircraft involved could well have come from bases in Thailand, and *Time* surmised that the North Vietnamese were circumventing U.S. attacks in Laos by channeling their support for the war through ports in Cambodia. Toward the end of the month, Senator Mike Monroney of Oklahoma arrived in Saigon with word that there was "general unhappiness in Washington" with news reporting from Saigon. Aware that Monroney was close to Johnson, Westmoreland saw him as the president's personal emissary and concluded that Johnson was becoming increasingly dissatisfied with the U.S. mission's failure to keep the Saigon correspondents in line.[33]

The air strikes on 6 and 11 February in response to the attacks at Pleiku and Qui Nhon only added to the problem. The first attack caught reporters off guard, but by the time the second occurred, more than twenty newsmen had congregated at Da Nang, the main base for air strikes on the North, in hopes of covering further raids. They counted the aircraft taking off for the second raid and had the news on the wire even before the planes reached their targets. As if that were not enough, shortly after the attacks, MACV announced the types of bombs dropped, released photographs of strike results, and allowed pilots who had participated in the raid to brief reporters. The airmen inadvertently revealed a potential target for attack and speculated on the possibility that enemy fighter aircraft might respond to a future raid. It was all too much for General Wheeler. He cabled Westmoreland to complain that the session not only had revealed sensitive information but also had made the strikes appear far more menacing than the facts warranted.[34]

The Defense Department immediately drafted guidance to restrict information on air strikes against North Vietnam. Those rules permitted release of the times of attack, the locations and general categories of the targets, the names of Americans killed and wounded after search and rescue operations were completed, and general characterizations of success, but they embargoed anything that might embarrass the military services, help the enemy, or increase discussion of the war. To keep the enemy from gauging the effectiveness of his radar, nothing was to be said about the number of planes involved in a raid, and the bombs employed were to be characterized only as "conventional." Official spokesmen were also to avoid revealing the use of napalm or other spectacular weapons such as antipersonnel bombs. In the same way, only photographs cleared by the Defense Department were to be distributed to the press lest reporters learn that some of the bombs had mistakenly hit nonmilitary buildings and facilities. Since the Thais objected to any indication that aircraft based in their territory might have been involved in attacks on North Vietnam, information officers were to characterize all aircraft originating in South Vietnam and Thailand only as "land based." On the side, Wheeler and Sharp advised Westmoreland to refrain from allowing pilots to brief the press and suggested that word of attacks involving aircraft based outside of South Vietnam should come from the office of the commander in chief, Pacific, in Hawaii.[35]

Zorthian agreed with the need for rules but found serious fault with the ones the Defense Department had issued. Anyone who knew anything about combat, he said, understood that enemy fighters might rise to meet an attack and that all targets of any significance in North Vietnam were on Johnson's list. As for the proviso banning the naming of air bases in South Vietnam, the enemy knew where they all were. Refusal to mention them in news releases would thus contribute little to military security while compelling official spokesmen to conceal the obvious. An unwillingness to provide at least round figures on the number of planes involved in a raid and the use of doublespeak to describe well-known

Barry Zorthian (left) with Carl Rowan (center). (Barry Zorthian)

types of armament would similarly achieve nothing beyond the destruction of official credibility. As for the pilots, reporters needed the colorful details they could provide after a raid and would interpret any attempt to sequester them as some sort of cover-up.[36]

Zorthian and the information officers at MACV requested that the Defense and State Departments convene a conference in Hawaii to discuss the direction future public affairs policies should take. When neither agency responded, Zorthian took action on his own. Concerned that the situation in South Vietnam was so open that restrictions of any sort would fail unless newsmen agreed to cooperate, he contacted the most important of the Saigon correspondents to obtain their promise to withhold information on air strikes until the planes returned. "This does not necessarily commit us to any announcement," he told his superiors, but to issuing "a go-ahead on information the news media may have obtained by personal observation and other sources." Receiving no objection, he spelled out the arrangement in a memorandum for the press that incorporated many of the rules covered in the Defense Department's draft guidelines. He requested voluntary compliance.[37]

Westmoreland was more cautious than Zorthian. Although he joined the counselor in calling for a conference on information policy, he also believed the military should exercise stronger control over the press. To that end, he suggested that the Joint Chiefs consider a system similar to the one that had prevailed during the Korean War, when reporters had submitted to formal censorship.[38]

The State and Defense Departments scheduled a conference for mid-March but postponed consideration of censorship. The idea nonetheless remained on everyone's mind, to resurface at the beginning of March, when Johnson finally decided to send two battalions of marines to Da Nang to defend the air base. Because the South Vietnamese government believed the move could trigger antigovernment demonstrations, it stipulated that the marines should arrive with as little publicity as possible, but reporters could hardly miss the flurry of construction that began at Da Nang and quickly surmised that an American troop commitment was in the offing. They filed dispatches to that effect on 2 March, causing consternation in Washington.[39]

Making matters worse, on that date the Johnson administration finally began a program of regular, gradually intensifying attacks on North Vietnam (Rolling Thunder). Until then, reporters had been able to discern U.S. attacks in Laos only from leaks, casualty announcements, and Communist propaganda. With the start of Zorthian's program and the advent of regularly announced attacks on North Vietnam, however, they had little difficulty determining when an attack on Laos occurred. If public affairs officers declined to confirm that a departing flight was targeted on North Vietnam, there was only one other place the fighters could go. The newsmen began to put the news on the wire just as soon as the planes returned.[40]

The front-page stories that followed brought a quick reaction from President Johnson. "Highest authority continues to be gravely concerned by speed and completeness of discussion of operational details of military missions in Laos and North Vietnam," the State Department told Ambassador Taylor. "We believe that if U.S. sources sternly refused details few reporters will seek out accurate facts by themselves. Should they persist, we believe you should consider placing the environs of airfields including even city of Danang off limits to unauthorized U.S. citizens."[41]

Public affairs officers in Saigon shared State's concern but were convinced that draconian measures would have little effect. The flight line at Da Nang Air Base, they noted, was easily observable from a commercial airline terminal at one end of the field and could never be completely closed off. As for censorship, it would have to involve the sovereign government of South Vietnam, and that nation's officials would almost inevitably attempt to tamper with news dispatches that had nothing to do with military activities. The cure might thus cause more problems than the malaise it sought to heal.[42]

Ambassador Taylor did believe, however, that action was necessary. In order to limit the amount of specific information reporters could acquire, he told the State Department, he had already approached the South Vietnamese government about closing the air bases at Da Nang and Bien Hoa to all but escorted newsmen. Since reporters were beginning to surmise that fighters based in Thailand were involved in strikes on the North, he then suggested that official spokesmen confuse the issue by limiting strike announcements to simple statements that American and South Vietnamese planes had attacked North Vietnam. There would be no indication of the size of an operation or whether the aircraft had been land- or sea-based. In the same way, he said, public affairs officers should say nothing when an aircraft went down in Laos unless a pilot was killed, wounded, or captured. Then they could dampen speculation in the press by merely stating that an airman had been lost in connection with operations in Southeast Asia.[43]

The deputy assistant secretary of state for public affairs, James L. Greenfield, questioned Taylor's recommendations. Communist wire services would announce raids in Laos no matter what the United States said, he remarked on 10 March, and the Saigon correspondents could verify the announcements by paying civilian South Vietnamese to count the aircraft leaving Da Nang. Admiral Francis J. Blouin of the Defense Department's Office of International Security Affairs agreed but noted that the problem would soon disappear on its own. "There will be so many air strikes," he said, " . . . the press will find it difficult to tie in communist announcements with specific missions."[44]

In the end, the Defense Department decided to withhold all information on the bases from which strikes originated but sanctioned occasional briefings for the press by pilots and routine mention of the most common types of bombs. Taylor was less flexible. Although he decided to announce the size of attacks on North Vietnam in round numbers, he closed Da Nang Air Base on 15 March to all but escorted reporters.[45]

When South Vietnamese security officers broke the news to correspondents, the move sparked an angry reaction in the press. Reporters for the AP pointed out that the rule required a military escort for each correspondent visiting the base, but that only two officers were available to serve the more than thirty reporters in the area. The association's managing editor, Wes Gallagher, asserted that the rule inhibited the American people's ability to obtain a true picture of the war by attempting to control what the troops said to reporters. Richard Starnes of the *New York World-Telegram* remarked that in earlier conflicts reporters had always been able to collect war news at its source by sharing the fighting man's lot at the front, but that would no longer be possible. The world would have to rely on Radio Hanoi for word of raids against North Vietnam.[46]

Arthur Sylvester, the assistant secretary of defense for public affairs, dismissed these complaints. The South Vietnamese had imposed the restrictions at Da Nang without notice to the United States, he told reporters. Indeed, the Defense Department continued its policy of "complete candor with newsmen."[47]

The conference Zorthian had requested met in Honolulu between 18 and 20 March. The assembled public affairs officers—Bankson; Zorthian; Greenfield; the new chief of MACV public affairs, Col. Benjamin W. Legare; and representatives of all the U.S. agencies concerned with the war—concluded immediately that the uproar over the closing of Da Nang Air Base would be only the beginning if the president imposed further restrictions on the press in Vietnam. American success depended on public support, they told their superiors, and that support would surely waver "if any significant number of our people believe . . . they are being misled."[48]

Working from that premise, the group rejected any form of censorship, opting firmly for the system of voluntary cooperation Zorthian had already adopted. Censorship would require not only the legal underpinnings of a declaration of war, it argued, but also an enormous logistical effort. The censors would have to control South Vietnam's mail, communications, and transportation facilities. They would have to employ multilingual military personnel to do the censoring and would have to develop expanded Teletype and radio circuits to move the censored material. Even if they could do all that, there was no guarantee that many of the correspondents who were foreign nationals and beyond the reach of American regulations would cooperate. Beyond that, there was the South Vietnamese government to consider. Its leaders would have to play a key role in the program, yet they lacked any concept of an American-style free press and would inevitably apply a heavy hand every time a reporter said something they disliked.

As opposed to censorship, the system of voluntary cooperation had many advantages. Besides retaining the policy of maximum candor that had done so much to reverse earlier problems with the press, the approach allowed for a measure of control over the Saigon correspondents. In return for accreditation to cover the war, military transportation around South Vietnam, and admission to important briefings and interviews, reporters would agree to abide by rules designed to protect military security. Those who accepted the system would have access to candid, sometimes classified, information. Those who declined would find their privileges at an end. Since the Saigon correspondents had already behaved responsibly by agreeing to withhold reports on air strikes in progress, the procedure had an additional merit. It paid tribute to the good faith and honor of the great majority of news media representatives.

The conference recommended rules for covering the air war that were identical to those already in effect. Everyone recognized that, at least for the time being, operations in Laos would have to remain unmentioned—"no answer," they said, "no lies"—but all others should be announced. If information had to be withheld for the sake of military security, it should be for sound reasons that could be revealed to reporters off the record. Almost as important as the information to be released was the way officials made the announcement. In the past, before briefing the press on a strike in North Vietnam, public affairs officers at MACV had released a communiqué that attempted to justify the attack by listing U.S. grievances against North Vietnam. Meanwhile, in Washington, the White House and sometimes the State and Defense Departments had held backup briefings to corroborate the news. The inconsistencies that resulted from so many release points, the conferees noted, drew attention away from the South Vietnamese contribution to the war, eroded the policy of maximum candor, and diminished Zorthian's authority. In addition, the coupling of strictly military information with obvious propaganda stretched official credibility and harmed relations with the news media. A far better approach would be one in which MACV became the principal point of release for all news of the war. For the rest, official statements justifying air attacks should be separated from strike announcements and find expression either in special briefings or in press releases on enemy provocations. With the advent of an approach free of political taint, Rolling Thunder would become routine and would cease to be the subject of sensational news stories.

The Johnson administration approved the conference's recommendations on 3 April with only one major change. The chairman of the Joint Chiefs of Staff, General Wheeler, refused to divorce announcements of air strikes against North Vietnam from their political justifications on grounds that anything of the sort would weaken the American position before the world. At the time, Wheeler's decision seemed little burden, but it marked, in fact, a critical divide in the history of the war. Ratifying the subordination of military spokesmen to the political demands of their civilian superiors, it left the way open for President Johnson and his successor, Richard M. Nixon, to exploit the military's credibility with the American people by drawing officers supposedly above politics into the business of selling the war.[49]

No one at the time, however, realized what was happening. Unwilling to delay approval of the report, all concerned went along with Wheeler's wishes. Zorthian briefed the Saigon correspondents on the rules, requested their voluntary cooperation, and then announced that Da Nang Air Base would be open to reporters who obtained identification cards, valid for one month, from the South Vietnamese National Press Center. From then on, the newsmen would have to submit to escort while on South Vietnamese portions of the base, but once they entered the American sector, upon receiving clearance from a newly established press center in Da Nang, they would have free access to all unclassified American areas.[50]

With that, the basic apparatus for dealing with the Saigon correspondents for the rest of the war was in place. Those who had formulated the policy had failed to separate military information from politics, but they had probably been naive in thinking they could. At the least, they had created a system capable of giving the American people a reasonably accurate picture of what was happening without at the same time helping the enemy. Whether the Johnson administration would use it in that manner remained to be seen.

4

The Ground War

The Honolulu conference addressed immediate issues: censorship and the air war. All concerned understood, however, that American forces might shortly become necessary. As early as 12 February, the Joint Chiefs of Staff had concluded that South Vietnam showed imminent signs of collapse and had requested a major commitment of U.S. troops. They renewed their request on 20 February, recommending the deployment of a full U.S. Army division. On 25 March, General Westmoreland joined them, calling for thirty-three thousand men immediately and more by midyear if the bombing of North Vietnam produced no weakening of enemy will.[1]

President Johnson again temporized. Concerned that the American public was as yet unprepared and that the presence of large American forces in South Vietnam might only kindle South Vietnamese xenophobia, he settled on a compromise that promised to postpone problems. Rather than send all the men the military had requested, he ordered some three thousand marines to Da Nang and Hue on 3 April and approved the commitment of a full army logistical command—twenty thousand men—to South Vietnam to lay the base for the buildup of men and matériel that would follow when the time was right. "We do not desire [to] give [the] impression of a rapid, massive build up," the press guidance that accompanied the decision avowed. While the marines were to deploy as soon as possible, all other deployments were to be spaced out "with publicity . . . kept at the lowest possible key." If reporters inquired, official spokesmen were to dismiss the movement of troop transports toward South Vietnam as routine fleet maneuvers.[2]

As for the marines, the Defense Department announced blandly that they had received instructions to guard the facilities at Da Nang. The classified orders the agency issued, however, were far different. The marines were not merely to guard the air base but to seek out the enemy aggressively in their area of operations.

45

The phrase used to describe their new mission, *counterinsurgency combat operations,* had been carefully designed to give Westmoreland the authority he needed to take to the offensive but to be vague enough to avoid the political problems that Johnson and his staff feared.[3]

Public affairs officers tailored their announcements to a three-phase program Westmoreland had devised to move his forces toward full combat. When the marines began patrolling around Da Nang Air Base, MACV announced that they were merely relieving South Vietnamese forces for duty elsewhere. Off the record, however, official spokesmen affirmed that the force would fight if attacked and would move out from the base's perimeter. When the marines stepped up their activities and began to respond to enemy initiatives within fifty miles of Da Nang, public affairs officers followed with routine observations that the marines had "a combat support role" in addition to their defensive mission. Only in May, when Westmoreland contemplated using the marines throughout South Vietnam's northernmost region, did the question of fully revealing the U.S. offensive role arise. Then Johnson once more temporized.[4]

The Saigon correspondents, for their part, had no doubts about the direction the United States was taking. Accepting it as the natural outcome of U.S. deployments, they paid great attention to the arrival of American troops but said little about the role of the marines. Indeed, they were so inattentive to what was happening that Zorthian became concerned the American public had been only partially informed that the American role in the war was growing.[5]

If reporters accepted the evolving nature of the American commitment to South Vietnam, there was no easing of tension between the press and officials. A case in point occurred at the very time Johnson was considering whether to commit American ground forces to combat, when South Vietnamese commanders laid down plans to employ tear- and nausea-producing gases if their use might assist in saving civilian lives or in rescuing allied prisoners of war.

Public affairs officers in the field recognized immediately that the development had great potential for problems and suggested as early as December 1964 that MACV inform the press and emphasize that the gases involved were standard riot-control agents in use around the world. Unwilling to give the enemy even the slightest propaganda advantage, the State and Defense Departments refused. Shortly afterward, AP reporter Peter Arnett heard rumors of the new tactic and approached information officers for an explanation. Following orders, the officers declined to respond, but they warned MACV that Arnett knew everything and that an explosion was imminent. The command did not respond.[6]

Arnett waited several months until he could tie the story to a specific incident. He used it on 20 March, when his partner, AP photographer Horst Faas, observed South Vietnamese troops going into combat with gas canisters in hand. Quoting a Radio Hanoi report that allied forces were using "poisonous chemicals" and that a twelve-year-old girl had suffered a swollen face in a recent gas attack, he observed that "by tacit agreement" gas had not been used in World War II or

Korea. He added that the compounds involved were nonlethal and that they might provide a humane way to rescue civilian hostages of the Viet Cong, but he then countered the point by quoting an American adviser who had said that the agents would still be difficult to justify to an American public that remembered the mustard gas of World War I. In the end, Barry Zorthian could only conclude that Arnett had written a deliberately negative story. "Even a neophyte journalist" would have known, he avowed, that the references to injured children, mustard gas, and tacit agreements would inflame anti-American sentiment around the world.[7]

The article was on the wire for several hours before Zorthian and MACV learned of it. When they did, official spokesmen went before reporters to explain that in situations where the Viet Cong intermingled with refugees or took noncombatant hostages, South Vietnamese forces used nonlethal riot-control gases instead of artillery and air strikes. Newspapers around the world paid little attention to the explanation, preferring to interpret it as confirmation of Arnett's story.[8]

Further attempts at clarification had little more success. "The argument that the non-toxic gas is more merciful than anti-personnel weapons has some merit," the *Washington Post* declared, "but not much. . . . Although the gas may not be poison, the word is, and all the propaganda resources in the world cannot explain away its employment as an act of Christian charity." Even a temporarily disabling gas could kill the sick and the very young, the *New York Times* asserted. In addition, gas in Vietnam was "supplied and sanctioned by white men against Asians," something no Asian would ever forget. The Federation of American Scientists, meanwhile, labeled the use of "weapons of indiscriminate effect" both "morally repugnant" and "incomprehensible," and Tokyo's *Asahi* charged that the United States was using Asians as guinea pigs.[9]

The reasons underlying the outcry were difficult to discern at the time because the agents involved were relatively harmless in comparison with the lethal gases banned by international agreement. In that light, as *Wall Street Journal* reporter Philip Geyelin observed, the true significance of the episode may have been less the gas than the uproar itself. The crisis seemed to indicate that the United States was much more alone on the issue of Vietnam than President Johnson and his advisers wished to believe. The world seemed nervous about what the United States was doing in South Vietnam, skeptical about its arguments, and eager for any solution that would head off a wider conflict.[10]

Whatever the controversy's cause, its effects endured. Ambassador Taylor withdrew Westmoreland's authority to employ tear gas in combat and postponed a program to spray herbicides on crops in Communist-controlled portions of heavily populated Binh Dinh Province. Other crop-control programs in less populated regions continued, but the Joint Chiefs of Staff still stipulated, "While 'gas crisis' is running its course, . . . it would be preferable that major crop destruction programs . . . be stretched out or otherwise reduced in visibility, provided this can be done without publicity and without serious problems [with the South Vietnamese]."[11]

More rules followed in July, long after the controversy over Arnett's revelations had ended. When Westmoreland asked at that time to expand the herbicide program, the State Department expressed concern that another outburst would arise in the press and insisted that both the ambassador and a senior South Vietnamese official approve the operations. Although targeted mainly at remote areas in which the enemy had difficulty finding food, the program might include more populated regions if compelling reasons arose, but only with prior authorization from Washington. In all cases, the people were to be warned. Meanwhile, the Viet Cong were to be blamed for any damage that occurred because they had made themselves responsible by refusing to abandon the targeted area.[12]

As the controversy over gas subsided, President Johnson sought ways to avoid similar problems in the future while preparing the American people for war. To that end, he drafted a key speech to emphasize America's desire for peace and the Communists' aggressive intentions. Delivering it at Johns Hopkins University on 7 April, he declared his willingness to negotiate "without preconditions" and proposed a massive program of American aid for Southeast Asia as an alternative to war. He had no expectation that North Vietnam would respond positively to his offer and had fielded it mainly to throw the burden of future escalations on the Communists by underscoring their unwillingness to negotiate. He was thus disturbed to learn shortly after making the speech that news reports from Saigon were counteracting the conciliatory image he wanted to convey. In one, a reporter had declared that "American war planes, swarming against North Vietnam in unprecedented numbers, wrecked three bridges and scored for the first time against Mig fighters. . . . South of the border, fresh landings of U.S. Marines . . . were in the offing. . . . The Navy and Air Force launched 220 planes laden with 245 tons of bombs and rockets."[13]

General Wheeler informed Westmoreland of the president's displeasure, stating that "highest authority is increasingly unhappy at press releases which forecast impending U.S. reinforcements to South Vietnam, discuss U.S. military actions to include targets and extension of target system, and represent magnitude and weight of . . . U.S. strikes against [North Vietnam]." He added that pressures on the president increased when reporters wrote stories of that sort and that censorship might well pose the best solution to the problem.[14]

Westmoreland responded that censorship might indeed be the answer but that, as the Honolulu conference had shown, "practical considerations" made it impossible. Admiral Sharp seconded him, remarking that as the war escalated, so would the reporting, and that censorship might only inflame what the press had to say.[15] These opinions notwithstanding, the deputy assistant secretary of defense for public affairs, Philip Goulding, declined to rule out the alternative and instructed Bankson to investigate the issue again. In response, Bankson resurrected all the arguments levied by the Honolulu conference, emphasizing that the

South Vietnamese government would never handle newsmen fairly. He added that reporters would exercise restraint if given good reasons for doing so because they shared a common goal with government: "the maximum release of information without endangering military security."[16]

In the end, the only change in policy that resulted from Johnson's concern was a ruling from the Defense Department forbidding the prior announcement of troop movements. That took care of premature disclosures, but it did nothing to remedy the president's basic problem. For with the United States driving deeper into war without the full consent of the American public and Congress, it would be only a matter of time until severe public relations problems arose.[17]

The issue became clearer during mid-April, when Johnson finally decided that air attacks against North Vietnam were having little effect on the enemy and that only an infusion of American troops would make a difference. Following a meeting with Westmoreland in Honolulu, McNamara recommended an increase of forty-four thousand men, bringing U.S. troop strength in South Vietnam to seventy-five thousand. A crisis in the Dominican Republic and questions about whether to call up the reserves kept Johnson from announcing the full troop commitment, but he approved deployment of the U.S. 173d Airborne Brigade and three more marine battalion landing teams. That was enough to prompt speculation in the press that American units might soon take a stronger role in the war. Reports also indicated that Australia would shortly commit a battalion to the conflict. Barred from revealing the true mission of U.S. forces, public affairs officers in Saigon could do little to answer questions. Instead, they affirmed developments as they occurred, in as routine a manner as possible.[18]

Washington officials, for their part, attempted to set up another diversion. In early May, the State and Defense Departments instructed Zorthian to deemphasize the American role in the war by underscoring South Vietnamese accomplishments and the American role in advising and supporting those efforts. "We would hope," officials said, " . . . eventually to turn reporters, who consider themselves 'war correspondents,' into 'counter-insurgency correspondents.' "[19]

Although official spokesmen moved to highlight nonmilitary developments, Zorthian cautioned his superiors that such subjects could never compete with the war for news coverage. Arthur Sylvester, however, insisted that American units were seeking "maximum visibility" for their own efforts and demanded that MACV give the South Vietnamese credit whenever possible. So directed, the command cut back on details of American efforts and inserted statistics on Viet Cong terrorism into its nightly communiqués. Zorthian, meanwhile, inaugurated briefings on nonmilitary topics and redoubled his efforts to have the South Vietnamese brief the press on their operations.[20]

Zorthian, Westmoreland, and the new MACV chief of information, Col. Benjamin Legare, were convinced, nonetheless, that any attempt to downplay the American role in the war would fail. Asserting that reporters could see for themselves that the marines and the 173d were actively seeking combat and engaging

Barry Zorthian (left) and Arthur Sylvester brief the press. (Barry Zorthian)

at times in full-scale offensive operations, Westmoreland informed the Pentagon on 11 May that he believed a comprehensive background briefing for selected newsmen on American operations was imperative. He added that he intended to deliver it within two days unless directed to do otherwise. Unprepared for the impact the session might have, the Johnson administration vetoed the plan.[21]

Procrastination continued until the end of May, when enemy forces mauled two South Vietnamese battalions in Quang Ngai Province, prompting hard-pressed South Vietnamese commanders to seek American help. They later with-drew the request, but by then it was clear that American forces might shortly have to enter combat to prevent a major South Vietnamese defeat. Agreeing with Zorthian that U.S. spokesmen would be better off if they could anticipate the event rather than endure the sort of questioning that had followed the tear gas affair, the State Department finally authorized a low-key announcement, which came on 4 June at the regular MACV briefing. Responding to a question Colonel Legare had planted with a trusted reporter, the command's spokesman stated that U.S. forces would supply combat support to the South Vietnamese when and if that became necessary. Observing that details of the arrangement had yet to be worked out, the officer changed the subject so deftly that no questions followed.[22]

Despite that avowal, when the State Department issued a communiqué of its own on the subject the next day, the release was less than forthcoming. "In establishing and patrolling their defense perimeters," it said, "[U.S. troops] . . . come into contact with the Viet Cong and at times are fired upon. Our troops, naturally, return the fire. It should come as no surprise . . . that our troops engage in combat in these and similar circumstances."[23]

Although Zorthian picked up the discrepancy between the two announcements—MACV had said that U.S. forces would undertake missions as circumstances required, while State had said all combat was defensive—the issue took several days to come to a head in the press. On 7 June, a reporter asked during a State Department briefing whether the South Vietnamese had ever sought combat assistance beyond what MACV was already supplying. The briefing officer, Robert McCloskey, responded that they had and confirmed in response to a second question that a U.S. marine battalion had been alerted. Competing with the first American walk in space by America's *Gemini IV* astronauts, the affirmation attracted little attention, but the subject again refused to die. The next day, newsmen pressed McCloskey for more information, and he finally admitted that American forces were available for offensive combat. The reporters wanted to know whether the change had been announced in Saigon. McCloskey thought that it had but could not be more specific.[24]

With that, complaints began to arise in Congress and the press that a dangerous and reckless departure from accepted policy had occurred. The White House sought to counter the allegation by announcing that there had been no change in the mission of U.S. ground forces and that the safeguarding of important military installations remained central to the U.S. role. Under the circumstances, however, it could not avoid adding that Westmoreland had the authority to employ his troops in support of the South Vietnamese if the appropriate Vietnamese commanders so requested. That avowal, along with another by Secretary Rusk to the effect that "obviously, we don't expect these men to sit there like hypnotized rabbits waiting for the Viet Cong to strike," countered the effect the administration had hoped to induce. As Kenneth Crawford noted in *Newsweek,* since the change in policy had been apparent for some time to anyone who followed daily casualty reports, the government's attempts at clarification served only to intensify an impression that a cover-up was in progress.[25]

Columnist Arthur Krock had the last word. "There is certainly fundamental 'change' in a 'mission,'" he said, "which begins as strategic counsel and technical assistance within a government territory, proceeds to bombing outside that territory, . . . moves onward to 'perimeter defense' that inescapably leads to ground combat, and finally is given authority for expansion into formal ground warfare." Quoting Lewis Carroll's *Alice in Wonderland,* he added: " 'The question is,' said Alice to Humpty Dumpty, 'whether you *can* make words mean so many different things.' "[26]

While the controversy continued, the Viet Cong increased their pressure on South Vietnam, leading Westmoreland to conclude that they possessed the resources to attack at will throughout South Vietnam and that he might shortly have no choice but to commit American forces to combat. Circumstances worsened on the night of 9 June, when the Viet Cong attacked a South Vietnamese Special Forces camp at Dong Xoai, some ninety kilometers north of Saigon. During the fighting that followed, the Communists ambushed two waves of South Vietamese reinforcements, causing some 650 government casualties. At one point, the situation seemed so serious that Westmoreland alerted portions of the 173d Airborne and warned Sharp that he might have to commit them to the battle.[27]

Sharp was appalled. In a telephone call and a later cable, he reminded Westmoreland that an American defeat at that point in the war, "particularly in the immediate wake of adverse publicity on the subject," might embarrass the president and "jeopardize or change the course of our present plans regarding the use of U.S. forces." He suggested that Westmoreland use a massive application of airpower rather than troops to relieve the camp. Indeed, if the general decided to commit ground forces, he was to notify his superiors in the chain of command before issuing any orders. Sharp's caution was well advised. For the Saigon correspondents were even then watching for any sign that U.S. forces might take the offensive. They informed their editors as soon as they saw the 173d going on alert, using commercial lines almost certainly subject to enemy monitoring.[28]

In the end, Westmoreland followed Sharp's advice and drove the enemy back with air attacks. Although he thus avoided the problems Sharp had predicted, Zorthian was distressed by the eagerness of the press to report the story and the security violation it had caused. Aware that something similar would occur if the 173d actually went into combat, he and the MACV command devised a set of rules to keep the press in check. MACV would announce any enemy attack on the unit at its regular daily briefing but would request that reporters voluntarily withhold casualty figures until the engagement was over. In that way it could keep the enemy from learning how effective his tactics had been. If the 173d entered combat, official spokesmen would confirm the news only when it was of no further use to the enemy and would discuss casualties only after the fighting had ended. Overall, briefers would hold to the official line on the mission of U.S. forces, confirming that the troops had acted at the request of the South Vietnamese government and that the deployment had been within Westmoreland's authority.[29]

Endorsing the guidelines as a temporary measure, the State Department directed the U.S. mission to reconsider the whole question of restraints on the press. Before starting, Zorthian consulted the Saigon correspondents. He found them as concerned as he about protecting military security but also unwilling to agree to rules that gave unscrupulous newsmen an advantage over those who cooperated. In order to ensure fair competition, a few were even calling for full press censorship.[30]

Convinced that the expedient would never work and that the reporters were clearly sympathetic to military needs, Zorthian in the end proposed a set of rules that met official requirements without doing violence to the press. Under that system, MACV would withhold word of deployments until the news was obviously in enemy hands, would announce only the general magnitude of operations without revealing participating units, and would release numbers killed and wounded only as weekly totals. Figures for individual engagements would never appear. Instead, MACV would describe day-to-day casualties as light, moderate, or heavy. If reporters attempted to circumvent the rules, MACV would have the right to exclude offenders from official briefings and facilities, and to deny them the right to accompany the troops in the field. In case the system broke down completely, the Defense Department would draft and have on hand a contingency plan for full censorship.

The State and Defense Departments delayed approving the new rules until they could consult the South Vietnamese. In the interim, General Westmoreland launched the first raid of the war with B-52 bombers, giving the Saigon correspondents an opportunity to demonstrate their sensitivity to any appearance of official news management. The general had been experimenting for some time with ways to destroy large enemy ground installations. When a massive assault by tactical aircraft against Communist positions northwest of Saigon proved ineffective, he sought permission to employ B-52s in hopes that the big aircraft would pack the punch the smaller bombers lacked. He advised against revealing the operation to the press, but Washington agencies disagreed on grounds that word of the attack would inevitably leak. If it did, reporters might conclude that the government was attempting to hide something and begin an outcry similar to the one that had accompanied the use of gas.[31]

To prevent that from happening, the Defense Department and the Joint Chiefs of Staff drafted a complicated plan to monitor the minute-by-minute progress of the bombers toward their target. As soon as the attack occurred, Secretary McNamara would inform the press, playing down the newness of the approach and emphasizing Communist provocations. When Zorthian objected that an announcement in Washington would undermine the policy of revealing combat operations in Saigon first, the Defense Department agreed that first word of the development should come from Saigon.[32]

Despite all the planning, nothing went as expected. When the bombs fell on 18 June, the Defense Department authorized release of the news by MACV but moved so quickly to make its own announcement that it preempted the news from Saigon. Then, when MACV finally released word of the attack but refused to give details until its scouts returned with definite information on the raid's effects, the press moved to fill the vacuum on its own by concentrating on the midair collision and crash of two of the bombers while en route. How, news commentators asked, could U.S. officials balance the loss of those expensive intercontinental bombers against the jungle huts that had been their targets?[33]

Because the raid had been designed in part to set a precedent for future B-52 strikes, the Defense Department stepped into the gap, again ahead of MACV. Official spokesmen at the Pentagon asserted that the raid had probably caused "numerous Viet Cong casualties" and had destroyed large quantities of enemy rice, a large communications center, and from twenty to thirty buildings. Nevertheless, the briefers could enumerate only three enemy casualties, all killed by the survey team, and they had no choice but to suggest that the team itself was responsible for most of the damage on the ground. They avowed that it was "extremely significant . . . that an area which had been considered unassailable has been entered," but the press dismissed the assertion. Instead, Walter Cronkite of CBS News charged that the Pentagon was "attempting to put the best possible light on . . . a mission that failed," and Peter Jennings of ABC News termed the raid "the most spectacular disappointment of the Vietnam War."[34]

By then, the Saigon correspondents were in full cry. Avowing that their employers maintained them in Vietnam at great expense in order to receive the earliest possible word of events, they charged that the Pentagon had taken the lead in announcing the mission in order to hide its failure. Official spokesmen responded that the survey team had covered only 10 percent of the area in question and that the bombers might have been "damn effective" in other portions of the target, but the reporters would have none of it. The point illustrated the problem, one remarked: "If you multiply no damage by ten you still have no damage." The briefers dismissed the comment at the time, but a few days later, the U.S. mission notified the Defense Department that "for your information, . . . no concrete evidence was obtained of either damage or casualties." On 24 June, MACV recommended that Saigon become the normal point of release for news of B-52 strikes. It took three weeks, but on 12 July the Defense Department agreed.[35]

Whatever the effectiveness of that first raid, it had added the B-52 to the American arsenal in South Vietnam. "What is now important," Sharp told Westmoreland, "is to get off a request for another, or perhaps a series of . . . missions before the political climate changes. . . . The main thing is to establish a pattern."[36]

Planning for a second strike began immediately, with elements of the 173d Airborne slated to conduct a postattack inspection of the target. Because the mission would be dangerous, MACV planned to keep the press on a tight leash in order to avoid security problems. Even so, since the ground portion of the operation would involve American troops in the controversial role of supporting the South Vietnamese in combat, Zorthian decided it would be best to allow reporters to see what was going on for themselves. To that end, he made room for a pool of six reporters to accompany the 173d in combat and told its members they could write what they wanted. The command would not release casualty statistics until the operation had ended, and everyone using pool reports would have to hold the story until MACV gave the word, but it would be a test of the principle of voluntary cooperation.[37]

In the end, on 28 June, MACV canceled the B-52 portion of the operation but sent the 173d into the target because the area housed an enemy base that threatened Bien Hoa. Since the attack was nothing more than a standard ground operation, the command at that time replaced the indefinite waiting period prior to release with a simple thirty-six-hour rule. Associated Press reporter Peter Arnett complained that the policy embargoed information already in enemy hands, but MACV denied the contention, and the rest of the press corps accepted the rule. "Hell hath no fury," Zorthian later remarked, "like a wire service scooped."[38]

If most reporters went along with Zorthian, they nonetheless had doubts. NBC News correspondent Sid White cataloged them. "In recent weeks," he said, "there have been several . . . attempts to withhold or distort the facts. The most recent . . . was the disclosure that military officials in Saigon will soon change their method of reporting ground combat casualties by providing weekly . . . rather than day-to-day summaries. . . . It appears that this is a move . . . to offset expected casualties as Americans are committed more frequently to combat. . . . That is to say . . . [officials] won't give a true picture which might make us look bad."[39]

Recognizing that reporters would continue to question every shift in policy until MACV adopted a consistent set of rules, the State and Defense Departments decided during the first week of July to go ahead with Zorthian's proposed system of voluntary cooperation. They had to wait until 12 July for the South Vietnamese to agree, but they then announced the decision. As planned, they told reporters, MACV would reveal casualties on a weekly basis with losses for particular engagements appearing only as *light, moderate,* or *heavy.* Officials would keep troop movements secret until the information was clearly in enemy hands and would never divulge the number and type of units involved in specific operations. If reporters learned details on their own, they were to keep them to themselves.[40]

During the question-and-answer session that followed, reporters concentrated on the criteria MACV would use to determine whether casualties were light, moderate, or heavy. Zorthian responded that no exact measurement was possible and that the media would have to rely on his judgment. He was willing to give the numbers off the record but warned that he would end the practice if they became public. If a reporter wanted to say that a fight had been hard with many casualties, that would be permissible as long as no statistical rundown appeared. It was when the numbers became finite that they rendered aid to the enemy.

The answer failed to satisfy the correspondents. "Everything is relative," one countered. "If we understand that there are twenty casualties in an engagement, off the record, it would make an enormous difference to us whether [they involved] . . . a platoon or a battalion; but since we're not allowed to say it's a platoon or a battalion, if it were a platoon we'd have to say . . . heavy." Although Zorthian failed to make much of the comment, in the months to come the issue would develop into a serious problem for MACV. For the rest, reporters reacted calmly to the new guidelines. The consensus seemed to be, as Keyes Beech of the

Chicago Daily News observed, that some restriction of information useful to the enemy was "long overdue."[41]

The willingness of the press to accept the guidelines reflected public attitudes in the United States. Although the antiwar movement was gaining momentum, Harris polls indicated that 62 percent of Americans approved of President Johnson's handling of the war and that 79 percent believed South Vietnam would fall to the Communists unless the United States held firm. A substantial 32 percent questioned whether the United States would win if the war grew into a major conflict, but the State Department was so impressed that it cited the figures around the world, wherever the American public's support for the war came into question.[42]

If public opinion polls can be misconstrued, the attitude of CBS News left no mistake about the public mood. Producing a series of "Vietnam Perspective" programs on the developing conflict, the organization filmed interviews with administration spokesmen—Rusk, McNamara, Wheeler, and Taylor, to name a few—but took no notice of critics of the war. It then allowed those officials to review and edit tapes of their comments prior to broadcast and published transcripts of their comments in book form at its own expense.[43] There were, however, those who questioned whether the mood would last. Speaking in London at a joint United States–United Kingdom Information Working Group meeting on 20 July, the assistant secretary of state for public affairs, James Greenfield, remarked candidly that the public's high regard for the war was based on low U.S. casualty rates and that the situation would change as the war heated up.[44]

Presidential counselor George Ball said the same thing the next day in a meeting with the president. "In a long war, I said the president would lose the support of the country," he recalled years later. "I showed him a chart. . . . As our casualties during the Korean War had increased from 11,000 to 40,000, the percentage of those Americans who thought that we had been right to intervene had diminished from 65% in 1950 to a little more than 30% in 1952." If the president had considerable support at that moment, Ball continued, everything would change "because it's a different kind of war and the American people are going to be profoundly shocked by their sons getting killed and you're going to have as great an opposition on your hands as occurred during the Korean War."[45]

Johnson seemed impressed, Ball recalled, but in the end "nobody really focused on the consequences of a lot of casualties." Instead, public support for the war seemed so high that when McNamara proposed a troop increase to 175,000 men and William Bundy suggested a broad public relations campaign to prepare the American people, the assistant secretary of state for international organizations, Harlan Cleveland, had little difficulty arguing against any promotional buildup. "I have the very definite impression," he said, " . . . that public opinion is already substantially conditioned to expect an increase in our force level. . . . The surprise would be if [the president] decided not to act." When Johnson approved

McNamara's proposal on 27 July—making his final, fateful decision for war—he adopted Cleveland's approach and played everything in low key.[46]

The approach succeeded for the time being, but in the end Ball was right. As he had warned, public approval of the Vietnam War fell in step with the rise in American killed and wounded, dropping 15 percentage points each time U.S. casualties increased by a factor of 10 (going from 100 to 1,000, 1,000 to 10,000, and so on). Some would say that the press, particularly television news, played a critical role in the process by publicizing the casualties, but the formula had worked just as well during the Korean War, when television news was nonexistent. As MACV's public affairs officers were well aware, there is no way to hide the burdens of war from the population of a modern state. Whatever the efforts of government officials to conceal the truth, the dead and maimed return home. And when their number mounts, as the leaders of the Soviet Union learned during their war in Afghanistan in the 1980s, word travels fast, even if a nation's news media are under total state control.[47]

The situation in South Vietnam was beginning to slide even as Johnson was making his decision to escalate the war. For despite the favorable public mood and the willingness of the news media to accept Zorthian's guidelines, reporters could see the contradictions that were beginning to accumulate at the heart of the war, and tensions were building between them and their official handlers. On one occasion, for example, during a visit to South Vietnam to coordinate relations with the press, Arthur Sylvester lost his temper at a late-night session with some of the Saigon correspondents and dressed down Jacques Langguth of the *New York Times,* Morley Safer and Murray Fromsom of CBS News, and several other reporters for supposedly relying too much on official handouts. When one of the newsmen questioned the credibility of government spokesmen, Sylvester became incensed. "Look," he said, "if you think any American official is going to tell you the truth you're stupid." In time of war, he added, the press had the obligation to be the "handmaiden" of government. Sylvester later termed the remark about handmaidens a joke, but by then several furious reporters had stomped out of the meeting.[48]

Disagreements flared again over the announcement of the first U.S. air attack on a North Vietnamese surface-to-air missile site. Seeking to decrease the impact of what many would consider an escalation, the Defense Department revealed the development during a Pentagon briefing rather than at MACV. As a result, the Saigon correspondents began to charge with considerable heat that domestic political considerations had motivated the move and that the entire system of voluntary cooperation would break down unless the government followed its own rules. Public affairs officers at the U.S. mission in Saigon underscored the point, avowing that "grave repercussions" might follow if Defense continued to set aside normal announcement procedures.[49]

That problem had hardly subsided when a new one arose having to do with

The marines come ashore at Da Nang. (Department of Defense)

the treatment of South Vietnamese civilians by U.S. forces. During July, the marines had begun to patrol densely populated areas to the south of the air base at Da Nang, a region dominated by the Communists for generations. Encountering stiff resistance, marine commanders decided to subdue what they considered one of the enemy's main strong points, the village of Cam Ne. Scheduling the operation for 3 August, they told their men to "overcome and destroy" every hedgerow, trench line, bunker, and hut from which the enemy fired.[50]

Viewing the town as a fortified obstacle, the marines followed orders. When they received fire from an estimated one hundred enemy hiding in and around the village, they responded with rockets and grenade launchers, setting off secondary explosions among mines and booby traps ringing the village. Many of the huts also went up in flames. The troops asserted that they made sure all civilians were out before they destroyed caves and tunnels in the houses. Even so, they reported that three civilians had been wounded and that a ten-year-old boy had been killed while in a hut from which Viet Cong were firing. The marines' commanders asserted that despite American mortar and artillery fire, "the VC were able to pop right back up out of the ground and fire. . . . That gives some indication of the extent of the fortifications in the town."[51]

Accompanying the operation, Morley Safer and his Vietnamese cameraman,

Ha Tue Can, saw a different story. Cabling CBS to inform his producers that a filmed report would follow within a few days, Safer said that an officer at the scene had told him the marines had orders to burn the village if they encountered resistance. After an enemy fired an automatic weapon from an unidentified direction, he continued, the marines responded with rockets, grenades, and machine guns. Despite the pleas of elderly villagers, they also used cigarette lighters and flamethrowers to destroy some 150 dwellings. The reporter added that prior to the burning, the marines had urged the townspeople to abandon their shelters, but the people were slow to move because the troops spoke only English. Safer's cameraman filled in as interpreter, but by then civilian casualties had occurred. The cable so distressed executives at CBS News that they introduced that evening's broadcast with a reading from it.[52]

Safer's film played two nights later. Showing a young marine, his rifle hanging casually at his waist, igniting a hut with a cigarette lighter, it disputed official contentions that most of the huts had been destroyed in an exchange of fire. As the film played, Safer enumerated the civilian casualties and told how 150 homes had been leveled in retaliation for a burst of gunfire. "Today's operation shows the frustration of Vietnam in miniature," he said. "There is little doubt that American fire power can win a military victory here. But to a Vietnamese peasant whose home means a lifetime of backbreaking labor, it will take more than presidential promises to convince him that we are on his side." CBS played a rejoinder by MACV's chief of public affairs, Colonel Legare, to the effect that the marines never burned houses unless they doubled as fortifications and that the hut in question had concealed the concrete entrance to a tunnel, but Safer's pictures and commentary dominated the news.[53]

Safer returned to the theme two days later with another filmed report, this one featuring interviews with marines who had fought at Cam Ne. "You're up against a lot of women, children and old men," the reporter said to one. "How do you feel about it?" The soldier responded: "You treat everyone like an enemy until he's proven innocent. That's the only way you can do it. . . . We are the only company that went in there that hasn't had people killed. . . . And . . . we're going to have to show these people . . . that we're done playing with them. . . . I think we proved our point." Turning to several other marines, Safer asked, "Do you have any private doubts?" One responded that he and his comrades were caught in the middle and that no one had any answers. Another was more blunt. "You can't do your job and feel pity for these people." Alluding to marines who had been killed or wounded, Safer then asked: "Do you go in with revenge in your hearts?" One trooper responded that he did because "I don't like to see a fellow marine . . . as much as scratched over here in this country." Contacted by investigators later in the week, all of the men interviewed claimed that they had been lured into indiscretions by misleading questions.[54]

The marines banned Safer from their area of operations but rescinded the order when Legare pointed out that MACV had responsibility for disciplining reporters. Arthur Sylvester was less discreet. When Safer broke MACV's new ground rules a short time later by revealing without official leave that U.S. airborne forces were moving to the Central Highlands because a Special Forces camp in the area was under attack, the assistant secretary contacted Fred Friendly, the president of CBS News. Alluding to Safer's Canadian origins, Sylvester suggested that the reporter had "no interest in our efforts in Vietnam" and that "an American reporter . . . would be more sensitive."[55]

Friendly refused to reassign Safer. The reporter's film showed clearly that huts had been destroyed without any indication of enemy resistance, he said, and MACV had yet to produce evidence of enemy fortifications at Cam Ne. As for the incident at Pleiku, Safer had been unable to contact MACV's office of information but had obtained clearance from the most senior officer present. Indeed, officers at the scene had told him that the enemy was well aware troops were arriving in the area.[56]

Sylvester's letter, Friendly continued, was an attempt at "character assassination." The suggestion that an American might be more suitable than a Canadian was really an assertion that an American would be "more sympathetic" to the official line. "You don't want anything you consider damaging to our morale or our world-wide image reported. We don't want to violate purely *military* security . . . [or to] endanger the life of a single soldier but . . . we must insist upon our right to report what is actually happening despite the political consequences. . . . In the long term, this, too, will help enhance our nation's position in the eyes of the world."[57]

Sylvester's attempt to have Safer recalled had hardly ended when another controversy involving the marines arose. On 14 August, an AP photographer gave the U.S. mission in Saigon pictures of South Vietnamese soldiers torturing enemy captives while U.S. marines looked on. Learning of the photographs, General Westmoreland directed General Walt to do everything possible to separate the American presence in Vietnam from brutality or violations of the laws of war. Even if Walt was unable to moderate the way the South Vietnamese treated their enemies, he could at least "try to keep Americans out of the picture."[58]

Reacting to pressure from the Joint Chiefs of Staff, who were concerned that news of atrocities might dampen public acceptance of larger troop commitments, Westmoreland in the end laid down guidelines to govern operations that involved civilians. These rules prohibited the indiscriminate destruction of populated zones. Instead, commanders, forward air controllers, and helicopter pilots were to select targets only after giving due consideration to civilian lives and property. Units in the field were to use loudspeakers and leaflet drops to warn villagers of imminent air and ground assaults wherever security allowed. South Vietnamese officers were to accompany large operations both to identify the enemy and to ensure close coordination between U.S. and local forces. When possible, South Vietnamese units were to fight alongside American forces down to the company level to serve as intermediaries with the people.[59]

By the time the directive appeared on 7 September, the marines were already putting many of its provisions into practice. On 9 August, for example, when marine units once more entered Cam Ne and suffered two killed and twenty-one wounded, Safer reported that the units involved searched for enemy hideouts but also gave full warning by dropping leaflets from helicopters. Then, before departing, they attempted to show their concern for the people by building shelters for the homeless. One marine officer told the reporter, "All of that bad publicity generated by the action at Cam Ne has done more good than harm."[60]

General Westmoreland could hardly agree. Believing that television had a powerful influence on the attitudes of Americans and that stories such as Safer's could only turn public opinion against the war, he instructed Legare to consider whether it would be possible to put television reporters under some sort of constraint. Recognizing that any attempt to discriminate between print and television journalists could well demolish official credibility, Legare passed the request to Sylvester. Six days later, in policy guidance for all military commands throughout the world, the Defense Department specified that information was to be "equally available . . . to all media and all media representatives" without discrimination.[61]

Although the furor over Cam Ne died down quickly, Safer's reporting resurrected talk of censorship in official circles. It became so heavy that Sylvester had no choice but to instruct the commander of the army reserve's field press censorship detachment, Col. Ervin F. Kushner, to devise a plan. Meanwhile, Bankson was to do another study on whether the expedient would work.[62]

Both the State Department and MACV objected. State pointed out that heavy-handed South Vietnamese officials might antagonize non-American correspondents, complicating President Johnson's attempt to win international support for the war. Colonel Legare, meanwhile, observed that the government would have to censor editorials and news analyses to stifle critical comment on the war and that any attempt to do so would violate the First Amendment. If that occurred, he said, Congress, the public, and the press might unite in opposition to the president and the war.[63]

Sylvester was convinced, but he still wanted to have a plan on hand in case his superiors inquired. When Kushner's design proved impractical—it failed, for example, to account for reporters' ability to file dispatches from outside of South Vietnam—Sylvester assigned the task to Charles W. Hinkle, the director of the Defense Department's Office of Security Review. When Hinkle declined to sign his name to a program he knew would fail, the assistant secretary then passed the task to the newly designated special assistant for Southeast Asia, Bankson's replacement, Col. Winant Sidle. Convinced that censorship would be counterproductive, Sidle proceeded to draw up a plan so ponderous that it could never become a serious alternative to Zorthian's voluntary guidelines. Under it, MACV would have to create a huge, multilingual establishment just to review news dispatches. Elaborate film-processing and film-viewing facilities would also have to be built to allow for the review of the thousands of feet of news film reporters produced every day. The mountains of letters and packages mailed daily from South Vietnam would also have to be screened. In the end, the system would employ hundreds.[64]

Transmitting an information copy of Sidle's plan to the State Department in August 1966, a year later than intended, Sylvester noted that the Defense Department had no intention of ever instituting censorship. With that, all consideration of the question ended. As the American buildup proceeded and the war lengthened, the Saigon correspondents would report as they saw fit, under only the lightest official scrutiny.[65]

5

Keeping a Low Profile

As the war accelerated, the press corps in South Vietnam grew from 40 correspondents at the beginning of 1964 to 282 in January 1966. Only 110 were Americans and 67 South Vietnamese. The remainder came from countries as diverse as Britain, France, Germany, South Korea, Japan, Ceylon, India, Canada, Italy, Australia, Ireland, Thailand, Denmark, the Republic of China, and New Zealand. No more than one-third were true, working reporters. The rest were support personnel—secretaries, interpreters, sound technicians, cameramen—or spouses who had gained accreditation in order to use the post exchange in Saigon. Nearly half were over the age of thirty-six.[1]

The increase created strains with the South Vietnamese, who resented the reporters' preoccupation with the American side of the war. The U.S. State and Defense Departments responded by instructing Westmoreland to include South Vietnamese units in every American operation and to credit them with victories whenever he could. Zorthian, meanwhile, attempted to highlight South Vietnamese exertions by pushing the Saigon regime to create a press center and to begin weekly news conferences. In the end, however, neither effort came to much. Intent on the growing American role in the war, the Saigon correspondents continued to write accordingly. Meanwhile, the South Vietnamese briefings were so boring and uninformative that most reporters sent their Vietnamese assistants to cover the sessions.[2]

The nature of the war compounded the problem. Characterized by sudden flare-ups and widely scattered action, it taxed the ingenuity of newsmen who were under instructions to report combat. Scrambling for any edge over the competition, the reporters concentrated on what they knew. In the process, much to President Johnson's chagrin, they not only emphasized the American side of the war but also sometimes distorted it by reporting engagements involving companies, platoons, and even squads as if they had involved the divisions and regiments of World War II.[3]

Although the stories aggravated U.S. commanders, some were clearly of benefit to the troops. When the AP revealed a shortage of boots in the 101st Airborne Division, commanders complained bitterly that the problem was routine, but the men still probably received replacements much more quickly than they would have if the press had said nothing. In the same way, when Jack Laurence of CBS News revealed that discarded live grenades were turning up in U.S. garbage dumps, where they were killing South Vietnamese scavengers, the story led to a redoubling of U.S. efforts to ensure proper garbage disposal.[4]

beneficial reporting

There were also occasions when news stories could work to the advantage of MACV itself. During the first week in September 1965, for example, an enemy force under attack by U.S. Marines barricaded itself in bunkers and tunnels behind some four hundred civilians, many of them women and children. The marine commander, Lt. Col. Leon M. Utter, used tear gas to drive the throng into the open, where his men eliminated the Viet Cong without harming the civilians. As luck would have it, an AP correspondent saw everything. Aware of MACV's rule barring the use of gas, the reporter asked Utter whether the command had approved the move. The officer, who may or may not have known of the prohibition, responded forthrightly that he had made the decision on his own.[5]

Learning of the incident, official spokesmen held a special briefing in Saigon to put what had happened into the best light possible. They stressed Utter's humanitarian motives, pointed out that the use of riot-control agents was morally preferable to the flamethrowers and grenades that the marines would normally have employed, and asked reporters to refrain from publicizing the incident in order to protect Utter's military career. The story, however, was too big to hold. It broke the next day. When it did, official Washington braced for an uproar, but nothing happened. Instead, UPI noted blandly that Utter had apparently been unaware of MACV's prohibition on the use of gas; Reuters brought out the officer's humanity; and the AP asserted that many officers believed that tear gas was the best means for handling situations such as the one the colonel had encountered.[6]

Realizing that the positive attitude of the press represented an opening, General Westmoreland immediately requested authority to reinstate the use of gas to clear caves, tunnels, and underground shelters. The tactic, he said, would have reduced American casualties at Cam Ne. Shortly thereafter, an editorial in the *New York Times* avowed that the employment of riot munitions was "obviously more humane than any other effective type of action." If the United States abandoned that tactic, the newspaper said, it would "condemn to death or injury many more Americans and Vietnamese than the absolute necessities of war demand."[7]

Moved by the lack of negative press coverage and the *Times*'s editorial, President Johnson tested the waters by authorizing Westmoreland to use gas during an attack scheduled for 25 September. McNamara instructed MACV to hold a briefing prior to the operation to explain the move and to emphasize the lack of risk it involved to both Americans and South Vietnamese. The command later canceled the operation, but Westmoreland rescheduled the first use of gas for 8 October, when portions of the 173d Airborne were to investigate an enemy tunnel complex in the Iron Triangle, an enemy base area located thirty kilometers northwest of Saigon.[8]

The news stories that followed the event bore little resemblance to the angry denunciations that had accompanied Peter Arnett's revelation earlier in the year. What criticism there was focused on the public affairs effort that accompanied the operation. An article by John Maffre in the *Washington Post* was typical. It underscored the humanity of the tactic but then noted acidly that the operation had occurred "with as much detailed planning in public relations as normally goes into a major operational assault." One day after it appeared, Westmoreland sought permission to employ tear and nausea gases at his own discretion. Three weeks later, in the absence of any further outcry in the press, the Joint Chiefs complied.[9]

In the end, if the controversy over the use of tear gas came out well for the government, it nonetheless augured ill for the future. For if the public consensus on the war was so fragile that Johnson and his advisers felt constrained to shape the courses of action they would take according to whether the press agreed or disagreed, what would happen in the future, when truly difficult choices had to be made?

There were no real solutions to the problem short of abandoning South Vietnam or deciding to go all out with the war, but the Johnson administration did adopt an approach that promised to provide a measure of leverage. Convinced that public support would erode as the conflict escalated and American casualties increased, it moved to reduce the impact of the events and decisions to come by tightening its hold on the news. The first steps dealt solely with information of value to the enemy. MACV announced during mid-August that it would no longer release figures on the number of aircraft attacking North Vietnam and tonnages for bombs dropped to keep the enemy from adjusting his defenses to meet American tactics. A second set of restrictions came later in the month, when Zorthian and Legare terminated the practice of revealing specific casualty figures off the record because reporters sometimes used the information to question MACV's characterization of losses as "moderate."[10]

The success of the measures led, perhaps inevitably, to pressure for others that were less easy to justify. An incident in which public affairs officers at MACV mistakenly revealed an air strike well within a thirty-mile no-fly zone the United States had set between North Vietnam and China provided the occasion. The criticism that followed in the press prompted General Wheeler to question whether MACV was required to incur self-inflicted wounds by revealing its own mistakes. Admiral Sharp advised against any attempt to hold back on grounds that if the press found out, the lack of credibility that would result "could cause

General Earle G. Wheeler. (U.S. Army)

problems far more serious than . . . the revelation of occasional mistakes." Westmoreland, however, agreed with Wheeler. Since reporters had no way of finding out about strikes in North Vietnam, he told the chairman, "an error in target can be protected until I feel it is to our advantage to notify the press."[11]

Later in the month, a reference by UPI to secret radio detection equipment aboard U.S. aircraft produced more discussion of restrictions. General Wheeler, in particular, declared his distress at the close associations newsmen had developed with some members of the military because they might lead to the revelation of classified information. The policy of maximum candor, he said, had "had its day." Westmoreland responded that the existence of radio detection aircraft in South Vietnam was no secret to anyone, but that he would instruct members of the military to keep "a friendly but dignified" distance from the press. He added that MACV was already taking steps to do that. The command's evening briefing was no longer a casual gathering but a formal news conference, and his own background briefings for selected newsmen had moved from their original informal setting in his office to a more decorous conference room.[12]

Despite the strides the U.S. mission was making in dealing with the press, officials in Washington remained dissatisfied and continued to push for changes. Arthur Sylvester, for one, complained during October that reporters tended to interpret the absence of a large body count as evidence that an operation had failed. He wanted MACV's briefers to begin stressing that military operations had many objectives, from disrupting enemy communications to freeing South Vietnam's peasants from the Communists. President Johnson, for his part, was concerned that reporters tended to concentrate on what their readers wanted most, news of U.S. troops in combat, and that the approach might ultimately limit public support for the war. He instructed public affairs officers in Saigon to play down combat and to highlight newsworthy nonmilitary activities such as road construction, well digging, and rice distribution.[13]

As Sylvester had perceived, most reporters did believe that numbers were the game, but so did some of the war's most important managers. One week after the assistant secretary lodged his complaint, for example, Secretary McNamara drew upon body counts at a Pentagon briefing to demonstrate that American forces in South Vietnam were achieving good results. In the same way, on 30 October, Admiral Sharp avowed in a message to Westmoreland that "figures reflecting Viet Cong casualties" were "of great significance in estimating Viet Cong capabilities." If the news media were clearly preoccupied with numbers, they were thus not alone.[14]

The same was true for Johnson's instructions to lower the profile of the war. Reporters paid great attention to combat, but so did their sources. At the end of October, for example, while Zorthian was pointing reporters to civic events and nation-building activities, officials in Washington were announcing that U.S. forces would shortly achieve a solid beachhead along the length of South Vietnam's northern coast. The event prompted Ambassador Lodge to tell his superiors pointedly that if military commanders were seeking to play down the American role in the war, officials in Washington were making far too much of it.[15]

For a time, slackening combat in South Vietnam drew reporters in the direction Johnson wanted, but the trend proved temporary. During October, the pace of the fighting quickened, with American forces entering combat in earnest. Reporters could see it all, and the conclusions they drew were of little consolation to officials.

During an engagement at Plei Me in the Central Highlands, Charles Mohr of the *New York Times* watched as a single enemy soldier armed only with grenades routed two platoons of government irregulars. In the stinging story that followed, the reporter quoted an American adviser who pointed to a Viet Cong captive and remarked, "We ought to put this guy on the north wall and throw out these government troops. He would probably hold it alone."[16]

A monthlong campaign mounted by Westmoreland to find and destroy the enemy regiments that had threatened Plei Me further diverted reporters. At first, the operation went well. Uncovering an enemy hospital, the troops discovered a map that detailed the Viet Cong's bases and trails. With it in hand, the U.S. First Cavalry Division (Airmobile) proceeded to demolish the Thirty-third North Vietnamese Regiment.[17] Even so, the enemy had his day. On 14 November, one of his reinforced regiments surprised a U.S. battalion at a landing zone code-named X-ray. After a harrowing day and night, all of it chronicled by UPI correspondent Joseph Galloway, the American force drove the enemy from the field and claimed victory. The following day, however, a battalion stumbled into a hastily devised enemy ambush near a landing zone named Albany. The attack almost annihilated an entire American company and rendered the battalion combat-ineffective. In all, the First Cavalry suffered 151 killed, 121 wounded, and 4 missing.

As the battle progressed, perhaps to give relief forces time to change the complexion of what had happened, the First Cavalry's officers concealed the disaster even from General Westmoreland, who visited their command post during the fighting but learned only that a battalion had repelled a determined enemy assault. The Saigon correspondents, however, had heard of the fighting from their contacts, and Neil Sheehan and Peter Arnett were already on their way to the scene. Although Westmoreland soon began to suspect that something was amiss because of the large number of casualties arriving at medical receiving stations, it was only when the reporters returned to Saigon to file their reports that he learned the details of what had happened.[18]

Despite his disappointment in his officers, Westmoreland disciplined no one. Instead, at a special background briefing on 20 November, he accused newsmen of informing the enemy of American mistakes, of discrediting the United States before its allies, and of lowering the morale of both the troops in the field and their families at home. In fact, he said, the operation in the Ia Drang valley had been an "unprecedented victory" because the enemy had fled the field and had suffered casualties far in excess of those of the United States. To the chagrin of reporters, MACV then balanced the carnage at Albany against the total number of troops in the area and labeled casualties for the operation "moderate."[19]

The combination of Westmoreland's remarks with MACV's comment about moderate casualties threw the press into full cry. Reporters in both South Vietnam and the United States alleged that the command was whitewashing its losses. One of the most telling commentaries came from *New York Times* correspondent Charles Mohr. Asserting that "a steady stream of misinformation" was emanating from the U.S. command, the reporter used the body count as an example. During the Pleiku campaign, he said, one battalion commander had seen his estimate of 160 enemy dead in a two-day operation grow to 869 by the time it reached the press. Australian war correspondent Denis Warner agreed. A veteran of every conflict in Southeast Asia since World War II, the reporter charged that a huge discrepancy existed between the enemy casualties claimed by Westmoreland's command and the number of enemy weapons actually recovered on the battlefield. Military reverses were acceptable to most nations, he said. "What no one will accept indefinitely . . . is the persistent attempt to win by pretense what has not been won on the ground." *Newsweek* concentrated on MACV's handling of American casualties. Since the command described losses in the context of the total force involved in an operation, the magazine's editors remarked, the terms *light, moderate,* and *heavy* could mean anything it wanted. A battalion might lose a platoon, but if that unit constituted only 1 or 2 percent of its total strength, the casualties would be announced as light.[20]

The furor over the Plei Me campaign came at an extremely inopportune moment for President Johnson. During November, secret administration testimony before Congress had leaked to the press. It indicated that a U.S. intervention in the Dominican Republic earlier in the year had not been an attempt to rescue Americans stranded in a foreign revolution, as official spokesmen had proclaimed, but instead was an attempt to prevent a Communist takeover. Then, on 30 November, CBS News commentator Eric Sevareid revealed in *Look* magazine that Adlai Stevenson, the former U.S. ambassador to the United Nations, had revealed in a conversation just two days before his death that during 1964 the United States had twice rejected North Vietnamese offers to discuss peace.[21]

By December 1965, those reports and others like them had thrown the Johnson administration's continuing assertions that it sought only peace in Vietnam into doubt. On 17 December, Seymour Topping of the New York Times and Keyes Beech of the Chicago Daily News used leaked information to reveal that the president had authorized American troops to fire across South Vietnam's border into Cambodia, and even to enter that country itself if that proved necessary for the self-defense of the troops. Inclined to say as little as possible on the subject, MACV spokesmen filed a no comment when first queried on the stories, but that only fueled speculation. In the end, the command had no choice but to conduct a backgrounder on the new policy attributable only to "authoritative sources." The State Department, meanwhile, announced quietly that American commanders throughout the world had authority to do what was essential to protect the lives of their troops.[22]

Neither the backgrounder nor the announcement did anything to stifle speculation that the United States was about to widen the war. Reporters in Washington asked sarcastically how the exercise of self-defense squared with the sovereignty, independence, and territorial integrity of Cambodia. In Saigon, R. W. Apple of the New York Times remarked that even if the new policy had logic on its side, the United States was still obviously "edging closer to . . . confrontation . . . throughout Southeast Asia."[23]

A series of news stories based on leaked information and appearing at the time bolstered Apple's point. On 13 December, Joseph Fried of the New York Daily News disclosed that American aircraft were spraying defoliants on enemy supply lines in Laos. Two days later, Fried revealed that a recent air strike against a North Vietnamese power plant had not been the routine mission MACV had depicted but retaliation for a recent enemy attack on a U.S. enlisted billet in Saigon. Then, on 18 December, UPI correspondent Ray Herndon divulged that B-52 bombers were conducting strikes against Communist infiltration routes in Laos. Herndon's story was particularly galling because the U.S. ambassador to Laos, William H. Sullivan, had never informed Laotian premier Souvanna Phouma of the raids.[24]

Realizing that the leaks behind the stories had come from high-level members of the U.S. Air Force who wanted their service to receive public credit for its efforts, and that the problem stemmed from the unrealistic public affairs policies surrounding the war in Laos, officials at the Defense Department suggested that the time had come for a change. With the Soviet Union willing to wink at U.S. efforts in Laos as long as they went unacknowledged, however, the Johnson administration refused. Instead, when the next B-52s departed for Laos, planners saw to it that the target straddled the border so that official spokesmen could tell reporters the strike had occurred in South Vietnam.[25]

Although unyielding on Laos, President Johnson understood the importance of good public relations. Polling important members of Congress, he learned that a number of legislators believed the American people were disturbed by lengthening casualty lists and were uncertain about the alternatives available. If the administration intended to enlarge the war, Senator Robert F. Kennedy observed, it would first have to build up support at home by making a bold move for peace. Many senators favored a pause in the bombing of North Vietnam as the best approach. As Senator Sam Ervin remarked, the United States should give the Communists a chance to stop their aggression—but then bomb them out of existence as soon as their ill will became apparent.[26]

Although Westmoreland opposed a bombing halt, arguing that the enemy was infiltrating troops into South Vietnam at a rate unmatched by the United States and that the president should step up the tempo of the air war rather than reduce it, President Johnson found the benefits to be gained from the move tantalizing. For if recent polls indicated that 73 percent of the American people favored a renewed effort for a cease-fire, they also showed that 61 percent would favor increased bombing if that pause failed to elicit a positive response from Hanoi. In that light, as Rusk observed in a message to Westmoreland, Wheeler, and Sharp, the pause would help to sustain support "for what has to be done in [the] months ahead." Meanwhile, the risks would be minimal. Bad weather over North Vietnam during January would preclude most air strikes anyway, allowing the bombers to concentrate on infiltration routes in Laos.[27]

On 27 December, without any announcement, Johnson decided to extend that year's Christmas bombing halt for an indefinite period. In the days that followed, as the truce expanded beyond its announced limits and ambassadors departed for every corner of the globe to bring international pressure to bear upon North Vietnam, the American news media had no doubt that some sort of initiative was under way. Although some reporters speculated that the halt was merely the prelude to larger operations if American moves for peace failed, the New York Times and other papers greeted it optimistically in hopes that it would lead to a lasting cease-fire.[28]

General Wheeler and Ambassador Lodge were not nearly as confident. Although air sorties in Laos had more than doubled since the beginning of the bombing halt, Wheeler told McNamara, the enemy had countered them by dispersing his forces and breaking up his supply depots. Meanwhile, the Communists were increasing the flow of men and matériel into South Vietnam. Ambassador Lodge was equally emphatic. MACV had recorded 1,122 overt enemy acts of aggression between 26 December and 1 January, he told President Johnson on 5 January 1966. That was the highest total since the beginning of American troop involvement in the war. In that light, whatever its effect on public opinion, the pause had "definitely caused losses."[29]

State Department analysts disputed Wheeler's and Lodge's assertions, contending that enemy activity levels in South Vietnam had changed little since

Christmas and that U.S. forces were in no immediate danger. Whatever the validity of the point, Johnson was willing to bear the risk. Although the fifteen hundred Americans already lost in the war represented a terrible responsibility, he told Ambassador G. Mennen Williams, as many lives were lost monthly in the United States in traffic accidents.[30]

As expected, the halt produced no worthwhile response from Hanoi. On 25 January, the Defense Department released a detailed report to the press documenting Hanoi's use of the interval to increase its infiltration of men and matériel into the South. When the bombing resumed five days later, few Americans were dismayed. Harris polls revealed that 60 percent even advocated the deployment of five hundred thousand men if that would shorten the war. The halt had achieved its goal.[31]

If Americans seemed supportive, however, public opinion on the war was hardly as clear-cut as it seemed. Interviewing a carefully selected cross section of Americans during February and March 1966, researchers at Stanford University found that although most approved of Johnson's handling of the war, those same individuals favored de-escalation. Eighty percent were open to bargaining with the Viet Cong, 70 percent approved of free elections even if the enemy won, and 52 percent would accept a coalition government in South Vietnam that included Communists. Forty-nine percent supported the status quo, 23 percent full-scale war, and 19 percent withdrawal. Asked to choose between withdrawal and a war that might cause hundreds of thousands of casualties, the 49 percent who favored the status quo chose war, but a majority of those who responded to the survey rejected tax increases or cuts in social services to finance the conflict.[32]

The poll's findings were used by all sides in the debate over the war, with each commentator interpreting them according to his own preconceptions. A number asserted that the survey had uncovered strong support for the conflict and attributed responses that disagreed with that conclusion to leading questions rigged by obviously antiwar academics. In fact, the study's authors asserted that its results favored neither the pro-war nor the antiwar position. Instead, they said, it showed that there was little backing in the country for either withdrawal or all-out war but substantial support for holding military operations steady while making new efforts to seek peace.[33]

That conclusion came close to the Johnson administration's own estimate of American public opinion. Although done with peace feelers for the time being and bent upon escalation, the president sought to cultivate an appearance of moderation in order to alienate as few voters as possible. To that end, on 29 December 1965, the Defense Department issued rules forbidding the release of advance information on deployments to South Vietnam. Ostensibly an attempt to deny information to the enemy, the order had the effect of presenting critics with a fait accompli each time new American units departed for Vietnam. In the same way, to avoid giving opponents of the war the slightest edge, General Wheeler instructed MACV to choose nonprovocative titles for combat operations. Within days, the name of Operation Masher in Binh Dinh Province changed abruptly (and with, perhaps, a touch of irony) to White Wing.[34]

At that point, the president made his first attempt to trade upon the army's heretofore high credibility with the American public by pulling Westmoreland into the politics surrounding the war. When the Associated Press Managing Editors Association invited the general to speak at an April luncheon, Johnson pressed him to attend. The meeting would be "an unusually good forum," Johnson said, to assist in drawing public opinion into line with official policy. Uncomfortable with the idea, Westmoreland declined.[35]

With the war escalating and the news media alert for any new development, the system for handling the press in South Vietnam was by then beginning to sag. MACV was barely able to cope with the nearly three hundred reporters on the scene, and there seemed little chance that it could handle the influx that would accompany the enlarged war President Johnson contemplated. Communications facilities were so deficient that a telephone call to a point more than fifteen miles outside of Saigon took hours to complete. As a result, public affairs officers had no quick way to gather details on fast-breaking news, and reporters in the field had no reliable means to move stories to their bureaus in Saigon. Meanwhile, with only a single helicopter available for the use of the press, reporters seeking to reach units in the field had to hitch rides, a process, Peter Kalischer of CBS News remarked, that required "gall, contacts, and steady nerves."[36]

The effort to remedy these problems began in November 1965, when Arthur Sylvester approved construction of a special Teletype system to link major military bases in South Vietnam with MACV in Saigon. He also authorized a special news flight each day from Saigon to Nha Trang, Qui Nhon, Da Nang, Pleiku, and back. Delayed until January 1966 by a shortage of cargo aircraft, the arrangement proved so inflexible that MACV replaced it within the month with a more adaptable approach in which four passenger flights made the circuit per day with fifteen seats each reserved for newsmen.[37]

While these adjustments were occurring, MACV was also fine-tuning arrangements for reporters in the field. Earlier in the war, most of the news had occurred in areas close to Saigon and easily accessible to the press. With the arrival of the marines at Da Nang, however, a number of correspondents had moved north. To accommodate them, MACV had created a press center at Da Nang staffed by the marines. It provided newsmen with short-term lodging, occasional briefings, and tips on stories. Later, when poor communications caused long delays in the release of news from Da Nang to correspondents in Saigon, MACOI designated the new center a semi-independent extension of itself. Under policy guidance from the U.S. mission, the facility became the sole release point for news of American actions in the northernmost regions of South Vietnam. It held a daily briefing and released a daily communiqué.[38]

As the war continued, MACV established three more press centers: at Nha

Television gear was cumbersome and difficult to handle in the field. (Don North)

Trang in the II Corps Zone, at Long Binh in the III Corps Zone, and at Can Tho in the Mekong delta. Only the one at Nha Trang survived. The others were too near to Saigon to attract many newsmen. Later, the army set up other press centers at Qui Nhon, Pleiku, and An Khe. For the rest, most major American units in South Vietnam made provisions of their own for visiting newsmen. The best-established provided comfortable facilities that featured private rooms, bars, and regular movies. In the field, however, reporters often received little more than a poncho, a sleeping bag, and the same rations as the troops for a small fee. "My own worst nights were spent in Plei Me Special Forces Camp, where rats kept running over our chests," New York Times correspondent Charles Mohr remarked, " . . . and in a flooded sugar cane field . . . where Jack Foisie of the Los Angeles Times bitterly contested the single, tiny, hip-sized patch of dry ground I had found."[39]

Public affairs officers were supposed to treat all reporters the same, but, in fact, differences in handling were sometimes pronounced. As Washington Post correspondent Peter Braestrup remarked, reporters for prestigious print organizations such as the New York Times and the Washington Post received considerable assistance from information officers, but television and wire service reporters received much less. The print reporters had time to cultivate their sources and tended to cover all sides of a story. The others were under short deadlines, had no time for niceties, and sometimes leaped to hasty conclusions. Rodger Bankson, the chief of MACV information during 1967, confirmed Braestrup's observation. He soon learned, he said, whom he could trust. He could vouch for newsmen such as Wendell "Bud" Merick of U.S. News & World Report without having to worry about a breach of security later, but newsmen who had embarrassed MACV, such as Peter Arnett and Morley Safer, received only what he was required to give, nothing more.[40]

MACV also streamlined the way it accredited reporters. Since all, prior to 1965, had received accreditation from the Defense Department, the command had left the paperwork to South Vietnamese officials, who issued an initial one-month approval but then never bothered to follow up with more. With three hundred reporters present in South Vietnam by late 1965, however, the system was under stress and needed to be formalized. At the end of November, therefore, MACV announced that newsmen with Defense Department accreditations would receive automatic credentials, while all others would have to fill out a personal information form, supply a picture, and provide a letter from a bona fide news organization stating that it would take responsibility for their conduct. Freelance reporters were to present a letter from one of their clients affirming that agency's willingness to buy their work. There were complaints at the time from officials in Washington that MACV was giving out accreditation cards rather too freely, but there was little anyone could do. In an open society, the press employs who it wants.[41]

Another series of attempts to tighten information policy accompanied the change in accreditation procedures. For a time, to limit details available to the enemy, the Defense Department pressed MACV to reduce the size of its daily communiqué by cutting the document to 350 words. It relented when public affairs officers pointed out that an absence of officially sanctioned news would force reporters to turn to rumors and hearsay. "If we are to retain the support of the public," they added, "it is essential that the people receive and believe they are receiving the facts."[42]

On another issue, however, MACV and the Defense Department were in full accord. Where pictures of the war appearing in the press and on television were concerned, both wanted them to further American ends. Because of that, the Defense Department dispatched a ten-man camera team to South Vietnam in July 1964 to depict subjects such as pacification that news photographers tended to slight in favor of military action. The program was too complicated for MACV to absorb at the time, but in the fall of 1965 the command resurrected the idea, adding a motion picture unit to the team to balance footage broadcast by the television networks. In the end, if most major news organizations preferred the work of their own correspondents and considered MACV's effort propaganda, smaller regional newspapers and television outlets became willing patrons.[43]

Officials were also concerned that guidelines had never been developed to cover news photography. No one wanted the family of a dead or wounded American to learn of its loss through a grisly film report on television or a picture in a newspaper. During the Korean War, censorship had largely solved the problem, but that was impossible in Vietnam. In addition, any attempt to restrict television crews would inevitably lower official credibility in the eyes of the rest of the press, an offense against one being, to most reporters, a threat to all. Indeed, even voluntary guidelines would not work. In the heat and action of combat, film crews had little control over what occurred in front of their cameras, and since facilities for developing news film were virtually nonexistent in Vietnam, they had no chance to review their work before it left the country. In the end, MACV and the Defense Department opted for an informal approach. On 24 April, Zorthian and Bankson, who had replaced Legare on 5 February, met with representatives of the three American television networks to warn them that if complaints about film footage of the dead and wounded arose, commanders in the field would almost certainly deny them the right to accompany troops into combat. Defense did the same in Washington, at a meeting with executives from all the major news film producers in the United States, from the television networks to organizations such as Metro-Goldwyn-Mayer.[44]

The news media went along, either because of the threat or, more likely, to keep gruesome pictures broadcast at the dinner hour from prompting viewers to change stations. The result was that American television viewers, contrary to allegations by critics of the news media, were rarely treated to scenes depicting the war in all its bloody detail. Indeed, according to researcher Lawrence Lichty, between August 1965 and August 1970 only seventy-six out of some twenty-three hundred television news reports originating in Vietnam showed heavy fighting— soldiers in combat, incoming artillery, or American dead and wounded within sight on the ground. Instead, as television analyst Michael Arlen asserted, viewers received a "distanced overview . . . composed mainly of scenes of helicopters landing, tall grasses blowing, . . . soldiers fanning out . . . , rifles at the ready, with now and then (on the soundtrack) a far-off ping or two, and . . . (as the visual grand finale) a column of dark, billowing smoke a half mile away, invariably described as a burning Viet Cong ammo dump."[45]

Upon arriving in South Vietnam, Rodger Bankson encountered a number of administrative problems within MACV's office of information that also needed remedies. At a time when reporters were demanding more and better information, for example, efficiency was diminishing within the organization because officers were arriving without the skills their assignments required. Bankson handled the problem simply, by notifying each of the services that if it failed to provide proper staffing for positions it had to fill, he would do it himself with people of his own choice, whatever their service. Unwilling to surrender positions of influence in the information program, the services began to give greater thought to their assignments.[46]

Bankson also discovered that there were problems with the nightly briefings, which newsmen and officials alike had by then dubbed "The Five O'Clock Follies." With tensions high and reporters constantly disputing official assertions, the professionalism of the officers in charge was critical. Briefers with combat experience seemed to do the best. Others rarely possessed the insight and experience necessary to satisfy the reporters. Moving quickly because the briefings were the single most important source of news for the press, Bankson eliminated much of the pressure on his people by increasing the number of spokesmen from one to four and by creating alternating teams of two briefers each. One officer dealt with the ground war, while the other handled air operations. Later Bankson added a third officer to cover actions involving the navy. He found over time that the switch of subjects and briefers had an unexpected benefit: it served almost invariably to cut off debate.[47] In the same way, Bankson made a special effort to identify briefers who had both combat and public affairs experience. He found that the arrival of the new men brought about a steady improvement in MACV's credibility, if only because reporters trusted line over staff officers. Overall, his changes were so well received by the press that reporters on one occasion jeered at a correspondent who had authored a story criticizing MACV's information effort because that individual had continued to use the command's facilities despite his so-called reservations.[48]

If Bankson succeeded in reorganizing MACV's handling of the press, he made little progress in removing the command's restrictions on acknowledging the use of napalm, defoliation, and sophisticated armaments such as cluster bombs and flechette ammunition. In the past, he observed, official spokesmen had declined to acknowledge the presence of those weapons in order to deny the Communists a chance to claim that the United States was waging a terror campaign. Yet by 1966, everyone in South Vietnam knew they were present and in use. Official confirmation of the obvious would eliminate an important bone of contention with the press while reassuring the families of the troops in the field that their sons were receiving the best America had to offer.[49]

Admiral Sharp denied the request—on grounds that he had no wish to give the enemy even the slightest advantage and that confirmation of such emotional topics could only fuel antiwar sentiment in the United States. Not to be deterred, Bankson took up the subject again two months later, asserting that American aircraft had recently dropped cluster bombs by accident on a friendly village, causing a large number of casualties. As a result, he said, exaggerated news stories referring to "some exotic new weapons system" were beginning to appear in the United States. Sharp again refused.[50]

Although the admiral managed to hold the line on controversial weapons and munitions, the Johnson administration did give way on another of its policies, the one mandating secrecy on virtually every aspect of the war in Laos. When the family of an airman killed during a strike in Laos went to the newspapers with the story in May 1966, the Defense Department finally admitted that some eleven airmen had died there over the previous two years. In order to give that portion of the war the lowest possible profile, however, the department neglected to reveal that eleven more had been killed prior to that time. The move disturbed Arthur Sylvester, particularly when stories began to appear in the press during July 1966 detailing what reporters called "the clandestine war in Laos" and alleging that the United States was concealing casualties. Sylvester appealed to McNamara for a change of policy, avowing that "the severe blow which could be inflicted by the revelation that we are hiding casualties could be a telling one in the November [off-year] elections."[51]

The secretary agreed. On 3 August he instructed MACV to change the lead sentence of its weekly casualty summary from "casualties incurred by U.S. military personnel in Vietnam" to "casualties incurred by U.S. military personnel in connection with the conflict in Vietnam." Although newsmen would inevitably link the change to the addition of casualties in Laos, there was to be no acknowledgment that anything was different. As always, the command's spokesmen were to decline to admit that the United States was conducting operations in Laos.[52]

To Sylvester's chagrin, the State Department partially nullified the effect of the change by specifying that casualties among the 125 military attachés assigned to the U.S. mission in Vientiane were not to be included in the report. The department took this step to keep reporters from surmising that the attachés were in fact advisers to the Laotian army, but the rationale it gave, that those individuals were unconnected with the war in South Vietnam, was far-fetched at best. Rather than indulge in a debilitating interagency argument, Sylvester sidestepped the problem by notifying the policy's creators that he would refer all questions on the subject to them for response.[53]

Less easy to remedy were the leaks of classified information that continued to appear in the press. Some had resulted from chance slips of the tongue and others from good detective work by skillful reporters, but many were clearly the work of persons well placed at MACV. Bankson believed that interservice rivalry was at the root of the problem. Constrained by rules such as the ones on Laos, individuals within the army, air force, navy, and marines had come to believe that the efforts of their services were going unnoticed by the American public. The leaks were their way of compensating.[54]

Bankson was willing to live with the complaints that emanated from the various service information offices in South Vietnam, especially those of army public affairs officers who resented the unique entitlements the marine press center enjoyed at Da Nang. When it became clear, however, that the director of information, Seventh Air Force, Col. William McGinty, with the connivance of high officers within his service, was behind many of the revelations involving the air war, he took immediate steps to have the officer reassigned. In the end, however, the episode proved an exception. Leaking continued, and no one except McGinty was ever apprehended. The problem of interservice rivalry also remained. At one point, MACV even had to station an official observer at the Da Nang press center to keep the briefers there from attempting to make the war seem an exclusively Marine Corps affair.

For the rest, if MACV had succeeded in streamlining its handling of the press in order to assist the Johnson administration in keeping the war in low profile, events would shortly show that there was little chance the effort would succeed. The conflict had gone too far for that.

6

The South Vietnamese Dimension

The low profile President Johnson sought became impossible shortly after the December bombing halt. During January 1966, the chairman of the Senate Foreign Relations Committee, Senator J. William Fulbright of Arkansas, questioned further escalation of the war and decided to hold public hearings on the president's Vietnam policies. To dilute the impact of the inquiry, McNamara and Wheeler immediately refused to testify in public session. Then, in a move that both Fulbright and the press interpreted as an attempt to steal the limelight, Johnson announced that he and his top advisers on the war would meet with South Vietnam's leaders in Honolulu. Whether the allegation was so or not, when the hearings started on 5 February, they attracted so much interest in the press that NBC decided to televise them in full.[1]

Over the days that followed, administration spokesmen fielded hostile questions from the committee on South Vietnamese refugees, unjustified official optimism, and the continuing need for social and political reform in South Vietnam. Retired U.S. Army Lt. Gen. James Gavin warned that U.S. policy in South Vietnam was dangerously out of balance and called for withdrawal to defensive enclaves until some political solution became possible. George Kennan, former U.S. ambassador to the Soviet Union, seconded Gavin, arguing for an American withdrawal as soon as conditions in the area permitted. Ambassador Taylor and Secretary Rusk defended the administration's position. Taylor explained U.S. goals. Rusk emphasized that the United States had to take a stand or the prospect for peace would disappear.[2]

The news media responded to the hearings along ideological lines. Journals that questioned the war, such as the *New York Times* and the *St. Louis Post-Dispatch,* praised the inquiry. Those that tended to support administration policy were less satisfied. The Johnson administration, for its part, concluded that the hearings had served its ends by helping to prepare the American public for war.

In fact, it thought so well of them that it attempted a few weeks later to have the government of France play tapes of the inquiry on the nation's state-controlled television network to encourage "objective reporting" on the issue. The French scorned the suggestion.[3]

Although the president had succeeded in turning aside Fulbright's criticisms for the time being, he still had a serious problem. He and his administration had worked incessantly to burnish the public image of America's ally, South Vietnam, but they had been thwarted time and again by the instability of the nation's government and by the unpredictable performance of its armed forces. Coups and countercoups had succeeded one another in the months since Nguyen Khanh had retired from the government in February 1965. Finally, in June, Air Vice Marshal Nguyen Cao Ky had taken charge as premier, while Gen. Nguyen Van Thieu had become chief of state. The two had seemed to turn the war around. With American B-52s keeping Communist forces off balance, U.S. and South Vietnamese forces had begun to enter formerly inviolate enemy base areas and to drive up enemy casualty rates.[4]

The hopes the advances encouraged began to fade, however, on 9 March 1966, when a North Vietnamese regiment attacked a South Vietnamese Special Forces camp at A Shau, some forty-five kilometers to the southwest of Hue. The enemy forced the garrison's defenders, seventeen U.S. advisers and 360 South Vietnamese and Montagnard irregulars, into one corner of the base. U.S. Marine helicopters arrived to evacuate the group, but the irregulars panicked and mobbed the aircraft, forcing them to back off empty. In the end, only 186 managed to escape through the jungle to safety. Five of the seventeen U.S. advisers were killed.[5]

Early news reports of the incident were based on official communiqués. They noted that the camp might have been betrayed but otherwise said little about problems. One quoted a U.S. adviser who praised his South Vietnamese and Montagnard comrades because, as he put it, "if they hadn't fought real hard, we'd have been overrun."[6]

The true story emerged on 14 March, when Scripps-Howard reporter Jim Lucas revealed that the commander of the American advisers at A Shau, Capt. John D. Blair, had emerged from the jungle cursing the camp's South Vietnamese defenders and charging that only the Montagnards had fought. "If I could get my hands on Chung Wei [a South Vietnamese lieutenant]," he declared angrily, "I'd kill him." On the same day, CBS broadcast a report by Jack Laurence, who had interviewed Lt. Col. Charles House, the commander of the marine helicopter squadron that had gone into A Shau. The officer had avowed, "So many people wanted to get out, they hung on the cables—almost pulled the helicopters into the [landing] zone. And it was . . . a hell of a thing to have to do: some of them had to be shot in order to maintain control."[7]

The reports caused immediate concern at the White House, which ordered a Defense Department investigation that ultimately substantiated the two news stories. In order to preserve what they could of the good image of the South

Vietnamese armed forces, U.S. Army spokesmen in Saigon played down Blair's statement as the product of great stress. The marines dealt differently with House. They awarded him the Navy Cross (second only to the Medal of Honor) for his valor at A Shau but then presented him with a letter of reprimand for his comments to the press. The move, which eliminated any chance House might have had for further promotion, was a clear warning to marine officers serving in South Vietnam to hold their tongues when dealing with the press.[8]

The controversy over A Shau was still unfolding in the press when a second problem arose, centering on the commander of the I Corps Zone, Lt. Gen. Nguyen Chanh Thi, who had long ruled South Vietnam's northern provinces virtually independent of the Saigon government. When the general sent troops to operate in the Demilitarized Zone separating North from South Vietnam despite orders to stay out of the area, Thieu fired him for insubordination in an obvious attempt to consolidate his own power. The U.S. mission in Saigon passed the move off as a routine change of command, but few reporters believed it. Within hours, Neil Sheehan called Lodge to assert that "a terrible row" had broken out among the generals and that a new era of instability was in store for South Vietnam. Lodge responded that the move was a blow against warlordism and a sign of the renewed vigor of South Vietnam's government.[9]

Lodge's avowal made sense and might have put all questions to rest, but for militant students who began to demonstrate in Da Nang on Thi's behalf. The radical arm of the Buddhist movement joined in, protesting official corruption, inflation, and the government's continuing disregard for the political rights of the people. Spurred by Communist agitators, who sought to destabilize the government by any means, the disorders soon spread to Hue, where mobs attacked the radio station and closed the schools. At first, affecting a neutral stance in case the students and Buddhists prevailed, the U.S. mission made no comment on the disturbances. Yet when the demonstrators began to cultivate the Saigon correspondents and the Ky regime held silent, it had no choice but to fill the vacuum. Otherwise, reporters would do it themselves, turning to unreliable sources for the information they needed.[10]

Although a few critical editorials appeared in the United States—the *New York Post,* for one, charged that Johnson was supporting a hated military clique that persecuted Buddhists—much of what appeared in the press was moderate in tone. Neil Sheehan reported that most of the people in Da Nang and Hue appeared indifferent to Thi; Wesley Pruden of the *National Observer* asserted that the relief of Thi was a sign that the Ky regime might be maturing; Dan Rather of CBS News noted that devout Buddhists were a minority in South Vietnam and that radical Buddhists constituted a minority within a minority.[11]

Even so, the Saigon correspondents were under orders to describe what was happening in South Vietnam, and they did so, detailing each new demonstration down to the slogans on the protesters' signs. Aware that nothing could be hidden, Ambassador Lodge warned Ky that unless his government restored order, public opinion in the United States would turn against the war. During the first weeks of March, he said, while the Buddhists had demonstrated, 228 Americans had died in combat and 850 more had been wounded. The American public would never tolerate tolls of that sort in the face of prolonged South Vietnamese "foolishness." Within the week, the *New York Times* added weight to Lodge's warning by asserting that even if Communists had infiltrated the demonstrations, a change of government in Saigon was clearly in order.[12]

As the disturbances continued, the U.S. mission and the State and Defense Departments attempted to divert the press from the political situation by highlighting an increase in enemy infiltration across the Demilitarized Zone and a series of heavy defeats the enemy had sustained elsewhere in South Vietnam. A few stories on enemy infiltration appeared as a result, but when Ky sent three battalions of his marines to occupy Da Nang Air Base and rebellious troops from the South Vietnamese First Division set up roadblocks nearby, news coverage once more shifted to the disturbances. Headlines—" 'Rebel City' Setting Up Defenses," claimed the *Washington Post*—made it seem as though Da Nang was about to explode. Stories also appeared suggesting that the crisis had affected the conduct of the war by slowing the pace of South Vietnamese operations in the critical region north of Da Nang. *Time* summed it all up. The rioting seemed, its editors declared, "a senseless and dangerous self-indulgence" for a country faced with possible extinction.[13]

The Johnson administration sought to counter the trend by declaring that the Buddhist-student struggle was an almost necessary by-product of the political consciousness that had begun to emerge in South Vietnam. The line held until 12 April, when word arrived in Washington that American casualties during the preceding week had topped those of the South Vietnamese for the first time in the war. Seeking to prepare the American public for the announcement, Arthur Sylvester at last acknowledged publicly that the riots had begun to disrupt military operations. To underscore his point, however, he attributed a bomb shortage in South Vietnam that had reduced air strikes by one-third to striking Buddhist dockworkers at the port of Da Nang. In fact, leaks to the press would reveal within the week that the shortage was actually the result of production deficiencies in the United States. Accompanied by charges in Congress that the Defense Department was once more misleading the American people, and coming at a time when a U.S. military policeman had reportedly waved a gun at Peter Arnett in an attempt to keep him from reporting a riot in Saigon, Sylvester's lack of candor left the press more distrustful than ever of official intentions and statements.[14]

The crisis appeared to ebb on 10 April, when Ky withdrew his marines from Da Nang Air Base. Four days later, Thieu promised an election within five months to select delegates for a constitutional convention, and the Buddhists agreed to allow the military to retain power until the new government could take control. Meanwhile, U.S. advisers reported that, except for the headquarters of the South Vietnamese First Division, the Buddhists and students were making little headway in gaining the support of South Vietnam's armed forces.[15]

Westmoreland underscored these themes in a background briefing for the press on 30 April, but all was not what it seemed. Shortly after the session, word arrived from a highly respected South Vietnamese colonel that morale within the units guarding the II Corps Zone had declined to such a level that the force was in grave danger. With the commander of the region playing it safe by declining to back either side, the officer said, the troops no longer had any idea of what they were fighting for. Meanwhile, Buddhist chaplains were subverting the force from within by telling the men that they were fighting only for the United States, not for South Vietnam.[16]

Although the chief of the South Vietnamese Joint General Staff, Gen. Cao Van Vien, confirmed most of the allegations, Westmoreland professed to believe that the situation was still relatively well in hand. On the premise that there was no immediate crisis and despite the fact that U.S. casualties had again exceeded those of the South Vietnamese during the first week in May, he flew to Hawaii on 12 May to consult with Admiral Sharp. Ambassador Lodge departed at the same time for meetings in Washington. Five days later, with Westmoreland and Lodge both conveniently out of the country, South Vietnamese marines under Vien's direct command flew to Da Nang to secure the city's civic center, radio station, and military installations. Four days after that, Vien drove the dissidents from their pagodas and secured the rest of the city.[17]

With their fortunes declining, the Buddhists reacted with fury. A number of bonzes set themselves on fire, and mobs ransacked the U.S. consulate in Hue. Some of the violence was clearly staged for the benefit of the press. On one occasion, agitators poured gasoline on the corpse of a burning nun in order to provide better pictures for reporters who had arrived too late for the immolation.[18]

The violence took a toll on American public opinion. Fifty-four percent of those queried by a Gallup poll at the time contended that if the crisis degenerated into large-scale warfare, the United States should withdraw from South Vietnam. Another 48 percent avowed that the country would never achieve a stable government. Reflecting on the trend, General Wheeler had to concede that there was a logic to the public's response. "I think I can feel the first gusts of the whirlwind," he told Westmoreland. " . . . Regardless of what happens of a favorable nature, many people will never again believe that the effort and sacrifices are worthwhile."[19]

Westmoreland and Lodge attempted to allay concern in Washington by blaming the press, which had, they said, blown the situation out of proportion. If some reporters had initially gone along with Buddhist allegations, however, they had recognized as the crisis lengthened that the demonstrators were attempting to manipulate them and had begun to treat Buddhist claims with considerable reserve. Denis Warner, for one, underscored the role of Communists in the demonstrations by noting that the Buddhist movement's propaganda in Hue was virtually indistinguishable from that of the Hanoi regime. To those reporters who remembered the Communist rise to power in Hanoi, he said, "every action, every manifesto, every decision taken in Hue seemed familiar."[20]

Ambassador Lodge admitted as much on 29 June, following the elimination of the last Buddhist holdout positions in Hue and Saigon. "In fairness," he told President Johnson, " . . . it must be known that the attitude of the press toward the Buddhists did undergo a marked change. Undoubtedly this was partly due to their own observations, but I hope that the ceaseless backgrounding done here and in Washington played a part."[21]

Although the threat from the Buddhists diminished, major public relations problems remained. Continuing news reports charged, for example, that the ineptitude of South Vietnam's bureaucracy had retarded the effort to win the peasantry to the government's side. Americans sometimes stepped in to double for local officials, Ward Just noted in the *Washington Post* on 6 November, but that did nothing to strengthen the country's ability to govern itself. Meanwhile, the reporter added, the nation's armed forces seemed oblivious to the danger confronting them. On many Friday nights, for example, U.S. Marines returning to base "bone tired and dragging their butts" encountered freshly shaved and dressed South Vietnamese junior officers heading in the opposite direction to Da Nang for the weekend.[22]

Convinced that the pacification program, the effort to win the peasantry to the side of the government, had failed to achieve its ends, President Johnson pushed for improvements throughout the latter half of 1966. When the endeavor continued to lag, in April 1967 he shifted it from civilian to military control and placed it under Westmoreland. At that time, the agency in charge of the effort received a proper military name, becoming known as the Office of the Assistant Chief of Staff for Civilian Operations and Revolutionary Development Support, or CORDS, for short.[23]

Long before taking control of the program, Westmoreland and Zorthian had begun a campaign to counter the news media's negative image of pacification. While Zorthian refined and released statistics on the effort's achievements, Westmoreland instructed his commanders (in language reminiscent of the old CONARC memorandum) to "indoctrinate" their men in such a way that they would "talk up" civic action even in their letters home. Whenever possible, in order to dispel the belief that the war was largely an American endeavor, officers were also to attribute whatever successes they could to the South Vietnamese.[24]

In the end, a few positive news stories appeared, but the image of pacification failed to improve. Bud Merick told why in a July 1967 article for *U.S. News & World Report.* The program had only fitful progress, he said, because the American military in South Vietnam had allowed combat operations to take precedence over purely civilian concerns such as pacification.[25]

Reporter Jonathan Schell provided a powerful example of what Merick meant in an article for the *New Yorker.* Summarizing Operation Cedar Falls, an Ameri-

The refugee camp at Phu Cuong. (U.S. Army)

can sweep during January 1967 through an enemy-dominated region south of Saigon known as the Iron Triangle, Schell described how the inhabitants of the village of Ben Suc had been terrorized by careless allied bombing and indiscriminate artillery fire. On the day of the operation, Schell continued, U.S. forces had rounded up all of the village's teenage and adult males and had detained some as Viet Cong on the barest of pretexts—good grooming, better than average clothing, or the lack of an identification card. South Vietnamese troops accompanying the operation, he said, abused some of these individuals.[26]

As these events transpired, other troops collected the women and children of the village and relocated them to a barren field miles away at Phu Cuong, where little had been done to prepare for them and confusion reigned. Those people with homes near roads had been able to transfer many of their belongings to trucks, but those who lived well off the roads had lost everything, often bringing out only clothing, a few cooking utensils, and a bag or two of rice. In the end, Schell said, once the people were gone, the army bulldozed broad swaths across Ben Suc, and air force jets then pulverized the rubble with bombs in an attempt to collapse tunnels under the village that ran too deep to destroy by other means.

The army officers in charge at Ben Suc would later take exception to Schell's characterization of the village as unoffending. In fact, they noted, the area had been a Viet Cong redoubt for years. The ground beneath Ben Suc was honey-

Viet Cong prisoners captured near Ben Suc. (U.S. Army)

combed with deep tunnels that housed a number of Viet Cong facilities, and a large enemy hospital amply stocked with medicine stood nearby. Indeed, the tunnels yielded up an intelligence bonanza: 285 pounds of enemy documents and reports that shed new light on Communist operations earlier in the war while compromising upcoming enemy initiatives in the Saigon region. As for the suspects the troops had detained, while some had indeed been abused, several turned out to be not only Viet Cong but also the highest political and propaganda cadre captured to that date.[27]

If Schell had distorted the military portion of the operation, however, his description of the chaos at Phu Cuong was only too accurate. The refugee camp had grown up in disorder because the commanders of Operation Cedar Falls, over the protests of U.S. pacification officials, had put military goals first and had kept knowledge of the operation from everyone, including the South Vietnamese, until a scant two days before the operation's start. On the surface, it was hard to fault them. They had engineered a major success for U.S. and South Vietnamese forces. But if the final outcome of the war depended on winning the hearts and minds of South Vietnam's people to the side of their government, the ultimate effect of the operation was still probably a setback.[28]

At the very time Schell's piece appeared, in fact, MACV was rethinking the whole idea of relocating villages sympathetic to the Viet Cong. Prodded by leaks to the press that had sparked a Senate investigation on the handling of refugees, the command had come to realize that disgruntled villagers forcibly separated from their homes were an excellent source of recruits for the enemy. In addition, South Vietnam's government clearly resented the forced relocation of its people by foreigners. The result of that reevaluation became policy in 1968, when MACV instructed all commanders to avoid creating any more refugees than necessary.[29]

If pacification remained a problem, the apparent reluctance of many South Vietnamese military units to pursue the war with vigor was perhaps an even stronger impediment to the effort to improve the South Vietnamese image. There were many theories about why those forces seemed to hold back, but most reporters agreed that, despite a few outstanding exceptions, the nation's military lacked the dedication and singleness of purpose necessary for victory. The entry of U.S. troops into the fighting, they added, had only made matters worse by prompting the country's officers to sit back and relax.[30]

General Westmoreland dismissed such claims out of hand. South Vietnam's armed forces were sorely pressed, he said, but they were improving in number and strength and only needed time to develop. In an attempt to counter the complaints of the press, he instructed Zorthian during January 1967 to develop a public relations program for those forces parallel to the one for pacification.[31]

Zorthian settled on a low-key campaign that promised to cultivate awareness of South Vietnamese accomplishments. Under it, American officers in the field were to compile lists of outstanding South Vietnamese operations in their areas of responsibility, direct reporters to them, and go along themselves, when possible, in order to steer them in the right directions. Meanwhile, MACV's information office was to step up its advice to South Vietnamese commanders on proper public relations techniques and to increase their efforts to train South Vietnamese information officers. They were likewise to include South Vietnamese successes in the news clips official photographic teams developed for release in the United States, and to begin producing background materials on South Vietnamese operations that Washington agencies could draw upon for briefings. Everyone involved was to depict South Vietnam's commanders as able and dedicated, and the nation's soldiers as first-class fighting men.[32]

Zorthian and MACV's efforts notwithstanding, little changed. American officers in the field were too busy to spoon-feed reporters, and South Vietnam's commanders continued to shun publicity much as they had during the Diem years, lest they give their superiors the idea that they were somehow promoting their own political careers or plotting a coup. As for the Saigon correspondents, the successes Westmoreland hoped to promote seemed remote and unreal. During nine of the first thirty weeks in 1967, U.S. casualties exceeded those of the South Vietnamese. During the six months ending in May 1967, U.S. casualties even surpassed the number of South Vietnamese drafted into the army. Meanwhile, at any given time, between 9 and 20 percent of the army's regular force personnel and from 17 to 30 percent of its irregulars were listed as deserters. By July, South Vietnamese battalion-size operations were lasting only eight battalion-days in the field, while those of U.S. forces were running thirty-nine, and South Vietnamese maneuver battalions were making contact with the enemy only 27 percent as often as their American counterparts.[33]

As with Harkins and Nolting, Westmoreland knew there were problems but excused them because he believed there were extenuating circumstances. Many South Vietnamese units were preoccupied with providing security for pacification, he said, and spent less time in the field than American units. As for the desertions, they were usually temporary and often involved soldiers who were homesick or who had gone home to help their families harvest crops. Most of what was wrong, he said, would diminish over time. In the interim, what the South Vietnamese needed was encouragement rather than criticism.[34]

Reporters understood what Westmoreland was saying, but they had only to visit the field to receive a different picture. After accompanying an operation just to the south of Saigon, *New York Times* correspondent Tom Buckley, for one, compared an American unit with a nearby South Vietnamese platoon. The South Vietnamese seemed well dressed and freshly shaved, he said, while the Americans were dirty and bone tired from days in the field. The Vietnamese may have seemed fresh because they were newly arrived replacements, but conversations with members of the American unit banished all doubt for Buckley. "We're not heroes," the men avowed, " . . . but we stay and fight if we have to. If there's trouble today, you just watch. . . . They'll *didi mow*. (The phrase is . . . known to every G.I. It means . . . 'bug out' or run away.)" Sure enough, the Vietnamese vanished as soon as firing began.[35]

Since South Vietnamese forces tended to kill as many of the enemy per day of combat as the Americans and fought fiercely when cornered, reporters could only conclude that their lack of aggressiveness stemmed less from cowardice or ineptitude than from a lack of motivation. David Halberstam, for one, underscored the problem in an account of a conversation he had held with a North Vietnamese major who had defected to South Vietnam. "I could command a division in North Vietnam," the officer said. "But a platoon here, even a squad, I could not do that. What can you do? They have no purpose."[36]

The low regard in which many American generals held South Vietnam's armed forces added to the problem. "We were really quite indifferent," one told a researcher after the war. "Most of us did not want to associate with them." Reporters sensed the attitude and confirmed it in conversations with the generals. "Every time Westmoreland makes a speech about how good the South Vietnamese army is," one told *New York Times* reporter R. W. Apple anonymously, "I want to ask him why he keeps calling for more Americans. His need for reinforcements is a measure of our failure with the Vietnamese."[37]

Westmoreland responded with more optimism, but by August 1967 there was growing concern in the United States that the war was in a stalemate, and journals everywhere were criticizing South Vietnam's armed forces. *Newsweek* was among the most pointed. If progress had indeed occurred, the magazine's editors remarked in a major article on the Mekong delta, South Vietnam's army still displayed "stupendous ineptitude" and a "distressing reluctance to fight."[38]

To counter the trend, Westmoreland once more chose to rely on public relations. Moving carefully to avoid charges that MACV was making propaganda, he quietly instructed his commanders to begin scheduling on-the-record press conferences to explain events in their areas of responsibility. In the meantime, MACOI was to make a major effort to move reporters to the scenes of important South Vietnamese actions and to keep a running tally of South Vietnamese successes for release to the press. If a South Vietnamese officer participated in a briefing, it was to appear to be his own idea. Otherwise reporters might suspect that a sales campaign was in progress and respond by stepping up their criticism.[39]

The effort drew the press to South Vietnamese operations, but public relations again failed to produce the results Westmoreland wanted. Instead, in mid-September, Peter Arnett charged that South Vietnamese forces were avoiding contact with the enemy and that South Vietnamese inefficiency was costing American lives. Everett G. Martin, *Newsweek*'s bureau chief in Saigon, echoed Arnett, alleging that U.S. claims of South Vietnamese progress were misleading and that MACV was seizing upon every action in which South Vietnamese forces as much as did their duty as evidence of improvement. He quoted an American colonel who had returned to Vietnam after three years. "Everyone must admit that militarily we are better off than we were three years ago," that officer said. "With five hundred thousand U.S. troops, more planes, and more artillery, we should be. . . . But otherwise, I don't see any change." *Newsweek* reporter Merton Perry followed a week later with an insulting article titled "Their Lions, Our Rabbits" in which he avowed that 360 pacification workers had been killed to that date in 1967 while South Vietnamese troops had idled nearby. Adding that a few units had given up their combat roles to provide beer, prostitutes, and laundry services to American troops, he avowed that South Vietnam's armed forces were as sick as the society that had engendered them—riddled with "factionalism, corruption, nepotism, inefficiency, incompetence, and cowardice."[40]

Official spokesmen at MACV refused to rebut the Martin and Arnett articles on grounds, they said, that the effort would only have called attention to the reporters' arguments. The South Vietnamese were so outraged by Perry's comments, however, that they banned the offending issue of *Newsweek* from sale in their country. Martin sought to excuse Perry by pointing out that *Newsweek*'s editors had altered the tone of the reporter's piece by editing out significant qualifications and explanations. Even so, because of those revisions and because the South Vietnamese were clearly considering further action, he advised both his employers and the U.S. mission to refrain from protesting. Unconvinced of Perry's innocence, the mission was more than happy to comply.[41]

Nguyen Van Thieu (center) and Nguyen Kao Ky (right) hold a press conference. (U.S. Army)

With the image of the South Vietnamese armed forces lagging and pacification just beginning to gain momentum because of the appointment in June of a new director for CORDS, the able Robert W. Komer, one final opportunity arose during 1967 to promote South Vietnamese progress. It involved the elections Ky and Thieu had promised the Buddhists. Between September 1966 and June 1967, local balloting had selected a constituent assembly, village councils, and hamlet chiefs. On 4 September, a final election was slated to choose a president and a senate. If it went well, U.S. officials reasoned, the South Vietnamese government's growing claim to the allegiance of its people would shine forth to the world.[42]

The U.S. mission had tested the techniques it would use during the election for a constituent assembly. Predicting that coverage would be heavy and that a swarm of newsmen would descend upon Saigon in search of irregularities, the mission had warned Ky and Thieu to keep the voting fair. When some five hundred reporters did indeed arrive, it then took pains to hold background briefings and to arrange interviews and transportation for all who wanted them. Although allegations arose that some South Vietnamese had voted only to avoid later difficulties with the authorities, few reports of irregularities followed.[43]

Public affairs officers took the same pains for the presidential election. Watching for signs of tampering, the U.S. mission kept close tabs on the candidates, particularly Ky. When reports surfaced indicating that Ky's ally Col. Nguyen Ngoc Loan, the director of the National Police, was instructing his subordinates to subvert the voting by bribing or blackmailing local officials, Ambassador Ellsworth Bunker put an end to the effort by speaking privately with Ky. In the same way, when friction arose between Thieu and Ky, Bunker took both generals aside to warn against any action that would discredit the election in the United States. Within the week, the two agreed to an accommodation in which Thieu became president and Ky vice president with control over the cabinet and the armed forces.[44]

As the election neared, reporters once more began to seek out irregularities, but the government responded by allowing candidates to pursue their activities with little official hindrance and even rescinded censorship of the local press in order to allow the competitors to criticize incumbents with impunity. Those moves had the desired effect. Disapproval of the government declined to such an extent in press dispatches that Bunker told President Johnson he considered the "balanced tone" of reporting from Saigon helpful.[45]

Although the situation seemed well in order, the Johnson administration insisted on taking a hand. When the South Vietnamese, at U.S. urging, invited a panel of prominent Americans to observe the elections, the White House instructed Bunker to minimize the group's exposure to the "emotional and slanted attitudes" of the Saigon correspondents. To that end, there were to be no news conferences and as little mixing as possible with cynical reporters.[46]

However, there was no stopping members of the delegation. A number—particularly politicians such as Governor Richard Hughes of New Jersey and Senators Edmund Muskie of Maine, Bourke Hickenlooper of Iowa, and George Murphy of California—discussed matters openly with reporters, at times carrying on a running debate. In the end, President Johnson's concern that the reporters' biases might rub off on the panel proved groundless. All of the group's members agreed that the election had been fair.[47]

The American news media agreed, for the most part, but the election had little effect on the long-term image of the South Vietnamese government. The defeated candidates charged that the voting had been rigged, and their supporters began a series of wild demonstrations in protest. The regime responded by arresting the runner-up in the election, Truong Dinh Dzu, the only candidate to run on a strong peace platform. The move made Dzu a martyr in the eyes of the press when, in fact, if all disputed ballots had been disqualified, he would have dropped to fourth place.[48]

By the end of September, the Saigon correspondents were once more reporting on the ineptitude of the South Vietnamese army and the lack of progress in pacification. As they did, the president's national security adviser, Walter W. Rostow, instructed the U.S. mission to start another public relations campaign. It was to present sound evidence of "the steady if slow progress" of pacification, economic progress in the countryside, and the improvement of the South Viet-namese armed forces because little of that was coming through in the American news media.[49]

The mission and MACV complied, making progress a dominant theme over the next three months. Nonetheless, the campaign, like all the others, failed to dispel the doubts of the Saigon correspondents. The chief of the MACV Office of Information at the time, Brig. Gen. Winant Sidle, was one of the few in govern-ment who understood why and would go on record about it. From mid-1966 on-ward, he told Westmoreland in September 1967, MACV had oversold success when, in fact, "we did not truly know whether we were making progress or not." He was speaking only of the pacification program, but his comment had far wider implications. For events would show that it applied as well to almost every other aspect of the war.[50]

7

Claims of Progress—and Counterclaims

William P. Bundy, assistant secretary of state for Southeast Asian affairs, warned President Johnson toward the end of 1966 that the South Vietnamese government and armed forces were adopting a caretaker mentality as the American effort grew. The lack of progress that would occur during 1967 as a result, he said, might undermine the president's chances for reelection. At the least, it would impair the government's ability to bring the war to a successful conclusion by dividing the American public against itself and by feeding the enemy's conviction that the United States would yield to Communist pressure in due course.[1]

The president and his advisers were well aware that problems were developing, and they did what they could to shore up public acceptance of the war. To that end, Lodge and Westmoreland began to cultivate influential visitors to South Vietnam in hopes of enhancing their pro-administration viewpoints. In the same way, MACV and the U.S. mission sought continually to temper news stories that might reflect poorly on the South Vietnamese government. As a result, when they learned during July that CBS was preparing to broadcast allegations that Prime Minister Ky was taking fifteen thousand dollars a week in kickbacks from the Saigon racetrack, the chief of the MACV Office of Information, Col. Rodger Bankson, moved quickly to counter the story. Although he was unable to keep CBS from airing the piece, he emphasized that the funds in question had gone to charity and that the track's ledgers were open to all. In that way, he sowed enough doubt to preempt a major scandal.[2]

The U.S. mission used similar care later in the year when AP reports alleged that up to 40 percent of American aid to South Vietnam was being diverted to the black market. Rather than issue a flat denial, Lodge and Westmoreland held a background briefing to underscore U.S. and South Vietnamese efforts to fight corruption. The stories that followed took the two at their word. Sources in Saigon acknowledged the problem, reporters said, but asserted as well that the success the United States had achieved in halting runaway inflation in South Vietnam would have been impossible if thefts on the scale alleged had occurred.[3]

In that case, rebuttals delivered with conviction and authority had the desired effect. Less easy to remedy were recurring allegations that U.S. and South Vietnamese operations were slaughtering innocent civilians. Zorthian attempted to divert the press to enemy atrocities by sending out teams at regular intervals to photograph and catalog enemy violations of the laws of war. Reporters, however, tended to take Communist terrorism as a given. They were much more interested in events they considered abnormal, as when U.S. aircraft or artillery leveled villages or killed civilians.[4]

In the end, there was little Westmoreland could do to distract the press from the issue, if only because mishaps involving civilians occurred with regularity. On 1 July 1966, for example, American aircraft hit a friendly village, killing seven civilians and wounding fifty-one. A week later, more aircraft struck a force of South Vietnamese civilian irregulars, killing fourteen and wounding nineteen. Other incidents followed, culminating on 9 August in an episode in which U.S. fighter bombers operating under MACV's new rules of engagement and with full South Vietnamese authority killed sixty-three civilians and wounded eighty-three more in a village to the south of Saigon.[5]

Correspondents understood that accidents happened, but they also recognized that there was too much of a margin for error in South Vietnam where firepower was concerned. As the *New York Times* noted in a 21 August editorial, American tactics had become so violent that the bomb tonnage dropped on South Vietnam each week exceeded that dropped on Germany at the height of World War II. In a separate article, *Times* correspondent Charles Mohr added that, whatever MACV's rules of engagement, they would have little value if they were widely ignored. Adding a touch of innuendo, the reporter then quoted an unidentified American officer who had said, "I never saw a place where so many military orders are disobeyed as in Vietnam."[6]

In the end, the Defense Department decided that many of the accidents during July and August had been the products of a decision President Johnson had made the year before to keep American public opinion in check by ensuring that American soldiers served only one year at a time in the war zone. Because of this policy, so the reasoning went, a large number of experienced officers had returned to the United States in June, July, and August, while new men unfamiliar with the rules had arrived. On top of that, it seemed clear that many South Vietnamese officials were inclined to respond favorably to every American request for air strikes, whatever the risk to their own people.[7]

Westmoreland called a press conference to explain what had happened. Emphasizing MACV's concern for civilian casualties and blaming human and matériel failures whenever possible, he announced that a board of inquiry would review the command's rules of engagement to identify areas that needed improvement. During the session, neither he nor any of the reporters present took notice of the fact that U.S. forces had become almost profligate in their use of firepower. That bombs and bullets would sometimes miss their marks and hit civilians appears to have been everyone's foregone conclusion, an unavoidable fact of war.[8]

Westmoreland's presentation had no appreciable effect on press coverage of civilian casualties. If anything, the continuing escalation of the air war fueled newsmen's interest in the subject. During June 1966, for example, President Johnson approved strikes against petroleum storage facilities near Hanoi and its port, Haiphong, in a region that contained at least one thousand people per square mile. At first, the attacks caused few public relations problems. Official spokesmen emphasized that all bombs had been on target, and the North Vietnamese chose that moment to infuriate many Americans by releasing photos of a mob jeering at captured American pilots—a violation of international agreements prohibiting the exposure of prisoners of war to public abuse.[9]

Nothing more happened until early December, when the United States launched Rolling Thunder 52, a campaign of air attacks against a large railroad marshaling yard at Yen Vien, 5.5 nautical miles north of Hanoi, and a huge vehicle depot at Van Dien, 5 nautical miles south of the city. Although the raids stood out sharply against a decline in air operations that had occurred during October and November, MACV received instructions to describe them as no substantial increase over the level of earlier raids. To counter enemy claims that the United States had escalated the war, public affairs officers were to stress that the pilots involved had taken pains to avoid hitting populated areas.[10]

The North Vietnamese reacted routinely when the strikes began on 2 and 5 December. When more followed on the thirteenth and fourteenth, however, Radio Hanoi denounced the United States for attacking residential areas. The State and Defense Departments declined at first to comment. Even so, when the Soviet news agency TASS seconded the North Vietnamese, the Defense Department broke its silence to declare that nothing new had occurred because all the targets involved had been hit earlier in the war.[11]

The approach might have worked, but for Western travelers visiting Hanoi who began to charge that the bombers had struck residential areas. Taking refuge in the lack of strong evidence, MACV again refused to comment. Reporters responded by attempting to determine whether any bombs had struck Hanoi itself, an essential step in judging whether an escalation had occurred. The State Department took a day to produce a map showing that all attacks had fallen outside the city's boundaries. A reporter later managed to produce a map from the French colonial period that showed much wider city limits, but by then the press was fixated on the possibility that pilot error might have occurred. In response to questions, official spokesmen confirmed that mistakes were always possible but then put the comment on background to keep anyone from using it as an admission of guilt. Deputy Secretary of Defense Cyrus Vance then contradicted even that limited affirmation by telling reporters no basis existed for any allegation that American bombs had hit Hanoi. The Johnson administration only conceded that an accident might have occurred on 22 December, declaring, almost as an afterthought, that "if" American aircraft had caused civilian injuries or damage, "we regret it."[12]

While officials in Washington and Saigon backed and filled, the press turned Hanoi's allegations into an exposé. The *Kansas City Star* asserted that raids within five miles of a city's center would inevitably endanger civilians. The *Chicago Tribune* alleged that the enemy's handling of the press appeared to have been more straightforward than that of American news managers. David Brinkley remarked on NBC, "For two days and more," Communist charges had gone around the world "with no clear word of denial or explanation . . . and it is doubtful that the denial will ever completely catch up with the original report." Shaken by the outburst, President Johnson quietly banned air strikes near Hanoi. "We were just starting to put some real pressure on Hanoi," Admiral Sharp told Wheeler angrily, a short while later. " . . . Then, Hanoi complains that we have killed a few civilians, hoping they would get a favorable reaction. And they did. . . . Not only did we say we regretted it . . . we also stopped our pilots from striking within ten miles of Hanoi."[13]

The outcry over Rolling Thunder 52 was just dying down when a series of stories filed directly from North Vietnam by Harrison E. Salisbury, the respected assistant managing editor of the *New York Times,* rekindled the issue. Salisbury had applied for admission to North Vietnam more than six months before, but the Communists had held back until they had a story worth telling. They made their move during December. Inviting Salisbury to interview their leaders, they took him to visit towns and villages where they said American bombers had harmed civilians.[14]

The reporter described scene after scene of desolation in his dispatches. The town of Nam Dinh, seventy-five kilometers south of Hanoi, had been targeted by American bombers for sixteen months, he said, even though it was of little military significance. At Van Dien, the reality of the bombing at ground level was far different from the sterile picture MACV imparted in its news releases. Although the bombers had supposedly targeted a truck park, they had in fact destroyed a senior high school, leading many North Vietnamese to suspect that the United States was conducting a hidden campaign against civilian facilities.[15]

The stories and others like them set off a furor in Congress, where opponents of the war called for a halt in the bombing while proponents urged stronger action. A similar split appeared in the press. George Hamilton Coombs and Fulton Lewis III of Mutual Radio News, on the one hand, contended that Communist forces were the ones guilty of targeting civilians because they had waged a continual terror campaign against South Vietnam's civilians for years. Walter Cronkite of CBS News, however, asserted that Salisbury's revelations had widened the credibility gap dogging the Johnson administration. Meanwhile, Max Lerner of the *New York Post* asserted that the only way to square Salisbury's assertions with those of the Pentagon without concluding that there had been deception on the part of the government was to assume either that American bombing runs were highly inaccurate or that American air crews had been careless. Whatever the truth, he said, the American people "ought to be told."[16]

Although the United States had never bombed civilian targets on purpose, the Defense and State Departments had known since October 1966 through reconnaissance photographs that mistakes had occurred. In the end, to cut off speculation, they had no choice but to admit it. When they did, however, they sought to save face by stressing the pains they had taken to avoid harm to civilians by reducing the size of bombs and by selecting targets carefully. They also attempted to pass some of the blame to the enemy by noting that damage caused by bombs was indistinguishable from damage caused by spent antiaircraft missiles falling to earth. Although the point about the care taken in planning the raids was true, the distinction between bombs and missiles was specious. Bombs usually penetrate structures and blow them from the inside out. Missiles tend to explode on contact and to work from the outside in.[17]

No one in the press picked up on the slip at the time. Instead, official spokesmen took to the offensive by accusing Salisbury of placing too much faith in North Vietnamese pronouncements. In that way, they said, the reporter had questioned whether Nam Dinh contained significant military targets when, in fact, it housed a petroleum storage facility, an important railroad yard, and a thermal power plant. These installations were so important that one of the largest concentrations of antiaircraft weaponry in North Vietnam defended them. In the same way, one of Salisbury's stories had alleged that areas near the seventeenth parallel had been devastated by bombs. In fact, the reporter had never visited the region and had once more used North Vietnamese information uncritically. Indeed, public affairs officers declared, most of his statistics on Nam Dinh had come from a North Vietnamese propaganda tract. Years later, in a letter, Salisbury denied that he had ever seen the pamphlet. "My data was either based on direct observation of Nam Dinh (and elsewhere) or upon figures provided by the local (Communist) officials. As *Times* editor Clifton Daniel noted at the time: It is not surprising that their figures and those of the pamphlet coincided." The comment clarified the reporter's sources but also tended to confirm the Communist origins of at least some of the statistics he used.[18]

In the end, the rebuttals had some effect. Learning that the reporter had used propaganda in his reports, the *Washington Post* questioned their reliability. Meanwhile, the *New York Times* itself pulled back. Besides allowing its military correspondent, Hanson Baldwin, to dispute Salisbury's conclusions in a front-page article, its editors rejected in print the "sweeping denunciations and false conclusions" some Americans had drawn from the reporter's stories. Although they remained critical of the bombing, they added, that was far different from saying that there was "even a shred of evidence" to prove the United States had deliberately bombed civilians.[19]

In the end, those hits notwithstanding, the U.S. government never truly caught up with Salisbury. Unaware of what the reporter would say until it appeared in print, official spokesmen met each new revelation as it came, but by the time their clarifications appeared, Salisbury had moved on to some new allegation. Making matters worse, early in the dispute government spokesmen had conceded only grudgingly that American bombs might have injured a few civilians, but by its end they were admitting, for example, that during one strike on Yen Vien, three bombs had hit the target and forty had fallen outside. If they had been more candid at the start, Goulding would later lament, they might have deflected most of the criticism that occurred.[20]

Salisbury's revelations wounded the Johnson administration's credibility at a time when it was coming under increasing attack, particularly from critics of the war who were charging that the bombing had done little or nothing to curtail enemy infiltration into South Vietnam. The president and his advisers sought figures that would strengthen their position, but official statistics on the war often contradicted one another, in part because they depended more on the preconceptions of their creators than on what was happening in the field.

A case in point occurred during March 1967, when General Wheeler suggested that Westmoreland brief correspondents on positive results the bombing had produced. He mentioned that MACV might feature a reduction in enemy battalion-sized attacks that had occurred over the preceding year as an indication that air attacks on the North had impaired the enemy's ability to mount large operations in the South. Westmoreland responded that Wheeler's figures were based on incorrect preliminary reports and that, in fact, more mature analyses showed a dramatic increase in the attacks. Wheeler was aghast. "If these figures should reach the public," he told Westmoreland, " . . . they would, literally, blow the lid off of Washington."[21]

He explained what he meant in a second message. Under the new figures, he said, major enemy attacks for 1966 had nearly quadrupled, going from 45 under the old estimate to 174 under the new. Meanwhile, U.S. and South Vietnamese forces had made 385 contacts with enemy battalions, mostly on the enemy's terms rather than their own. The implications the figures entailed were dangerous. The decline in large-scale enemy attacks had been emphasized in presentations on the war's progress to the president, the Congress, and the news media. The new estimate meant that, despite everything that had been said in those briefings, the enemy's combat capabilities had been increasing all the time. Implying that Westmoreland was attempting to inflate the size of the war in order to justify larger troop increases, Wheeler indicated that a special intelligence team would have to evaluate the whole matter. "I cannot go to the president," he said, "and tell him that, contrary to my reports and those of the other chiefs . . . we are not sure who has the initiative in South Vietnam."[22]

Westmoreland stood by his statistics. The figures had resulted from procedures settled upon at a recent intelligence conference in Honolulu, he told

Wheeler, and they were the best available. In addition, they were altogether consistent with the nature of the war. The enemy could be expected to exercise the initiative where battalion-sized attacks were concerned because his battalions included no heavy equipment and rarely comprised more than 180 men. They were thus easy to hide and could choose their moment to attack.[23]

From that point onward, the record is for the most part silent. The chief of MACV intelligence, Maj. Gen. Joseph A. McChristian, would later assert that the reviewing team upheld his figures. Westmoreland himself would avow cryptically in a message to Sharp that Wheeler's reviewers and MACV's analysts had settled on an acceptable new definition for the enemy's large-unit assaults. Even so, the Defense Department's count of the enemy's battalion-sized attacks for 1966 remained unchanged, standing at forty-five for the rest of the war.[24]

Although Westmoreland and the others, in that case, declined to speak out because of the trouble it would have caused for the military services, the public affairs officers who served them in Washington and Saigon were less inhibited. Watching the effects of their government's policies playing out in the field, they spoke their minds when necessary. In the case of MACV's policy for describing American casualties, for example, they recognized that the modifiers *light, moderate,* and *heavy* had little meaning for reporters because most had no idea how many troops were involved in any given operation. As a result, the newsmen sometimes decided that heavy casualties had occurred when only ten men in one platoon had been wounded out of dozens of platoons in contact with the enemy. On top of that, when MACV attempted to set the record straight, some reporters inevitably concluded that the command was indulging in a cover-up. Recognizing that the problem had become a major threat to official credibility, Colonel Bankson and Col. Willis Helmantoler, USAF, the director of public affairs for the Office of the Commander in Chief, Pacific, took it upon themselves in early 1967 to corner Westmoreland and Sharp at a reception in Saigon in order to argue for a change in policy. Goulding did the same in Washington with Secretary McNamara.[25]

In the end, despite concern that the move might aid the enemy, the Defense Department decided to let the facts speak for themselves. On 7 March, as a result, MACV began announcing casualties for significant combat actions if the disclosure would pose no threat to the units involved. The change had the desired effect. News stories and editorials across the United States applauded it, and MACV's credibility improved.[26]

Although the Saigon correspondents sometimes jumped to erroneous conclusions, it would be a mistake to assume that they were unwilling to give MACV any benefit of a doubt. A case in point occurred in early 1967, after the United States began to arm U.S. forces with the new M16 rifle. When rumors began to circulate that the weapon was costing American lives by jamming in combat and a subcommittee of the House Armed Services Committee decided to investigate, a few news stories detailed the allegations, but little sustained critical comment appeared. Two reports by CBS correspondent Murray Fromson were typical. In the first, after interviewing a young marine who expressed little confidence in the rifle, Fromson turned to the marine commander in South Vietnam, Lt. Gen. Lewis Walt, who observed that the M16 was the finest rifle the Marine Corps had ever received and that morale among his men would decline if they came to believe their basic weapon was defective. In the second story, the reporter presented criticisms by individual marines but then ran a test comparing the M16 with its predecessor, the M14. After burying each rifle in a pile of sand, a marine retrieved and fired each. The M16 was equipped with a standard dust cover and fired upon demand. Lacking a cover, the M14 jammed. Judging from this limited evidence, Fromson announced that the M16 was the better weapon, exactly the opposite of what some of the troops were reporting from the field.[27]

The conclusion was technically correct, but evidence compiled by the House Armed Services Committee indicated that the M16 indeed had problems. Because of changes in the propellent prescribed for its ammunition, it fired hot and fast and sometimes jammed. In addition, it required more frequent cleaning than other rifles, but because maintenance equipment had failed to reach some units in the field, at least a few of the troops had improvised cleaning rods out of materials at hand, particularly old clothes hangers. All of this information was well suited for exposés, but according to journalists and public affairs officers who were there, reporters took little note of it both out of goodwill for the military and because they had no wish to undermine the confidence of the troops in their basic weapon. Stories on the subject appeared from time to time, especially after the House Armed Services Committee charged the army with "criminal negligence" for its failure to correct the rifle's deficiencies, but the issue never received the sort of play in the news media that it could have.[28]

In the end, the lack of a strong outcry in the press left military managers with little incentive to fix the weapon. As a result, a year later, despite an army-mandated reconditioning program to correct what was wrong and reports from virtually all U.S. component commanders in South Vietnam that repairs were complete, an army review team found that many M16s had yet to be touched. In addition, 38 percent of the men interviewed reported rifle malfunctions within the preceding four months. Although adequate stocks of cleaning supplies existed in military depots, the troops also complained that the materials were difficult to get. A few had even resorted to diesel fuel and insect repellent to replace bore cleaner for their rifle barrels. All this occurred in February 1968, at the height of the Tet offensive. If reporters knew about what was happening, they said nothing about it.[29]

If the press sometimes deferred to the military, it declined to extend the privilege to the Johnson administration. Westmoreland and Zorthian saw the tendency and attempted to divorce MACV from domestic politics by playing down justifications for the president's policies in the command's official statements. They also managed to deflect two attempts by Johnson during 1966 to have Westmoreland travel to the United States to shore up public support for the war. By 1967, however, with antiwar sentiment increasing in the United States, Johnson was not to be denied. When he asked Westmoreland to go to New York during April to address the annual meeting of the Associated Press Managing Editors Association, he phrased the summons in such a way that the general felt he had no choice but to comply.[30]

Westmoreland's misgivings proved correct. When the general avowed during the speech that the Communists interpreted antiwar protests in the United States as a sign of crumbling morale and hardened their resistance, his words caused an uproar in Congress and the press. Fulbright and Senator George McGovern charged that Johnson had brought the general home to stifle dissent and that the president and his military leaders were blaming their failures on their critics. A *Chicago Daily News* headline asserted, "Dissent Is Not Treason," and columnist Walter Lippmann suggested that the justification of administration policy should be the responsibility of politicians rather than generals.[31]

Despite these complaints, many congressmen and editorial writers sided with Westmoreland. The *Washington Star* termed the uproar over the speech "nonsense," the *Washington Post* saw no reason that the government should refrain from responding to its critics, and Senator Mike Mansfield of Montana disagreed with Westmoreland's remarks but still contended that the general had as much right to express his views as anyone else. A speech by Westmoreland before Congress also went well. Mansfield called it "soldierly," and Senator Eugene McCarthy of Minnesota, who opposed the war, conceded that it was an "objective appraisal."[32]

Despite the favorable remarks, Col. Winant Sidle, Goulding's special assistant for Southeast Asia at the time, could only conclude that Westmoreland's trip constituted a long-term loss for the military. Before the trip, Sidle said, reporters and editors had so trusted the general that many journals had reprinted his background sessions for the press almost word for word. Afterward, suspecting that he had become a tool of the president, they greeted his pronouncements with more skepticism.[33]

It was probably unrealistic, however, to expect that the news media would go along with Westmoreland indefinitely, if only because important members of the official community itself were beginning to raise questions, and their misgivings were bound to spread to the press. As early as September 1966, for example, intelligence analysts had begun to doubt that the bombing of North Vietnam was creating insurmountable difficulties for the enemy. Then, in November, Secretary McNamara himself had claimed that the bombing of the northernmost portions of North Vietnam hardly justified the cost.[34]

The doubts remained submerged for a time, but they began to surface in public during August 1967, when the Preparedness Subcommittee of the Senate Armed Services Committee held hearings to investigate whether air attacks on North Vietnam were having much effect. Meeting in executive session, the Joint

Chiefs of Staff and other witnesses advocated mining the enemy's ports and lifting the restrictions that had held the air war in check to date. On 25 August, however, McNamara contradicted them, asserting that enemy forces in South Vietnam required only fifteen tons of supplies per day from North Vietnam, an amount that would slip through even the heaviest of air campaigns. Meanwhile, the economy of North Vietnam was so primitive that it could sustain the worst damage with only minor adjustments, and the nation's people were so inured to hardship that nothing short of all-out attacks on population centers would shake them. As for mining the ports, the effort would fail. The enemy's supply requirements

Barry Zorthian with Brigadier General Winant Sidle. (Barry Zorthian)

were so small that North Vietnam could receive most of what it needed through nearby harbors in China or by ferrying supplies from ship to shore across its own beaches at night.[35]

McNamara's testimony leaked to the press almost immediately and made headlines around the world. Building on allegations already rising that the war was in stalemate, editors asserted that if the secretary was to be believed, after two and a half years of effort and a buildup of five hundred thousand troops, the United States was no better off than it had been when it first started fighting. The stalemate had merely escalated along with the war.[36]

Proposals began to rise within the administration on ways to rebut these allegations. General Wheeler, for one, wanted Westmoreland to hold a special briefing for the press to present a factual case for progress. The session would cover the number of enemy base areas U.S. forces had overrun, the many miles of roads and waterways they had opened, the huge amounts of equipment and supplies they had captured or destroyed, and other facts and figures of the sort. Admiral Sharp disagreed. "We have trapped ourselves," he said, "with our obsession to quantify everything. . . . I suggest that we attempt to move away from . . . numbers and concentrate on the less tangible but more important results of our operations."[37]

Sharp was right. More numbers were not the answer. As appraisals coming from within the Defense Department's Office of Systems Analysis showed, the Johnson administration's claims of progress were under attack because they failed to stand up to close scrutiny. In the case of the body count, the office's analysts noted, MACV professed to have killed or captured over one-fourth of the men coming of military age in North Vietnam every year. Even if those figures were to be believed, they said, the enemy could sustain damage of that magnitude indefinitely. The British had absorbed a loss of half their men in a five-year age-group during World War I and had gone on fighting.[38]

American commanders, the analysts continued, had failed to come to grips with the way the enemy fought. Holding the initiative, North Vietnamese and Viet Cong forces sought to hurt their opponents while keeping their own casualties low. As a result, they usually employed small squads in surprise attacks that took down one or two Americans and then escaped before artillery and air strikes could respond. American forces could legitimately claim a kill ratio of 5 to 1 when Communist troops charged en masse or stood and fought, but the enemy's attacks by stealth, along with ambushes, mines, and booby traps, accounted for three out of every four American casualties. When included, such encounters reduced the kill ratio to 1.5 to 1, hardly enough to break the enemy's will. Compounding the problem, the counts of enemy dead submitted to higher headquarters seemed routinely to double at each level as they moved up the chain of command. The analysts concluded that the degree of delusion within the U.S. government had become so great it was a matter for national concern.[39]

General Westmoreland disputed the analysts' contentions and dispatched teams of investigators to monitor the body-counting process. Although the officers reported back that the count was largely honest, Bankson's replacement as chief of the MACV Office of Information, newly promoted Brig. Gen. Winant Sidle, recognized that the units surveyed might have followed proper procedures only because inspectors were present. He moved immediately, on that account, to downplay tallies of the enemy's dead and all other statistics in MACV's briefings for the press.[40]

Sidle was convinced that the military had overplayed the progress of the war and that time and patience would be required to reestablish MACV's credibility with the press. He understood, however, that the task would be difficult because the corps of correspondents in Saigon had become increasingly unmanageable as 1967 progressed. Many of the influential veteran reporters who had sympathized with the military in the past had departed, to be replaced by an unwieldy mass of more than 450 journalists that could surge to over 500 in times of crisis. Of those, a few veterans remained—Arnett, for example, and Faas, Mohr, Sully, Merick, Shaplen, and Deepe—but many of them were already deeply suspicious of the military. The rest were often unknowns with little experience in journalism or limited knowledge of war.[41]

Reasoning that MACV's team of briefers had "a chip on its collective shoulder," Sidle began the process of change by replacing it with individuals more likely to get along with reporters. He also made certain that a small press liaison office located in Saigon was manned around the clock by knowledgeable officers.

In that way, correspondents under deadlines would be able to check their facts without having to deal with the bureaucracy at MACV's headquarters at Tan Son Nhut Air Base. Since reporters placed more trust in lower-ranking officers than in generals who often had something to sell, Sidle also made a special effort to identify talented young officers who could replace high-ranking briefers in periodic backgrounders on special developments.[42]

If Sidle was willing to work with the press, he still believed there were limits to how far he or any information officer could go. Convinced that Zorthian was giving away "the family jewels" at the U.S. mission's weekly backgrounders, he made it a point to attend each one of the sessions. Reporters complained that the presence of a general in uniform put a damper on the proceedings, but that was the very effect Sidle sought. Since unthinking soldiers who acted or spoke improperly on camera were often the guilty parties when disagreeable news stories played on television, he also took steps to ensure that official escorts accompanied network reporters and cameramen when they visited units in the field. With an officer present, he reasoned, soldiers would think twice before doing or saying anything improper. Understanding, nevertheless, that negative news stories would still get by, he attempted to limit the damage they caused by setting up a system to monitor blatantly erroneous reporting. Besides compiling a list of "hardheads" to track worst cases, he took pains to speak with particularly biased correspondents to "straighten" them out. If no change followed, he would transfer the case to the Defense Department, which would contact the individuals' employers.[43]

Sidle's innovations had been in effect for hardly a month before the Saigon correspondents demonstrated how hard change would come. On 9 October, CBS newsman Don Webster and cameraman John Smith visited units of the First Infantry Division at the scene of a nighttime firefight. The two separated to cover different parts of the battlefield, with a military escort accompanying each. Webster encountered no problems, but Smith observed a dead enemy body lying to one side with an ear slashed from its head. In an exchange that remains less than clear to this day (Westmoreland asserted that Smith "persuaded" the soldier, but Smith denied it), the cameraman furnished his enlisted escort with a knife and then filmed the man as he duplicated the atrocity on another nearby body. The rarest of happenings, a violation of the laws of war filmed as it occurred, the episode played on the CBS Evening News with Webster narrating.[44]

The commander of the First Division arrested the culprit and sought to proceed against Smith as an accomplice, but the U.S. embassy in Saigon declined. Any move against the cameraman could only make trouble with the news media at a time when the president needed the goodwill of the press to demonstrate that progress was occurring in the war. In the end, subpoenas were issued for Smith and Webster to testify at the trial of the enlisted man, but both had left the country. During the trial that followed, the soldier was convicted, fined, and reduced in rank.[45]

Although Smith went undisciplined, the U.S. mission in Saigon did manage to temper the work of at least a few reporters by appealing to their editors. When Ambassador Bunker, for example, learned in December that Orville Schell, the older brother of Jonathan Schell, would shortly publish an article in the *Atlantic Monthly* scoring the violence of U.S. tactics, he cabled McNamara. The secretary in turn contacted Schell's editor, former assistant secretary of state for public affairs Robert Manning. In the end, according to McNamara, Manning edited the article, making the version that appeared in press "less troublesome in tone and content" than the original.[46]

Sidle's adjustments, particularly his determination to devalue statistics, promised to remedy MACV's main public relations problems, but they were too slow and undramatic for President Johnson. At a time when the press and television seemed dominated by stories of the South Vietnamese army's ineptitude and allegations of stalemate, he wanted action. On 28 September, as a result, he ordered Westmoreland to begin amassing statistics to demonstrate that the war was succeeding.[47]

The program the U.S. mission devised in response was antithetical in spirit to Sidle's low-key approach. Under it, senior mission officials would hold special briefings to compare the situation in 1967 with those that had prevailed in 1965 and 1966, MACV would sponsor visits by reporters to areas of South Vietnam that showed progress in pacification, and public affairs officers would hold hardhitting briefings to allay public concern about controversial topics in the press. The U.S. mission would also accelerate the release of captured enemy documents that admitted by word or inference that Communist forces were having problems.[48]

The plan received wide support within the Johnson administration, but McGeorge Bundy took exception. Asked during October to suggest ways for the United States to strengthen its public image, he warned against initiatives that built upon appearances rather than substance. The president would have to defend his record in his next campaign for reelection, Bundy said, leading reporters to scrutinize his statements on the war for signs of political maneuvering. Bundy's remarks appear to have had some effect. Although the administration went forward with its campaign, official spokesmen concentrated on general trends rather than hard statistics in making their points.[49]

Barry Zorthian also attempted to move the administration toward moderation by rationing the number of captured enemy documents he released to the press and by ensuring that only the most credible appeared. When the White House pressured him to step up his efforts, he made a great show of effort, but he still took care to provide only the most significant materials. As a result, the press continued to take captured enemy documents seriously whenever they appeared.[50]

The president was nevertheless of his own mind. When he encountered an extremely optimistic appraisal of the situation in the II Corps Zone, for example,

General William Westmoreland briefs President Johnson and his advisers in Washington, D.C. (Department of Defense)

he insisted that the commanders of the other three corps write similar reports so that he could use them in his dealings with the press. In the same way, he quoted CORDS's statistical summaries in his conversations with newsmen despite warnings that the figures were at best rough indicators.[51]

The U.S. mission in Saigon was more successful in dealing with the president where combat was concerned. When the enemy experienced a major defeat at Loc Ninh in the III Corps Zone, Johnson pressed for a statement praising South Vietnamese accomplishments during the battle. Aware that the operation had been largely an American affair, Westmoreland declined to make what he termed a "hard sell." It was fortunate that he did. Several days later, South Vietnamese troops pillaged Loc Ninh and several plantations nearby, a development that might have come to light if reporters had been following their activities more closely. In the end, General Wheeler placated Johnson by giving Orr Kelly of the *Washington Star* enough information to write a favorable piece on the South Vietnamese role in the battle.[52]

Shortly after the battle at Loc Ninh ended, American forces fought a second battle at Dak To, located near the Laotian border in the Western Highlands. The three-week engagement involved some of the hardest fighting of the war and seemed to many reporters a less than clear-cut American victory. Both the AP

American troops pinned down at Dak To. (U.S. Army)

and UPI dispatched stories on how for three days enemy fire had driven off helicopters attempting to evacuate scores of American wounded. Aware that the development was complicating the president's success campaign, Westmoreland instructed his deputy, Gen. Creighton Abrams, to do what he could to refute allegations that U.S. units had been surrounded and slaughtered.[53]

Abrams could do nothing of the sort. The fighting at Dak To had been little less spectacular than the press reports depicting it. Occupying well-fortified positions on heavily jungled slopes, the enemy had stood and fought with fury, laying down such intense fire that he kept helicopters at bay for two days before they could land to assist several large groups of badly wounded Americans. In the end, the enemy pulled back with some sixteen hundred estimated dead, but U.S. forces still lost three hundred killed and over one thousand wounded.[54]

The Johnson administration placed little importance on press coverage of Dak To because it was preoccupied with its latest public relations endeavor, a second visit by Westmoreland to the United States. The official line had it that the general was in town to program the next six months of the war, but all concerned understood that the true purpose of the trip was public relations. During his time in the United States, Westmoreland testified before the House Armed Services Committee, delivered an address to the National Press Club, and appeared on the

NBC News program *Meet the Press*. On each occasion he stressed that American forces were gaining the upper hand in South Vietnam and that they would begin to turn the fighting over to the South Vietnamese within two years. "It is significant," he told the National Press Club, "that the enemy has not won a major battle in more than a year. In general he can fight his large forces only at the edges of his sanctuaries."[55]

Reporters and editors had no doubt that another of the president's public relations campaigns was beginning. Ward Just of the *Washington Post* expressed the views of many. Scoring the president's "hard sell" on Vietnam, he asserted that statistics could never measure intangibles such as the loyalty of a people to its government. When official spokesmen such as Westmoreland claimed that the Saigon regime controlled 67 percent of the South Vietnamese people, they were thus opening themselves to a possible public backlash. What would happen "if a year from now we have, say, eighty-five percent of the Vietnamese people under Saigon control," the reporter asked, "and the war has not abated and American casualties remain about the same?"[56]

Despite the criticism, Westmoreland's remarks once again played well in some segments of the news media. Reviewing Westmoreland's themes, for example, columnist James Reston disagreed with the general's emphasis on military action and asserted that resolution of the conflict rested ultimately with North Vietnam's Communist allies, but he then commended Westmoreland for his careful estimates and modest demeanor.[57]

Westmoreland's message received further enhancement when AP reporters George MacArthur and Horst Faas published a detailed story on the enemy's increasing use of Cambodia as a sanctuary. After the account appeared, in order to put the story into context, Westmoreland requested and received permission to hold a background briefing on the evolution of the Cambodian port of Sihanoukville on the Gulf of Thailand into a major logistical hub for enemy forces in South Vietnam. When the briefing appeared in the press—attributed to Westmoreland despite a stipulation that reporters name only "military sources"— it stole the limelight from the president's critics.[58]

The president's campaign continued on into December, with Johnson himself asserting in an interview with CBS News that the enemy had yet to win a single victory on the battlefield but still sought a way to break the will of the American people. Toward its end, MACV made a final attempt to demonstrate the success of American efforts by mustering U.S. troops to secure South Vietnam's main north-south road, Highway 1, from the Cambodian border in the south to the Demilitarized Zone in the north. Vice President Ky then drove the length of the road from one end to the other with newsmen to prove how safe it had become. No one in the press noted at the time that the troops departed after Ky passed, leaving those portions of the road that were of little use once more to the enemy.[59]

Although the president's popularity rose some 11 points in polls during this period, critics of the war were hardly silent. Antiwar demonstrations occurred at locations across the United States, and Senator Fulbright revealed during extensive hearings in Washington that the Johnson administration had prepared a draft resolution justifying military action in South Vietnam even before the Gulf of Tonkin attacks had occurred. Meanwhile, in Congress, a number of legislators moved from support for the war to positions of doubt. Prominent among them were Senator Thurston Morton of Kentucky and Congressman Thomas P. "Tip" O'Neal of Massachusetts, who advertised their changes of heart publicly in a series of comments to the press. Meanwhile, many legislators admitted privately to reporters that they had suspended judgment on the war and that they intended to "stay loose" for as long as possible before the next election campaign forced them to make up their minds.[60]

The administration responded by pressing its public relations campaign in every forum possible. On television, in speeches before traditional Democratic constituencies such as the AFL-CIO, and in articles for well-disposed publications, high-level officials such as Dean Rusk, Walter Rostow, and William P. Bundy asserted that enemy casualties were increasing and that the need to repair damage caused by the bombing had deterred enemy infiltration into South Vietnam. They added that if the United States had failed to act to save South Vietnam, all of Southeast Asia would by then have been in jeopardy.[61]

The campaign continued into 1968, when Robert Komer held a news conference in Saigon on the pacification program. Specifying that much still needed to be done, Komer noted that all trends were still "significantly upward." Year-end reports on 12,277 hamlets showed that 67 percent of South Vietnam's people lived in secure areas. The rice harvest was richer than in the previous year; more tractors were to be seen in the fields; and people in the hamlets were buying Honda motorcycles. "You don't start buying tractors with your piasters," Komer said, "unless you expect you're going to be able to use them." The briefing marked the end of President Johnson's public relations campaign. Five days later the enemy launched the Tet offensive.[62]

8

The Tet Offensive

Despite the optimism of their public statements, neither the president nor Westmoreland was convinced that all was well. At the very time when the administration's progress campaign was reaching its height, three North Vietnamese division headquarters and seven regiments—a total of more than fifteen thousand men—were taking up station near the marine outpost at Khe Sanh in Quang Tri Province. Meanwhile, an unprecedented volume of supplies and troops was moving down the Ho Chi Minh Trail, the enemy's main infiltration route through Laos into South Vietnam. On 21 December, Johnson predicted quietly at a meeting with allied leaders in Australia that he expected a major enemy attack in the near future. Meanwhile, concerned that MACV might not have the resources to respond if a massive enemy force crossed the Demilitarized Zone into South Vietnam, Westmoreland began transferring American troops into the nation's northernmost provinces. He also sought and received permission to begin contingency planning to use tactical nuclear weapons.[1]

The invasion Westmoreland expected never materialized. Instead, on the evening of 30 January, as the South Vietnamese people celebrated Tet, their most festive holiday, enemy forces attacked the main cities and administrative centers in the country's northernmost provinces. More than seven hundred of the enemy fell in the assaults, but those attacks proved only a prelude. Late the next night, the enemy launched simultaneous attacks against South Vietnam's most important cities, towns, and hamlets. In Hue, eight battalions seized most of the city. In Saigon, eleven local force battalions launched coordinated attacks on many politically important targets, including the presidential palace, Tan Son Nhut Airport, and the newly constructed U.S. embassy.[2]

Westmoreland viewed the offensive as a diversion in preparation for the long-awaited attack in the I Corps Tactical Zone. Confident in his ability to repel it, he told Wheeler that the enemy's concentration on high-visibility targets

Bodies of two Viet Cong lie where they fell during an attack on the U.S. embassy in Saigon. (U.S. Army)

indicated a desire to have some sort of psychological effect on world public opinion. Hanson W. Baldwin made the same point in the *New York Times* the next morning.[3]

If Westmoreland was composed and well collected, the Saigon correspondents were aghast. Unable to reach most of the fighting around the country, they centered their attention on Saigon and the target most accessible to them, the U.S. embassy. Hearing great volumes of fire coming from the building's direction, they took the word of officers and military policemen at the scene and concluded that Communist commandos had penetrated at least the lower floors of the facility. In contact with the embassy at all times and aware that it remained sealed to the enemy, the State Department attempted to correct the erroneous reports that followed. Westmoreland did the same at an impromptu press conference at the scene shortly after U.S. forces regained control of the compound. Coming in the wake of the president's optimism campaign, the offensive had nonetheless so wounded official credibility that some in the press continued to place their reliance in the word of their initial low-level sources, who in theory had nothing to sell. As a result, CBS played Westmoreland's comment on the 1 February edition of the morning news, but NBC News anchorman Chet Huntley told his audience that enemy snipers in the embassy and on nearby rooftops had fired down on the rescuers in the court-yard—the exact opposite of what had happened. As late as 2 February, the *New York Times* was still willing to publish an article assert-ing that guerrillas had penetrated at least the first floor of the embassy. The newspaper added in an edito-rial that the success of the enemy's offensive threw both the adminis-tration's claims of progress and the competence of the South Viet-namese armed forces into serious doubt. Other journals were just as harsh.[4]

A news conference Westmore-land held on 1 February did little to ease the reporters' concerns. Under instructions from President John-son to provide a brief personal com-

General William Westmoreland
talks to embassy military personnel
following a Viet Cong attack. (U.S. Army)

ment to the press each day in order to reassure the American public, the general claimed that MACV had foreseen attacks during the new year even though it had failed to predict an initiative during Tet itself. He then explained that the enemy was in the midst of a three-phase campaign. The first had been intended to bleed allied forces at Loc Ninh and Dak To. The second, in progress, targeted govern-ment facilities. The third would be an all-or-nothing effort in South Vietnam's northernmost regions. Overall, Westmoreland said, the enemy had lost fifty-eight hundred killed in the first days of the offensive alone—so many that it would take him weeks and months to recover.[5] When Robert Schakne of CBS asked for an assessment of the situation, the general responded that the Viet Cong had ex-posed themselves to American firepower and had suffered a great defeat. He added that the attacks were only diversions from the enemy's main effort, which would come across the Demilitarized Zone and around Khe Sanh. To many re-porters, Westmoreland seemed to be mouthing platitudes while the wolf was at the gate.[6]

Gloom pervaded the news stories that followed. Orr Kelly of the *Washing-ton Star* stressed that the United States had been caught off guard. Mike Wallace remarked on CBS that the offensive had "demolished the myth" that allied strength controlled South Vietnam. *New York Daily News* reporter Jerry Greene characterized the attack as a "potent propaganda victory" for the enemy that had clouded a steady stream of official American optimism. The *New York Times* observed, "These are not the deeds of an enemy whose fighting efficiency has 'progressively declined' and whose morale is 'sinking fast,' as United States military officials put it in November."[7]

According to Westmoreland, the Johnson administration fell into "great consternation" at the news from Saigon. The U.S. mission attempted to restore balance by assuring the president that the situation was under control, but as Westmoreland observed, the effort was more than offset by the "doom and gloom" emanating from South Vietnam. Adding to the effect was a chorus of alarmed comments from Congress, where supporters of the war sided with Westmoreland but numerous middle-of-the-road members expressed shock and dismay. Even the supporters were none too happy. "What happened?" one stalwart remarked. "I thought we were supposed to be winning this war."[8]

Public affairs officers in Saigon could do little to counter the trend. With communications from the field lagging by as much as a day, they had only fragments to work with. On the morning of 1 February, as a result, they could announce only that there had been firing around Hue and that some portions of the city's northern sectors had been surrounded. They had little more to say that evening, by which time almost the entire city was in enemy hands.[9]

MACV's information officers attempted to clarify the situation at Hue and elsewhere by having the director of the command's operations center, Brig. Gen. John Chaisson, USMC, brief reporters. Although predicting erroneously that Hue would be cleared in a few days, Chaisson admitted that U.S. intelligence had failed to predict the full dimensions of the attack. He then credited the enemy with "a very successful offensive, in its initial phases." The general's candor did not sit well with some. The next day, the chief of MACV intelligence, Brig. Gen. Phillip B. Davidson, Jr., attempted to explain away the general's admission that the breadth and violence of the offensive had been a surprise. American commanders had recognized the enemy's ability to attack at Tet, he declared, and had expected some sort of offensive all along. Chaisson, he said, had admitted only that he *personally* had been surprised.[10]

President Johnson also spoke. At a White House ceremony on 1 February and at an impromptu news conference the next day, he asserted that the enemy would fail again and again because America would never yield. Indeed, he said, even if the enemy attempted to twist what had happened into some sort of psychological victory, Communist forces had lost 10,000 men, while at most 249 Americans and 500 South Vietnamese had fallen. Although time lines would have to be adjusted, he added, he saw no reason to revise his assertion that "we have made progress."[11]

Comparing the various versions of what had happened, many in the press questioned the body counts Johnson had cited and proclaimed their suspicion that the attacks had hardly been as well anticipated as Davidson and others had said. Cynthia Parsons, for one, made it a point to remark in the *Christian Science Monitor* that although one general had admitted the attack had been a surprise, another had all but denied it. If MACV had been so certain that the enemy would attack, the *New Republic* added in an editorial entitled "Misled in Every Sense," why had U.S. and South Vietnamese forces been so ill prepared to repel the assault? "Or is forewarned," the magazine asked, "not forearmed in this weird war?" Quoting *New York Times* columnist James Reston, the magazine's editors went on to charge, "We are the flies that captured the flypaper."[12]

General Westmoreland responded to the criticism by instructing his public affairs officers to screen measures of progress carefully. Even so, he believed that Hanoi had exposed its forces to the full fury of American firepower and that MACV's body count was more than plausible. "We seldom know the number of killed . . . resulting from B-52, tactical air, and artillery strikes," he told reporters on 25 February, " . . . [or] how many die from their wounds. . . . These unknowns more than offset the relatively small inaccuracies of our accounting system."[13]

Although time and events would ultimately convert many reporters to Westmoreland's point of view, for the enemy had indeed suffered grievous casualties during the offensive, there was little the general could do about another aspect of the offensive that drew the attention of the press—apparent violations of the laws of war. The issue arose on the morning of 2 February, when AP photographer Eddie Adams photographed Brig. Gen. Nguyen Ngoc Loan, the chief of South Vietnam's National Police, in the act of summarily executing a newly captured Viet Cong officer. The AP filed a brief story, quoting Loan, to accompany the picture. The Viet Cong had "killed many Americans," the general said, "and many of my people." A film of the incident by NBC News cameraman Vo Suu, slightly edited to eliminate the gore, played that evening on NBC's Huntley-Brinkley Report. Limited by time, correspondent Howard Tuckner contributed only the barest commentary. Noting little more than that the victim had been the commander of a Viet Cong commando unit and that he had been "roughed up," the reporter let the film speak for itself. The man approached. The general fired. The man fell.[14]

Adams's picture appeared in virtually every important newspaper in the United States. Many of the journals that commented attempted to balance it with some allusion to enemy atrocities. The *New York Times*, for example, published it with a photograph of a South Vietnamese officer holding the body of his murdered child. Both the *New York Daily News* and the *Chicago Daily News* implied that Loan's act paled in the context of the violence occurring in South Vietnam on both sides. The *Chicago Tribune* charged that the antiwar movement was quick to exaggerate allied atrocities but said little when the Viet Cong obliterated whole villages.[15]

These attempts at balance were lost in the reaction that set in almost immediately. A report by the AP led the way. If the enemy kept lists of men to be killed, it maintained, government troops also executed enemy prisoners, sometimes with the approval of their American advisers. To demonstrate the point, the story's

Eddie Adams's photo of Brigadier General Nguyen Ngoc Loan executing a Viet Cong prisoner. (AP/Wide World Photos)

author quoted an anonymous U.S. Army sergeant. "If I had my way," the man had said, "we would execute on the spot every Viet Cong and Viet Cong suspect we catch."[16]

General Wheeler responded in a widely publicized letter to Congressman Henry S. Reuss of Wisconsin. Alluding to the picture of the officer holding his murdered child, he contended that the South Vietnamese army was far more scrupulous in its handling of civilians and prisoners than the Communists. The U.S. mission, meanwhile, warned the South Vietnamese on their treatment of prisoners and obtained the removal of several execution posts they had erected in Saigon's central market.[17]

Despite these efforts, the issue of American and South Vietnamese atrocities gained rather than lost momentum. On 19 February, the *New York Times* and the *Washington Post,* along with a number of other papers, published an AP photograph of a South Vietnamese marine shooting an enemy captive. An accompanying article quoted an unnamed American adviser who had told newsmen, "We usually kill the seriously wounded Viet Cong. . . . The hospitals are so full . . . there is no room for the enemy . . . [and] when you've seen five-year-old girls with their eyes blindfolded . . . and bullets in their brains, you look for revenge. I saw two little girls that dead [sic] yesterday. One hour ago I shot a Viet Cong." The State and Defense Departments warned MACV that if the soldier was telling the truth rather than merely attempting to impress a gullible newsman, a serious violation had occurred that could implicate U.S. commanders if they failed to investigate. The command did what it could, but with eyewitnesses unwilling to come forward, legal action against offenders proved impossible.[18]

In the end, the pictures of General Loan's atrocity probably had little effect on American public opinion. Twenty million people watched Huntley-Brinkley on the night Suu's film played, but NBC received only ninety letters on the subject. Fifty-six accused the network of bad taste. The rest complained that the film had appeared at a time when children could watch. Few alluded to the conflict in Vietnam. War, apparently, was war.[19]

By the end of the first week in February, heavy fighting was continuing in Saigon's suburbs and other areas, and the enemy retained possession of much of Hue, but the Communists had failed to achieve their main military objectives. Although they had sought to spark a general uprising among South Vietnam's people, none had occurred. Instead, the bulk of the nation's armed forces had fought hard.[20]

The offensive, however, had still done drastic damage to South Vietnam's economy and to many of its cities. South Vietnamese troops had looted parts of Can Tho, My Tho, and Chau Duc in the Mekong delta, and they and their American allies had brought so much gratuitous firepower to bear in rooting out the enemy that they had devastated towns such as Can Tho and Ben Tre. The net effect was that the inhabitants of many areas and the government functionaries who served them seemed immobilized by shock. General Westmoreland set up a special working group to speed recovery, but over the short term the going was difficult. Money ran out and red tape abounded.[21]

The press covered it all, particularly the suffering both sides had imposed on innocent civilians. "At what point do you turn your heavy guns and fighter bombers on your own city?" Peter Arnett asked after visiting Ben Tre. "When does the infliction of civilian casualties become irrelevant as long as the enemy is destroyed?" Observing that the South Vietnamese command had declined to authorize air strikes and artillery fire at Ben Tre until the total destruction of their forces seemed imminent, the reporter answered the question with a comment by an unnamed U.S. adviser who had said, "It became necessary to destroy the town to save it." The *New York Times* seized upon the remark as soon as it appeared. So did *Time*. From there it passed into the lore of the war, to become one of the most serviceable icons of the antiwar movement.[22]

Reporters also began to evaluate the damage the offensive had caused to pacification. While some observed cautiously that the effects of the attack on the pacification effort had yet to be gauged because conditions in the countryside were still unclear, Lee Lescaze and Ward Just of the *Washington Post*, Charles Mohr of the *New York Times*, and the editors of *Newsweek*, to name just a few, all agreed that the program was a shambles. That the enemy had moved through the countryside without betrayal by the people, *Newsweek* claimed, made a mockery of Robert Komer's claim prior to the attack that 67 percent of South Vietnam's people lived in secure areas.[23]

A report by the Office of the Assistant Secretary of Defense for Systems Analysis agreed with the reporters' analysis, noting that the enemy largely controlled South Vietnam's countryside and that pacification "as currently conceived" was dead. The U.S. mission was of a different mind. If pacification teams had withdrawn from the countryside to fight in the cities during Tet, Ambassador Bunker observed on the 18 February edition of the CBS News program *Face the Nation,* so had enemy forces. Tet was a revered tradition among the Vietnamese people, Bunker added, and had not been violated in over a thousand years. In that sense, by breaking with custom, the enemy had forfeited the respect of many South Vietnamese.[24]

Robert Komer attempted to give reporters a framework for judging the program at a 24 February news conference. Conceding that pacification had been damaged, he noted nevertheless that the enemy had bypassed secure areas in order to ensure that his plans remained secret. By so doing, he had left up to 80 percent of all pacification teams undisturbed. Komer claimed that the main effects of the offensive in the countryside were psychological, with many people living in fear that the Communists would come back. Although six months might elapse before the situation returned to normal, he added, pacification would recover.[25]

Komer's message was lost on the press. Concentrating on the negatives the administrator had admitted to, the *New York Times,* for one, headlined its account of the session "U.S. Admits Blow to Pacification." In all fairness, Komer's points were difficult to see at the time. Although the Office of Systems Analysis ultimately retracted its conclusion that pacification was dead, for example, it refused to relinquish the idea until well into September.[26]

Circumstances in the northern portion of South Vietnam tended to confirm the opinion of many journalists that the war was going sour. Reporters had only to look toward the old imperial capital at Hue and toward the marine base at Khe Sanh to its west for evidence that seemed to confirm that conclusion. For if MACV continued to issue optimistic bulletins on Hue until as late as 8 February, every reporter knew that the enemy held most of the city and that the fighting there had been bitter.[27]

Involving the sort of house-to-house fighting that had occurred during World War II, the battle for Hue was, in fact, relatively easy for the press to cover. Although the South Vietnamese did most of the fighting and suffered four times more casualties than the U.S. Marines at the scene, reporters found the easiest going with the Americans, where they at least knew the language and where the American public expected them to be. As a result, with a few exceptions, most exaggerated the marines' role in the battle, describing how the Americans were

Television crewmen film the fighting at Hue. (Don North)

fighting "foot by blood soaked foot" while saying little about the South Vietnamese and their efforts. In the end, nonetheless, the circumstances may have worked to the benefit of the South Vietnamese. For if many of their units did well in the battle, others did so poorly that, at one point, three battalions of South Vietnamese marines—the strongest force in Hue's Citadel—took three days to advance less than half a city block. The Saigon correspondents never noted that failure and others like it because they were preoccupied with the American effort.[28]

As the fighting continued, Hue's Communist captors began to execute government officials, student leaders, priests, bonzes, ministers, and anyone else who might ultimately question their aims, consigning, in all, as many as four thousand noncombatants to mass graves. Informed by the city's mayor that executions were occurring, the AP carried the story on 11 February along with the *Washington Post* and the *New York Times,* but the rest of the press was slow to follow. On a slow news day the story might have received more of a hearing, but the mayor was well known as an incompetent, and reporters already had more than enough to do. Even MACV hesitated when it heard the word. Unable, at first, to confirm the mayor's account, it waited until 9 March, two weeks after the fighting in Hue had ended, before issuing a communiqué on what had happened. By then the story was out of date, and MACV's statement seemed just another attempt by U.S. spokesmen to publicize enemy atrocities.[29]

If the battle for Hue received heavy coverage, the press paid far more attention to events at Khe Sanh. Westmoreland had predicted that the main enemy threat would come from the north. Looking in that direction, the Saigon correspondents recognized that the enemy was on the defensive at Hue but saw as well that his forces surrounded some six thousand marines at Khe Sanh. They assumed that a climactic battle was in the making similar to the one that had occurred during the French Indochina War in which Communist forces had trapped a large French force at Dien Bien Phu. President Johnson was thinking the same thought and becoming increasingly disturbed. With criticism of the war rising in the United States and with his own political fortunes at stake, he could ill afford the bad publicity that would accompany the annihilation of a major American force.[30]

Westmoreland and Wheeler attempted to reassure the president. In fact, they noted, the situation at Khe Sanh was hardly as dire as the one at Dien Bien Phu. The United States could reinforce and resupply the base by air, and B-52 bombers could pound the enemy's positions at will. Johnson was unimpressed. Aware that Westmoreland was preparing contingency plans for the employment of nuclear weapons, he told Wheeler he had no wish to use them to save the base. Westmoreland responded by telling the president that ample nonnuclear means existed to protect the base. He told Wheeler privately, however, that he was unprepared to rule out the option if the enemy launched a major invasion across South Vietnam's northern border. His troops were stretched too thin.[31]

For that reason, Westmoreland continued planning for the possible use of nuclear weapons, but by then too many knew what he was doing. On 5 February, an anonymous telephone caller informed the Senate Committee on Foreign Relations that one of the foremost experts on nuclear weapons in the United States had recently traveled to South Vietnam with several other scientists. Suspicious, the committee took up the issue in closed session, where several senators expressed concern that the president might feel compelled to use an atomic bomb if Khe Sanh were in danger of falling. Shortly after the meeting, the antiwar candidate for the Democratic presidential nomination, Senator Eugene J. McCarthy of Minnesota, brought the issue into the open at a news conference.[32]

With the press playing the story in full and with a crescendo of criticism developing around the world, the Johnson administration labeled McCarthy's allegation false and unfair speculation. The president himself told newsmen that the secretaries of state and defense had never "considered or made a recommendation in any respect to the employment of nuclear weapons." Meanwhile, Admiral Sharp quietly instructed Westmoreland to discontinue planning and to lock up all written materials generated by the project.[33]

While the controversy over nuclear weapons played itself out, the situation at Khe Sanh grew ominous. Early on the morning of 7 February, Communist forces employing tanks for the first time in the war attacked the Lang Vei Special Forces camp, eight kilometers southwest of the base. Two hundred of the facility's five hundred South Vietnamese defenders went down, along with ten of their twenty-four American advisers. Artillery and rocket fire pounded Khe Sanh itself, and the enemy launched a series of bitter assaults against marine outposts on nearby hills. Although the marines defending the base were never in danger of annihilation, they were well within range of the enemy's artillery, which cost them 125 killed and 812 wounded between 1 January and 25 February.[34]

The situation proved irresistible to the American news media, particularly after 24 February, when the enemy's withdrawal from Hue left Khe Sanh the only major combat story in South Vietnam for reporters to cover. Like the president, the Saigon correspondents were particularly interested in the similarities between the battle and the siege at Dien Bien Phu. MACV attempted to put the issue to rest by adopting the same line with them that Westmoreland had taken with Johnson, but reporters found the topic too compelling to drop as long as a chance existed that an attack would occur. As late as 8 March, when it was becoming clear that no enemy attack on the base would materialize, reporter Charles Mohr felt justified in observing that U.S. firepower had yet to silence the enemy's artillery and that the Communists' delay in attacking resembled the slow strangulation that had befallen the French force at Dien Bien Phu fourteen years earlier.[35]

Although the battle figured in 38 percent of all stories on Vietnam filed by the AP from outside of Saigon during February and March and played heavily in newspapers across the United States, television news far outstripped the print media in the prominence it gave the subject. CBS, for example, devoted 28 percent of its filmed reports from Vietnam during the period to the battle. Constrained by the nature of television to show action but unable to feature combat because none occurred within camera range, many of these reports featured the damage the enemy was causing to the marines while neglecting the havoc American artillery and B-52s were inflicting on the besiegers. "Here the North Vietnamese decide who lives and who dies," CBS correspondent Murray Fromson intoned solemnly from the base on 14 February, " . . . and sooner or later they will make the move that will seal the fate of Khe Sanh."[36]

Television correspondents also exaggerated aircraft losses at the base. During the course of the fighting, several C-123 and C-130 cargo planes went down, as did a number of marine helicopters. These losses were well within expectations for a battle of that size, but when reporters used them time and again to build dramatic tension, they took on a symbolism far larger than their actual importance. Describing a group of eighteen-year-old marines waiting for a flight out of the base, ABC correspondent Don North told his viewers that the men's main aim in life at that moment "was to become nineteen—a final dash across the runway into . . . cargo planes for a flight back to the world." Along the runway, the reporter added ominously, were "the skeletons of cargo planes that didn't make it."

The same sort of report was still appearing a month later. Describing the crash of yet another C-123, CBS correspondent George Syvertsen remarked, "From now on, it's going to take even more courage" for an air force pilot to fly into Khe Sanh.[37]

As negative press coverage of the battle continued, Gallup polls reported that public approval of the president's performance in office had dropped 7 percentage points. In response, President Johnson set off on a cross-country tour to solidify his support, and public affairs officers in South Vietnam redoubled their efforts to publicize South Vietnamese heroism and to bat down particularly pessimistic news reports. On 20 March, they also released a remarkable captured enemy assessment written on 1 February in which Communist commanders confessed that they had missed their main objectives during the attack and had failed in particular to spark the general uprising among the South Vietnamese that they had sought.[38]

Although these efforts had their effect, high officials in Washington were by then becoming increasingly concerned that sensitive information was appearing in the press. Reporters were counting the enemy rounds hitting Khe Sanh, Admiral Sharp told Westmoreland, and they were also publishing the exact number of American casualties that resulted. This was information that could help the enemy gauge the accuracy of his guns.[39]

Westmoreland was also concerned. With a record 636 reporters accredited to MACV at the end of February, he considered his public affairs officers overburdened and believed that a loosening of standards in dealing with the press had set in as a result. On these grounds, he changed MACV's guidelines for correspondents. From then on, reporters would have to generalize the number of incoming enemy rounds and would have to revert to the terms *light, moderate,* and *heavy* in describing casualties incurred in enemy attacks on fixed positions. Since facilities for handling the press at Khe Sanh were crowded, the number of reporters who could visit the base at any one time would be limited to fifteen: two for each of the American television networks, two apiece for the AP and UPI, one for Reuters, and a pool of four Americans to represent all other newspapers and press agencies. Similar allocations were to apply to other large American base camps in the I Corps Zone. If these steps failed to improve the situation, Westmoreland said, he would seriously consider some form of field press censorship.[40]

The general's moves all focused on restricting the press. McNamara's replacement as secretary of defense, Washington lawyer Clark Clifford, was convinced that official agencies were equally to blame for the problems that had occurred. Exaggerated official optimism in the months preceding Tet had contributed to the shock Americans had felt when the attack began, he told Wheeler. If the administration continued to play that game and the enemy attacked again, the backlash that would follow in the United States would demolish for good what was left of the president's credibility. Citing as a case in point an interview at MACV in which a "senior military spokesman" had avowed that the Communists had been hurt but then proceeded to warn that they still had huge forces left and might attack again, Clifford instructed Wheeler to tell Westmoreland he wanted such statements to stop. There were to be no more forecasts of allied or enemy plans, predictions of victory, or projections of difficult fighting ahead. Instead, moderation was to be the rule. With that approach in place, reverses in battle would seem less shocking and successes would appear all the sweeter.[41]

Clifford's instructions were well considered, for by the end of February 1968, pessimism pervaded the American news media. Cataloging an accumulation of woes from high crime rates to a "looming bloodbath" at Khe Sanh, a *Life* headline on 23 February avowed "Wherever We Look, Something's Wrong." Shortly after that, following a two-week fact-finding trip to South Vietnam, CBS anchorman Walter Cronkite aired his own misgivings in a widely discussed television documentary. "To say we are closer to victory today," he said, "is to believe . . . optimists who have been wrong in the past. To suggest we are on the edge of defeat is to yield to unreasonable pessimists. To say we are mired in stalemate seems the only realistic yet unsatisfactory conclusion. . . . It is increasingly clear . . . that the only rational way out would be to negotiate—not as victims, but as an honorable people who . . . did the best they could."[42]

Newsman Howard K. Smith provided one of the few counterpoints to the mood. Charging that the press was "contributing to the confusion and frustration now damaging the American spirit," he resigned his position at ABC News because he felt he was no longer participating in an age of great journalism. Press coverage of Eddie Adams's picture of General Loan executing the Viet Cong was an example of what he meant, he said. No one had made "even a perfunctory acknowledgment . . . of the fact that such executions, en masse, are the Viet Cong way of war."[43]

Whatever the pessimism of the press, however, the majority of Americans went their own way. Queried by the Gallup Poll on whether they considered the war a mistake, 45 percent responded "yes," the same percentage as in December 1965; 43 percent said "no," a drop of 3 points; and 12 percent had no opinion. Even more telling, the number of those who considered themselves "hawks" on the war rose 4 percentage points between December and February, while those who saw themselves as "doves" fell by the same percentage. The number of those expressing confidence in the government's military policies in South Vietnam rose from 61 to 74 percent. Queried by Louis Harris on whether a bombing halt would hasten the chances for peace, 71 percent of respondents favored continuing the bombing, a rise of 8 points over the previous October, while the number of those favoring a halt fell from 26 to 15 percent.[44]

If Americans were unwilling to repudiate the war, they nonetheless appeared increasingly dissatisfied with their president. Willing to back any decision he made, they saw little forward motion on his part. Instead, after making a few public comments after the start of the offensive, he left all efforts to marshal public opinion to his staff and aides. The air of indecision that hung about his policies as a result took a toll on his standing in the polls, where disapproval of his handling of the war rose from 47 to 63 percent by the end of February. By the end of March, the figures were even worse. The number of those expressing confidence in U.S. military policies in South Vietnam dropped from 74 to 54 percent, while the number of those who deemed the war a stalemate rose from 38 to 42 percent.[45]

If the gloomy reporting of the press had little effect on American public opinion, it nonetheless reinforced doubts already circulating within the Johnson administration. Presidential speechwriter Harry McPherson described his own feelings:

> I was extremely disturbed. I would go in two or three mornings a week and study the cable book and talk to Rostow . . . and get from him what almost seemed hallucinatory from the point of view of what I had seen on television the night before. . . . Well, I must say that I mistrusted what he said. . . . I put aside my own interior access to confidential information and was more persuaded by what I saw on the tube and in the newspapers. . . . I was fed up with . . . the optimism that seemed to flow without stopping from Saigon.[46]

The military recognized what was happening but had no answers. They were convinced that while the allies had suffered losses, the enemy was on the verge of a catastrophic defeat. All that was needed, the chief of staff of the army, Gen. Harold K. Johnson, told Westmoreland, was "a little bit of a push from us." Johnson added, however, that a revival of confidence in Washington would be necessary before that could happen, and that it would be "an uphill fight all the way."[47]

General Johnson expected no help from the press, and little was forthcoming. Instead, throughout March and April, American newspapers ran articles on Westmoreland's alleged lack of confidence in the marine units fighting in South Vietnam's northernmost regions. During the Battle of Hue, *Los Angeles Times* correspondent William Tuohy wrote, marine battalions had been understrength and poorly supplied; the marine chain of command had been confused; and little coordination had existed between marine and South Vietnamese units. Thoroughly dissatisfied, Tuohy said, Westmoreland had put his deputy, Gen. Creighton Abrams, in charge to remedy the situation.[48]

All the more annoying because it was painfully close to the facts, the article galled Wheeler, who labeled it "unfounded and deleterious speculation." Westmoreland agreed. Failing to refer to a 22 January message he had sent to Wheeler in which he had questioned the marines' professionalism and their ability to defend Quang Tri Province in an emergency, he dismissed the report as just another attempt by the press to manufacture news.[49]

General Sidle managed to divert a number of negative stories by convincing the reporters involved that interservice rivalry was a problem only at the lowest levels and that relationships at command levels were completely harmonious. Even so, the *Washington Star* published a story titled "The Army-Marine Feud" in Vietnam on 14 March. In April, George Wilson of the *Washington Post* reported that U.S. Army officers at Khe Sanh had alleged that the marines there were so psychologically defeated that "they were seeing shadows outside [the] . . . wire and wouldn't go out to pick up their dead." Westmoreland considered discrediting Wilson because the article had also revealed the general's desire to use Khe Sanh as a springboard for future operations into Laos, but he reconsidered when he learned that Gen. Robert E. Cushman, Jr., the marine commander in South Vietnam, had revealed those plans in an on-the-record briefing—an indiscretion on the part of the general, not the reporter.[50]

As the controversy over the marines ran its course, a more damaging subject caught the eye of the press. Early in the offensive, at Wheeler's prompting, Westmoreland had requested the deployment of an additional army division and half of a marine division. He did so not because he feared defeat but because he believed he needed the troops to seize the initiative from the enemy and to ensure that he would have ample resources to repel the enemy offensive he expected from the north. Wheeler, however, had larger stakes in mind. Since the buildup for the Vietnam War had sapped the ability of U.S. forces to respond to potential crises elsewhere in the world, he intended to use the offensive as an excuse to reconstitute the U.S. strategic reserve. To that end, in passing Westmoreland's request along, he replaced the general's rationale with a more forceful one that stressed the uncertainties confronting U.S. forces in South Vietnam. He then appended a request for the call-up of enough reservists to provide for the increased requirements of all the services.[51]

Unwilling to take any action that would spark a public outcry or require congressional approval, President Johnson dispatched only a portion of the force Westmoreland had requested, a single brigade from the army's Eighty-second Airborne Division and a marine regimental landing team, about 10,500 men.[52] A short while later, Wheeler visited South Vietnam to confer with Westmoreland. The two decided that 205,000 men could be deployed in three stages over the next year. Of these, 108,000 would go to South Vietnam, while the rest would become part of the strategic reserve. Reporting to the president upon returning to Washington, Wheeler again neglected to mention that Westmoreland felt no immediate need for a deployment of the size requested and painted the situation in South Vietnam in the starkest terms. If the enemy synchronized the coming offensive in the north with attacks around the country, he said, Westmoreland's margins would be "paper thin."[53]

Far from making a case for more troops, Wheeler's report drew out the many doubts that had haunted the Johnson administration over the previous year. At a meeting to discuss Westmoreland's request, Rostow and Rusk supported the dispatch of at least some reinforcements, but former secretary of defense McNamara questioned the economic, political, diplomatic, and moral consequences of a larger American buildup. Ambassador Bunker observed that a large increase in troops might destroy what was left of South Vietnamese initiative, and Clifford avowed that the move would leave an inevitable impression that Johnson was "pouring troops down a rat hole." It was time, Clifford said, for the United States to reevaluate its entire position in Southeast Asia.[54]

Taking Clifford at his word, Johnson asked him to chair a study to determine the least objectionable course in South Vietnam. Clifford made his report on 4 March. "We can no longer rely just on the field commander," he said. "He can want troops and want troops. . . . We must look at . . . our other problems in the world . . . ; we must consider whether or not this thing is tying us down so that we cannot do some of the other things we should be doing." Clifford recommended the dispatch of no more than twenty-two thousand men, just enough to cover problems that might arise over the next four months.[55]

Aware that his administration was divided on the issue and concerned as well that the dispatch of 205,000 troops would be politically difficult, Johnson held back. While he was still deliberating, on the morning of 10 March, Hedrick Smith and Neil Sheehan revealed Westmoreland's request in the *New York Times.* Basing the story on a number of sources rather than on a single massive leak, they detailed the discussions under way within the administration and the doubts that accompanied them. The story went around the world.[56]

Shortly after it appeared, opponents of the war in Congress seized upon it. Senator Mike Mansfield asserted, "We are in the wrong place and we are fighting the wrong kind of war." Senator Robert Kennedy warned that it would be a mistake to commit more troops without the support and understanding of Congress and the American people. Senator Frank Church told reporters dramatically that the president seemed "poised to plunge still deeper into Asia, where huge populations wait to engulf us and legions of young Americans are being beckoned to their graves." Senator Fulbright held a nationally televised hearing to grill Secretary Rusk. Pressed on whether the administration was considering escalation, Rusk responded that the president was considering his options but would consult with Congress before sending additional troops to South Vietnam.[57]

Obliged to make a decision but under the lash, Johnson quietly authorized a limited call-up of reserves and the deployment of some 35,000 men. Shortly afterward, however, he reevaluated his decision. When Westmoreland revealed a plan for a major offensive to relieve Khe Sanh using only the troops at hand, he decided that additional deployments were hardly as necessary as Wheeler had said and sent only 13,500 support troops.[58]

On 12 March, the day Fulbright's hearing ended, Eugene McCarthy came within a few hundred votes of defeating Johnson in the New Hampshire Democratic primary election. Although pollster Louis Harris and others warned that the vote represented popular dissatisfaction with more than Johnson's stand on the war and more than half of those who voted against the president considered themselves hawks, the election seemed to signify a swing in popular opinion toward McCarthy's antiwar position. A Gallup Poll released on the day after the election reinforced that conclusion. It revealed that 69 percent of all Americans favored a phased withdrawal of American troops as soon as the United States could train and equip enough South Vietnamese to take over.[59]

Viewing it all from a distance, General Westmoreland was amazed. As far as he was concerned, the troop request had been an academic exercise. That the three troop increments he and Wheeler had discussed totaled 205,000 men, he later related in his memoirs, had never even crossed his mind.[60]

By the end of March, the president and his advisers were urgently seeking some way to regain the political initiative. A bombing halt seemed the best approach, but President Johnson hesitated. Since the weather in North Vietnam during April was usually too poor to make air attacks profitable, he was concerned that the North Vietnamese would view the move only as an empty gesture. By 31 March, however, he had made up his mind. As General Wheeler explained to Westmoreland at that time, public and congressional support for the war had decreased at an alarming rate over the preceding weeks, while many of the strongest proponents of forceful action in Vietnam had begun either to waver or to head for neutral ground. Johnson hoped a unilateral move toward peace would reverse the trend, the general said, and, as a result, would probably announce a halt during a speech he had slated for that evening.[61]

Although Wheeler considered the speech a public relations ploy, Johnson had other ideas. As the general had predicted, Johnson announced a partial bombing halt in his speech that evening, but then he emphasized his hope that it would lead to early negotiations. Adding that there would be no time limits and no conditions for the North Vietnamese to fulfill, he spent the rest of the speech describing the accomplishments of his administration and pleading for national unity. At its conclusion, he then electrified the world by declaring that he would neither seek nor accept nomination for a second term as president in order to spend the rest of his time in office in the pursuit of peace.[62]

Confronted by Johnson's move and having little to lose, the North Vietnamese went along. Three days later they announced their readiness to talk, engendering hopes around the world that the war would soon end. No one realized at the time that four more years would elapse and tens of thousands of additional casualties would occur before the promise of the moment would find fulfillment.[63]

9

"War in a Goldfish Bowl"

If the Tet offensive and the decisions following it marked a turn in the direction of the war, press coverage followed suit. When President Johnson announced his bombing halt and espoused the search for peace, he lost his ability to discipline members of his party who disagreed with him on the war. It became acceptable for longtime supporters of the war in Congress to criticize events in South Vietnam. As the debate broadened, the subject found a ready market in the press, where journalists, following normal procedure, replayed what their sources said.[1]

The result was readily apparent on television. According to researcher Daniel Hallin, spokesmen for the war predominated over critics on network news programs prior to the Tet offensive by 26.3 to 4.5 percent. After Tet and the president's turn, the critics achieved a rough parity of 26.1 to the supporters' 28.4. Forty-nine percent of all the criticism came from public officials, while only 16 percent originated in commentaries by reporters. When protest against the war moved "from the left groups, the antiwar groups, into the pulpits, into the Senate," Max Frankel of the *New York Times* explained, " . . . it naturally picked up coverage. And then naturally the tone of the coverage changed."[2]

The broadening of debate affected the attitudes of network anchormen and reporters. Earlier in the war, anchorman Walter Cronkite had thought nothing of referring to the North Vietnamese and Viet Cong as "the Communists." After Tet he did so rarely. In the same way, television reporters prior to Tet described the war in terms of "our side" versus "their side" and alluded frequently to the fight against Communist aggression and for democracy in South Vietnam. After the offensive those references disappeared.[3]

Personnel changes within the press added to the effect. As the war lengthened, senior editors and columnists moved up or out, making room for younger men who often were less sympathetic to the official point of view. When Phillip Geyelin replaced Russell Wiggins as the director of the *Washington Post*'s editorial page, the newspaper's editorials began to show less sympathy for the Johnson administration's policy on war. In the same way, many of the correspondents covering the war in South Vietnam also moved on, relinquishing their places to recent college graduates who tended to reflect the antiwar sentiments of America's college-age generation. Most of the new people performed professionally, attempting to cover both sides of any controversy that arose, but their personal opinions of necessity colored the selections they made.[4]

It is difficult to assess the effects of these changes over the long term. Theories of the news that attribute the slant an event receives in the press to bias, the economic interests of owners, or a publisher's policies fail to account for the nature of the news media. The reporter, the publisher, the editor, and even the owner work together, not as soloists. So many people contribute to the fabrication of a news story that the point of view of any individual is usually difficult to see when the final product appears. The *New York Times* provides an example. If a few radically antiwar individuals found employment at the paper, its publisher, Iphigene Sulzberger, was a traditional liberal and no threat to the status quo. The executive editor, Clifton Daniel, was the son-in-law of former president Harry S. Truman, and the foreign editor, James Greenfield, had been an assistant secretary of state for public affairs during the early 1960s.[5]

Adjustments in the way the U.S. government dealt with the news media also had an effect on what the press reported. Secretary Clifford's instructions to Wheeler and Westmoreland to avoid all forms of exaggerated optimism and to take a low-key approach when assessing events or theorizing about the future tempered the news by lowering the shock effect of problems in the field. Meanwhile, in Saigon, the U.S. ambassador, Ellsworth Bunker, decided to de-emphasize the public affairs effort. When Barry Zorthian's tour of duty in Vietnam ended, Bunker split Zorthian's job, giving responsibility for the psychological warfare activities of the Joint U.S. Public Affairs Office (JUSPAO) to a career officer with the U.S. Information Agency while awarding control of the mission's press relations to an expert in politico-military affairs with little experience handling the news media. A rogue of sorts, Zorthian had often sided with the press out of concern that any attempt to cut off reporters would throw them onto their own devices and remove the restraining influences official agencies could exert. The new man, "a sophisticated substantive officer of senior rank," as Bunker observed, "not a public relations or press affairs specialist," was more rooted in bureaucratic procedure and more likely to go along with his superiors' points of view. Shortly after taking office, indeed, he declined to host the regular background briefings for the press that Zorthian had found so useful and terminated the practice.[6]

If Tet changed the Johnson administration's approach to the press, North Vietnam's acceptance of negotiations on 3 April complicated General Westmoreland's conduct of the war. From then on, since victory on the battlefield seemed essential to the maintenance of a strong American position in the negotiations, there could be no letup in the fighting. But since the enemy would respond by using every device to appeal to world public opinion, General Westmoreland had to maintain the forward motion of his command while doing as little as possible, as he put it, "to rock the negotiations boat." Over time, the general's problem became, as Wheeler put it, "just one more example of conducting a war in a goldfish bowl."[7]

Restrictions on the press presented one avenue to a solution, but political considerations took precedence. For example, when reporters responded to Johnson's announcement of a bombing halt above twenty degrees north latitude by concentrating their attention on U.S. air operations in North Vietnam below that line, Johnson began to complain. The stories, he told Clifford, gave opponents of the war a club by revealing too many details about sophisticated weapons. Clifford was unsympathetic. By showing that U.S. attacks were indeed limited in extent, he responded, those reports contradicted charges by Hanoi that the United States had been unfaithful to the halt. The revelations about weapons, moreover, were of some comfort to the American people. By showing that the government was providing for the security of its troops, they contradicted claims that the bombing halt was risking the lives of American fighting men.[8]

In the absence of firm guidance on restrictions from Washington, Westmoreland attempted to put as good a face as he could on the American effort. Aware that the phrase *search and destroy* had come to connote indiscriminate violence against hapless civilians, he replaced the term in his command's lexicon with neutral phrases such as *spoiling attack* and *reconnaissance in force*. He also instructed his generals to keep communications open with newsmen they trusted so that they could identify issues of concern to the press and offer explanations. Even so, they were to wield the phrase *no comment* liberally and were to provide newsmen "beyond conversion" with only what was necessary, nothing more. Westmoreland likewise limited the release for background use, and not for publication, of information MACV's guidelines for the press normally banned. From then on, public affairs officers used not-for-publication information only occasionally in briefings and only in advance of truly important operations.[9]

The first word of MACV's changes reached the press toward the end of April, at the beginning of Operation Delaware, which took place south of Hue in the A Shau valley, a major enemy supply route and entrepôt. In order to cover the insertion of a battalion-sized force into Laos to guard the flank of the operation (a technical escalation of the war) but also on grounds that the attack involved a dangerous enemy base area untouched by allied forces in years, Westmoreland embargoed news of the operation for an indefinite period. The announcement agitated reporters, who had already spent five dangerous days in the field preparing background reports, but they went along reluctantly after receiving assurances that the Defense Department would keep home offices from breaking the news. A short while later, however, one of the military's favorite reporters, syndicated columnist Joseph Alsop, broke the embargo in an article dispatched from

Secretary of Defense Clark Clifford confers with President Johnson. (Department of Defense)

Hong Kong. Incensed because MACV appeared to do nothing to discipline the reporter, who was by then out of the command's reach in the United States, the Saigon correspondents raised such a howl that Westmoreland lifted his embargo after only eight days.[10]

The controversy over Operation Delaware was one of the last Westmoreland would have to endure as MACV commander. On 28 March, President Johnson named him to become the next chief of staff of the army. A week later, he announced that Gen. Creighton W. Abrams would become U.S. commander in South Vietnam; that Lt. Gen. Andrew J. Goodpaster would take Abrams's place as deputy U.S. commander; and that Adm. John L. McCain, Sr., would succeed Admiral Sharp as commander in chief, Pacific. All appointments were to become effective on 30 July, but since Westmoreland left South Vietnam on 30 May to prepare the testimony before Congress that would precede ratification of his nomination, Abrams assumed effective command of all U.S. forces in South Vietnam on that date.

The Saigon correspondents immediately began to speculate on how Abrams might approach the war. Some felt he would lay a renewed emphasis on the pacification program. Others believed he would make few changes. Abrams himself said nothing. Adopting an approach that would characterize his style in dealing with the press from then on, he told reporters laconically, "I look for more fighting."[11]

During the interval between commanders, problems continued with the press. They centered on one of the highest-ranking enemy officers ever to defect to the South Vietnamese, Col. Tran Van Dac. Providing details on a second wave of

President Johnson announces that he will not run for reelection. (LBJ Library)

Communist attacks that U.S. commanders had long suspected was in the offing, Dac had presented the United States with a rare opportunity to inflict a major defeat upon the enemy. The intelligence was so sensitive that Westmoreland instructed everyone who knew anything to keep Dac's defection secret. Even so, someone immediately leaked word to AP reporter George McArthur, who put the news on the wire. The reporter described Dac accurately as a North Vietnamese colonel and commissar, named him and his unit, and then added that the officer had passed along detailed plans for a forthcoming enemy offensive. An investigation began immediately to find out where McArthur had got his information, but since the infraction was not covered by the MACV guidelines the reporter himself went unscathed.[12]

In the end, the revelation made little difference. Beginning on the night of 4 May, waves of enemy troops struck Saigon as planned. Although most failed to break through U.S. and South Vietnamese defenses securing the city, enough reached their objectives to cause fierce fighting in the suburb of Cholon. They held out for days, burning buildings in order to create large numbers of refugees. By the end of the month, more than 125,000 people were homeless and some

Rubble clogs the streets of Cholon following house-to-house fighting. (U.S. Army)

eleven hundred Americans lay dead, the highest toll of any comparable period in the war.[13]

Unlike the Tet offensive, the May attack came as no surprise to the Saigon correspondents, whose bureau chiefs received off-the-record briefings well before the assault. After laying out the enemy's capabilities and U.S. preparations to meet the attack, General Sidle had sworn everyone to secrecy on grounds that even with McArthur's breach a chance remained that the United States might achieve a significant victory.[14]

When events played out much as Sidle had predicted, reporters accepted official assertions that the enemy was losing ground and suffering serious casualties. They nonetheless complained about the body counts MACV released to them and the lag between events in the field and official communiqués to the press. So close to the action that four of them were executed by an enemy squad on a Saigon street corner, they also asserted that the violence of the American response to the attack had done immeasurable damage not only to the city itself but also to the allegiance of its citizens to their government. "A handful of snipers in houses around an intersection are wiped out or driven back at the expense of major damage to nearby buildings," Lee Lescaze of the *Washington Post* remarked. *Newsweek* agreed, adding that American helicopters had demolished an entire city block of low-cost housing originally constructed to demonstrate the South Vietnamese government's concern for the well-being of its people. *U.S. News & World Report* described Saigon as a "city of the homeless."[15]

Pacification officials agreed with the press. Although the enemy appeared to be losing on the battlefield, they said, he had gained the political edge by generating resentment among civilians who had lost relatives and homes to American air strikes and artillery. Official spokesmen blamed the enemy, noting that he was attempting to draw American fire into civilian zones in order to create a backlash against the United States in South Vietnamese and world public opinion. Other officials suggested in private, however, that larger issues were at stake. The question was, one observed in a cable to the State Department, "How long this can be endured without threatening all that has been achieved here."[16]

The news stories peaked on 2 June, when a misfired American rocket killed the chief of the Saigon police, Col. Nguyen Van Luan, and five other high-ranking South Vietnamese officers. Relying on preliminary information, MACV at first denied any U.S. involvement, but it later reversed itself when the facts proved otherwise. The Saigon correspondents, meanwhile, passed along rumors circulating in Saigon that the United States was deliberately trying to kill supporters of Vice President Nguyen Cao Ky because Ky was becoming increasingly anti-American in outlook. They also gave heavy play to the possibility that the incident would further damage already strained U.S. relations with South Vietnam. The affair echoed well into August, when the *Nation* published an article by Karl Purnell entitled "Operation Self-destruction," which quoted a comment by Luan shortly before his death to the effect that "the Viet Cong has no air force of his own, so he uses ours."[17]

Prodded by the uproar and shaken by a report from a U.S. pacification official in Saigon describing the devastation in Cholon as "far worse than I had seen in any location in Hue," Secretary Clifford asked General Wheeler to see if there was some way to keep from destroying so much property. Wheeler passed the request to Abrams, underscoring "the very real concern here in administration circles and the bad play we are receiving in the news media."[18]

Abrams responded that as a result of the incident involving Luan he had banned U.S. air strikes, attacks by armed helicopters, and artillery fire from Saigon unless he himself, the commander of the Saigon region, or the commander of the U.S. forces fighting within the city had personally approved. Although confirming allegations of serious damage to Cholon, Abrams questioned whether many civilian casualties had been inflicted and suggested that the transmission of raw, unevaluated pacification reports to Washington agencies hardly served the U.S. effort in South Vietnam. "We have nothing to hide," he said, "but neither should we be constantly on the rebuttal." He added that he lacked the benefit of press and television to show him the horror of war, but "I live with it twenty-four hours a day."[19]

Abrams's remarks infuriated Clifford. He could never accept the general's contention, he told Wheeler, that responsible officers within the U.S. embassy should await clearance from the military before reporting matters of concern to Washington. "Am I to interpret this to mean that I am not to ask him to look into an appropriate matter or to investigate a situation or to consider other ways of accomplishing the national purpose?" If that was so, he said, alluding to the decision to give Abrams command, "it is essential we know this now."[20]

Informed of Clifford's anger, Abrams backed down. Admitting

General Creighton W. Abrams. (U.S. Army)

that he had been wrong to say that his command was constantly on the rebuttal and that military commanders ought to review reports from the embassy to the State Department, he excused his remarks as an attempt to indicate that the news media in the United States seemed to paint a "significantly more gruesome picture of the war than one gets being here." In the end, nothing came of the matter. The general remained in command and went on to make the protection of Saigon and its civilians one of his main concerns. Indeed, when the regional commander asked for permission later in the month to restore the ability of division commanders to call in heavy weapons, he rejected the suggestion out of hand. Paraphrasing Peter Arnett's report on Ben Tre, he added, "I have tried to make it clear that our military forces must find a way to save Saigon without destroying it."[21]

As Abrams settled into his job, he wasted little time before issuing a memorandum on MACV's relations with the press. "Effective now," he told his commanders on 2 June, "the overall . . . policy of this command will be to let results speak for themselves. We will not deal in propaganda exercises in any way but will play all of our activities in a low key." There was to be no talk of future plans and operations because the information assisted the enemy and might backfire if something went wrong. Instead, achievements were to predominate in contacts with the press, and commanders were to make "considerably more extensive use" of the phrase *no comment.*[22]

Recognizing that erroneous news stories had often appeared because public affairs officers, under heavy pressure from the press, had released word of events before all the facts were in, Abrams set to work with Sidle to fine-tune MACV's system for reporting both good and bad news. Under the approach they developed, the first member of the MACV staff to receive word of something bad—for example, the destruction of an American unit in combat—was to inform the command's chief of staff and its Operations Center. While the center pushed to determine what had happened, official spokesmen were to tell reporters only that they would have no comment until after an investigation. If the inquiry confirmed that something bad had indeed occurred, they were to tell the truth. The same policy was to hold in the case of good news. Since initial reports of favorable events were often exaggerated or incorrect, an announcement in those cases would occur only when the Operations Center was convinced that the facts were correct. Abrams recognized that his approach would create tensions with the press. He believed, however, that allegations about lies were far more damaging to MACV than bad news, and that good news would have more effect with reporters if it came without embellishment.[23]

Obliged, like Westmoreland, to fight while negotiations were in progress, Abrams had little choice but to take that aspect of the war into account. An article by Keyes Beech in the *Chicago Daily News* provided the occasion. On 27 May, Beech claimed that MACV had ordered field commanders to go all out in the next three months so that U.S. emissaries could have a decisive say at the Paris peace talks. As a result, the reporter said, Americans could expect some of the heaviest fighting of the war after peace negotiations began. Information officers denied that a directive of the sort had ever existed but conceded that MACV had called upon the troops to redouble their efforts. It had been, they said, a pep talk.[24]

A short while later, Abrams issued a circular message to all his commanders. Although the *Daily News* story had been mistaken on some points, he observed pungently, MACV was obviously suffering from "diarrhea of the mouth." Since the press was hungry for stories bearing on the Paris peace talks, he continued, repeating guidance he had received from the Defense Department, all concerned were to refrain from releasing any information that might influence the negotiations.[25]

Abrams's efforts notwithstanding, it was impossible to give the war the low profile the Johnson administration would obviously have preferred. Instead, during mid-June, the North Vietnamese reinforced their units in the I Corps Zone in an attempt to do all they could to cause American casualties. If they succeeded, as one enemy directive observed, they would establish conditions "for the pacifist movements in the United States to expand and the doves to assail the hawks thereby forcing the United States radically to change its Vietnam policy." Recognizing that he would have to counter the threat, Abrams decided to free up the units at Khe Sanh by dismantling the base. The enemy was bound to publicize the move as an American defeat, but it seemed essential if the United States was to avoid the increase in American casualties that would occur otherwise.[26]

On 22 June, Abrams informed General Wheeler of the steps he intended to

The military base at Khe Sanh. (Department of Defense)

take to minimize adverse comment. To enforce silence among the Saigon correspondents, he planned to embargo all news reports on plans, operations, and troop movements near Khe Sanh for an indefinite period. If reporters discovered that the base was closing, MACV would brief Saigon bureau chiefs but would respond to all other questions with a no comment. When the command finally announced the operation, official remarks would follow prepared scripts. There would be no backgrounding or follow-up, and MACV's public affairs officers would do all they could to direct the attention of the press away from Khe Sanh to events elsewhere in South Vietnam.[27]

The Defense Department accepted Abrams's arrangements but suggested that the official communiqué announcing the move play up the success of the American effort at Khe Sanh and stress the need to exploit the enemy's weakness elsewhere. Abrams demurred. Since it was "not quite true" to say that the United States was reinforcing success, he responded, the announcement should stick to the real reason for the move, the need to gain a better position to meet an enemy threat. In the end, Defense backpedaled. "Our education is advanced," Wheeler later told Abrams, "by your low-keyed approach."[28]

Although there seemed some hope at first that the embargo might succeed in downplaying news of Khe Sanh's closing, the possibility proved an illusion. On

26 June, John Carroll of the *Baltimore Sun* broke MACV's ground rules to reveal that the base was closing. The Defense Department attempted to contain the damage by keeping the rest of the press from reprinting Carroll's revelation, but the word was out, and few editors complied. "We have no actual control as long as they only reprint the *Sun* story," Phil Goulding told Abrams, "and they are all most aware of that."[29]

Goulding discussed the situation with Clifford and Wheeler. All agreed, Wheeler told Abrams, that the longer MACV delayed before making an announcement, the greater the criticism would be. Both the enemy and critics of the war would use the issue to erode public support for the war, and all sides would interpret MACV's delay as an attempt to cover up an American defeat. President Johnson, Wheeler said, was himself concerned. Abrams made the announcement shortly after he received Wheeler's message. In a separate communiqué, General Sidle announced that Carroll had been disaccredited for an indefinite period because he had revealed future plans of the marines in the Khe Sanh area. Other correspondents, Sidle said, honored the rules.[30]

The news media were already making the points Goulding, Clifford, and Wheeler had predicted. Shortly after Carroll's story broke, David Brinkley of NBC News repeated North Vietnamese assertions that the withdrawal was de facto recognition of "a most serious American defeat." Newspapers throughout the United States followed by dissecting Westmoreland's original decision to defend Khe Sanh. As the controversy gained momentum, military analyst S. L. A. Marshall entered the fray. Khe Sanh had never been of enough military value to justify the effort expended in its defense, he said. In that light, Carroll's article had jeopardized little. Lee Lescaze of the *Washington Post,* meanwhile, questioned Abrams's push for secrecy: "Was it essential to the security of the troops in the area, as MACV said, or was it a politically motivated policy? . . . If Carroll is correct that the enemy could observe the preparations for evacuation from the hills surrounding Khe Sanh and if the news embargo was politically inspired, there was good reason for him to write his story."[31]

The news media went on to criticize the indefinite length of Carroll's sentence, observing that no disaccreditation had ever lasted for more than one month. When MACV reduced the suspension to six months, Maryland's two senators, Daniel B. Brewster and Joseph D. Tydings, took up the case, with Tydings condemning Carroll's suspension as vindictive and unjustified. In the end, yielding to the pressure, MACV reduced Carroll's suspension to sixty days.[32]

If Abrams had clearly made an example of Carroll, he was equally firm with the Department of Defense. A case in point occurred during August, when intelligence revealed that the enemy was preparing yet another offensive for South Vietnam. The Office of the Assistant Secretary of Defense for Public Affairs drafted an elaborate contingency plan for handling the press. There were to be frequent briefings, unscheduled news releases, and off-the-record backgrounders during the initial stages of the attack. Abrams would meet with reporters personally to verify that MACV had anticipated the offensive. After the enemy's effort failed, the general would hold yet another briefing to emphasize that South Vietnamese forces had played a major role. Abrams demurred. Barring specific guidance to the contrary, he said, he intended to conduct special backgrounders and briefings only if the news warranted. As for the press conference and backgrounder, they would add little to what the press already knew, and they might only feed the inclination of reporters to divine the enemy's intentions. Instead, all concerned should avoid overemphasizing MACV's success in predicting the attack. Too much could go wrong.[33]

The enemy's effort began on the night of 17 August, so quietly that MACV found it difficult to convince reporters a major attack had even occurred. Although Saigon was again a target, the Communists concentrated on installations in outlying areas, apparently in hopes of drawing U.S. troops away from the city so that sappers could slip past checkpoints undetected. To prolong the offensive while preserving their strength, enemy commanders relied mainly on mortar and rocket assaults against selected targets. Even so, it was all over within nine days.[34]

Press coverage of the attack was so restrained that it drew the attention of Secretary Clifford. Attributing the effect to Abrams's low-key approach rather than to the fact that news reporting had reflected an indifferent effort by the enemy, Clifford cabled his congratulations to the general. In the process, he emphasized his approval of Abrams's basic approach to the press, "particularly," he said, "that MACV should not predict, claim, or characterize but should . . . let the actions speak for themselves."[35]

For the time being, all seemed well. By the end of the offensive, the news media's criticism of the war had begun to fade. If complaints continued about body counts and official obfuscation, most reporters acknowledged that South Vietnam was growing stronger while North Vietnam, as Beverly Deepe reported in the *Christian Science Monitor,* continued to spend thousands of lives for no commensurate gain. In the past, Deepe added, alluding to word games the North Vietnamese were playing in Paris to disguise their heavy involvement in the South, time had always inclined to the enemy. With South Vietnam growing stronger, Communist stalling might at last begin to favor the United States.[36]

Although the enemy's failures seemed grounds for optimism to some, Clifford refused to concede that time favored the allies. Despite all the talk about how the South Vietnamese armed forces had improved, he told President Johnson in July after visiting Saigon, better leadership, training, and equipment were still required. Since the Tet offensive, he noted by way of example, the government of South Vietnam had authorized an increase of eighty-four thousand men to its armed forces, but no one had made any attempt to find the four thousand new captains and one thousand new majors who would be required to handle the influx.[37]

Clifford elaborated on his views at a meeting in Honolulu with Rusk, Rostow, and George Christian, the president's press secretary. Although American and

South Vietnamese forces were more than able to defend themselves, he said, they would have to shift to the offensive to defeat the Communists. The enemy, however, was building permanent installations out of their reach in Cambodia and Laos and could retreat into them whenever pressed. The South Vietnamese government, for its part, had little incentive to bring the war to an end through negotiation. American troops did much of the fighting, and American money continued to pour in. The political corruption that resulted from it all ate at the nation like a cancer.[38]

The American public shared the secretary's reservations. Polled by the Gallup organization during August, more Americans than at any time in the past (53 percent) considered the war a mistake. By a margin of more than two to one, those interviewed also asserted that the Republican presidential nominee, Richard M. Nixon, would do a better job of handling the war than either of the contenders for the Democratic nomination, Vice President Hubert H. Humphrey and Senator Eugene J. McCarthy of Minnesota.[39]

The president and his advisers were well aware of the public mood, but they were caught in a dilemma. In order to dampen speculation accompanying every lull in the fighting that the enemy was signaling his desire for an accommodation, they pressed MACV and the U.S. mission to do everything possible to drive home to the press the likelihood that the peace talks might be long and hard. Yet, in hopes of placating enough antiwar delegates to win the nomination for Humphrey, they also felt they had little choice but to maintain at least the appearance of forward motion in the peace talks. As Clifford observed in his notes of a high-level meeting on 25 May, that seemed the "only way for H.H.H. to make it."[40]

In the end, the peace talks remained in session, and Humphrey won his party's nomination, but only after a week of angry debate on the floor of the Democratic convention and violent antiwar demonstrations outside. When security officers within the convention hall and the police on the streets attempted to restore order, they assaulted a number of newsmen in the process. News coverage of the event became so harsh as a result that many Democrats concluded they had little chance of winning the November election. Public opinion surveys taken shortly thereafter, however, revealed that, whatever the news coverage, a majority of Americans had sided with the police against the rioters.[41]

While the Johnson administration remained preoccupied with the peace talks and the election campaign, General Abrams and his commanders were becoming acutely aware of the enemy's vulnerability. Estimates put Communist losses during the first week of the August offensive at about fifty-four hundred men even before the results of air strikes and B-52 attacks were tabulated. In that light, there seemed little doubt that the morale of enemy forces would sink.[42]

On 1 September, Abrams attempted to press his advantage by requesting permission to pursue enemy forces if they attempted to retreat across the border into their sanctuaries. When the Johnson administration put the matter under study but made no decision, he repeated the request, pushing throughout October and November for leave at least to bomb those areas. With the November election in the offing, however, the president's hands were tied. Johnson could hardly have approved Abrams's request without causing irreparable divisions within his party. He thus instructed Abrams to put "constant, relentless, persistent pressure" on the enemy but to avoid any dramatic increase in out-of-country operations.[43]

Under the circumstances, Johnson was sorely tempted to expand the partial bombing halt of 31 March into a total cessation of all bombing in North Vietnam. Undercutting enemy contentions in Paris that the United States was the sole aggressor in South Vietnam, the move would demonstrate anew his dedication to peace while galvanizing support for Humphrey and other Democratic candidates in the election.

On 11 September, Johnson asserted publicly in a speech that he would not halt the bombing unless Hanoi agreed to reciprocal military restraints. Informed a week later that the president was nonetheless toying with the idea of a unilateral halt, Abrams objected emphatically. "There exists at this time among our commanders and troops a noticeable sense of confidence both in what has been done and in what lies ahead," he told Wheeler. "To a discernable degree the Vietnamese military are showing this, too." In that light, a bombing halt without a compensating move by the enemy "would come as quite a shock to some of the troops and their commanders." In fact, he added in a later message, the absence of some sort of agreement putting the Demilitarized Zone off limits to all parties would allow the Communists to develop within two weeks of a halt a military capability in the area five times the size of the one they possessed earlier.[44]

Faced with Abrams's reservations, President Johnson held to his demand that the North Vietnamese agree to mutual restraints. In exchange for a halt to all bombing of North Vietnam, he told the Soviets, the Hanoi regime would have to stop its abuse of the Demilitarized Zone and refrain from attacking South Vietnam's cities, provincial capitals, and major population centers. In addition, the authorities in Hanoi would have to enter promptly into serious political discussions that included the elected government of South Vietnam.[45]

With Richard Nixon leading Humphrey in preelection polls, pressure for some sort of halt nevertheless continued to build in Democratic circles. On 11 October, Hanoi's delegation in Paris introduced the issue into official discussions by approaching Ambassador Harriman to ask whether the United States would stop the bombing if it had an answer to the question of South Vietnamese participation in the peace talks. The State Department polled Bunker and General Abrams for their opinions. The two agreed to go along if the North Vietnamese accepted American conditions on the Demilitarized Zone and the cities.[46]

In the end, following better than two weeks of wrangling in which all sides backed and filled, the Communists agreed—at least in the eyes of American negotiators—to a three-part understanding. First, they would begin serious negotiations that included representatives of the South Vietnamese government. Second, the bombing cessation would depend both on their respect for the Demili-tarized Zone and on a halt to attacks against South Vietnam's major cities. Third, the United States would continue reconnaissance flights over North Vietnam after the bombing ceased. The halt itself was to begin on 29 October at 7:00 P.M. Eastern Standard Time.[47]

It did not. Instead, the South Vietnamese declined to associate themselves with the halt on the grounds that Hanoi had portrayed the National Liberation Front, the Communist political organization in South Vietnam, as an indepen-dent party to the negotiations when it was entirely controlled by North Vietnam. In private, South Vietnamese diplomats told Bunker that Johnson was obviously dragging their country into peace talks just days prior to the U.S. elections in or-der to improve his party's prospects.[48]

President Johnson went ahead with the halt on 31 October without South Vietnamese agreement. Galled, the Thieu regime responded with an emo-tional campaign designed to sow doubts about the decision among the American people. One of the Saigon correspondents, Keyes Beech of the *Chicago Daily News,* became its vehicle. In a widely quoted 31 October article, Beech reported that "shocked and angry South Vietnamese had hurled the word *sellout* at their American allies after learning of the halt."[49]

Beech returned to the subject two days later when he dutifully visited the U.S. embassy in Saigon to check his facts. To the horror of those present, he leafed through pages of notes containing fragments of President Johnson's letters to Thieu and other exchanges between members of the U.S. mission and South Vietnamese officials. Although Ambassador Bunker complained that some of the details Beech had received were slanted or distorted, he had to concede that most of the information was accurate. It was obvious, Bunker later observed in a cable to the State Department, that someone intimately involved with the nego-tiations had briefed the reporter. He corrected what he termed the "worst distor-tions and misrepresentations" in Beech's version, but he could not stop the re-porter from suggesting that the Johnson administration had halted the bombing five days before the U.S. presidential elections in return for a breakthrough in the Paris talks. Resorting to "high-pressure salesmanship," Beech said, President Johnson had then urged Thieu to accept the arrangement.[50]

Numerous news reports from Saigon took up Beech's themes. Beverly Deepe emphasized in the *Christian Science Monitor* that the Thieu regime feared the seating of a separate National Liberation Front delegation in Paris because the act might lead both to a coalition government and to an eventual Communist takeover. *Newsweek* asserted that "U.S. officials were guilty of a gross miscalcula-tion: they thought they could bring the Saigon regime [around] in time, and they were wrong." *U.S. News & World Report* avowed that the Johnson administra-tion's plans had collapsed because the South Vietnamese had decided they were being "dragged to Paris on an equal footing with the Viet Cong," without any guarantee that Hanoi would abide by its agreement.[51]

Despite the publicity, the American public agreed, 55 to 28 percent, that Johnson had done the right thing. Humphrey benefited. In late October, according to pollster Louis Harris, he had trailed his Republican opponent by substantial margins, but by 4 November, Nixon's lead had narrowed to only 2 percent. In the end, Nixon won, but by only four-tenths of 1 percent.[52]

The impasse between the United States and South Vietnam continued for several more weeks. Finally, on 25 November, faced with a threat that the United States would go to the talks alone and having received a letter from President-elect Nixon backing Johnson's efforts, Thieu agreed to join the talks. The face-saving press release that announced the development emphasized that the negotiations with Hanoi would be essentially two-sided and that the South Vietnamese delegation would be the main spokesman on all matters of principal concern to the South Vietnamese people.[53]

Although the agreement with the Thieu regime bolstered hopes that serious discussions with Hanoi might at last begin, little in fact changed in the weeks that followed. Instead, despite the so-called understanding leading to the bombing halt, Communist forces continued to probe the Demilitarized Zone to determine how much provocation the United States would tolerate. By 4 December, General Abrams had launched at least one American foray into the zone to eliminate an enemy threat and had requested permission to conduct full-scale operations in the southern portion of the area. President Johnson refused because he considered the American position weak. The understanding with the North Vietnamese, he reasoned, had been predicated on the start of negotiations, but the temporizing of the South Vietnamese had frustrated that end. In addition, combat operations in the Demilitarized Zone might engender the sort of large engagements that would jeopardize continuation of the talks.[54]

As the halt lengthened, MACV intelligence analysts threw the Johnson administration's hope for peace further into doubt by reporting that enemy forces had accelerated deliveries of ammunition and other supplies into Laos and the southernmost portions of North Vietnam. Before the halt, on 13 October, Abrams had reported that the enemy's logistical arrangements in North and South Vietnam were a shambles and that the United States faced a moment of supreme opportunity. By 17 November he had little choice but to withdraw that conclusion and to observe that the North Vietnamese had reversed the trend. Within a few short weeks, he said, Communist forces would be prepared to push their forward supply depots into the northernmost portions of South Vietnam, where they might alter the strategic balance.[55]

It seemed clear in light of everything that had transpired that the United States intended to end the war and was willing to put up with much more than it had in the past, as long as it saved face. What was not so clear was how the decision to halt the bombing and to begin negotiations would affect the policies of Johnson's successor, Richard M. Nixon.

10

"I Will Not Warn Again"

Laird was his own entity allowed to do what he wanted

Richard Nixon assumed office on 20 January 1969. A seasoned public official who had served as vice president under President Dwight D. Eisenhower, he had attempted during the campaign to divorce himself from the controversies that had afflicted his predecessor. The aura of professionalism and quiet competence that settled around him as a result won the admiration of many. The new president had stated during his campaign that he had a plan to end the war. Most Americans appeared willing to give him time to develop that strategy.

Although many Americans seemed supportive, the new secretary of defense, Melvin R. Laird, was convinced that limited time remained before the nation turned against the war. If Nixon attempted to prolong the fighting in order to achieve victory, he reasoned, the political strife that would follow would obstruct the achievement of an honorable negotiated settlement. For Laird, only one alternative seemed possible: American combat involvement in the war had to cease as soon as practical. Since achieving that end would be difficult and Nixon would suffer pressure from many directions, Laird decided the process would need an advocate and that he would have to be the one. To preserve his independence, he thus insisted before accepting office that the president sign a letter of agreement stating the length of his term of service, his authority to pick his aides without White House interference, and the fact that Defense would play the lead role in the withdrawal of American forces from the war. Nixon agreed. Laird was well connected with Congress, and two other candidates, for reasons of their own, had already turned down the job.[1]

Once in office, Laird moved swiftly to set his agenda in place. Suspicious from the beginning of the president's subordinates, he instructed his staff to pass all requests from the White House for assistance to him for his personal approval. In the same way, seeking to enhance the Defense Department's ability to mold discussion of the war, he established a daily briefing for Pentagon correspondents that came early in the morning, well before briefings at the State Department and the White House. Convinced that information on many aspects of the war was far too restricted, he also instructed his associates to be more forthcoming when they could. For his own part, he attempted whenever possible to avoid off-the-record meetings with reporters. Unlike the president's special assistant for national security, Henry A. Kissinger, and others at the White House—and much to the chagrin of at least a few correspondents who loved the sense of cachet it gave their work—he rarely requested that reporters attribute his remarks only to "official sources."[2]

Secretary of Defense Melvin Laird.
(Department of Defense)

More open to reporters

The approach made good sense as far as public affairs was concerned, but it came into conflict with an attitude at the White House that considered secrecy essential to the conduct of foreign policy. A case in point arose early during Laird's tenure, when the secretary attempted to change the way official agencies described U.S. attacks on the Ho Chi Minh Trail in Laos. He argued that since the press knew full well the attacks sometimes involved B-52s and that they were hardly defensive in nature, the attempt to pass them off as reconnaissance flights returning fire only when fired upon posed a major threat to official credibility. Assisting the new administration during the transition period, William P. Bundy at the State Department denied the request. The news media not only knew about the bombing, he said, but also understood the reasoning behind the refusal to confirm it. Thus, a new policy could only complicate efforts to cut the trail by increasing pressure on the United States to extend the bombing halt to Laos.[3]

Bundy's assurances notwithstanding, reporters had little to say about the war in Laos only because they had no day-to-day news of the subject. When information became available, however, they could cause a considerable stir. During March, for example, when MACV stationed a company of marines on a hill in Laos to protect the flank of Operation Dewey Canyon, they learned of the event almost immediately from troopers in the field. Official spokesmen attempted to direct reporters toward the large quantities of enemy supplies and equipment uncovered during the operation, but few went along. Instead, a spate of articles appeared on the border violation.[4]

To put the issue to rest, Laird decided to make an immediate statement. Out of deference to policy, he refused to confirm that U.S. forces had been in Laos, but he still managed to amplify the public record by responding vaguely, "I would certainly say that there had been operations in which it has been necessary in order to protect American fighting forces that undoubtedly that border, being a very indefinite border, may have been transgressed by American forces." Confronted by the comment, the State Department had little choice but to loosen its rules. Going no further than Laird, it permitted official spokesmen from then on to confirm that U.S. forces might have crossed the border to protect other American units or in pursuance of their right of self-defense.[5]

In the end, the story died for lack of nourishment and because the press had very obviously sought to give the new president room to set his policies in motion. Even so, as Laird had perceived, time was short. During March, the Gallup poll reported that the lack of progress in the war had begun to polarize American public opinion. Twenty-five percent of those responding to a recent survey favored escalation of the war, while another 21 percent opted for withdrawal. Meanwhile, if 15 percent recommended fighting on as the Paris negotiations ran their course, another 15 percent wanted the war to end as soon as possible. A strain of pessimism was also apparent. Only 17 percent thought the peace talks were making headway, and only 28 percent believed they would end in an honorable settlement.[6]

Whatever the results of the polls, President Nixon refused to be rushed. Counting on the initial period of grace that always follows the inauguration of a new president, he rejected suggestions that he make some dramatic gesture to prove his peaceful intentions. Instead, he issued National Security Study Memorandum (NSSM) 1, a list of twenty-nine questions designed to determine how well the war was going, to all of the U.S. agencies involved with the conflict. Then, on 22 January, rather than surrender the least military advantage, he instructed Abrams to do what he could to improve the American position in the negotiations by increasing pressure on the enemy. Abrams responded that MACV's efforts were at their peak. If the president wanted more, he could increase the bombing of the Ho Chi Minh Trail, accelerate equipment deliveries to the South Vietnamese armed forces, and permit American forces to begin attacking the enemy's base areas in Cambodia.[7]

Although the president postponed any decision on Abrams's recommendations for the time being, the general's request for attacks on the enemy's sanctuaries in Cambodia was attractive. During the Johnson era, an assault on the bases had seemed unthinkable, if only because the country's volatile head of state, Prince Norodom Sihanouk, appeared capable of allying his country with North Vietnam if the United States provided an excuse. By early 1969, however, Sihanouk had made it plain in conversations with American diplomats that he was concerned about the North Vietnamese presence in his country. Communist forces operating along Cambodia's border with South Vietnam were a menace, he had told U.S. presidential emissary Chester Bowles in December 1968. Thus, the United States would be doing his country a favor if it raided areas inhabited only by those units. Courting resumption of diplomatic relations with the United States— broken off since 1965—Sihanouk repeated his overture during a 6 March 1969 press conference, all but implying that he would welcome bombing of the sanctuaries as long as no Cambodian civilians came to grief.[8]

Given Sihanouk's stance and Nixon's interest, General Abrams continued to press for the attacks. Intelligence sources had revealed,

National Security Adviser Henry Kissinger.
(National Archives)

he told Wheeler on 9 February, that the main enemy headquarters directing the war in the southern portion of South Vietnam, the Central Office for South Vietnam (COSVN), was located just across the border in the so-called Fishhook area of Cambodia. A B-52 strike on that target would inevitably disrupt a coming enemy offensive in South Vietnam and might even forestall the attack. Nixon instructed Abrams to send a secret team to Washington to brief concerned officials, but in the end he once more dropped the idea.[9]

He returned to it, however, on 23 February, when the enemy launched the offensive Abrams had predicted and proceeded to shell or probe some 117 military installations and population centers throughout South Vietnam. Since the attacks violated the three-part understanding that had led to Johnson's bombing halt, Abrams proposed resumption of the bombing of North Vietnam as the best response, but Nixon preferred an attack on the sanctuaries as a more pointed alternative. He backed off once again, however, when Kissinger objected that it would be impossible to hide the raid, and that the antiwar outpouring the move would spark might shake public support for the war.[10]

Adding weight to Kissinger's warning, allegations were already rising in the press that MACV had attempted to cover up important details of the enemy's February offensive in order to deny the Communists a psychological victory. A 13 March article in the *New York Times* by correspondent Charles Mohr and another two days later by UPI reporter Jack Walsh were particularly telling. Mohr alleged that MACV had refused to admit that enemy forces had overrun the town of Song Be, eighty-seven kilometers north of Saigon; that the command had failed to reveal the destruction of nine large transport helicopters at Cu Chi, thirty kilometers northwest of Saigon; and that when enemy sappers had blown up a Canadian hospital at Quang Ngai in Military Region 1, briefers had waited for questions from the press rather than volunteer information about the loss. Walsh, meanwhile, revealed that following a 23 February attack on the U.S. Ninth Infantry Division's air base at Dong Tam in the Mekong delta, official spokesmen had alleged that neither casualties nor damage had occurred. In fact, he said, two fuel tanks containing fifty thousand gallons of gasoline had gone up in flames, and fourteen helicopters had been damaged. In the same way, MACV had reported only five Americans killed in an attack at Dau Tieng, seventy kilometers northwest of Saigon, when reporters had counted more than twenty-one bodies.[11]

The reporters had most of their facts correct, but rather than indulge in a cover-up, official spokesmen had merely followed Abrams's instructions to let the war speak for itself. Questioned by the Defense Department, MACV's information officers pointed out that according to rules promulgated after the Tet offensive of 1968, official statements described damage caused by rockets and shelling only as *light, moderate,* or *heavy* in order to keep the enemy from confirming the results of his attacks. As for the twenty-one bodies, only five were from Dau Tieng. The base was a central collection point for casualties from the entire area. The rest had fallen elsewhere.[12]

Whatever the criticism in the press, Nixon became increasingly impatient as the enemy's offensive continued. Turning to the press himself, he made the point at a 14 March news conference that American casualties were running at between three and four hundred per week. He would not tolerate continued North Vietnamese violations of the three-part understanding, he then remarked. "We have issued a warning. I will not warn again."[13]

Abrams had recommended combined ground and air attacks on the sanctuaries. Given the carping of the press, Nixon decided that a B-52 strike on the sanctuaries would be easy to defend because it countered an obvious threat to American forces. He made his move the next day, 15 March, when the enemy fired five rockets into Saigon, a clear violation of the understandings. In order to give the attack a low profile, he instructed all concerned to make "absolutely no comment" on the strike. Although security was to be stringent and President Thieu was to be informed only an hour before the raid, there was to be no attempt to conceal the escalation behind a cover strike in South Vietnam, as had been the case for some earlier B-52 operations in Laos. Should the press inquire, a flat "no comment" would suffice.[14]

Code-named Breakfast and occurring early on the morning of 18 March, the raid produced some seventy-three secondary explosions, many of them very large. The enemy said nothing, perhaps to draw as little attention as possible to his own use of Cambodian territory. Sihanouk was also reticent but nonetheless attempted to cover himself by remarking at a 28 March news conference that "no chief of state in the world placed in the same position I am in would agree to let foreign aircraft bomb his own country." Three months later, he resumed diplomatic relations with the United States.[15]

Lacking notification from either North Vietnam or Cambodia, the American news media failed to mark the event, but on 25 March UPI did publish a report by Jack Walsh recounting Abrams's original request to bomb the sanctuaries. Based on so-called informed American sources, the story received headline treatment in the *Washington Star,* which avowed: "Military Asks to Hit in Cambodia; Presses Nixon to Knock Out Red Sanctuary; Points to Hints by Sihanouk That He Won't Object."[16]

Defense declined to comment, and State denied any knowledge of a possible escalation, but General Wheeler cabled Abrams to note, "We all needed this exercise like a hole in the head." Terming the report "a disaster," Abrams responded that he was attempting "with the utmost discretion" to find the source of the leak. Even so, he added, "I would rather not know, than . . . let the press know I'm looking."[17]

More jolts followed. On 1 April a UPI report by correspondent David Lamb quoted the commander of the Third Marine Division at Da Nang, Maj. Gen. Raymond Davis, to the effect that "it makes no sense to watch 400 trucks a day moving through Laos with ammunition to kill Americans. . . . The quickest way to shorten this war is to destroy these sanctuaries." Two days later, UPI correspondent Robert Kaylor revealed that throughout the previous year the U.S. Special Forces had conducted secret forays into Laos and Cambodia. A second UPI article by Walter Whitehead repeated Kaylor's charges and added that Sihanouk had given tacit approval for those operations. Confusing the situation, a story by Reuters appeared at the same time alleging that the Cambodian government was aware of the attacks and would shortly issue a public protest.[18]

Abrams began another discreet investigation. In the case of General Davis's statement, he found that Lamb had broken faith with the general by publishing excerpts from an interview never intended for public release. The origins of the other stories were more difficult to determine because so many people knew what was happening. In the end, Abrams had to content himself with a message to his commanders advising all concerned to refrain from saying anything, even on background, that might be misconstrued as counter to national policy. On the side, he instructed the teams penetrating Cambodia to avoid killing Cambodian citizens if at all possible, because there were opportunities for "large stakes" in the near future that might be jeopardized if Sihanouk turned hostile.[19]

Little stir developed in the press over Kaylor's revelations because most journals were preoccupied with the negotiations. That lack of publicity, together with Sihanouk's silence, opened the way for more strikes. Between April and August 1969 they occurred intermittently, always with White House approval and always with simultaneous cover strikes in South Vietnam. After that, Abrams received general authority to conduct the raids, and they became a closely held but regular feature of the war. The program lasted until April 1970, when the United States and South Vietnam invaded Cambodia. By then, the U.S. Air Force had flown some thirty-six hundred sorties in support of the program.[20]

The press guidance accompanying the strikes was designed to camouflage the attacks. When a raid occurred, routine press releases referred only to targets in South Vietnam. Official spokesmen then included the strike in a list of cover strikes so that it would merge unobtrusively into the mass. If newsmen inquired, briefers were to confirm that routine operations sometimes struck near the Cambodian border but that there were no further details. If questions continued, they were to neither confirm nor deny but to avow that the matter was under investigation. Only if the Cambodians protested would the U.S. government acknowledge that a strike had occurred. Then it would apologize and offer compensation.[21]

The Defense Department's public affairs officers considered the approach a formula for disaster. If the operations were handled in a forthright manner, they told Nixon, the public would side with the president. The only justification necessary would be a statement that the attacks were designed to save American lives and to pave the way for U.S. withdrawals. Preferring secrecy, Nixon demurred.[22]

As was often the case, however, the press learned of the raids almost immediately. On 9 May, crediting "Nixon administration sources," William Beecher of the *New York Times* authored a detailed account of the strikes. Other stories followed in the *Wall Street Journal,* the *Washington Post,* and *Newsweek.* Confronted by the revelation, MACV's spokesmen volunteered that B-52s had struck areas adjacent to the Cambodian border. When the questions persisted but the Cambodian government once more remained silent, Daniel Henkin, the assistant secretary of defense for public affairs, cleverly ended the discussion without telling an outright lie. "This is a speculative story," he told newsmen, "and as such I have no comments on it." A short while later, President Nixon inaugurated wiretaps on the telephones of officials he suspected of having informed the press.[23]

At the end of March 1969, just as the bombing was beginning, Col. L. Gordon Hill replaced General Sidle as chief of the MACV Office of Information. A highly skilled public affairs officer, Hill faced circumstances far different from the ones that had prevailed during his predecessor's watch. With government institutions hardening to the press, official spokesmen were doing less than ever before either to sell the war to the American public or to ensure that the news media had the information they needed to construct a rounded picture of events. Meanwhile, if Laird and the Defense Department were preoccupied with preserving the credibility of the armed forces by advocating policies in Laos and elsewhere that allowed all dimensions of the war to speak for themselves, the White House, as with the Cambodian bombing, appeared much less open and much more willing to break rules when expediency so required. There was no excuse for the direction the president and his advisers were taking, but it seemed easy to rationalize at the time. As Laird had seen so sharply, the war had the capacity to tear the United States apart. Special times seemed to require special measures.

That something had to be done, indeed, seemed apparent from the responses to NSSM 1 that reached the White House just prior to the Cambodian bombing. They revealed startling disagreements among the agencies responsible for the war. The Joint Chiefs of Staff; the Office of the Commander in Chief, Pacific; MACV; and the U.S. embassy in Saigon were all hopeful. Without forecasting victory, they asserted that the South Vietnamese were fighting better than ever and that the enemy had responded by assuming a low profile on the battlefield. The Department of De-

Lots of disagreement about war in cabinet

Colonel L. Gordon Hill. (Hill family)

fense, the CIA, and, to a lesser extent, the Department of State, however, were more pessimistic, avowing that American efforts in South Vietnam had at best prolonged a stalemate.[24]

Although they differed, the two sets of estimates agreed that the South Vietnamese armed forces would be unable for the foreseeable future to stand alone against both the Viet Cong and the North Vietnamese. They also tended to doubt that the South Vietnamese government would survive a peaceful election if Communist candidates participated. In the same way, no one suggested that Communist objectives had changed or that the enemy was incapable of pursuing them. Instead, he had gone to Paris to cut costs and to pursue his aims through negotiation, not because he faced defeat. In the end, Hanoi would continue to rely on Communist China and the Soviet Union for the resources it needed to carry on the fight, but it would pursue its own ends, independent of each.[25]

Nixon clearly understood the problem that confronted him. Although he pushed for the sort of reforms that would give South Vietnam a chance at survival, he had little choice but to weigh that nation's weakness against his own aspirations. Since a precipitous American withdrawal from the war—tantamount to defeat—would jeopardize his desire to shape a new foreign policy for the United States by triggering a swing away from post–World War II predominance toward isolationism, he had to adopt a fallback position. As Henry Kissinger observed later in the war,

> We recognized from the beginning the uncertainty that the South Vietnamese could be sufficiently strengthened to stand on their own within the time span that domestic opposition to American involvement would allow. Therefore a negotiated settlement has always been preferable. Rather than run the risk of South Vietnam crumbling around our remaining forces, a peace settlement would end the war with an act of policy and leave the future of South Vietnam to the historical process. We could heal the wounds in this country as our men left peace behind on the battlefield and a healthy interval for South Vietnam's fate to unfold.[26]

With little forward motion occurring in the peace talks, an effort to buy time became imperative to Nixon. By mid-March, pressure for an accommodation with North Vietnam had begun to build in the United States, with commentators of all political persuasions assuming that the new administration intended to put a swift end to American involvement in the war and expressing disappointment when nothing happened. "Where are the fresh ideas and the new start," Tom Wicker of the *New York Times* remarked on 20 March, "let alone any 'plan' to end the war?" Syndicated columnists Rowland Evans and Robert Novak responded that while the president could hardly telegraph his intentions to the enemy, their sources indicated that he had in fact adopted an antiwar strategy that would shortly resolve itself into substantial troop withdrawals.[27]

As the tension rose, the administration began to seek some way to relieve the pressure. By the beginning of April, all concerned had decided that the casualties U.S. forces were suffering held the key and that they should be reduced. The subject "is being thrown at me at every juncture," Wheeler told Abrams, "in the press, by the Secretary of Defense, at the White House, and on the Hill." To cut the chances that the president might have to abandon offensive operations or seek a settlement detrimental to U.S. objectives, he continued, Abrams had to "get more mileage" out of the South Vietnamese armed forces.[28]

The enemy, for his part, was well aware of Nixon's problems. By April 1969, U.S. intelligence intercepts and public statements by North Vietnam's leaders all indicated that the Communists intended to exploit what they called "the contradictions in the enemy's camp." Playing on U.S. sensitivity to further American casualties and on South Vietnam's many infirmities, they planned so to tire the American public and so to discredit the Thieu regime that American withdrawals would become inevitable. In that way, they could ensure that the sort of coalition government they could control would come into being in South Vietnam, ensuring a Communist victory.[29]

Pursuing these goals, between January and June 1969, the enemy avoided large-scale ground assaults and conducted artillery, rocket, and sapper attacks in order to kill as many Americans as possible while suffering no more casualties than necessary. In the process, as compared with 1968, while nearly doubling his assaults on South Vietnamese installations, he tripled those conducted against Americans. General Abrams responded by instructing his generals to continue to put as much pressure as possible on Communist forces but to do so with an awareness that needless American casualties were detrimental.[30]

By that time, the Nixon administration was inaugurating a government-wide austerity program to cool the overheated American economy. As far as the war was concerned, it included reductions in B-52 strikes, cutbacks in destroyer patrols along South Vietnam's coast, and cuts in the number of South Vietnamese civilians employed by the army. American troop reductions were also in the offing. Whatever the mistakes of the past, the president and his advisers reasoned, the United States had to show that South Vietnam was taking charge and releasing Americans to return home. Once that happened, the administration could use the withdrawals to demonstrate how well the president's policies were working.[31]

The military, from the Joint Chiefs of Staff on down, greeted the prospect of withdrawals with misgivings. The commander of the U.S. Ninth Infantry Division, Maj. Gen. Julian Ewell, was among the most outspoken. Informed by visiting newsmen that his unit would be among the first to go, he warned Abrams that South Vietnamese forces were unready to take control of the areas his forces patrolled. "The GVN holds the towns," he said, "the Viet Cong hold the people, and the GVN moves anywhere it wishes in battalion strength and even then gets racked up every few months."[32]

On 17 April, General Wheeler notified Abrams that the first departure of an American unit would probably occur on 1 July or shortly thereafter. Abrams was astounded. Recognizing that the withdrawals represented the virtual abandonment of American goals in South Vietnam, he responded emphatically that while he appreciated the need for troop withdrawals, "my impression was that it would be reasonably deliberate so that U.S. objectives here would have a reasonable chance of attainment." The projected date for the initial withdrawals, he said, implied "an acceleration of troop reductions not previously contemplated here in the light of the . . . anticipated capabilities of the Vietnamese, . . . [who have yet to come to grips with] the realities of what they must do."[33]

Discussions followed on the date for the first withdrawal, with Laird pressing for an early announcement while Abrams held out for 1 July. While those discussions were going forward, news broke that the U.S. 101st Airborne Division had engaged a major enemy force at Dong Ap Bia, a small mountain located about two kilometers from Laos near the A Shau valley in the region west of Hue. The news stories that followed virtually ensured that Laird would have his way by turning all eyes once more to the question of American casualties.[34]

Code-named Operation Apache Snow, the action at Dong Ap Bia (Hill 937) began on 10 May, after intelligence revealed that the enemy was developing a chain of concealed, fortified positions along routes leading toward Hue from the A Shau valley. When probes established that a North Vietnamese regiment had fortified Dong Ap Bia, American commanders decided to attack. During the nine-day battle that followed, U.S. air strikes and artillery hammered the mountain with more than 3.5 million pounds of bombs, while American and South Vietnamese troops made some twelve combat assaults. According to official tallies, 56 Americans and 5 South Vietnamese were killed. Estimates, always questionable, put the enemy's losses at 630 men.[35]

Early news reports of the battle were bland, the products of briefings in Saigon. That changed after 16 May, when reporters arrived at Dong Ap Bia and discovered the details of what had happened. Associated Press correspondent Jay Sharbutt described the scene. The mountain was "almost bare," he said, "its heavy jungle cover blasted apart by artillery, rockets, bombs, and napalm." He continued that the Americans fighting there became more frustrated with each futile assault to gain the top. "After all these air and artillery strikes," one told him, "those gooks are still in there fighting. All of us are wondering why [U.S. forces] . . . can't just pull back and B-52 that hill." Another soldier, badly wounded, declared in a CBS News report, "My God, that hill is absolute suicide." The term *Hamburger Hill* seemed to appear out of nowhere, the product of a soldier's cynicism or a reporter's morbid wit. It became the name of the battle.[36]

Senator Edward M. Kennedy of Massachusetts drew national attention to the event on 20 May. Denouncing President Nixon's policies on Vietnam as "counter to our . . . intentions in Paris," he termed the army's tactics at Dong Ap Bia "senseless and irresponsible" because they sent young men to their deaths to capture positions that had no bearing on the end of the conflict. American lives were being wasted, he said, merely to preserve military pride. An array of comments followed in the press. The *Baltimore Sun,* the *New York Post,* the *Boston Globe,* and the *St. Louis Post-Dispatch* supported Kennedy. Others—the *Wall Street Journal,* the *New York Times,* the Hearst syndicate—questioned Kennedy's qualifications as a critic of military tactics but agreed that it was time to lower the level of violence in South Vietnam.[37]

Military spokesmen refused to rebut Kennedy directly, but they made the commander of the operation, Maj. Gen. Melvin Zais, available to reporters for questioning. Zais defended his tactics forcefully, observing that a ground attack had been necessary because the enemy had built bunkers deep enough to withstand the heaviest air strike. American troops suffered the most casualties, he added, when they failed to take the offensive: "It is a myth . . . that if we don't do anything nothing will happen to us. . . . If we pulled back and were quiet, they'd kill us in the night. They'd come in and crawl under the wire and they'd drop satchel charges . . . and they'd mangle, kill, and maim our men." Of Kennedy, Zais would only say, "I know for sure he wasn't here."[38]

The controversy over the battle ran for weeks. On 23 May, television commentator Martin Agronski refused to criticize either Kennedy or Zais, blaming in-

stead those American decision makers who had committed American forces to
an impossible task in South Vietnam. On 1 June, the *New York Times* charged that
while MACV had told newsmen only forty-five Americans had been killed at
Dong Ap Bia, reporters at the scene had counted sixty. On 11 June, David
Culhane of CBS News interviewed a survivor who had since left the army. He
had felt misgivings about the attack from the beginning, the man said: "They just
kept sending us up there, and we weren't getting anywhere. They were just slaughtering us, like a turkey shoot, and we were the turkeys."[39]

When the criticism continued, the government counterattacked. In a speech
before the Navy League on 4 June, Gen. Lewis W. Walt, the former commander
of all marines in South Vietnam, complained that he considered news coverage of
the battle and of the war in general "inaccurate and misleading." A short while
later, at a second Navy League function, the chief of naval operations, Adm.
Thomas L. Moorer, commented, "Bad news too often attracts the headlines. . . .
In my opinion, we sell ourselves short by . . . focusing on the bad, the bizarre, and
the big." Henry Kissinger also spoke out. Concerned that reporters might interpret operations such as the one at Dong Ap Bia as proof that the United States
was escalating the war, he emphasized at a 26 May backgrounder that if American casualties remained high, enemy-initiated actions rather than American operations were to blame. The number of American battalion-sized attacks had remained steady for a year, he said, and accounted for up to 150 Americans killed
per month. Beyond that, there was a direct correlation between the number of
enemy attacks in any given week and the level of American casualties for the
same period. Questioned on whether American forces at Dong Ap Bia were
fighting on their own terms or those of the enemy, Kissinger sidestepped the issue by responding that the battle fell into "a gray area."[40]

Although Hamburger Hill remained in the news, a White House announcement on 21 May that President Nixon would travel to Midway Island on 8 June to
confer with President Thieu rapidly overshadowed it as a story. The president had
called the meeting ostensibly to coordinate U.S. policies with those of the South
Vietnamese, but he appears, in fact, to have viewed the conference mainly as a
backdrop for his first announcement of a troop withdrawal. He wanted, he told
Laird on the very day he revealed the Midway trip, to base the move on the improvement of South Vietnamese military capabilities as agreed between Thieu
and himself rather than on pressures from within the United States. He nonetheless paid homage to those pressures by asserting that the number of troops involved should be odd rather than even because that would seem more plausible
to the American public. He added that although the first units to depart would go
mainly to American bases on Okinawa, some would have to return to the United
States for publicity purposes.[41]

The same sort of ambivalence characterized planning for the public affairs
initiative slated to accompany Nixon's announcement. Information officers in
South Vietnam and the United States began work on position papers and press

releases to counter allegations that the reduction was insignificant or a public relations ploy. Nevertheless, an effort also began, as Admiral McCain put it, to develop "a coordinated program . . . to ensure maximum political and psychological benefit from this reduction."[42]

Nixon and Thieu met at Midway as planned on 8 June, with Nixon announcing that twenty-five thousand American troops would leave South Vietnam by the end of August. Ten days later, the Defense Department disclosed the identities of the units involved and announced that most would go to either Okinawa or Hawaii. As Nixon had stipulated, however, one group of men, the Second Brigade of the Ninth Division, along with some twelve hundred reservists called to active duty during the 1968 Tet offensive, would return to the United States. It arrived in Seattle, Washington, on 8 July.[43]

The public affairs guidance accompanying the redeployment was geared to stress both the accomplishments of the departing American units and the ability of South Vietnamese forces to carry on. All concerned were warned to concentrate in their dealings with the press on themes indicating progress. Once the units destined for Seattle had arrived, they were to parade through the city's streets to demonstrate that U.S. troops were indeed coming home. Although heckling was expected, Seattle seemed an excellent site for the event because of its moderate size and lack of a large antiwar movement.[44]

The redeployment itself took place as planned. After leave-taking ceremonies at Saigon's Tan Son Nhut Airport, the troops traveled to Seattle, participated in a parade attended by General Westmoreland, and listened to welcoming speeches. On the surface, as *Newsweek* commented, "all the sights and sounds were of success," but underneath, many in the press saw disparities. Where most of the returning veterans "felt they had gone to Vietnam to do a job and had done it," *Newsweek* thus reported, others were "clearly disenchanted." One had asserted that the ceremonies were "just a gimmick." A few had seemed disturbed that they were receiving a victor's send-off before the war itself had been won. When the troops arrived in Seattle, some fifty antiwar demonstrators waving signs reading "It's a Trick, Dick" and "Bring the Other 500,000 Home" claimed the attention of reporters. So did comments by disgruntled bystanders. The *Washington Post* devoted only a small amount of space on page 10 to the ceremonies but headlined the article "Returnees Jeered." The *New York Times* noted that on the same day the troops arrived in Seattle, a thousand other men were departing the city for duty in South Vietnam. In the end, the Defense Department decided that coverage of the event had been so negative that it would be unprofitable to hold similar receptions for returning troops in the future. The Second Brigade of the Ninth Division and a few reservists thus became the only Americans returning from the war ever to receive a formal welcome home.[45]

In the days that followed, the press spent considerable time speculating on whether the South Vietnamese armed forces would be able to stand alone. Information officers at MACOI responded by publicizing South Vietnamese achievements in battle, but if they succeeded in winning coverage for stories they wanted told, they never overcame either the lack of aggressiveness of the country's military leaders or the preference of the Saigon correspondents for derogatory information.

Shortly before the first American withdrawals, for example, fighting broke out at Ben Het, a camp located near the point where the borders of Laos, Cambodia, and South Vietnam meet. The battle received little attention in the press until mid-June, when enemy pressure against the facility mounted.[46] First reports in the press were routine, but on 26 June Peter Arnett filed a story that became a major source of irritation to both the Nixon administration and MACV. Since the defense of the camp was entirely in South Vietnamese hands, Arnett concentrated on the American battalion that provided artillery support. The unit, he said, had become the victim of a logistical foul-up. Lacking water for five days, the troops had been reduced to drinking sodas and rainwater, and they were firing three rounds of ammunition for every one they received. Meanwhile, the battery's members had not only to fire the guns but also to guard their perimeter themselves because the South Vietnamese force defending them had suffered high casualties. Since the U.S. command viewed the battle as a test of the South Vietnamese ability to stand up to the North Vietnamese, however, it was reluctant to step in. The artillerymen felt, Arnett concluded, that they were being "sacrificed in an experiment that seemed to be failing."[47]

Following close upon Arnett's allegations, UPI revealed that during the battle U.S. artillery and tactical air support had returned the fire of enemy batteries located across the border in Cambodia. The article then noted allegations that U.S. B-52 bombers were already bombing that country. That evening, when MACV's briefers responded "no comment" to questions on the bombing, the assembled reporters hooted in derision.[48]

Officers at MACV later contended that Arnett, while partially correct, had built his story on the word of men at the scene without seeking a broader perspective. During early June, for example, the camp at Ben Het had in fact experienced a water shortage, yet no one had gone thirsty. Beer and soda had been in ample supply. Ammunition, on the other hand, had never been a problem except on one or two brief occasions. During the week before Arnett's report, the unit had fired 3,154 rounds while receiving 3,076 replacements. Perimeter defense had also been adequate, involving personnel from the battery itself and some sixty civilian irregulars. As for the South Vietnamese units fighting at Ben Het, the command believed that their conduct of the battle had indeed been less than commendable. They had dallied before relieving the base, and one of their regiments had come close to collapse. Even so, the force had still kept the enemy from attaining any of his objectives. Arnett, for his part, stood by his story.[49]

Although MACV made these findings available to the press and even conceded—without admitting to B-52 strikes—that the artillery had fired into Cambodia, it could do little to counter the impression of reporters that the battle was somehow a test of South Vietnam's ability to fight. For General Abrams himself considered it that, and he had so informed the commander of the U.S. artillery at the scene, his former chief of public affairs, General Sidle. As a result, as every reporter at the scene knew, nearby American forces that could have intervened left the fighting entirely to their ally.[50]

As press coverage of the battle continued, interest in the battle on Capitol Hill rose to a high pitch. Following a trip to Washington in late June, Admiral McCain cabled Abrams to inform him that "a reverse at Ben Het at this critical time will raise a hue and cry. The military from General Wheeler on down will be scapegoats. On the other hand, a sound trouncing of the enemy, particularly if it is accomplished by the [South Vietnamese] . . . , even if it is accomplished with U.S. fire and logistic support, would have far-reaching favorable effects."[51]

Abrams, of course, had no intention of losing the battle. Between 5 May and 26 June, he authorized some seventy-three B-52 strikes in defense of Ben Het, a number far in excess of what might have been expected. When MACV's deputy commander, Gen. William B. Rosson, visited the base on 29 June, he was thus able to tell reporters in all honesty, "We've punished the enemy severely. The camp is intact, fully manned, well supplied, and the morale of [the] forces [is] very high."[52]

The controversies surrounding the battles of Dong Ap Bia and Ben Het raised concern in Washington about whether MACV was doing enough to promote South Vietnamese operations. In response, Abrams instructed Colonel Hill to make the promotion of South Vietnamese achievements a top priority. On the side, he also decided to play down the American role in large operations. From then on, only the names of combat actions that developed "substantial news value" were to be released.[53]

Reporters recognized the change almost immediately. On 4 August, UPI reporter David Lamb dispatched a story outlining the policy and quoting unnamed U.S. officers to the effect that, with the Paris peace talks focused on troop withdrawals, it hardly served American interests "to ballyhoo a multi-battalion drive in search of the enemy." Another reason for the change, the reporter theorized, was that U.S. commanders had occasionally been embarrassed when a highly publicized operation had failed to achieve its goals. He noted as an example an operation near Hue several months earlier that had never been revealed because the 101st Airborne Division, during five weeks in the field, had managed to claim only two enemy killed. The story was so accurate that Abrams at first suspected a breach of security had occurred. He learned later, however, that Lamb had merely combined shrewd deductions with information already on the record.[54]

On the day after the story appeared, MACV cabled the Da Nang press center to clarify its policy. The effort to play down U.S. operations, it noted, hardly indicated a change in the practice of revealing significant operations. It merely meant that "we should not go out of our way to publicize them if they do not contain substantial news value. . . . If an operation achieves significant results, and its existence is probably very well known to newsmen, it would not be in our best interest to deny its existence." The memo was a masterpiece of circumlocution, denying any change while confirming that one had occurred.[55]

If that was so, however, it was more a reflection of the complexities confronting the Nixon administration than a mere attempt to dissemble. For the United States in 1969 was beset by contradictions. It had to fight while taking as few casualties as possible, to negotiate successfully with an enemy who was convinced he could win, and to withdraw from South Vietnam without appearing to abandon the South Vietnamese. Given the enemy's perception of America's problems and his desire to exploit them in any way possible, it was understandable that MACV would attempt to deny him that advantage by tightening its hold on information about the war. No one recognized at the time that the situation in South Vietnam, as Lamb had demonstrated, was far too open for the effort to succeed.

11

Keeping Control

By September 1969, President Nixon's public opinion ratings were beginning to drop. His personal popularity remained high, and two out of three Americans supported his decision to turn the war over to the South Vietnamese, but only 35 percent approved of his handling of the conflict. In that light, it seemed clear that they would tolerate the status quo in South Vietnam only for as long as they considered the nation worth saving. If its image before the world deteriorated or if the United States appeared to be losing control, they might abandon the long-term commitment that Nixon considered essential to a face-saving peace agreement and push for settlement on any terms.[1]

Nixon might have possessed a significant advantage in dealing with the problem if the press had been as compliant for him as it had been for Lyndon Johnson during the early years of the war, but changes were occurring in that institution. Trends in the print media had for years led away from traditional channels of news gathering—the press conference, official news releases, reports of official proceedings—and toward methods less susceptible to the government's point of view. By 1969 they were well advanced. Reporters were doing more independent research, conducting more interviews, publishing more analytical essays, and paying more attention than ever before to sources who questioned the war.[2]

The same was true for television news. During 1965 and 1966, ABC had broadcast interpretive stories on the war only 13 percent of the time, but by 1969 that figure had risen to 47 percent. Similar percentages prevailed at CBS and NBC. Administration spokesmen still dominated the news because they ranked high as authoritative sources, and the opinions of individual members of Congress and antiwar critics rarely, if ever, outweighed the president in their ability to attract coverage, but individuals inclined to criticize the war had a better chance of being heard than ever before.[3]

As news coverage changed, so did the language journalists used to describe the war. Prior to Tet, for example, journalists on television in particular had described the war as "our side" versus "their side" and had cast it in terms of the so-called good war, World War II. After Tet, they still rarely questioned the honesty of American motives, but "our war" became "the war," and references to World War II faded. By 1971, many reporters were no longer referring to North Vietnam as "the enemy."[4]

The break with cold war ideology led to sometimes telling commentaries. In June 1969, with the controversy over Hamburger Hill raging, *Life Magazine* printed the pictures of 242 Americans who had died in Vietnam during a recent week. In the same way, NBC News anchorman David Brinkley introduced a routine roundup of casualty statistics by saying, "Today in Saigon they announced the casualty figures for the week. And though they came in the form of numbers, each one of them was a man, most of them quite young, each with hopes he will never realize, each with families and friends who will never see him alive again." It was one of the strongest comments Brinkley ever made about the war.[5]

The effect on American public opinion of remarks such as Brinkley's and of television news in general is hard to tell. Anchormen rarely questioned the official news releases and statements that continued to be their main sources for information on the war. In Brinkley's case, moreover, the reporter's attitudes were more than balanced by those of the less antiwar cohost of NBC's evening news, Chet Huntley, who read 60 percent of the program's stories on Vietnam. In addition, of the 57 million households in the United States that possessed televisions in 1969, only 24.3 million had them tuned to the news on any given evening. Of the two persons per home who supposedly watched, 51 percent, according to one survey, failed to recall after an hour even a single story out of a possible nineteen that had aired.[6]

As for the print media, their hold on public opinion has long been in doubt. Walter Lippmann pointed out in 1921 that if newspapers succeed in telling people what to think about, they have little influence over the shape of the conclusions that result. Instead, readers filter the information they receive through people important to them—parents, supervisors, teachers, respected associates—before finally coming to a conclusion themselves. The conditioning imposed by society plays an important role in the process. In one study, researchers found that while the kin of those serving in Vietnam paid more attention to the war than others, they were far more likely to base their opinions on symbols acquired gradually throughout their lives—whether they were liberal, conservative, ardently anti-Communist, favorably disposed toward the military or suspicious—than on their supposed self-interest.[7]

The changes occurring in public opinion and the news media weighed heavily on the president as 1969 advanced. Caught between public distaste for a protracted conflict, the enemy's obvious abilities, and the need to maintain the U.S.

government's credibility as the leader of the free world, the president sought some means to enhance South Vietnam's chances for success while shielding the United States from the consequences that would arise if the nation failed.

He addressed the problem at a 30 July 1969 meeting of U.S. chiefs of mission in Southeast Asia. The way the war ended, he said, would have an enduring impact on America. For if the war went sour, sentiment favoring isolationism would increase in the United States, with possibly disastrous implications for the nation and the world. As a result, the United States would henceforward require the countries of Asia to handle their own subversion and insurgency problems. Their leaders "should be under no illusion" that the United States would step in to counter anything less than a large-scale external attack. "If a country can't handle its internal security, it is scarcely capable of being saved."[8]

The public affairs surrounding the portion of the program that related to South Vietnam had been months in preparation. The twenty-five-thousand-man troop withdrawal Nixon had announced at Midway Island was meant to show that the United States had ruled out a purely military solution to the war. Meanwhile, Laird had carefully intimated during March that Nixon had a plan to turn the war over to the South Vietnamese. That American forces would remain involved in the fighting for the time being was clear, but so was the president's intention to pull back.[9]

Publicized later as "the Nixon Doctrine," the approach embodied both advantages and disadvantages. As applied to Vietnam, on the one hand, it promised not only to keep costs within limits but also to alleviate public and congressional concern about an unending war. It would also bolster South Vietnam's self-esteem; demonstrate that the United States could withdraw from the war while honoring obligations to its ally; and undercut the antiwar movement, which was calling for commitment to a total U.S. withdrawal. On the other hand, there was no certainty that the South Vietnamese possessed the ability to do what had to be done. Meanwhile, the morale of the American troops who remained in Vietnam to cover the withdrawal would probably decline, and the first departures would induce pressure for more, destroying any incentive for the enemy to negotiate on terms favorable to the United States.[10]

The challenge facing the Nixon administration seemed clear. It had to ease antiwar pressures at home by reducing draft calls, cutting casualties, and withdrawing American combat forces; persuade Thieu to broaden the base of his government, reform the military, and eliminate corruption; and all the while convince the enemy that the United States was determined to fight for as long as necessary to gain an honorable peace. If the task seemed daunting, there were few plausible alternatives, and only one thing seemed clear. The control of appearances would be essential. There would have to be a careful balance between statements to the press highlighting the withdrawal for the benefit of the American public and those emphasizing the president's willingness to stay the course to preserve leverage in the negotiations. There might also be times, Nixon avowed in a message to Thieu, when statements might have to be made to the press that differed from private assurances the administration had given the South Vietnamese government. In those cases, he said, "We must trust each other."[11]

With appearances so important, the public affairs policies that disguised U.S. support for the embattled government of Laos seemed particularly threatening to many within the administration. Over the years, official spokesmen, at Laotian premier Souvanna Phouma's behest, had continued to describe U.S. air attacks on the enemy's supply routes through Laos as reconnaissance operations in which American pilots fired only when fired upon. Journalists recognized that the assertion was a sham, but they reported only intermittently on the subject because the fighting in Laos was spasmodic and difficult to cover. Their interest grew, however, following the bombing halt in North Vietnam. They could see that the number of military flights leaving American bases in Thailand remained the same even though air strikes in North Vietnam had ended and the tempo of operations in South Vietnam remained constant. The only conclusion possible was that the United States had escalated the war in Laos. Recognizing the problem, Laird requested a change in policy, but the State Department remained reluctant to do so, since any affirmation that Americans were fighting in Laos would allow the Communists to depict Souvanna as an American pawn.[12]

There matters stood until the middle of 1969, when insurgents supplied and advised by North Vietnam began to put increasing pressure on Souvanna's armed forces. That led to a possibility that the United States would have to increase its support for the premier and to an increase in news coverage of what the New York Times began to call the "twilight war." One of the most important stories came during November, when Newsweek published a wide-ranging survey of American involvement in Laos. Observing that hundreds of members of the U.S. Army's Special Forces "in mufti" played a role in the fighting, the magazine quoted a U.S. diplomat in Vientiane who had asked, "How can you hide all this? . . . It's like trying to hide an elephant under a handkerchief."[13]

Recognizing that U.S. credibility was at stake, President Nixon tried to compromise by affirming at an 8 December news conference that the United States was attacking enemy infiltration routes in Laos. The avowal, however, had no effect because Nixon declined to give details. The criticism continued.[14]

By mid-February 1970, the situation in Laos had deteriorated so drastically that the president had little choice but to approve an unprecedented B-52 strike in the country's northern region. The attack caught enemy forces in the open and stalled their offensive. (Indeed, the rotting bodies of the soldiers caught in the attack fouled so many streams that a shortage of drinking water ensued over a broad area.) Word of what had happened leaked immediately to Walter Whitehead of UPI. At that point, recognizing that continued stonewalling would be fruitless and could only harm the government's credibility, the president at last

Jerry Friedheim briefs the press on Laos.
(Jerry Friedheim)

Disatisfaction Kept growing

resolved on a change. On 6 March, in a public declaration on U.S. involvement in Laos, he confirmed that American aircraft had been flying sorties in the area for years.[15]

The announcement proved unsatisfactory to critics of the war in Congress, who immediately began to allege that the president was indulging in half measures and that the administration was covering up U.S. casualties that had resulted from air operations in Laos and from secret U.S. combat missions against the Ho Chi Minh Trail. In response, administration spokesmen announced on 9 March that they would begin to reveal aircraft losses in Laos and any casualties that resulted from enemy action against American personnel stationed in that country. Since, however, Souvanna had never received formal notification that ground penetrations of Laos were occurring, casualties from those operations continued to be carried as part of the total for South Vietnam. In the same way, although the Nixon administration revealed that some fifty American civilian support personnel had been killed in Laos over the six previous years, it refused to discuss details of incidents that had occurred prior to the president's inauguration in 1969.[16]

Planners at the State and Defense Departments understood that any statement on Laos would attract the attention of the press, but they failed to anticipate the reaction that developed when information on the subject began to open up. Ordinarily, two correspondents and three stringers covered the news from Vientiane. After the president's announcement, that number grew to more than ninety. The dislocations that resulted strained not only the capacities of the U.S. embassy at Vientiane but also the patience of reporters.[17]

The U.S. ambassador to Laos, G. McMurtrie Godley, worked hard to satisfy the visitors. Although unable to provide the sort of facilities the military command in Saigon supplied, he sponsored a number of field trips for reporters to areas that had potential for stories. One group of fifty correspondents flew over a road the Chinese were building in northern Laos. Others visited refugee centers and public works projects. A few rode into combat with Laotian air force fighter aircraft. Since the Laotian Ministry of Information had little experience in dealing with American reporters, Godley and his staff also provided advice and assistance to various members of the local government. As a result, reporters were able to conduct a number of interviews with prominent local military leaders and politicians.[18]

The ambassador's attitude toward the press was conditioned by his own perception that reporters could be of value to officials for the insights they provided. Although attempting to keep newsmen out of areas where American advice and support to Laos were too apparent, he saw little benefit in discouraging them from accompanying operations in regions where the American role was less visible. They might learn something of use.[19]

Although Godley tried, in the end he was unable to take hold of his problem with the press. The only true combat stories that appeared in all of March came because CBS and ABC television news teams, traveling from Thailand to Pakse on the Laotian Plateau des Bolovens, arrived at their destination shortly before an enemy attack and filmed the action. Lacking access to similar events because of poor transportation, most reporters had no choice but to exploit the few unambiguous details of the fighting that were available. The oversimplifications that resulted whetted the appetites of editors for more and created pressure for newsmen in the field to find something else that was new, unique, or exciting. The result, Godley said, reminded him of the *New Yorker*'s tribute to military analyst George Fielding Eliot, "who could make collision of two row boats in Central Park Lake look like Battle of Jutland."[20]

With time, the number of the correspondents resident in Vientiane declined. Although Godley and the State Department remained sensitive to news stories on Laos, the dire predictions about what the Soviet Union and China would do and say if the U.S. role in that portion of the war were acknowledged never came to pass. Instead, by changing its policy, the Nixon administration had finally removed a long-standing impediment to official credibility.

As the administration's policies on Laos fell into place and Vietnamization gathered momentum, President Nixon became increasingly sensitive to situations that opened South Vietnam to criticism. Early in June 1969, for example, CBS News ran two reports back-to-back. In the first, Secretary of State Rogers observed that the South Vietnamese were taking over more of the burden of the war. In the second, a reporter in the field alleged that the men of a South Vietnamese Regional Forces company had panicked under fire and run off in all directions. Galled, Nixon requested a full report. He learned in response that the company in question had indeed done poorly but that several days later, unattended by television cameras, several members of the unit had earned the American Bronze Star for valor.[21]

With White House interest at a peak, General Wheeler began an inquiry into the U.S. effort to publicize South Vietnamese achievements. Finding that MACV had for months required South Vietnamese spokesmen to brief the press on their own nation's military operations, he decided that the program was premature because the South Vietnamese were unsophisticated in dealing with reporters. He suggested that MACV do more on its own to highlight the South Vietnamese role and that it release background information on programs to modernize the South Vietnamese military.[22]

General Abrams had no intention of supplanting South Vietnamese news releases with announcements by American briefers, but he told Wheeler he would reinstate MACV's earlier practice of noting in American news releases significant South Vietnamese actions that involved U.S. artillery or air support. He would also encourage his allies to conduct periodic background briefings on important subjects even if they involved problems, to provide reporters in the field with more extensive information, and to increase the number of public affairs officer billets in their armed forces. As for U.S. forces, he would instruct commanders to augment South Vietnamese public affairs efforts with U.S. personnel during significant operations.[23]

Wheeler's push for changes came at a time of increasing financial stringency for U.S. public affairs activities in both the United States and South Vietnam. Although legitimate budget cutbacks were involved in the reductions that occurred, politics was also a factor. Nixon wanted to shrink the size of MACV's office of information because, he told Kissinger, its members resembled their counterparts in the press, tended to "lean to the left," and posed "particularly difficult" problems on that account. In response, Abrams, with Laird's concurrence, made a great show of cutting 130 spaces from MACV's information apparatus but took steps behind the scenes to ensure that half of the cuts came from functions that had nothing to do with press relations. In that way, the command's fifty-three-member public affairs staff would remain intact to support press coverage of Vietnamization.[24]

The South Vietnamese, for their part, bent somewhat to the pressure MACV applied. Although they remained suspicious of the press and avoided releasing bad news, the chief of their information directorate sought English-language training for his officers and began to staff his command center on a twenty-four-hour basis in order to provide better service for the press. Toward the end of the year, the Joint General Staff also dropped an irritating requirement that had forced correspondents to submit a letter of introduction from the Directorate of Information every time they sought to visit a South Vietnamese unit in the field.[25]

In the end, the South Vietnamese never did develop the kind of sophistication in handling the media that might have furthered their cause with the Saigon correspondents. Whatever their insufficiencies, however, the effort to publicize the progress of Vietnamization went forward. As it did, both the Defense Department and MACV took pains to avoid overoptimism and to allow reporters to see for themselves. The news dispatches that resulted often pointed up difficulties, but, as Henkin told Laird, the criticism created a realistic picture of the program and helped to allay suspicions that it was a sham. In addition, articles and commentaries on South Vietnamese successes began to appear. One of the most telling was by Peter Kann of the *Wall Street Journal,* who told of how he and two other journalists had set off on a four-hundred-mile automobile journey across the Mekong delta to test official claims of progress. The trip produced no grand conclusions, Kann said, but "three unarmed Americans were able to spend a week driving through rural Vietnam without being shot at. That, perhaps, is progress." Meanwhile, a report produced by Charles Collingwood for CBS News that featured an interview with Thieu seemed so advantageous to U.S. ends that the U.S. Information Agency purchased it for show abroad to foreign dignitaries and opinion leaders.[26]

While the effort to promote Vietnamization appeared reasonably successful, the Nixon administration recognized that its ability to maintain control depended on many imponderables, the foremost being the South Vietnamese themselves. The United States had lavished equipment and advice on them, but during all the years of the war to date, succeeding governments in South Vietnam had failed to make the changes necessary to put the nation on an effective war footing. The result was plain to see in the news media's coverage. Reporters replayed official comments that a turn for the better was in prospect, but an undertone of disbelief also festered. In an article widely circulated during July, for example, columnist Jack Anderson described the operations of the Saigon black market and highlighted the open lifestyles of some of its millionaire operators. Meanwhile, in a report that echoed the work of David Halberstam six years earlier, Harry Reasoner of CBS News pointed out that junior officers were the ones who directed South Vietnamese operations in the field because most of their superiors stayed consistently in the rear.[27]

The stories continued as the year advanced. During September, *Time-Life* photographer-correspondent Larry Burrows wrote that if the war was to be won, much depended on the effectiveness of South Vietnam's government: "I asked a friend if he knew of a dedicated and honest village chief. 'They are as rare as the autumn leaves,' he said. There is no autumn in Vietnam." During October, *U.S. News & World Report* published a broad assessment of the South Vietnamese government by a high-ranking, unidentified U.S. intelligence officer who summarized the problems confronting the United States and then quoted a South Vietnamese colonel. American aid was like opium, that officer had said: "Our people have become dependent upon it and have let the Americans do what we ought to be doing for ourselves." Meanwhile, John E. Woodruff of the *Baltimore Sun* revealed that official reports in his possession indicated a decline in the combat efficiency of South Vietnam's armed forces over the preceding year. The information, he said, stood in marked contrast to the optimistic briefings he and other reporters had received.[28]

President Nixon and the members of his administration read these comments with dismay. In response to their questions, however, the Defense Department could do little more than confirm that much of what the reporters had to say was true. The long war, heavy casualties, poor leadership, inadequate family benefits for the military, and the American withdrawal had all taken their toll on South Vietnamese morale, and there were few short-range solutions.[29]

The South Vietnamese themselves did little to remedy matters. Although they opened more of their operations to reporters, they insisted on interpreting every news story that criticized the Thieu regime as a threat to their national security. On 24 June, for example, they issued warnings to Reuters and Agence France Presse and banned the 23 June edition of *Newsweek*. Reuters had alleged erroneously that Thieu planned to invite Communists to join a committee supervising the next year's general elections. Agence France Presse had asserted accurately, however, that the regime had forced Prime Minister Tran Van Huong out of office in order to give the job to a member of the military clique, Gen. Tran Thien Khiem. And in a story that was also well-founded, *Newsweek* had alleged that the wives of President Thieu and other members of the government were buying villas abroad, possibly in preparation for a Communist victory. Publicly, the U.S. embassy urged reporters to remember that a nation at war had a right to protect the morale of its citizenry. Privately, Ambassador Bunker and General Abrams agreed that the Thieu regime would have to curb corruption, improve the leadership of the armed forces, and find a formula to incorporate an opposition party into the life of the country before the South Vietnamese image in the United States could improve.[30]

President Thieu and his associates, for their part, appear to have had little sense of urgency. According to knowledgeable South Vietnamese insiders, they and their subordinates declined to take the negotiations seriously and remained unconvinced that an accommodation with the Communists would ever occur.[31] Ambassador Bunker wrangled continually with them in an attempt to bring change, citing the imprisonment of political opponents, censorship of the local press, and compelling evidence that the country's bureaucracy was rife with corruption. The failure of the regime to prosecute black marketeers was a case in point, he noted, even those who made no secret that they specialized in the illegal marketing of American currency or openly displayed stolen U.S. Post Exchange goods in their stalls. "A corrupt society is a weak society," Bunker told Thieu on one occasion. "It is a society in which everyone is for himself, no one . . . for the common good."[32]

Thieu was cooperative and took many notes, but nothing changed. Corruption was one of the means he used to retain power. As Bunker knew, the president employed South Vietnam's inspectorate to investigate his generals. When an officer stepped out of line, the president would produce a dossier and threaten him with arrest unless he cooperated. The system was hardly perfect, since the investigators commonly confronted their subjects with offers to suppress evidence in return for bribes, but everyone benefited. The generals maintained their lucrative side concerns, and Thieu kept control. On occasion, the president would replace a corrupt officer to placate the Americans, but that individual rarely suffered more than a transfer to new duties and a promotion.[33]

In truth, however, more was involved in the Thieu regime's failure to reform than ineptitude and greed. Over time, the United States had progressively relegated the South Vietnamese to a subordinate position in their own land. American troops fought the enemy's main forces, leaving inglorious secondary tasks to the South Vietnamese armed forces. Meanwhile, American dollars fueled the nation's economy and, along with it, graft and corruption. The U.S. mission's news releases emphasized the South Vietnamese role in everything, and Bunker and Abrams took care to consult with the nation's leaders on major decisions, but the policies that determined the course of the war almost always took the shape the United States wanted.

From time to time the South Vietnamese government attempted to assert its prerogatives. During September 1969, for example, the local Saigon press began to complain bitterly that an article in *Newsweek* had alluded to a contingency plan for American troops to fight the local armed forces if that became necessary in connection with the U.S. withdrawal. They also criticized American news stories that questioned South Vietnam's ability to take control of the war. If the United States wanted their country to do the fighting, they said, it should give the nation more of a say in decisions that governed its future.[34]

Sensitive to the U.S. practice of selecting units for redeployment with only a nod to what he conceived of as South Vietnam's requirements, President Thieu took up the theme. He wanted more say in the process, or, at least, to create the appearance of say to enhance his own standing with his people. To that end, despite American urging, he refused to participate in a three-day cease-fire announced by the enemy in observance of Ho Chi Minh's death. He also declared that he was dissatisfied with the timing and size of the second installment of the U.S. withdrawal, and he threatened to withhold approval unless his generals agreed that it would have little effect on territorial security. Reassured by his officers, he approved the plan the next day, but that evening Vice President Ky reasserted South Vietnamese prerogatives by informing reporters at a cocktail party that President Nixon would shortly announce a 40,500-man troop reduction. He added that the United States might withdraw as many as 200,000 troops by the end of the year.[35]

The leak threatened to increase pressures rising in the United States for larger and faster redeployments and jeopardized the administration's stance in the peace talks by suggesting that Nixon might withdraw U.S. forces whether or not progress occurred in the negotiations. In the end, Nixon regrouped by stressing that only 60,000 Americans would depart South Vietnam by 15 December. Henry Kissinger, meanwhile, noted in a Washington backgrounder that if the United States intended to replace its forces as rapidly as feasible, it had never established a fixed schedule of withdrawals.[36]

Over the weeks that followed, Thieu remained contentious. He was obviously concerned that both he and South Vietnam might lose face before the world if Nixon appeared to be the one who made all the decisions on withdrawals. The

President Nixon with President Thieu. (U.S. Army)

issue finally came to a head toward the end of October, when Bui Diem, South Vietnam's ambassador to the United States, approached the State Department with a proposal. It might be prudent, he said, if the next announcement of a redeployment came from Thieu rather than President Nixon. Thieu would make a public declaration to the effect that the South Vietnamese armed forces were prepared to replace a given number of Americans. Nixon could then follow with a statement acquiescing to the suggestion. Secretary of State William P. Rogers rejected the idea out of hand. If approved, he said, the proposal would "put us in the position of letting the basic decisions be made by the Vietnamese." The remark unwittingly highlighted the contradiction between American rhetoric and the reality of the American role in Vietnam.[37]

If the Nixon administration found it difficult to repair the image of the Thieu regime, it had its own public relations to consider as well. The president had to guard continually against any occurrence in South Vietnam that might either force the pace of withdrawals or throw into question the sincerity of his well-publicized desire to pull back.

During August, for example, in an attempt to emphasize to U.S. commanders that American goals had changed, the administration had revised MACV's statement of mission. Where the old one had indicated an intention to defeat the enemy, the new one emphasized the desire of the United States to assist the South Vietnamese in assuming an increasing share of the combat burden. During the months that followed, U.S. commanders found it difficult to adjust to the revised objective and persisted in following the old attrition strategy. "In reading Abrams' analysis of the military situation in South Vietnam," President Nixon thus told Henry Kissinger during November, "I get the rather uneasy impression that the military are still thinking in terms of a long war and an eventual military solution."[38]

The difference between the president's intention to Vietnamize the war and the attitude of the generals found its way into the press. On 3 November 1969, the *Washington Star* published an article by Donald Kirk alleging that the advent of Vietnamization had made little difference in the way U.S. forces fought. Referring to a recent remark by Laird that American units were following a policy of "protective reaction" rather than "maximum pressure," Kirk asserted that as far as the men of the U.S. First Cavalry Division (Airmobile) were concerned, the two terms meant exactly the same thing. On the very evening the report appeared, General Wheeler hurriedly instructed Abrams to reemphasize to his commanders that Vietnamization was their goal, and Nixon himself announced during an address to the nation that he had in fact changed the mission of U.S. forces in South Vietnam several months before.[39]

The reluctance of American commanders to abandon the attrition strategy became less important as the size of U.S. forces in South Vietnam diminished, but the good image of the war still remained at risk. For an ill-advised act by one or several Americans serving in South Vietnam could find its way into the press, where it could impair the ability of the president to achieve his ends. An episode of this sort occurred during July, when investigators implicated the commander of the Fifth Special Forces Group in South Vietnam, Col. Robert B. Rheault, and seven of his subordinates in the murder of a suspected enemy spy. The incident was sensitive for a number of reasons. The Special Forces were involved in highly classified intelligence-gathering operations subject to compromise if court proceedings became too detailed. In addition, allegations were circulating that the murder had been instigated by a CIA station chief.[40]

Over the days that followed, the CIA denied any involvement in the affair but declined because of the sensitivity of its operations to cooperate with either the prosecutors or the defense. Abrams, for his part, became infuriated with Colonel Rheault, who appeared to have lied to him in a personal interview when asked about the whereabouts of the victim. As a result, he took the highly unorthodox step of placing the suspects in solitary confinement at the American military prison at Long Binh.[41]

Given the dimensions of the case and the obvious intention of the suspects to defend themselves with vigor, the general had little doubt that the episode would eventually take on major proportions in the press. He succeeded in withholding word of it for several days, but on 4 August *New York Times* reporter Juan Vasquez heard rumors and filed a request for information with the Pentagon. Defense passed the query to MACV, which responded by naming the suspects and clarifying points of military law. But the command revealed no details on grounds that any further release of information might infringe upon the rights of the accused. "There's gotta be two sides of the story," Col. James Campbell, the chief of information for the U.S. Army, Vietnam, asserted at the time. "Someday you'll know the story and you'll see the Army wouldn't press charges without cause."[42]

Lacking authoritative information, newsmen turned to unofficial sources and began to publish rumors, some of which suggested that the United States was conducting a program of assassination against South Vietnamese officials.[43] Recognizing, meanwhile, that publicity could only assist their clients, the attorneys for the accused were only too willing to fill the vacuum. A civilian lawyer representing one of the suspects, George Gregory, told reporters that military authorities were engaging in some sort of vendetta. "I measured my client's cell very carefully today," he said. "It's 7 by 5, with a tin roof and hot as hell. The metal cot leaves only a foot between it and the wall and there's a foot square peephole. He has to bang on the door if he wants to go to the lavatory." The military lawyers for the accused were also outspoken. One issued a press release authored by his client. Another alleged on network television that Abrams had become personally involved in the case. Although the civilian lawyers were free to say what they wanted, the military members of the court were in violation of military regulations and subject to discipline. MACV's judge advocates, however, declined to take action lest any suggestion arise that the command was indulging in an attempt at intimidation.[44]

On 18 August the U.S. Army, Vietnam, released the suspects from pretrial confinement, eliminating one cause of controversy. By then, however, the families of the accused had contacted their congressmen, who had immediately sided with their constituents. The CIA sought to placate the congressmen by holding private background briefings for members of the House and Senate Armed Services Committees, but the effort had little effect. On the day following the first of the sessions, Peter W. Rodino, Jr., of New Jersey, Carl B. Albert of Oklahoma, and six other members of Congress signed a letter to the secretary of the army expressing "distress and indignation" over the way MACV had handled the whole affair. As pressure mounted, the lawyers for the defense attempted to subpoena classified manuals, publications, and instructions on the activities and operations of the U.S. Army Special Forces in Vietnam. When the CIA declined to provide documentation under its control and the accused responded that they had been denied materials necessary for an adequate defense, it became clear to all concerned that the defendants expected MACV to drop its charges rather than compromise sensitive intelligence activities.[45]

By then, divisions were growing within the Department of Defense itself.

Stanley Resor, the secretary of the army, was inclined to back Abrams on grounds that the U.S. Army should never condone murder. The office of the Defense Department's general counsel agreed. Dismissal of the case would constitute a grave failure to observe the Geneva Conventions governing the conduct of war at the very time the United States was urging North Vietnam to adopt a policy of moderation toward American prisoners of war. Laird, Westmoreland, Wheeler, Deputy Secretary of Defense David Packard, and the director of central intelligence, Richard Helms, however, wanted to drop the case. "You have a chain of command involved here and some of their defense is that [the suspects] . . . carried out their orders," Westmoreland told the vice chief of staff of the army, Gen. Bruce Palmer, Jr. "If you use the illegal order theory, the whole Army will start thinking twice about this, particularly the intelligence people, who are risking [their] lives all the time."[46]

On 23 September, with Congressman Rodino claiming on the floor of the House of Representatives that the case represented "one of the weirdest—and probably cruelest—trials in the military history of this nation," the CIA, with the approval of a beleaguered president, refused for a final time to participate in the case. Convinced that a fair trial would be impossible without CIA documentation and that further controversy could only harm the nation, Secretary Resor dismissed all charges against the accused.[47]

Although the case had ended, the interest of the press held firm. The *New York Times* and the *Los Angeles Times* prepared investigative reports that threatened to spill over into other areas of intelligence gathering. The *Philadelphia Bulletin* charged that the affair contained "a whiff of self-corruption dangerous to a democracy." *Washington Post* columnist Carl Rowan observed that "the shrewdest agent in the Soviet Union's 'bureau of dirty tricks' could never have dreamed up a plot that would do so much damage to America's reputation in the world." In that sense, he added, the case had cost the United States much more than the $6,472 it paid to settle with the victim's widow.[48]

With the end of the Green Beret affair, General Abrams became acutely sensitive to any portion of the American effort in South Vietnam that threatened to cause public relations problems, particularly the CIA-assisted Phoenix program. Established in July 1967 to assist in the elimination of the Viet Cong's shadow government, the effort had succeeded in neutralizing a few enemy leaders but had otherwise put the most pressure on the least important of the enemy's supporters, those who followed the Communists less out of conviction than because they had no choice. Powerful local bureaucrats sometimes used Phoenix to intimidate personal enemies, and numbers of innocent persons spent long periods in custody without hearings. Meanwhile, dangerous Communists regularly bribed their way to freedom, and those who were convicted often received prison terms of less than a year. The United States supported the program because the destruction of the enemy's infrastructure seemed essential to the outcome of the war, but MACV understood the risks and warned Americans involved in it to refuse to participate in questionable activities and to report all instances to superiors.[49]

As the controversy over the Green Beret affair ran its course, General Abrams decided that MACV could no longer support one aspect of Phoenix, the Provincial Reconnaissance Unit program (PRU). Employing Viet Cong defectors advised by Green Berets, these forces were noted for their violent methods. Rumor had it that the South Vietnamese government paid their members a fixed amount for the ear of a Viet Cong and more for the head of a leader. Convinced that the effort operated on the fringes of morality and that MACV would find it difficult to discipline American advisers who became involved in war crimes while serving under agencies beyond its jurisdiction, Abrams resolved to withdraw his command from the program as quickly as possible. By January 1970, as a result, MACV's support for the PRU had ceased.[50]

As with all the other efforts by the Nixon administration to preserve the public image of the American effort in Vietnam, Abrams's attempt to shield his command from bad publicity was fated to disappointment. For with the Thieu regime unwilling to change and the American public and Congress increasingly restive, time was growing short. As the Green Beret affair suggested, the war itself was out of hand and beginning to spin beyond control.

12

Questioning Begins

When President Nixon took office and pledged to end the fighting in South Vietnam, the antiwar movement in the United States stepped aside to draw breath. By the fall of 1969, however, those who opposed the war were losing patience with Nixon's policy of gradual withdrawals. During August a coalition of organizations advocating peace began planning a nationwide day of discussion and protest—a "Moratorium on 'Business as Usual'"—for 15 October to dramatize public disenchantment with the war. Work also began on a second, much larger, protest for 15 November in Washington, D.C. The movement gained in strength and respectability over the weeks that followed. Prominent academics endorsed it. The Roman Catholic archbishop of Boston, Richard Cardinal Cushing; the president of the Synagogue Council of America, Rabbi Jacob Rudin; and the general secretary of the World Council of Churches, Reverend Eugene Carson Blake, also spoke out.

If opposition to the war appeared extensive, American public opinion continued on its own track. While six out of ten of the individuals interviewed by pollsters considered the war a mistake, relatively few advocated hasty withdrawal from South Vietnam. Instead, most respondents rated protests by the young the country's largest problem after the war, and 84 percent advocated a crackdown on student demonstrations.[1]

Aware that the enemy would interpret the rise in antiwar dissent in the United States as a sign of weakness, President Nixon began a search for some means to solidify the credibility of the effort in South Vietnam. At first, he toyed with the idea of launching a major air assault on North Vietnam, the sort of move that in the past had galvanized public support while underscoring the nation's determination to continue the war. In the end, however, he saw more potential in an attempt to play on the American public's distrust of both the protest movement and the news media.[2]

Nixon meets with reporters before his 3 November 1969 speech. (National Archives)

To that end, he and the members of his cabinet stepped forward early in October to upstage the moratorium. Secretary Laird confirmed publicly that U.S. commanders in South Vietnam were no longer under orders to keep maximum pressure on the enemy. Secretary of State William P. Rogers declared on *Meet the Press* that the president had de-escalated the war and that troop withdrawals would continue. Then, on 10 October, Nixon himself stepped forward to announce the reassignment of the outspoken director of the Selective Service System, a particular target of the antiwar movement, Lt. Gen. Lewis B. Hershey. He also announced, three weeks in advance, that he would deliver a major address to the nation on 3 November.[3]

The October protest went as planned, with demonstrations occurring around the nation, but Nixon was not far behind. His 3 November speech also came off well and produced much of the effect he sought. During the talk, he outlined the effort to turn the war over to the South Vietnamese, underscored a decline in American casualty rates over previous months, and appealed to "the great silent majority" for support. Although the Hanoi regime termed the speech a "perfidious, . . . gunpowder-stinking address [that] had only added to the fire of [antiwar] struggle that is burning intensely throughout the United States," governments around the world extended their congratulations. The American news media were hardly as enthusiastic. The *New York Times*, for one, noted that Nixon had condemned North Vietnam's recalcitrance in the negotiations but had avoided any mention of South Vietnam's failure to liberalize its institutions. Seventy-seven percent of Americans, according to a Gallup poll, sided with the president.[4]

While Nixon was elated by the reaction to his speech, he understood that public patience was wearing thin. For if, according to the Harris poll, 51 percent of the American people disagreed with the antiwar movement's methods, 81 percent had still concluded that the demonstrators were raising legitimate questions. By a margin of 50 to 37 percent they also agreed that the war was morally indefensible and that the United States had erred by becoming involved. Indeed, when the 15 November march on Washington took place, more than 250,000 citizens turned out, making the demonstration the largest to occur in the nation's capitol to that date.[5]

Although public approval of the president's handling of the war rose 6 percentage points following the moratorium, Nixon was disgusted with the way the press had covered his speech. At NBC, David Brinkley had remarked that the president had finally made Lyndon Johnson's war his own, and ABC had played comments by Ambassador W. Averell Harriman in which the outspoken critic of the president's policies had called upon Senator Fulbright to launch another investigation of the war.[6]

The president retaliated over the weeks that followed by moving subtly to intimidate the television networks with hints of possible Federal Communications Commission investigations and by launching a series of harsh attacks on the press through his vice president, Spiro Agnew. Relying on the news media themselves to spread the word, Agnew criticized the press in general but especially television news for its "instant analysis and querulous criticism." His remarks drew a vehement reaction from the press, but the public greeted them warmly. Tens of thousands of television viewers contacted the networks to complain about news coverage, and the president's standing in the polls rose by some 5 percentage points.[7]

Although Americans complained, they were hardly as upset as they seemed. In a poll sponsored by ABC shortly after Agnew's speech, 51 percent of those who knew of Agnew's charges agreed that television news was biased, but 66 percent favored the networks' practice of commenting on presidential speeches. By a wide margin, the majority also agreed that network news programs should continue to criticize government. Nixon was aghast when he read the poll's findings. "My God!" he scribbled in the margin of the news summary that reported them.[8]

Nixon's alarm was appropriate. For even as the president strove to strengthen his base of support, circumstances were combining to weaken it. Military officers in a position to know—Westmoreland among them—had become privately convinced that the withdrawals Laird and Nixon planned were too sweeping and arbitrary to provide the South Vietnamese with the time they needed to reform. Despite their doubts, those officers obeyed their orders and pushed ahead to salvage what they could of their nation's honor. Their soldiers, however, were hardly

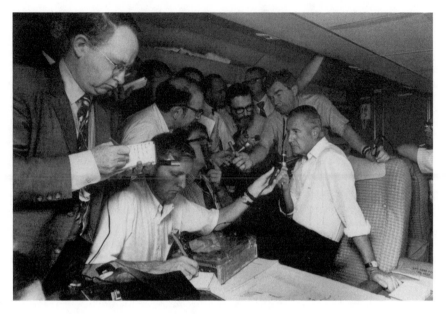

Vice President Spiro Agnew briefs the press. (Department of Defense)

as compliant. Reflecting American public opinion and increasingly doubtful about the war, they were becoming restive. As debate grew and public support weakened in the United States, it was becoming increasingly difficult for many to see much sense in the sacrifices they were making. Troops in combat held up well. They had to or they died. But President Nixon's decision in 1969 to cut casualties and to begin withdrawals drew an increasing number of soldiers into rear areas, where they had little to do. With social tensions already rising in the United States, drug abuse growing, and traditional values under siege, it was all too easy for some to take out their frustrations on soldiers of different races or to seek refuge in drugs they had known before entering the service and to introduce them to their friends. Even the members of the vast majority who avoided trouble often resolved to do nothing more than get by.[9]

The press caught the mood. Reporter Georgie Ann Geyer of the *Chicago Daily News* speculated during January 1969 on the possibility that increasing antiwar sentiment in the United States might infect the soldier in the field. In April, *Newsweek* reported that if outright dissent was rare among the troops, the men were hardly as single-minded or clean-cut as in the past. Many sported the trident-in-a-circle peace symbol, hanging it from their necks or inscribing it on helmet covers and liners. By November, Donald Kirk of the *Washington Star* could allege that "the worn out cliche of generals and master sergeants that 'morale over here is great' no longer seems to apply to men in the field." Many soldiers believed that the United States should leave South Vietnam as soon as pos-

sible, Kirk said. Others felt a repug-
nance even for the people they were
supposedly trying to save. During
February 1970, *Newsweek* revealed
in a report on the so-called new GI
that the troops had even jeered Bob
Hope during his annual Christmas
tour of South Vietnam when he
had alluded favorably to President
Nixon's plan to end the war.[10]

The first solid indications that
something was wrong seemed to
arise out of nowhere, in an area
both the military and the news media had long considered firmly under control: race relations. Young
black Americans had grown up with
the civil rights movement in the
United States and resented the in-
equities that had long seemed the
lot of their race. They carried their
concern into the army. A series of
articles in the *Washington Star* during May 1968 by a black newsman,
Paul Hathaway, caught what was

Bob Hope entertains the troops at Long
Binh, Christmas 1971. (U.S. Army)

happening. Hathaway had spent several months in South Vietnam interviewing
black soldiers. He reported that from 80 to 85 percent of the men he had talked
to were proud of their service but troubled by the military's treatment of blacks.
If racial integration seemed successful in the combat zone, he said, it was much
less apparent in rear areas, where black enlisted men often encountered narrow-
minded whites. Some wondered, he added, whether they should be home fighting
for their own people.[11]

That the problem ran deep became apparent as 1968 lengthened. During August, black prisoners rioted at the U.S. Marine Corps brig in Da Nang and at the
U.S. Army jail at Long Binh. The marine episode ended quickly, but at Long Binh
the rioters clubbed a white prisoner to death and injured many others. Two hundred and twenty prisoners were collected by guards into an open area within the
jail's compound, but problems continued for three more weeks because the rioters had destroyed most of the jail's records and few would volunteer their names.
Over the months that followed, more confrontations occurred at Seventh Air
Force headquarters in Saigon, at American air bases in Thailand, and on the aircraft carrier USS *America* in the South China Sea.[12]

A special team of Defense Department investigators traveled to South Vietnam to see firsthand what was happening. After interviewing a large number of black servicemen in private, the leader of the group, a black, L. Howard Bennett, wrote an alarming report on the conditions he had found. Interracial tensions, he said, had reached disturbing proportions in rear areas. Communication up and down the chain of command was difficult; officers often seemed insensitive to the needs of black servicemen, the majority of whom lacked confidence in official procedures for settling grievances; and many black enlisted men believed that the system of military justice discriminated against them. Bennett's conclusions were apparently too emphatic to be well received at the Defense Department. It took until March 1969 for General Abrams to learn of them, and then the information came as an afterthought, because Secretary Laird happened to mention the report during a trip to South Vietnam. It took nine months more before Defense, at the prodding of a congressional subcommittee investigating racial disturbances, began to develop an educational program on race relations applicable to all of the armed services.[13]

The public affairs handling of issues involving race was initially unfocused. Although there never appears to have been much inclination on the part of military spokesmen to hide anything, some civilian officials attempted to hold back. During October 1968, for example, when a black enlisted man at Da Nang went berserk with a gun after a racial confrontation with whites, accidentally killing a black guard, information officers were forthright. They detailed restrictions on the sale of alcohol to American servicemen that resulted from the episode and made the commander of the installation available to the press. Shortly afterward, however, Jack Moskowitz, the deputy assistant secretary of defense for civil rights and industrial relations, attempted to gloss over what had happened. Moskowitz conceded that young black servicemen were increasingly unwilling to suffer indignities because of their race, but he also stressed that the same problems afflicted civilian society and that racial incidents on military property were bound to be noticed.[14]

Following the inauguration of Richard Nixon, a greater recognition prevailed that problems existed, but inertia remained. When a team headed by Bennett visited South Vietnam again in November 1969, it found that if commanders were more willing than before to admit to racial polarization, many of the equal opportunity messages the team reviewed were dated close to its visit and that the signs marking the doors of equal opportunity officers were sometimes freshly painted. Meanwhile, if high-level officers seemed genuinely concerned, black soldiers continued to assert that the system of military justice favored whites and that MACV was marginally attuned to their needs.[15]

Months earlier, when the first reports of racial problems had surfaced, General Abrams had set up watch committees to monitor potential racial flashpoints. When Bennett's second report arrived, he redoubled his efforts. To eliminate unnecessary points of friction between officers and enlisted men, he began an examination of MACV's policies and procedures and issued guidance emphasizing the importance of effective communication within the chain of command. From then on, reporters would later note, racially insensitive officers in South Vietnam risked permanent damage to their careers.[16]

These efforts notwithstanding, a review of personnel problems at MACV in May 1970 reemphasized that communication among the ranks continued to limp. Meanwhile, in practice, the full extent of the problem with race seemed almost impossible to estimate because officers found it difficult to separate fact from rumor where allegations of discrimination were concerned. Out of a concern for career preservation, local commanders were also reluctant to discuss what was rapidly becoming, as one army personnel specialist remarked, "a war which is being fought every night in . . . places where our soldiers gather."[17]

Public affairs officers, for their part, were caught between their superiors' inability or reluctance to define the scope of what was happening and the reality of the racial problem. As a result, although they handled the press forthrightly when problems occurred, they were unwilling to go too far without a better understanding of what was happening. Learning of an increase in the number of racial incidents during the summer of 1970, for example, the chief of information for the U.S. Army, Vietnam, Col. Alfred J. Mock, argued vehemently against any announcement to the press. The army needed accurate facts and figures, he said, not only to document the problem but also to demonstrate that it had comprehensive, effective programs to remedy what was wrong. At that time, however, MACV had nothing to offer that was convincing enough to satisfy either the press or the public, let alone its own personnel.[18]

Whether or not the army revealed the increase, the Saigon correspondents recognized what was happening and followed the subject closely. They tended to agree with the military, however, that most blacks and whites in South Vietnam lived together without measurable difficulty. The two groups were much farther apart when allegations of widespread marijuana use by the troops began to arise in 1967. Military spokesmen acknowledged that marijuana was indeed present, but they failed to see a serious problem. Releasing statistics that indicated that marijuana usage had increased from a rate of slightly less than 1 user per 1,000 men in 1966 to 2.5 per 1,000 by the end of 1967, they asserted that none of the culprits were addicted to hard narcotics such as heroin and that none used marijuana in the field.[19] Reporters who went often into the field, however, were with the troops enough to know what was going on and made the subject one of their staples.

If known involvement rates seemed low, military commanders were still concerned. During February 1968, the Defense Department inaugurated a program to curtail marijuana use. In the campaign that followed, MACV released films and reading materials on the subject to the troops, special investigators identified South Vietnamese businesses that dealt in illicit substances, and Ambassador Bunker prevailed upon the Thieu regime to ban distribution of the drug.[20]

Reporters followed the effort with sympathy but also gave full play to their own findings. When the Defense Department released revised drug statistics in February, the *Washington Daily News* took pains to observe that the figures were probably less than accurate because cautious marijuana smokers rarely came to the attention of investigators. In the same way, during March, the *Washington Star* highlighted testimony before a Senate subcommittee by John Steinbeck IV, son of the novelist John Steinbeck. A Vietnam veteran, Steinbeck said that about 60 percent of American soldiers between the ages of nineteen and twenty-seven smoked marijuana when they could. He added that the U.S. command itself promoted drug abuse by distributing "pep pills" (amphetamines) to soldiers in combat. Military spokesmen could only confirm that MACV had indeed distributed amphetamines in survival kits. They said the pills sometimes spelled the difference between life and death for men who had to stay awake for long periods in the field. The *Star*, for its part, sided with the military. Its headline read: "Steinbeck's Son Quotes Self as Expert on Drugs, Vietnam."[21]

Although the Defense Department admitted that marijuana smoking was, after larceny, the second most widespread criminal offense among U.S. troops in South Vietnam, it continued to downplay the extent of the problem. When the department revealed at the end of the year that marijuana usage had grown to 7.99 cases per 1,000 men, the chairman of its drug abuse control committee, Frank A. Bartimo, thus noted that the figures compared quite favorably with drug use rates as high as 15 and 25 percent at high schools and colleges in the United States. Other official spokesmen added that there was virtually no addiction to hard narcotics such as heroin and that the rise in marijuana investigations was attributable to increased awareness of the problem and more vigorous enforcement of existing rules.[22]

The press dutifully replayed these assertions, but it also covered the opposite point of view. On 21 April, for example, *Newsweek* ran an article indicating that drug abuse had created a subculture among the troops. "A battalion of the U.S. Army's First Cavalry Division trooped into division headquarters at Phuoc Vinh one day recently after a month in the field," the story's authors noted. "The men showered and shaved and ate a hot meal in the mess hall. 'Then when the sun went down,' recalls one GI, 'about 200 of us went into the nearest field and had a damn good smoke.' But the scene was pure marijuana rather than Marlboro Country." Although a count of drug users was difficult to come by, the magazine continued, a recent report by an army psychiatrist estimated that 35 percent of the troops indulged in the practice: "The lower-level unit commander is reaching an accommodation with pot smokers. If he stopped them all it would decimate his outfit. So he sees no evil and as long as they stay out of trouble he doesn't bother them."[23]

Official spokesmen made little effort to refute *Newsweek*. Studies were beginning to show that drug use was much higher than government statistics indicated. Public affairs officers nonetheless resented the article and the point of view it represented. One suggested angrily in a memo that the story was "a fine example of the press focusing on the unfavorable."[24]

News stories on marijuana continued to appear over the months that followed. During September, Drummond Ayres of the *New York Times* observed that drug abuse was so extensive among American troops that marijuana had become a cash crop for South Vietnam's farmers. On 13 October, the *Baltimore Sun* reported that, according to an article in the *Journal of the American Medical Association,* some American soldiers in Vietnam were experiencing severe mental disturbances after using marijuana, a condition all the more dangerous because it existed in a war zone. Army spokesmen could only respond that if up to 30 percent of U.S. troops in South Vietnam smoked marijuana, confidential surveys indicated that only 9 to 11 percent did so three or more times per week.[25]

The evidence of drug abuse nevertheless continued to mount. During November, the Office of the U.S. Army Surgeon in South Vietnam conducted a controlled survey of soldiers entering and departing the war zone. Guaranteeing anonymity, the interviewers found that approximately 30 percent of the men arriving in South Vietnam and 45 percent of those departing had used marijuana at least once. Although the development seems dramatic in hindsight, few outside of the medical community in South Vietnam had any knowledge of the study. As late as 30 March 1970, indeed, the army surgeon at Long Binh who had conducted the test lacked access to a computer and so had failed to make more than a preliminary analysis of his data. The study apparently came to the attention of the Pentagon only when an army psychiatrist testified before a Senate subcommittee that in his experience 50 to 80 percent of all army personnel in South Vietnam had used marijuana at least once. Anticipating questions, the chief of U.S. Army public affairs, General Sidle, cabled MACV for information, only to learn that if the doctor's statistics seemed excessive, the best figures available in the field were bad enough.[26]

Signs that a major problem existed increased in the months that followed. By October 1970, even the comforting thought that hard drugs were not involved had disappeared. Investigators found that all statistics on the subject had underestimated the problem because hospital personnel had routinely attributed drug-related illnesses to the primary medical conditions involved—hepatitis, pneumonia, personality disorders—rather than to the ultimate cause, heroin or some other highly addictive substance. In addition, since the computer program that tallied the causes of noncombat fatalities made no provision for drug abuse, doctors coded cases of that sort as "unknown" or "accidental self-destruction." When official agencies revised their reporting methods, the magnitude of the lapse became apparent. Whereas during all of 1969 the army had identified only sixteen drug-related deaths in South Vietnam, between January and October 1970 it recorded ninety-three. Word of the finding came as no surprise to the Saigon correspondents. Their reporting on the subject had been impressionistic, but it had still been more accurate than that of the military.[27]

Official spokesmen contended that MACV's problems with race and drugs stemmed from the slowing pace of the war and the inactivity and boredom it bred among the troops. They took consolation from the fact that neither racial

If troops bored, why not bring home.

tensions nor drugs had rendered any unit in the field combat-ineffective. Even so, from 1968 onward, the military services' difficulties with race and drugs proved to be only an introduction to a whole range of other morale problems. The facts in those cases were as difficult to define as the ones involving race and drugs, but all came, in time, to take on great significance for the press because they seemed to bear upon the meaning of the war itself.

The Saigon correspondents had long known, for example, that corruption was rampant in South Vietnam. Indeed, some among their own number had been disaccredited for illegal trading in currency on the black market, and many more had been involved. It came as no surprise to them, therefore, when the Defense Department announced during August 1969 that the army had begun a probe of irregularities at officer and noncommissioned officer clubs in Europe and South Vietnam. What was shocking was the extent of the conspiracy that began to unfold and the importance of the high-ranking officers and enlisted men who were involved, one of whom was a former sergeant major of the army and MACV's principal noncommissioned officer, Command Sgt. Maj. William O. Wooldridge. In that case, public affairs officers attempted to keep the issue in low key in order to preserve both the rights of the accused and the good image of the armed forces, but they made no attempt to dissemble. All concerned understood that lies would only postpone the inevitable.[28]

The club scandal created hardly a stir, however, in comparison with another incident that surfaced at almost the same time. On 12 August 1969, during an enemy attack on a U.S. fire base some fifty kilometers south of Da Nang, a helicopter carrying eight persons, including AP photographer Oliver Noonan, went down killing all on board. A major effort ensued to reach the crash. Over the five days of fighting that followed, one of the most heavily engaged American units, Company A of the Third Battalion, Twenty-first Infantry, Twenty-third Infantry Division, lost ten men killed and twenty wounded. When it received orders to continue the operation for a sixth day, its men refused to go.[29]

Associated Press photographer Horst Faas was within hearing distance when the unit's commander, 1st Lt. Eugene Shurtz, radioed his superior, Lt. Col. Robert C. Bacon, to inform him of what was happening. Faas told what he had heard to Peter Arnett, who wrote it down and put it on the wire:

"Repeat that, please," the colonel asked without raising his voice. "Have you told them what it means to disobey orders under fire?"

"I think they understand, but some of them simply had enough—they are broken. There are boys here who have only 90 days left in Vietnam. They want to go home in one piece. The situation is psychic here."

"Are you talking about enlisted men or are the NCO's also involved?" the colonel asked.

"That's the difficulty here," Shurtz said. "We've got a leadership problem. Most of our squad and platoon leaders have been killed or wounded."

Quietly the colonel told Shurtz: "Go talk to them again and tell them that ... the enemy has withdrawn.... Please take a hand count of how many really do not want to go."

The lieutenant came back a few minutes later: "They won't go, colonel, and I did not ask for the hand count because I am afraid that they will all stick together, even though some might prefer to go."

After instructing the lieutenant to take his command post element and move off toward the objective, Bacon told his executive officer ... and an experienced veteran, Sgt. Okie Blankenship, to fly to the company's position, survey the situation, and reason with the men. "Give them a pep talk and a kick in the butt."[30]

Quoting Blankenship, Arnett described the meeting that followed. The men said they were sick of the heat, the sudden firefights by day, and the mortaring by night. The sergeant responded that another company was down to fifteen men but still on the move. He later admitted that the comment had been a lie. When someone asked why that unit went on, he replied, "Maybe they have got something a little more than what you have got." One man began to run toward the sergeant with his fists raised. "Don't call us cowards," he howled. "We are not cowards." The sergeant coolly turned his back and walked away. Behind him, the men picked up their rifles and began to fall in. The company went back to the war.[31]

Military spokesmen denied that the entire company had balked. Instead, they said, only five men were involved, and they had yielded to good leadership. They added that Lieutenant Shurtz had been doing the job of a captain even though he had been in South Vietnam for only two weeks and lacked experience. Although he remained an officer in good standing, his superiors had relieved him of command even before they had learned of Arnett's dispatch.[32]

In the days that followed, MACV made Shurtz and Blankenship available to the press. Stressing that the actions of a few men should not detract from the good performance of the three thousand others who had participated in the operation, they supported the official interpretation. Reporters also gained access to the new company commander, who said the incident had been "something that came up on the spur of the moment and nothing that would last."[33]

Testing the truth of these assertions, newsmen went into the field to interview the men of Company A. The soldiers denied that only five of them were involved. Instead, they said, the entire unit had balked, and the five had emerged as spokesmen. The men were vague about their motives. Some cited fear, others inexperience, but most apparently agreed with one soldier who said that the incident had come about because "morale was at rock bottom."[34]

Reporters were torn between the military's point of view and their own misgivings. James Sterba remarked in the *New York Times* that the reason behind Company A's refusal to fight seemed simple to the soldiers he had interviewed,

Peter Arnett. (Peter Arnett)

and none of the explanations involved fighting for lost causes, antiwar sentiment, troop withdrawals, or the peace talks in Paris. The men always complained until the shooting started, one soldier told him. Word of it never reached the press or the public because a good company commander would "give you hell and then plead with headquarters to get you some relief. . . . But it's all a lot of bull—it really is." Richard Threlkeld of CBS News, James Reston of the *New York Times,* and Kenley Jones of NBC disagreed. "Soldiers, as well as civilians, can perceive the developing strategy of the U.S.: to disengage itself from the war in Vietnam," Jones said, "even though its side has not won and even though the other side has refused to make concessions. That point is not lost on the men . . . who are being asked to gamble their lives. . . . Some of them may decide the stakes are too high." The *Washington Star,* meanwhile, sided with the military. "There have been suggestions from some quarters," it stated in a 30 August editorial, "that . . . draftees serving in Vietnam . . . are unwilling to die in an admittedly unwinnable war. . . . [In fact,] there have been similar incidents in every conflict since the Punic Wars." David Lawrence of *U.S. News & World Report* blamed the press. The publication of Arnett's dispatch before the military had a chance to clarify what had happened, he said, had played into the hands of the Viet Cong, whose radio broadcasts had made ready propaganda of the episode. "Again and again," he added, "information is disclosed in the press which could later reduce our military effectiveness."[35]

None of the commentators except for veteran correspondent Neil Sheehan noted that the incident with Company A was a first. In earlier battles at Plei Me and the Ia Drang valley, Sheehan said, soldiers had seemed to accept their lot as bitter but necessary, a matter of duty. At Dak To, officers had shouted, "Airborne," and the men had called back, "All the way," as they rushed again and again into the enemy's bullets and grenades until 158 were dead and the North Vietnamese were driven from the summit. Nevertheless, Sheehan said, "there comes a time in some wars when the killing, or just the manner of dying, appears so senseless that even the obedient soldier . . . begins to question the meaning of his sacrifice." Whatever the explanations for Company A's refusal, he concluded, "men had suffered equally before and had not balked when ordered to endure more."[36]

Some editorial writers, ever supportive of the American soldier, warned that so isolated an incident had little meaning beyond its immediate context. Yet, only nine days later, the unheard of happened again. A second unit refused a lawful order to advance. And this time the ringleaders were not green, frightened enlisted men but experienced noncommissioned officers.[37]

Word of what had happened reached the press two months after the event, when UPI correspondent Tom Tiede revealed that a platoon from Company B, Second Battalion, Twenty-seventh Infantry, Twenty-fifth Infantry Division, had refused to move out on a routine patrol. The reporter told how the unit's twenty-one members, all with extensive combat experience, had refused their commander's order because they considered it unfair to have to go on another patrol. "I never did get those men to obey me," the officer said. "I tried but they just wouldn't go. I had to bring charges against all of them." Tiede added that the men had received very light sentences, leading to speculation that the military were so battered by accusations that they had begun to back away from unpleasant duties rather than risk confrontation.[38]

The incident was more complicated than the reporter had realized. The battalion had lost three of its commanders to wounds in four months, and a new company commander had just replaced an officer who had been relieved for cause. The turbulence that had accompanied these shifts had given rise to practices in the unit that were contrary to good order. For example, soldiers had come to believe that those with less than thirty days to go before returning home were exempt from participation in combat operations. When the new commander attempted to reinstate proper practice, they became upset. On the day of their refusal, when ordered individually to obey, nineteen had declined, but that evening, all had participated in a dangerous night ambush. In the end, the army had been lenient not because it feared confrontations but because of those extenuating circumstances and the men's exemplary performance before and after the event.[39]

Company B's refusal received little play in the press. By the time it appeared, the news was stale, and many major stories competed for attention, particularly news that members of the U.S. Americal Division had massacred some three hundred civilians at a village named My Lai in South Vietnam's I Corps Zone. The incident involving Company A, however, became a model for reporters. Spurred by Arnett and Faas's example, they remained on watch for new combat refusals in hopes of determining whether the patience of the American soldier was indeed wearing thin. The military, for their part, resented the attention. Putting loyalty to the institution they served first, they continued to assert that MACV's problems with drug abuse, race relations, and indiscipline were hardly as bad as media reports made them appear. The Saigon correspondents had already demonstrated, however, that the best of them, by virtue of their many contacts, sometimes had a better grasp of the war's unmanageable human essence than the policy makers who supposedly were in control.

13

My Lai and Other Atrocities

The Military Assistance Command's difficulties with morale had little effect at first on President Nixon's effort to rally support for his policies. The full extent of the drug problem had yet to become apparent, and racial incidents in South Vietnam were mild in comparison with the rioting and burning that had occurred in the United States following the assassination of Dr. Martin Luther King, Jr. The news, however, is never static. On 3 November 1969, shortly before the president issued his appeal to the silent majority, both CBS and NBC ran film reports purporting to show American infantrymen standing by while South Vietnamese troops abused or mutilated enemy prisoners. Then, on the morning before Vice President Agnew delivered his attack on television news, Seymour Hersh published the first detailed account of charges that American soldiers had massacred hundreds of South Vietnamese civilians at a hamlet near Da Nang named My Lai. In each of these cases, the unthinkable had become real. The carefully cultivated image of the good American soldier who sheltered orphans and distributed candy to children was falling into doubt.

On the surface, the two television reports seemed indisputable. Reported by Robert Hager, the NBC story showed an American major and lieutenant colonel making no move to stop the beating of a Viet Cong prisoner by South Vietnamese interrogators. The CBS story, narrated by Don Webster, was even more appalling. After showing a South Vietnamese soldier stabbing a prone North Vietnamese captive, Webster remarked that the atrocity had occurred in the presence of U.S. military personnel who made no effort to object. Both reports showed violations of the laws of war, which prohibit acts of violence against prisoners, and both were particularly unfortunate from the Nixon administration's standpoint because the White House had worked for months to highlight the abuse of American prisoners of war by North Vietnam.[1]

Responding immediately, the State Department instructed the U.S. mission in

Saigon to investigate. Since neither report had indicated the units involved or where and when the incidents had occurred, MACV contacted Hager and Webster for assistance. When both declined to cooperate on grounds that their sources required protection, the Defense Department contacted NBC and CBS to request copies of the filmed reports and all footage deleted during editing. There was a "general consensus," the agency's representatives noted in their letters to the networks, that the two reports did not represent continuous actions but were the products of clever splicing. NBC released its film. CBS declined. "I am sure that you understand," the president of CBS News, Richard S. Salant, responded, "that we must jealously guard our roles as journalists." Outtakes, "like a reporter's notebook, are sacrosanct."[2]

With NBC's films in hand, MACV readily established that the incident had occurred. The officers involved were disciplined. In the case of Webster's allegations, however, nothing could be done. The Defense Department blamed CBS for the stalemate, reaffirmed the conclusion that the report had been a montage, and suspended further inquiry until more information surfaced.[3]

The controversy over the two television stories was just beginning when Hersh published his article on the massacre at My Lai. Alerted by a telephone caller who had alleged that the army was court-martialing a lieutenant at Fort Benning for killing a large number of civilians, the reporter had confirmed the facts of the case through sources on Capitol Hill and had then interviewed the officer accused of the slayings, 1st Lt. William Calley.[4]

The report caused an international sensation but came as no surprise to the army. The service had first learned of the atrocity in April 1969, when Ronald Ridenhour, a veteran who had heard of the incident during his tour of duty in South Vietnam, had written letters to General Westmoreland and a number of congressmen and officials to request an investigation. Over the months that followed, the army's inspector general had confirmed that on 16 March 1968 members of Company C, First Battalion, Twentieth Infantry, Eleventh Brigade, of the Twenty-third Infantry Division (Americal), had murdered up to 350 South Vietnamese noncombatants. What especially disturbed Westmoreland was the possibility that a cover-up had occurred. General Abrams should have learned of what happened almost immediately, he asserted, but nothing had been reported, "not even the suspicion."[5]

When the full dimensions of what had happened became apparent, there was little inclination on the part of the Defense Department to hide anything. All concerned understood that the incident would sooner or later come to light, and that lies and circumlocutions would lead to allegations that the Pentagon had condoned an atrocity. Yet neither was Defense willing to incur self-inflicted wounds. Rather than make a forthright announcement, it held off until September, when the army filed charges against Calley. Then it released the news at Fort Benning in Georgia, where the trial was to take place, rather than in Washington, where the news media congregated and where the splash would have been greater.[6]

The maneuver succeeded too well. On 5 September, a public affairs officer at Fort Benning revealed during a briefing that Calley had been charged with offenses against an unspecified number of South Vietnamese civilians. Officials at the Defense Department braced for more questions, but none came. Although the AP picked up the story, the rest of the news media paid scant attention. It appeared the next day on page 2 of the *Washington Star* and page 11 of the *Atlanta Journal*, but the *Washington Post* waited until 7 September to publish it on page A14. The *New York Times* carried a shortened version the next day, on page 38. NBC's Huntley-Brinkley Report made a brief mention on 10 September, but no other stories appeared until 13 November, when Hersh's article finally broke across the United States.[7]

The two-month delay is difficult to explain. The Defense Department's low-key announcement was part of it, but four months prior to the army's news release, Ridenhour had offered his story to major newspapers and magazines, including *Life, Look, Newsweek, Harper's,* and *Ramparts.* Only *Ramparts* had shown an interest, and Ridenhour had ultimately rejected the offer because the appearance of his information in such a rabidly antiwar magazine might have tainted his story. His desire to write the article himself for a fee may have told against him in the eyes of editors. Yet even then, he had placed more than enough information on the record to prompt inquiries to the Pentagon from curious reporters. None came.

Hersh himself had difficulties. He contacted *Life* and *Look* to no avail before the antiwar Dispatch News Service agreed to carry his material. He later hypothesized that self-censorship on the part of the press may have been to blame. There was little market, he said, for atrocity stories about American troops. In addition, the American news media were far more inclined than foreigners at the time to give their countrymen the benefit of the doubt. Most reporters discounted as enemy propaganda allegations that American units had committed major war crimes in South Vietnam. Thus when Radio Hanoi had announced on 17 April 1968 that a brigade of the U.S. Eighty-second Airborne Division had recently slaughtered 501 civilians at My Lai, the Saigon correspondents accepted out of hand MACV'S response that the Eighty-second had been nowhere near the area.[8]

At first, official agencies continued to hope that they would be able to contain the story. MACV thus steered clear of acknowledging the names of the members of Calley's company, the number of the dead, and other details in order, it said, to preserve the rights of the accused and to curb pretrial publicity. On the side, it also released a captured enemy document whose authors had admitted that Communist forces were responsible for the massacres at Hue during the Tet offensive.[9]

The line held through 14 November, when the army announced that a second member of Calley's company, S.Sgt. David Mitchell, had been charged in connection with the incident. Then it began to give way. The next day, the service disclosed that Mitchell had been a squad leader in Calley's platoon and authorized the release of general details on the various investigations in progress. The general counsel of the army, Robert E. Jordan, then disclosed at a high-level news conference that nine current and fifteen former members of the Americal Division were under investigation, and the Defense Department confirmed that Calley had been accused of murdering approximately one hundred South Vietnamese civilians.[10]

A flood of revelations followed. The *Washington Post* reported on 20 November that the commander of the Eleventh Brigade, Col. Oran Henderson, had conducted a brief inquiry into a massacre at My Lai but that nothing had come of the investigation. On 24 November the CBS Evening News ran an interview with a former member of Calley's platoon, Paul Meadlo, who admitted remorsefully that he had killed ten or fifteen villagers himself. CBS was later criticized because it paid Dispatch News to arrange the interview. Photographs of the massacre by a combat correspondent, Ronald Haeberle, who had accompanied the assault on My Lai also appeared. Published on 20 November, they showed dead women, children, and old men scattered along the trails surrounding the hamlet. Haeberle had used his own camera at My Lai and had taken his pictures with him when he mustered out of the army. Keeping quiet until Hersh's story appeared, he sold the photos to the *Cleveland Plain Dealer, Life,* and a number of European publications.[11]

The South Vietnamese Ministry of Information responded to the flood by declaring that the allegations about My Lai were "completely untrue." President Thieu, for one, contended privately that since the people of My Lai sympathized with the Viet Cong and sometimes took hostile action against American forces by planting mines and setting booby-traps, it made perfect sense that some of them might have been killed during a U.S. operation. When Ambassador Bunker warned, however, that the announcement could only play into the hands of the war's opponents, Thieu went on record to stress his harmony with the American position.[12]

Editorial writers and commentators in the United States were not necessarily unsympathetic to Thieu's point of view. Declining to lay the blame squarely on the men of Company C, some underscored the brutalizing effects of the war and cited the massacre as an important reason for ending the conflict. Others compared My Lai to mass killings that had occurred at Dresden, Hiroshima, and Lidice during World War II, and most distinguished between murder as a national policy and the isolated act of a few soldiers. Conservative columnists, in particular, made much of the fact that Haeberle had profited from the sale of his pictures.[13] Kenneth Crawford of *Newsweek* warned that it would be one of the ironies of history if an outrage committed by a few soldiers exposed South

Dead villagers at My Lai. (Time-Life)

Vietnam to the "systematic massacre" that could be expected if Nixon withdrew American forces prematurely from the war. The *Wall Street Journal* reminded its readers that the North Vietnamese had practiced a policy of atrocity against civilians throughout the conflict. John Wheeler of the AP noted that the Communists had already murdered as many as three thousand noncombatants at Hue during the Tet offensive. "You can't look war in the face with the kind of emotional responses we use in the states," he added, quoting an officer he had met. "You would go mad."[14]

These stories notwithstanding, editorial writers across the country asked again and again why it had taken almost two years for the facts in the case to become known. The same question was much on the minds of officials within the army and the Defense Department. On 24 November the secretary of the army, Stanley Resor, announced the appointment of Lt. Gen. William R. Peers to explore the possibility that a cover-up had occurred. The credibility of official spokesmen had by then fallen so low, however, that the news only generated more controversy. Headlines trumpeted "Who Will Investigate the Investigators?" and the chairmen of both the House and the Senate Armed Services Committee announced that they would hold separate investigations of their own.[15]

Individual Americans, for their part, appear at first either to have greeted the news with disbelief or to have judged the incident in accord with their own commitment to the war. On 21 December the *Minneapolis Tribune* thus reported that 48 percent of the respondents in a statewide poll refused to believe that an atrocity had occurred, and that 11 percent more were undecided. The *Wall Street Journal,* meanwhile reported that, "to a man," those who sought an immediate end to the war affirmed that they were appalled by what had happened, but that a surprising number of those who supported the conflict contended that "war is war." By January, most Americans had accepted the reality of the massacre, but 55 percent contended that Calley was a scapegoat for officers higher up in the army.[16]

Concerned that the affair might damage the president, White House spokesmen moved early in the crisis to emphasize that the "alleged incident" had occurred during Lyndon Johnson's tenure and to refer all questions to the Department of Defense.[17] With that stance firmly established, they then began to reconsider the hard line they had adopted toward the news media. For some time, the president had been planning to augment Agnew's attacks on the press with a series of antitrust suits against journals and television networks that could be accused of monopolistic business practices and tax audits against news executives he considered enemies. There would be "no sacred cows," presidential adviser John Ehrlichman wrote at the time. Katherine Graham of the *Washington Post,* David Sarnoff of NBC, William Paley and Frank Stanton of CBS, and Arthur Sulzberger of the *New York Times* were all to feel the sting of the Internal Revenue Service.[18]

Whether the White House went forward with the tax audits is unknown, but with My Lai casting its shadow, the antitrust suits became less than desirable. "This case could develop into a major trial almost of the Nuremberg scope and could have a major effect on public opinion," the White House director of communications, Herbert Klein, told Haldeman on 21 November. " . . . I called [Attorney General] John Mitchell this morning and suggested that special care be taken that the Justice Department does not move in any actions which might be regarded as intimidation of the media during this particular period of time. He assured me he was . . . on top of it." In the end, the administration postponed its moves until the fall of 1971, when the furor over My Lai had died down.[19]

Although thoughtful articles and commentaries continued, news coverage of My Lai remained so heavy that at the end of November both the prosecutor and Calley's counsel asked Lt. Col. Reid Kennedy, the military judge in the case, to order reporters to back off. Kennedy warned the press to avoid stories that might prejudice the outcome of the case and instructed potential witnesses to avoid news interviews, but he declined to impose prepublication restraints. When reporters insisted on interviewing witnesses who were beyond military jurisdiction, he suggested that the aggrieved parties seek a ban on press coverage from a higher court. They petitioned the U.S. Court of Military Appeals, which rejected their request on 4 December. By then, the American Civil Liberties Union had itself grown concerned and called upon the army to dismiss all charges against Calley because, its representatives charged, the news media had rendered a fair trial for the lieutenant impossible.[20]

Although press coverage left much to be desired, the situation was hardly as simple as it seemed. Some of the defendants had contributed to the problem by playing to the press in order to gain public support. One of them, Calley's immediate superior at My Lai, Capt. Ernest Medina, would later charge that profiteering publishers exaggerated the massacre to sell newspapers. Yet Medina himself made so many statements to reporters prior to Kennedy's restraining order that the judge enjoined him specifically from giving interviews. Without Medina's support and that of other defendants, there would have been a much smaller story for reporters to tell and far fewer excesses.[21]

First Lieutenant William Calley (UPI/Bettman)

As it was, once American war crimes had become an issue, there was no way anyone could have kept the subject in check. Claims began to arise from every direction that other atrocities besides the one at My Lai had occurred. The *Chicago Sun-Times* printed pictures purporting to show an enemy prisoner falling to his death after being pushed from an American helicopter during an interrogation; Congressman Lionel Van Deerlin of California claimed that American servicemen had shot a number of civilians near Dong Tam in the Mekong delta; and Robert Kaylor of UPI alleged that the U.S. Ninth Infantry Division had wantonly killed many civilians through the "indiscriminate use of mass firepower" in the same region. Then, on 9 January, word surfaced in the press that a classified study by the Rand Corporation had confirmed that South Korean troops operating in South Vietnam had committed outrageous crimes against civilians.[22]

Recognizing that allegations would continue, Secretary Laird instructed the military services to investigate every atrocity story that surfaced and to acknowledge those that were true. Following these instructions, MACV verified a few of the stories but found many more to be false. In the case of Van Deerlin's story, on the one hand, the command confirmed that a platoon leader, acting on orders, had ordered his men to fire all their weapons across a canal into a group of occupied huts. Since the act resulted in several civilian casualties, the officers involved were charged and tried. The helicopter story, on the other hand, proved to be distorted. Although the episode had indeed occurred, investigators found that the supposed victim had been dead when loaded onto the aircraft. The soldier who had photographed the incident had passed copies of his pictures to another enlisted man, who had mailed them to his girlfriend along with a false account of what had happened. She, in turn, had given them to her brother, who had informed the press. In the end, the aircraft's commander received a reprimand.[23]

Although most of the allegations yielded readily to Laird's forthright policy, some were difficult to handle. Kaylor's article on the conduct of the Ninth Division in the Mekong delta was a case in point. It made little impression at the time, but it still asked an important question: Had American tactics in the delta contributed to an inhuman waste of civilian life? The Ninth Division's commander, Maj. Gen. Julian Ewell, claimed his unit had killed at most six thousand enemy in the delta rather than the thirty-three thousand Kaylor had counted, and he asserted emphatically that his unit had exercised stringent rules of engagement to avoid civilian casualties. He termed Kaylor's article "the biggest collection of malicious innuendo I have ever seen."[24]

While the reporter's numbers may have been incorrect, Ewell had in fact conceived of the conflict in the delta as a manufacturing operation—he called it "mass-production guerilla war"—and appears to have linked recognition for achievement within his command to the number of enemy neutralized. "With respect to awards for valor," one of his directives stated, "a reasonable rule of thumb is an award for . . . every enemy eliminated." Indeed, in one case, during the trial of a lieutenant accused of murdering an enemy captive, witnesses from the Ninth Division testified that the stress on body counts was so strong within the unit that at least one company had been informed it would not receive necessary supplies until it had killed more of the enemy.[25]

The results of these policies are open to interpretation. They may have led, on the one hand, to inflated body counts. On the other, officers may have decided to inflict as many casualties as they could upon the enemy and, in case of doubt, to shoot first. Pacification reports clearly chose the latter interpretation. "It was felt by advisory personnel," one province adviser stated in March 1970, "that the high body counts achieved by the 9th were not composed exclusively of active Viet Cong . . . [and that] many . . . bystanders were also eliminated." Whatever the validity of that conclusion, the uncertainties affixed to the division's record in the delta worked to the official advantage. When *Newsweek* reporter Kevin Buckley began to research Operation Speedy Express during 1971, MACV's public affairs officers provided statistics and answered questions but took refuge as well behind the "very limited records of the operation in question."[26]

The allegations of South Korean atrocities were even more difficult to avoid, particularly since the conclusions in an army study paralleled those in the one by Rand. On 9 January 1970, Terry Rambo, the researcher who had directed that project, informed reporters that he had uncovered evidence that South Korean soldiers, following a deliberate and systematic policy, had killed hundreds of civilians in South Vietnam. Rambo added that when he had attempted to pursue the matter, an officer at MACV had ordered him to drop it.[27]

Army investigators dismissed the methodology employed in both studies as "based on rumor and hearsay," but there were still complete reports on the subject in official files, some accompanied by gruesome photographs. In one case, the Korean government had admitted fault and had paid an indemnity, but in most it had denied responsibility. Under the circumstances, the United States had little choice when reporters pressed but to retreat behind the technicality that the Korean force in South Vietnam was a separate entity unconnected with the U.S. command.[28]

In the end, however, even the Korean atrocity story paled beside some of the revelations that continued to arise from My Lai. During February, for example, allegations appeared that a second company from the American Division had committed a similar atrocity. During March, claims arose that 60 percent of Calley's men had been chronic or occasional smokers of marijuana, leading to speculation that drug abuse may have been to blame for the massacre.[29]

The army denied that drugs were involved, but the story about the second atrocity appears to have been true. The commander of the First Platoon of Company B in Task Force Barker, 1st Lt. Thomas K. Willingham, was charged with war crimes in an incident involving the deaths of up to ninety women and children that occurred two days prior to the one at My Lai. The case was later dropped for lack of evidence, but General Peers never doubted that the episode had occurred. "It was," he said, "an almost total cover-up."[30]

Although the dismissal of charges in that case made it seem as though the army was attempting to hide the truth, there continued to be little inclination on the part of the military to hide anything. The facts were undeniable. Instead, what concerned officers was how best to minimize the damage. When the Defense Department decided to go forward with a press conference on the Peers commission's findings, for example, Peers wanted to use the word *massacre,* but public affairs officers sought to avoid the term lest it harm the army's image. The discussion had reached a deadlock, with Peers refusing to present a watered-down version of his conclusions and declining to appear, when a member of the general's staff suggested that he substitute the phrase *tragedy of major proportions* for *massacre.* When all concerned agreed to the compromise, the session went forward as scheduled.[31] In the end, Peers's instincts were better than those of the public affairs officers. Although criticism of the Army and its values followed in the press, many journalists were pleased that the service had addressed its problems so forthrightly. "The Army is probably the last place," remarked Frank Reynolds of ABC News, for one, where "those who have lost faith in the establishment . . . would expect to find this kind of soul searching."[32]

If the army had held its own, the contest with the press over atrocities dragged on. On 21 May 1970, responding to charges by syndicated columnist Richard Wilson that CBS was under investigation for fabricating horror stories about the war, Walter Cronkite resurrected the controversy over Don Webster's story on the stabbing of the Viet Cong captive by devoting half his broadcast to a rebuttal

Lieutenant General William R. Peers.
(S. L. A. Marshall Collection, U.S.
Army Military History Institute)

by Webster. Responding to Pentagon suggestions that the helicopters involved appeared to be Australian rather than American, the reporter conceded the possibility but noted that the markings on the aircraft resembled even more those of a U.S. assault helicopter squadron based in Tay Ninh Province. In the same way, MACV had claimed that it was unable to determine anything about the men who were supposedly present at the incident, but Webster asserted that CBS had readily identified the man who had done the stabbing. He was Sfc. Nguyen Van Mot, who had been named Soldier of the Year in 1969 for all regional forces in South Vietnam's III Corps Zone. The reporter interviewed Mot through an interpreter. The soldier admitted to stabbing his prisoner but claimed he had done so only after the man had reached for a weapon on the ground beside him. Webster conceded that there appeared to be an enemy rifle on the ground near the victim but added that Mot had stabbed the man a second time, when he was giving no resistance. The reporter then played one of the outtakes that CBS had declined to release. It showed the prisoner's body being mutilated. "The Pentagon may wish to believe this story never happened," Webster said, "but it did."[33]

Although CBS clearly believed that Webster's account was correct, the Defense Department refused to give in. Reinvestigating the incident, it concluded instead that the victim might well have been dead when stabbed, that the terrain on the film failed to match the area identified by Webster, and that American helicopters almost never accompanied the operations of South Vietnamese irregular troops. MACV's inspector general, Colonel Robert Cook, would later suggest that since Webster had narrated the story but had not been present when it was filmed, the whole affair may have been concocted by a freelance South Vietnamese cameraman intent upon selling his film to a major American network. Although Cook's reasoning carries weight—as Senator Fulbright alleged and General Sidle confirmed, MACV's own film production teams were sometimes tempted to fabricate stories—the issue will always remain unresolved. For MACV had been quick to attribute NBC's atrocity report to similar manipulation until subsequent information had established beyond a doubt that the episode had occurred.[34]

In the end, Webster's allegations were spectacular, but they made little impression in comparison with My Lai, which continued to unfold week by week. Over the next two years, the press documented every bend in the case, chronicling its ebb and flow and speculating on each new development.

During January 1970, for example, a series of clashes developed between the House Armed Services Committee and the army, when Congressman F. Edward Hebert of Louisiana, the chairman of a subcommittee examining My Lai, called witnesses who were also being interviewed by the army's Criminal Investigation Division. Hebert even threatened to use his power of subpoena if the army refused to allow certain witnesses to testify. More controversy followed when the committee's conclusions appeared. Noting that a tragedy of major proportions had indeed occurred, the probers charged that the cover-up was so extensive and involved so many individuals that it was unreasonable to conclude that it had been without plan or direction. The report evoked considerable comment in the press, most of it favorable to the subcommittee.[35]

The House Armed Services Committee generated more headlines in October, during the trial of Sergeant Mitchell, when the judge in the case ruled that under a law known as the Jencks Act, four witnesses for the prosecution could not testify unless defense lawyers received access to their comments before Hebert's subcommittee. Hebert and the committee's chairman, Congressman L. Mendel Rivers of South Carolina, refused to release their remarks on grounds that promises of confidentiality had been given to all witnesses. "These boys have tasted enough . . . persecution from the 'objective press,'" Rivers explained, " . . . and I'm not contributing anything to its continuation."[36] Confronted by the committee's refusal, military prosecutors called only three witnesses and were unable to confirm that Mitchell had killed civilians at My Lai. The sergeant went free.[37]

Worse was to follow. The commander of Fort McPherson, Georgia, Lt. Gen. Albert O'Connor, who had custody of many of the defendants in the case, dropped the charges against six on grounds of insufficient evidence. The rest were tried by court-martial and declared not guilty. Of the twelve officers accused in connection with the cover-up, none, except for the Eleventh Brigade's commander, Col. Oran Henderson, ever came to trial. Between June 1970 and January 1971, Lt. Gen. Jonathan O. Seaman, commander, First U.S. Army headquarters at Fort Meade, Maryland, dismissed the charges against them because the allegations were, to his mind, unsupported by the evidence. As for the American's commander, Maj. Gen. Samuel W. Koster, Seaman noted that only two of seven charges seemed to have any foundation. Although he issued a letter of censure, as a result, he dismissed all charges against the general in light of the officer's "long and honorable career," and because Koster was not guilty of any "intentional abrogation of responsibilities."[38]

The army recognized that the decision posed large public relations problems, but it made no comment at the time. Seaman was the commander in charge and had final say under military law. Later, in May, after a thorough review, the service registered its unhappiness with Seaman's decision by taking the only action left to it. Secretary Resor demoted Koster to the rank of brigadier general and stripped him of his Distinguished Service Medal.[39]

Seaman's move caused an uproar in the press. Robert MacCrate, the lawyer who had served as Peers's civilian adviser during the army's investigation of the cover-up, told reporters that the decision had the effect of clearing an officer while his subordinates were still under investigation. Meanwhile, during a long speech from the floor of the House, one of the congressmen who had served on Hebert's subcommittee, Samuel S. Stratton of New York, charged that Seaman had acted in response to pressures from the Pentagon, which had obviously decided to "let General Koster off the hook." The congressman added in a subsequent article for the *New York Times* that the "steady progression of dropped charges" made it unlikely that the truth about My Lai would ever emerge.[40]

Stratton's contention that the generals wanted light punishment for a brother officer was understandable, but Peers himself, while disagreeing vehemently with Seaman's decisions, saw little to commend in the allegation. General Westmoreland was very sensitive to such matters, he wrote, "and, knowing the moral code of Secretary Resor, I do not believe he would have had any part of it." Whatever happened, if it happened, occurred "without their knowledge and approval."[41]

Although many of the defendants went free, no command intervention occurred in Calley's case, and the judge refused, as was his right, to allow the Jencks Act to govern the testimony of essential witnesses. As a result, on 29 March 1971, a military jury found the lieutenant guilty of premeditated murder, and the judge sentenced him to life imprisonment at hard labor.

The verdict caused as much turmoil for the army as Seaman's decision on Koster. Public opinion surveys found that by a score of 36 to 35 percent, with 29 percent undecided, a plurality of Americans disagreed with the ruling. Eighty-one percent believed that other atrocities on the scale of My Lai had occurred, and 43 percent asserted that they would follow orders to shoot civilians suspected of aiding the enemy. Meanwhile, Senator Abraham A. Ribicoff of Connecticut called upon President Nixon to overturn the sentence; members of the Illinois, Kansas, and Arkansas legislatures introduced resolutions seconding the senator; and Governor Jimmy Carter of Georgia called upon motorists to drive with their headlights lit on 5 April to show support for the soldier in Vietnam.[42]

Although many officers, according to *Baltimore Sun* correspondent Charles Corddry, were pleased with the verdict because it had reasserted military discipline, President Nixon decided that the mood in the country required action. Invoking his constitutional powers as commander in chief, he removed Calley from the stockade at Fort Benning at the beginning of April, placed him under house arrest on base, and announced his own intention to review the case, once it had gone as far as it could in the courts.[43]

Official spokesmen issued a white paper summarizing the legal rationale behind all of the government's moves in the case but made no comment on the president's decision. On the side, however, army lawyers drew up an eloquent list of arguments against presidential intervention. The evidence was neither ambiguous nor doubtful, they said. Thirteen thousand lieutenants had served in Vietnam since 1965. None had ever done anything approaching the enormity of Calley's crime. It stood "alone in infamy." The press agreed. "How Can Justice Be Impartial," a headline in the *Philadelphia Inquirer* asked, "With Nixon in Calley's Corner?" Often supportive of the president, the *Washington Star* added that "the day this country goes on record as saying that unarmed civilian men, women and children of any race are fair game . . . will be the day that the United States forfeits all claims to any moral leadership of this world."[44]

White House staff members, for their part, recognized almost immediately that the president had made a mistake, but they counseled patience in any attempt to undo the damage. The country was beginning to turn on the Calley issue, Patrick Buchanan said. "We should catch opinion as it shifts. Get in front of it—not reaming Calley, but defending the Army, the process of law in this country, our belief that excesses in combat will not be tolerated—and giving a good scourging to the guilt-ridden, war-crime crowd that is on the other side of our fence."[45]

Following his advisers' suggestions, Nixon waited until 29 April to defend his actions. He then observed at a news conference that many Americans had been concerned that Calley might not receive due justice. The announcement of his review, he said, had served to cool the issue down.[46] The news media had little good to say about the president's remarks, but that made hardly any difference. Over the months that followed, public attention shifted away from Calley to the trials of Medina and Henderson. In the end, both officers were cleared.[47]

The Calley case hung on for four more years. On 20 August 1972, the commanding general at Fort Benning reduced the lieutenant's sentence from life imprisonment to twenty years. More than a year later, on 21 December 1973, Calley lost the final appeal of his conviction. With only sentencing reviews remaining, his lawyers took the case into civilian courts to argue that he had never received a fair trial. On 27 February 1974, a U.S. district court judge freed him on bail pending final determination of his sentence. On 16 April, the secretary of the army, Resor's successor, Howard Callaway, reduced Calley's sentence to ten years, making him eligible for parole in six months. President Nixon in turn announced on 4 May that he had reviewed the sentence and deemed no further action necessary. Calley then entered the federal prison at Fort Leavenworth, Kansas, to serve the remainder of his sentence.

The lieutenant's lawyers pressed on. As a result of their efforts, on 25 September 1974, the U.S. district court in Columbus, Georgia, reversed the lieutenant's conviction on grounds of massive, adverse pretrial publicity. The court devoted two-thirds of its 132-page written opinion to a critique of media coverage, noting in particular the way reporters had continued to interview witnesses despite the protestations of the judge. The army, for its part, rejected the verdict out of hand, refused to release Calley, and appealed.

On 10 September 1975, the U.S. Fifth Circuit Court of Appeals in New Orleans found against Calley by a vote of 8 to 5. Any harm the lieutenant might have suffered from adverse press coverage, the majority asserted, had been more than offset by the trial court's scrupulous attention to detail and its care in selecting a jury. The five dissenting justices agreed but argued that the House Armed Services Committee, by refusing to release the testimony of important witnesses, had withheld crucial evidence that might have turned the jury against the government's case. By then Calley was home on parole.

Although the court, in effect, found in favor of the press and the army by upholding the verdict, neither institution came out of the affair looking good. The dismissal of charges against Koster and all of the high officers in the case except for Henderson marred the image of the army for years to come. Meanwhile, the continuous scrambling of reporters for every scrap of information on the case made it seem as though the press was out to make every last dollar it could from the issue, whatever the needs of the nation.

Appearances notwithstanding, neither the army nor the press had, in fact, done that poorly. Although more than willing to avoid self-inflicted wounds, the service had been forthright in its handling of the case. Seaman's failure to prosecute Koster and the others may have indicated personal prejudice on his part, but it is questionable whether the evidence existed to find any of them guilty. Even the two strongest cases, against Medina and Henderson, proved inadequate in the end. As for the press, the overenthusiasm of some reporters and the judgmental nature of some commentaries to the contrary, much of what the public read and watched about the case was factual and undistorted. Indeed, with antiwar sentiment running high in the country and the war's supporters digging in, the massacre was bound to become a major political issue. In that light, there was no right way to tell the story. Whatever a reporter said was bound to offend someone.

14

Incursion into Cambodia

The My Lai massacre harmed the image of the war, but it was hardly the only threat to President Nixon's effort to retain public support for the conflict. As a result of American withdrawals and the Vietnamization program, the antiwar movement seemed lethargic, but its leaders were looking for an issue to reenergize the effort. If they could find one, they might be able to speed up withdrawals and deny Nixon the face-saving settlement he sought.[1]

The word from South Vietnam was also less than encouraging. Intelligence estimates indicated that although the intensity of the war had subsided, the enemy's confidence remained high. Meanwhile, the flow of enemy supplies through Laos appeared greater than in previous years; the Phoenix program had failed to weaken the Viet Cong's network of subversives; the government's main bulwark in the countryside, its irregular forces, remained uneven in quality; and the next set of American withdrawals promised to cut deeply into the bone and sinew of allied fighting power. These assessments paralleled the reporting of the Saigon correspondents, who noted the continuing corruption of South Vietnam's officer corps, the poor esprit and fighting ability of the nation's armed forces, and the fact that Americans could not continue to fill the gaps that resulted.[2]

The commander in chief, Pacific, Admiral McCain, and General Abrams were more upbeat. While conceding that the Communists had advantages, McCain, in particular, emphasized that many of them grew from the enemy's possession of sanctuaries in Cambodia and the supplies and armaments that flowed with impunity into South Vietnam through the Cambodian port at Sihanoukville. The situation would continue, McCain told General Wheeler in January 1970, until the United States took action.[3]

Wheeler agreed but did nothing. Cambodia's ruler, Prince Sihanouk, had overlooked American B-52 attacks on the sanctuaries and was allowing his nation's press to highlight North Vietnamese violations of his nation's neutrality. It seemed possible, in that light, that he might break with the Communists and pursue genuine neutrality.[4]

McCain continued to push for action, calling for "plausibly deniable covert operations," if that was what it took, to destroy the enemy's supply system and the corrupt Cambodian officials who were profiting from the bribes it generated.[5] Before any decision could be made, however, the Cambodians themselves acted. Increasingly concerned about the Communist presence in Cambodia, the nation's prime minister, Lon Nol, backed by other government ministers, took advantage of Sihanouk's absence in Paris to institute currency reforms that cut the Communists off from money they needed to support their resupply effort. Then, between 8 and 11 March, with government connivance, rioters sacked the North Vietnamese and Viet Cong embassies during anti-Communist demonstrations in Phnom Penh. When Sihanouk attempted to save face by refusing to meet with government emissaries and began to threaten Lon Nol and his supporters, the Cambodian National Assembly removed him as chief of state and installed Lon Nol in his place.[6]

These developments prompted a reassessment by U.S. policy makers. At first, thinking centered on what the United States could do to assist Cambodia by providing advice and support to its armed forces. Then, on 25 March, President Nixon instructed the Joint Chiefs to draft plans for a U.S. or South Vietnamese assault into Cambodia to relieve pressure on Phnom Penh if the Communists attacked the city. Three days later, Admiral McCain suggested that Nixon use the opportunity to neutralize the enemy's sanctuaries.[7]

On 30 March, at the president's request, General Abrams submitted plans for nearly simultaneous, U.S.–South Vietnamese operations against enemy bases just to the west of Saigon in Cambodia's Svay Rieng Province, the so-called Parrot's Beak, and in a Cambodian region known as the Fishhook, some seventy-five miles to the north of Saigon, near Loc Ninh. Besides disrupting any threat to Phnom Penh and demolishing the enemy's logistics, the operation promised to disrupt the enemy's Central Office for South Vietnam (COSVN), located in the Fishhook, which coordinated Communist operations in the southern portions of South Vietnam.[8]

Although the State Department received no formal word of the planning that was occurring until much later, Abrams informed the chief of the South Vietnamese Joint General Staff, General Cao Van Vien, who initiated discussions with the Cambodian military. Within a short time, Cambodia and South Vietnam began occasional joint operations along the border. Although the South Vietnamese at first confined their activities to providing artillery and air support, by the end of March their forces, minus American advisers, were attacking across the border. One battalion penetrated three kilometers into Cambodia, where it claimed fifty-three enemy dead.[9]

The attacks alarmed the White House, which agreed to condone them only if they occurred at low levels after careful coordination with the Cambodians. The

South Vietnamese troops enter Cambodia. (Stars and Stripes Collection, U.S. Army Military History Institute)

restriction, however, carried little weight. On 5 April, a South Vietnamese armored cavalry contingent charged into Cambodia along with two battalions of infantry. Although the assault uncovered a trove of enemy documents and weapons, it agitated Laird, who believed the attacks would fire opposition at home. Informed of the secretary's concern, Abrams suggested that "we should not talk with [the] press about these operations" in order to avoid embarrassing Lon Nol.[10]

If Abrams truly believed that silence would obscure the attacks, he was mistaken. Over the days that followed, so many newsmen moved into the Cambodian countryside in search of action that it seemed, at times, as Glenn Currie of the *Washington Daily News* remarked, that there were as many newsmen and photographers present as Cambodian soldiers. The reporters took many risks. Two of them, Sean Flynn and Dana Stone, freelancers on assignment for *Time* and CBS News, disappeared while traveling a remote country road. Fifteen more followed over the next thirty days. Among the few ever to return were Richard Dudman of the *St. Louis Post-Dispatch* and Elizabeth Pond of the *Christian Science Monitor*. By the end of the war in 1975, indeed, a total of twenty-five correspondents would be listed as missing or dead in Cambodia.[11]

The reporters who remained had little difficulty finding out what was happening. A district chief in Svay Rieng Province, for example, confirmed that South Vietnamese units were entering Cambodia. In the same way, when the Cambodians, in an outburst of xenophobia and fear, massacred thousands of ethnic Vietnamese living in their country and drove many more into South Vietnam, correspondents counted the bloated bodies floating in the Mekong River and reported everything.[12]

Although what had happened would have come out anyway, whatever the restrictions imposed by government, official spokesmen were at first no more candid than they had to be. When General Wheeler authorized special B-52 strikes in Cambodia, he ordered public affairs officers to respond to questions with a cover story that characterized the operations as a response to threats against American forces in South Vietnam. In the same way, when newsmen discovered that the South Vietnamese were shipping captured enemy arms to Cambodia and queried the U.S. mission in Phnom Penh, official spokesmen denied everything. As late as 22 April, when the South Vietnamese commander in III Corps, Lt. Gen. Do Cao Tri, asked how to counter negative press coverage, his American advisers encouraged him to deny that his forces were engaging in cross-border operations.[13]

With time, all concerned realized that the approach was counterproductive and gave ground. Rather than deny outright that they were operating in Cambodia, South Vietnamese spokesmen adopted a policy of no comment. White House Press Secretary Ron Ziegler, meanwhile, admitted that captured enemy arms were going to Cambodia. He justified the move as an attempt to cope with an emergency.[14]

The move to candor notwithstanding, reporters got little more than they had before. U.S. field commands near the South Vietnamese border with Cambodia, for example, willingly transported reporters to their fire bases. Yet those journalists who made the trip learned quickly that they might be detained by the South Vietnamese if they moved off of American positions into Vietnamese-controlled territory. The news stories that resulted were predictable, laying almost as much importance upon the effort to give operations in Cambodia a low profile as they did on the fighting itself. A report by CBS News on 17 April was typical. In it, a newsman confronted an American military policeman barring the way into Cambodia. "ARVNs [South Vietnamese Army troops] can go into Cambodia but no GI's, no civilians, no Americans," the soldier said. "But we have ARVN press cards," the reporter responded. "That doesn't mean anything. You are an American citizen. . . . [The Vietnamese] don't want anybody in there right now."[15]

As the operations continued, the Nixon administration was upbeat, asserting in public that enemy force levels had declined in South Vietnam. Privately, it was much more somber. Intelligence reports reaching the White House indicated that the enemy had responded to Lon Nol's moves by systematically cutting all of the major roads and waterways leading into Phnom Penh. Massive intervention, according to Admiral McCain, appeared to be the only remedy.[16]

On 23 April, President Nixon approved a plan submitted by Abrams for a large-scale South Vietnamese attack into the Parrot's Beak supported, if necessary, by American tactical aircraft and artillery but involving no U.S. ground forces beyond the few necessary to coordinate air attacks if they occurred. In order to maintain the lowest possible profile for what some would inevitably interpret as an escalation of the war, the White House for a time considered banning not only reporters but also public relations personnel from any contact with the operation. Realizing that such measures would cause more problems than they solved, the president backed away from the approach, but the press guidance that went to MACV was still designed to keep a tight hold on word of what was happening. "It is hoped," Admiral Moorer told Abrams, "that publicity can be handled in as low [a] key as possible . . . [and that everything] practicable will be done to prevent . . . media representatives from accompanying forces."[17]

General Abrams declined to make any changes in MACV's normal handling of the press on grounds that actions of the sort would prompt questions. Instead, he said, reporters who requested information on American participation in the operation would be greeted with no comment until the South Vietnamese decided to reveal what was happening. Then the press would receive a relatively complete picture of what was going on.[18]

Although the president had decided in favor of a South Vietnamese operation, he remained troubled about committing American troops. "I have been enjoined," General Wheeler thus told Abrams privately, alluding to the abortive U.S. attempt to launch an invasion of Cuba in 1961, "to reiterate the president's concern that, if the operation fails, he will be subjected to the same kind of criticism evoked by the Bay of Pigs." Even so, Nixon was intrigued by the idea of somehow dealing a telling blow to the enemy. "During the course of our discussions," Wheeler told Abrams, "on several occasions the highest authority [Nixon] spoke of: the need to get the job done using whatever is necessary to do so; . . . use all the force necessary; if we get caught with our hands in the cookie jar we must be sure to get the cookies, etc."[19]

In the end, on 26 April, concerned that the objective was too important to place sole reliance on the South Vietnamese, Nixon decided to launch a double incursion. South Vietnamese forces would enter the Parrot's Beak as planned, but a combined U.S.–South Vietnamese force would probe the Fishhook. To deflect criticism, the president specified that American forces were to penetrate no more than thirty kilometers into Cambodia and that U.S. spokesmen were to lay heavy stress upon South Vietnamese portions of the operation. Even if the attack went poorly, all talk was to be of success.[20]

The decision was controversial from the start. Westmoreland opposed a large American troop commitment because it seemed unnecessary, and Abrams appears to have wanted the troops employed selectively, against only the most lucrative targets. Informed of the decision a day after the president made it, Secretary of State William P. Rogers and Laird also objected.[21]

At a stormy meeting on 27 April, the two attempted to change the president's mind. In return for potentially small gains, Rogers said, the operation exposed U.S. forces to the risk of severe casualties. As for any chance that the operation could neutralize COSVN, the headquarters was so widely dispersed that even a knockout blow would fail to silence it for long. Laird added that if the assault sparked widespread opposition in the United States, it might only give North Vietnam an excuse to delay serious negotiations. Since the enemy could adjust his base areas and replace combat losses quickly, and since the plan for the operation had already been leaked to him, he had the sort of advantages that could inflict many casualties on the attackers. In response, President Nixon concentrated on Rogers's remarks about COSVN. He understood, he said, that the headquarters was composed of many small bureaus spread over a large geographic area and that each of its cells had a backup in case of disaster, but none of that made much difference to him. For without the search for COSVN as justification, he was convinced that neither the preservation of the Lon Nol regime nor the attack on the sanctuaries would carry enough weight in the eyes of the American public to compensate for the increase in casualties that the operation might entail.[22]

With Laird's and Rogers's objections out of the way, the South Vietnamese attack into the Parrot's Beak began on the evening of 28 April. Since the president wanted to use a televised speech he planned for the evening of 30 April to set the tone for the operation, the press release that accompanied the attack contained few details. It specified only that the incursion was designed to save South Vietnamese and American lives by destroying important enemy bases, that the troops were under orders to preserve Cambodian lives and property, and that all forces would return to South Vietnam in due course.[23]

In an attempt to reassure reporters, who would inevitably turn to unreliable sources for information that the government failed to supply, the Defense Department issued a communiqué designed to show that it had their best interests at heart. Although pool arrangements would probably be necessary and the South Vietnamese would continue to have jurisdiction over areas under their control, it said, the press would have access to the American personnel supporting the attack. The South Vietnamese commander in the Parrot's Beak, Lt. Gen. Do Cao Tri, for his part, authorized some thirty newsmen to accompany his forces.[24]

The reactions of the press and of many in Congress were predictable. Ignoring the avowal that the troops would return to South Vietnam in due course, news reports persisted in describing the operation as an invasion. If the attack was necessary to protect " 'free world forces' in Vietnam," the *New York Times* avowed, "how long will it be before we are told that American troops must move into Cambodia to protect the American advisers and the 'free world forces' that are now there?" In Congress, meanwhile, leading members of both parties vowed to cut off funds for American operations in Cambodia, and even some supporters of the war were cautious. Senator John Stennis of Mississippi, for one, spoke in favor of the president's decision but still made it clear that he opposed the provision of extensive military aid to Cambodia's government.[25]

Aware that the news media and Congress would be even more critical once a large American force became involved, General Wheeler instructed Abrams to play down the U.S. role and to focus on South Vietnamese contributions. In order to emphasize the importance of the sanctuaries, he said, MACV was to provide "thorough pictorial coverage of these base areas once we get into them, to include condemning pictures of enemy installations, caches, captured materiel, documents, etc., which can be used to validate the impression we wish to convey."[26]

On the morning of 30 April, in preparation for the president's speech that evening, columnists supportive of administration policy such as James J. Kilpatrick, Holmes Alexander, and Roscoe Drummond received advance notification that the president's remarks would be important. White House staffers, meanwhile, prepared fact sheets for distribution to sympathetic opinion makers, advertisements for newspapers across the country, mass mailings to Americans who had supported administration programs in the past, and lists of prominent newsmen who were to receive calls after the speech.[27]

The president's remarks themselves were carefully crafted to justify the incursion to the widest possible audience. Although the bulk of the fighting would be in the hands of the South Vietnamese, Nixon said, a combined American–South Vietnamese force would be looking for COSVN, a "key control center . . . occupied by the North Vietnamese and Viet Cong for 5 years in blatant violation of Cambodia's neutrality." The move was "not an invasion" but a necessary extension of the Vietnam War designed to protect American lives and to guarantee the success of Vietnamization. Although it involved political risks, whether the Republican party gained in the coming November elections was "nothing, compared to the lives of 400,000 brave Americans fighting for . . . peace and freedom in Vietnam."[28]

Following the speech, Defense Department spokesmen attempted to counteract the president's overemphasis on COSVN by pointing out to reporters that the headquarters was an elusive target whose personnel rarely occupied any position for long. They also stressed that the main justification for the operation was the threat the sanctuaries posed to American lives. These assertions notwithstanding, the effort to find COSVN so appealed to the press that reporters made it an important gauge of the incursion's success.[29]

There were other problems with the president's announcement. Nixon believed, for example, that the incursion would do significant damage to the enemy, but he may have been too optimistic. As General Westmoreland pointed out after a meeting at the Pentagon on 1 May, the area involved was enormous; the days of good weather that remained before the monsoons began were limited; and General Abrams lacked the troops, helicopters, and logistics to do a thorough job within the time allotted. In the same way, although the move into Cambodia might have been logical two years earlier, it was no longer politically feasible. Shortly after it began, indeed, when Secretary Laird met with congressional leaders to explain the decision, the president's strongest allies stood by him, but many other stalwart Republicans broke ranks. As a result, it soon became clear that the Senate might pass a measure proposed by Senators John Sherman Cooper of Kentucky and Frank F. Church of Idaho to cut off funding for future American involvement in Cambodia.[30]

The press also voiced concern. *Chicago Today* commended Nixon for his courage in taking a "politically suicidal step," and the *Atlanta Journal* declared the move the "only honorable course," but the *Cleveland Plain Dealer* labeled the president's speech a "maudlin appeal to patriotism," the *New York Post* added that the president was leading the nation down "another dangerous dead-end road," and *Long Island Newsday* termed the attack "utterly pointless." Meanwhile, the editors of the normally hawkish *Chicago Tribune* seemed to have been torn between their misgivings and a desire to support administration policy. Although they later welcomed the incursion as an attempt "to protect the lives of our men," they failed to make any remark at all on the day the attack began.[31]

Over the weeks that followed, President Nixon attempted to muster all of the resources at his command to marshal support to his side, but he found the task daunting, in part because of the Saigon correspondents. As a group, the reporters present in South Vietnam at the time were far more opinionated than those of the past. Although a majority remained concerned with telling all sides of the story, the views of some were very strong, both for and against the attack. An influential minority, often those with lengthy service in South Vietnam and strong connections to the military, were elated when the operation began. Many newcomers, younger and more finely attuned to the dissent spreading in the United States, tended to question it. Whatever their points of view, however, most reporters followed Nixon's lead and judged the operation by its success in finding COSVN. They also kept watch for war crimes and for poor morale among the troops.[32]

Officials in Washington were well aware of the news media's concerns and warned MACV to be alert for any opportunity to reduce the operation's impact on the American public. Abrams was to do what he could to give the South Vietnamese maximum exposure and to see to it that his troops observed proper procedures in dealing with Cambodian civilians. Since undue emphasis on casualties might affect American public opinion, MACV was to refrain from releasing statistics on killed and wounded in Cambodia and was to combine the numbers with those for the operation as a whole. The command was also to counter stories rising in the press that some of the troops were less than enthusiastic about entering Cambodia by quietly emphasizing that the operation had "buoyed the spirit of the troops."[33]

Abrams did as he was told but also took pains to follow established policy in handling the press. Although some South Vietnamese commanders barred reporters from accompanying their forces, he provided them with as much access as he could. At his instruction, MACV organized special flights to move correspondents near the fighting and arranged for couriers to transport television news film to Saigon. Aware, as well, that the destruction of COSVN would be a major plus in the eyes of the press, he also exerted every effort to obliterate the headquarters. One of his B-52 strikes came close, but the enemy received at least seven hours' advance notice of the attack and was able to escape. Enemy prisoners of war would later reveal that their forces sometimes learned of B-52 strikes up to twenty-four hours in advance, long before the bombers had even left the ground.[34]

As the incursion progressed, Abrams likewise attempted to impose common sense upon suggestions he was receiving from Washington. He thus refused to participate in a news conference requested by the Defense Department that might have been interpreted by reporters as an attempt to massage the image of the operation. He also declined to underscore the high morale of his troops and allowed nature to take its course. As a result, reporters in the field encountered unhappy soldiers, but they also noted others who genuinely believed, as Frank Reynolds of ABC News observed, that the United States was at last doing something to shorten the war.[35]

The Nixon administration's attempt to orchestrate public acceptance of the incursion had little effect on the American people. Some 51 percent of those interviewed by the Gallup poll rallied to the president's side when Nixon announced the incursion. Yet, when pollsters switched to questions that omitted the role of the president, 53 percent approved the dispatch of weapons to Cambodia but disapproved by 58 to 28 percent of sending troops. Harris polls revealed similar reservations, and a plurality even avowed that it believed Nixon had started another Vietnam War. Discontent was particularly apparent among the young. Seventy-six percent of college students criticized the president's handling of the war, and 67 percent asserted that his administration was out of touch with the mood of America. Asked to react to a comment Nixon had made that student protesters were little more than "bums," the young, whether or not enrolled in college, rejected the claim by a score of 60 to 36 percent.[36]

During the week that followed Nixon's announcement, enough violence flared on America's college campuses to prompt several state governors to order out the National Guard. On 4 May, at Kent State University in Ohio, one of those units reacted to the taunts and rock throwing of protesters by firing into a crowd. Four students were killed, all of them unoffending bystanders. By 7 May, student strikes had occurred on 441 of America's college campuses, and demonstrators were converging on the nation's capital.[37]

As disorder spread across the country, measures to repeal the Gulf of Tonkin Resolution or to cut off funding for the war surfaced in the House of Representatives. Most failed to gain much of a following, but the Cooper-Church amendment to cut off funds for the incursion gained momentum. In an attempt to dampen the passions that were beginning to rise, President Nixon announced on 5 May that he would keep American forces in Cambodia within twenty-one miles of the South Vietnamese border and withdraw them within three to seven weeks.[38]

The president's assurances fell short for Secretary Laird. Intent on reducing the American presence in Cambodia, he announced on 12 May that several thousand American troops had already left the country and that more would depart within the week. Only the arrival of General Haig from Washington slowed the withdrawal. As Haig later explained to Kissinger:

> Abrams . . . has been told to reduce US presence in sanctuaries and to provide comfortable cushion to ensure all forces are out by June 30. I gave him clear picture of President's thinking. This guidance arrived just in time since he was preparing response to SecDef containing specific plan for withdrawal of all US forces. . . . Discussions with Abrams's staff also confirm they were under impression US forces should be withdrawn as early as practicable.[39]

Many of the pressures that afflicted Abrams reached down to his officers in the field. Informed abruptly, for example, to move forces into Cambodia's Rotanokiri Province, the U.S. commander in the II Corps Zone, Lt. Gen. Arthur S. Collins, Jr., recognized that the president might have to pull the troops back before they could accomplish anything. He pushed his commanders to cross the border before all preparations were complete, and in his haste caused the troops to outrun their fuel supplies. As luck would have it, a large group of reporters then arrived to cover the operation. "Well," Collins remarked later, "with . . . all these soldiers lying around the airstrip . . . [the newsmen] just had a field day. . . . Naturally the soldiers told them that we didn't have enough fuel." Adding an air of crisis to the situation, one of the platoons that reached Cambodia lost several men to enemy fire. The resulting news stories, describing fuel shortages, casualties, and swirling clouds of red dust, prompted Abrams to travel to Collins's headquarters at Pleiku, where he arrived, according to Collins, in a billow of cigar smoke, "grim and glowering."[40]

The Saigon correspondents missed little. Some learned from Lon Nol himself that the United States had failed to consult with Cambodia's leaders before committing troops to the country, and Max Frankel of the *New York Times* revealed that both Rogers and Laird had opposed the attack. Correspondents also uncovered profound divisions within the U.S. embassy in Saigon, where usually circumspect diplomats were freely criticizing the incursion in private conversations with correspondents.[41]

A number of favorable reports appeared, particularly when U.S. forces uncovered a vast enemy complex in Cambodia filled with tons of weapons and ammunition. The effect of these stories, however, was often ruined by other reports that brought up the controversies surrounding the operation. In one case, following a story by CBS reporter George Syvertsen on the ammunition dump, a second story appeared showing Gary Shepard interviewing a soldier about to enter Cambodia. The trooper indicated that he would follow orders only to avoid a bad-conduct discharge. In another instance, a soldier about to depart for Cambodia responded to what some officers considered a newsman's leading question by remarking that whether or not he obeyed the order to enter Cambodia would depend on what the rest of his unit did. In that case, General Westmoreland suggested that MACV withdraw the offending reporter's accreditation, but Daniel Henkin demurred. He might consider imposing restrictions on interviews prior to the commencement of an operation, he told the general, but reporters would replay a disaccreditation "hour by hour. . . . We've got to wince and let it fly by."[42]

In fact, however ill-advised, the reporter's question was perfectly logical in context. For at a time when violent protests were occurring in the United States, a few genuine combat refusals were also occurring in South Vietnam. In one, an infantryman protesting the incursion bound himself with a rope and then sat in the middle of a heavily traveled road. In another, widely reported by the press, six soldiers announced their refusal to go into combat but later joined their unit. All things considered, that reporters would have failed to bring up the subject was simply unthinkable.[43]

Conditions were different on 7 May, when AP reporter George Esper broke MACV'S guidelines for the press by revealing not only that a flotilla of American and South Vietnamese gunboats was about to move up the Mekong River into Cambodia but also the number and armament of the craft involved. Esper would later contend that South Vietnam's foreign minister, Tran Van Lam, had announced the operation, but MACV's chief of public affairs, Col. Joseph F. H. Cutrona, insisted there was a great difference between Lam's announcement and the fine details Esper had provided. It all meant little to the reporter. By the time the disaccreditation took effect, he had departed for the United States on leave.[44]

A story broken by AP reporter Peter Arnett and Leon Daniels of UPI was more difficult to handle. Describing an attack by the U.S. Eleventh Armored Cavalry on the Cambodian town of Snoul, a major transshipment point for enemy supplies moving down the Ho Chi Minh Trail, the two charged that several civilians had been killed in air strikes preceding the incident and that the regiment had looted the town. Arnett, in particular, described how one GI had emerged from a Chinese grocery clutching a bottle of brandy and how "another broke into a watch shop and came out with a handful of wrist watches." A third "lashed a Honda [motorcycle] to the top of his A-CAV [armored personnel carrier] before his troop moved off down the road."[45]

Public affairs officers could do little to contradict the story. For if a chance existed that Arnett and Daniels might have exaggerated what happened, their account was still close to the facts. Indeed, it differed from the conclusions of a later official investigation less in substance than in emphasis. The military considered the episode the sort of thing that had happened in battle since time immemorial.

American forces enter the village of Snoul. (U.S. Army)

For the reporters it was, as the *Washington Post* observed, "an instant editorial" on the war.[46]

A flurry of secondary press reports grew out of the AP and UPI accounts, but within a week or so they were gone. There the matter might have ended, except for the AP, which had run Arnett's report unedited in its international dispatches while removing all mention of the looting from the version it distributed in the United States. In a cable informing AP's Saigon bureau of the decision, the organization's general manager, Wes Gallagher, explained that he had decided to cut "inflammatory stories" of the sort in view of the turmoil erupting in the United States. The move was controversial but hardly extraordinary. The publisher of the *Washington Post,* Katherine Graham, had done much the same thing at the time by asking her editors to "cool down" coverage of the slayings at Kent State lest it somehow inflame the situation. Even so, Gallagher's decision angered AP's correspondents in South Vietnam, who responded by declining briefly to go into the field. Arnett himself was so offended that he leaked details of what happened to *Newsweek*'s Kevin Buckley, who gleefully reported the whole affair.[47]

If some within the news media were prone to caution, President Nixon was still angry at the way the press was covering the incursion. He intensified the search for ways to demonstrate the operation's importance. Seeing his chance when the troops began to find large stockpiles of food and ammunition, he instructed Wheeler to have MACV describe the development in ways the simplest American could grasp. Shortly thereafter, Wheeler cabled MACV to suggest that the command report ammunition as rounds of various types rather than in tons. "In certain significant caches," he added, "it might be possible to . . . report . . . in terms of days of supply for the enemy."[48]

Laird warned Nixon that the technique might turn the operation into a statistical exercise that could backfire if the numbers proved suspect. He added that it also might lead to charges that the president had bargained the lives of American soldiers for commodities North Vietnam could replace with ease. A better alternative, he said, would be to justify the incursion in terms of Vietnamization and the withdrawal, goals the American people could accept. Nixon demurred. What he wanted, he told Haldeman, was a coordinated program to communicate the incursion's achievements. Everyone, he said, had to "talk optimistically, confidently about the success of the operation in capturing enemy equipment."[49]

Public affairs officers at MACV did as they were told. By the middle of May, they announced, allied forces had captured 10,898 rifles, more than enough for an entire Communist division; over 2,700 tons of rice, a stock sufficient to feed 90,000 enemy regulars for better than forty days; and 1,505 tons of ammunition, at least a four months' supply for 126 enemy battalions. Army photographers validated everything by documenting enemy supply caches and rushing their film to Saigon for transmission to Washington. When American units uncovered a huge depot overflowing with arms, ammunition, and rice, MACV rushed newsmen to the scene. The reporters dubbed the area "the city" and gave it heavy play in their dispatches.[50]

American intelligence analysts in Saigon were considerably more cautious. Washington agencies should refrain from placing too much reliance on reports tabulating captured enemy equipment, they noted in their assessments, because battlefield appraisals were sometimes "embarrassingly misleading." Whatever the drain on the enemy's supplies, they added, the Communists could still attack at will. These remarks had little effect in Washington, where political motivations predominated. When MACV attempted to reduce its estimate of the amount of ammunition captured in Cambodia, General Wheeler canceled the step because the new statistics would have contradicted the far more optimistic information Washington agencies had already released.[51]

If MACV'S analysts were guarded in their estimates of the campaign's effect on the enemy, those of the Office of the Assistant Secretary of Defense for Systems Analysis were blunt. Rice was by far the largest component of the materiél captured to date, they warned on 16 May, but it was easy to replace. At least eighty thousand tons of it were at that moment available in Communist-controlled areas of Cambodia. As for the impact of captured ammunition on the enemy's capabilities, if estimates were correct, the amounts captured during the first two weeks of the operation were at best 15 percent of the total stockpiled in Laos and South Vietnam, an amount that would meet the enemy's needs for up to four years. Although the North Vietnamese would have to compensate for the

"The City" received heavy play in the press. (U.S. Army)

losses the incursion had inflicted, they could rebuild quickly. Between November 1969 and April 1970, indeed, they had moved over one hundred tons of supplies per day through Laos into South Vietnam, and they only needed to move twenty-five tons per day for sixty days to replace all of the ammunition and equipment they had lost to date. These warnings notwithstanding, the White House continued to insist that the Defense Department translate raw statistics into examples that would, as Haldeman put it, "hit home to the American people."[52]

For a time, the Saigon correspondents responded as officials wished, taking their cues from their official sources. Their early reports spoke of heavy enemy casualties and huge stacks of captured enemy arms and ammunition. Orr Kelly of the *Washington Star,* for example, relayed official estimates that some 4,543 enemy—one-eighth of the Communist force in Cambodia—had been killed. Gary Shepard of CBS News quoted an unidentified American who had said that one captured depot contained at least six months' worth of supplies and perhaps more.[53]

Similar reports continued in the weeks that followed, but questions nevertheless began to rise. According to its sources, *Time* noted, enemy forces were far from crippled: "Food is as close as the nearest paddy field. There is ample evidence, too, that the Communists, anticipating an assault, carted off substantial supplies." The lead article on Cambodia in the 25 May issue of *Newsweek* was even more pointed. It carried, boxed and in large type, what purported to be a top secret cable from Laird to Abrams. "Dear Abe," that document read, "in light of the controversy over the U.S. move into Cambodia, the American public would be impressed by any . . . evidence of the success of the operation: (1) high ranking enemy prisoners; (2) major enemy headquarters, such as COSVN; (3) large enemy caches."[54]

Official spokesmen labeled *Newsweek*'s story "phoney" and denied that Laird had ever sent the cable. Although the response appears to have been the truth—*Newsweek*'s supposed cable has never yet come to light—the "phoney" label was disingenuous. For the magazine's cable contained the heart, if not the wording, of General Wheeler's many messages to Abrams on how to play the incursion to the press. On grounds, indeed, that a broadening of the discussion could only weaken the official position, MACV's office of public affairs dropped the issue, allowing the whole affair to die from lack of nourishment.[55]

By that time, as the intelligence analysts had feared, the press was questioning MACV's statistics. On 29 May, John Woodruff of the *Baltimore Sun* remarked that the United States was pursuing an operation calculated to pay off in months, while the enemy conceived of his program in terms of years. *Time,* meanwhile, noted that the numbers military spokesmen released were sometimes misleading. That the force in Cambodia had captured 11,805 rifles, pistols, and submachine guns was true, but most of the captured rifles were outdated models replaced by the fully automatic AK47. As for the seventeen hundred tons of ammunition MACV claimed, the haul was indeed huge, but two-thirds of it was large-caliber antiaircraft ammunition of limited use in South Vietnam rather than the small-arms type most often employed. A 30 May article by James Sterba in the *New York Times* was even more telling. Conceding that the amount of captured matériel was impressive, the reporter noted that his own sources in the military had told him that they were being required to hail the incursion publicly as a "tremendous strategic victory" when they personally believed that the most they had gained was "a short-term tactical advantage."[56]

The president's advisers considered ways to respond to the criticism. A few urged caution. Inappropriate statements by Agnew and others, they said, might spark a crisis of national unity or spur antiwar zealots to violence. Others agitated for action. Ignoring attempts at restraint by individual editors and publishers, Patrick Buchanan, for one, told Nixon that over the first two weeks in May, CBS News had mostly run footage that depicted "fumbling South Vietnamese troops, shattered and burning hideouts, a few soldiers who bad-mouth America, some pitiful refugees of war and a few looters." It was an example, he said, of "how the media can manipulate public information and opinion without appearing to do so."[57]

Convinced that only the most emphatic measures would have any effect, President Nixon instructed his staff on 11 May to cut the *New York Times* and the *Washington Post* from all but the most routine White House contacts. There would be no interviews and no returned calls. Instead, publications that competed with the *Post* and the *Times,* such as the *Washington Star* and the *New York Daily News,* were to receive special interviews and other signs of presidential favor. Beyond allowing his staff to badger network news managers every time a particularly unfavorable story aired, Nixon made no moves against the television networks. Any attempt to ban camera crews would have denied the administration valuable day-to-day publicity.[58]

Nixon also began a public promotional effort to rally support for his policies by announcing that he would deliver a special speech to the nation on 3 June to report on the progress of the incursion. Meanwhile, Agnew stepped up his criticism of the news media, and preparations began for a special "Honor America Day" in Washington on the Fourth of July. Involving tens of thousands of common Americans in a day of patriotic entertainment and demonstrations, the event would showcase the silent majority's support for the president and his aims. These efforts, but particularly the speech, appear to have gone over well. "Relatively light response to RN's speech (1 paragraph in *Time*)," one White House news analyst crowed, "but next day's headlines dominated by 'success,' 'all objectives reached,' etc."[59]

On the day of the speech, 3 June, as part of the effort to establish the success of the incursion, a special deputation of dignitaries departed Washington to visit the war zone. The president's director of communications, Herbert Klein, had at first resisted the trip, on grounds that problems with the press would inevitably arise. Nixon had overruled him, but just the sort of incident the adviser had feared occurred when the party visited the U.S. Ninth Infantry Division at a location in Cambodia identified only as "Shakey's Hill." Narrated by CBS correspondent Jack Laurence, the story that followed described an elaborate tableau the Ninth had prepared to impress the delegation. Personnel from the unit had gone to great lengths to polish captured enemy weapons and to lay them out on tables covered with clean white linen. Then each member of the committee had met with "carefully chosen, dressed, shaved and briefed" soldiers from his home state. Finally, the visitors proceeded down a jungle path to inspect two bunkers that had held some of the captured weapons. They were not told that the weapons they were looking at in the holes had been placed there, having once been removed, to impart an impression of reality. Laurence concluded the piece by noting that the soldiers involved had been unfazed by all the attention. "We live like animals," one had asserted, "until someone comes. . . . [Then] we get all dressed up." The Nixon administration considered the report an example of television's bias but made no attempt at refutation. The damage had been done.[60]

Although the State and Defense Departments had made it clear on 24 and 25 May that South Vietnamese forces would continue operations in Cambodia after the American departure, American forces themselves withdrew from the country on 29 June, one day ahead of a 30 June deadline announced by Nixon. Fifty newsmen and five congressmen greeted the last American units to withdraw from Cambodia.[61]

As with everything else about the incursion, the event was marred by controversy. Morley Safer filed a report for CBS stating that MACV had brought out a band and refreshments to greet the returning troops but that only soldiers within

General Ngo Dzu (center) leads a VIP tour. (U.S. Army)

the view of the press and assembled dignitaries had participated in the festivities. In that light, he charged, the command had obviously indulged in a public relations extravaganza to underscore the withdrawal for the American public. No one doubts that Safer saw what he described, but the celebration was probably the concoction of officers in the field rather than MACV, which had sought specifically to give the operation's final moments as little fanfare as possible.[62]

Safer's report was indicative of public relations failures that had dogged the incursion from the very beginning. For if, as *U.S. News & World Report* correspondent Wendell Merick observed, the operation was clearly justified as a means to save American lives, the president and his advisers had decided that the public needed more and had sought to rationalize the operation in concrete terms as a search for COSVN headquarters. When that portion of the effort failed and when the importance of the arms, ammunition, and rice uncovered in Cambodia fell into question, they had little to fall back on but more exaggerations. The story thus became, in the eyes of the press, not the operation itself—most reporters conceded that it had harmed the enemy to some extent—but its long-term results and the gimmicks that both the military services and the president had resolved upon to make their points.

Patrick Buchanan and others claimed that, by highlighting contradictions, the press had shown bias against the president. Whatever the truth of the assertion, the official point of view had still come across well in the news media. During the first week of the incursion, Vice President Agnew defended the president's position on the popular *David Frost Show.* Herbert Klein appeared on the *Dick Cavett Show,* Ambassador Bunker on *Meet the Press,* Under Secretary of State Elliot Richardson on *Issues and Answers,* and Admiral Moorer on *Face the Nation.* Meanwhile, administration supporters spent one hundred thousand dollars on a major radio campaign, and the president's stalwarts in the House and Senate appeared daily on radio news programs. Similar activities followed the next week and from then on until the operation ended. The result was plain to see. During the first weeks of the incursion, in particular, the president's positions sometimes dominated the news.[63]

As for the success of the operation, it remained a matter of debate. Over the next year, the president and his staff would refer often to the advantages the attack had brought, but during February 1971 the Defense Department's office of systems analysis would report that the enemy's logistical units had survived intact in Cambodia. Meanwhile, a wider war had come into being. Isolating Phnom Penh both from the sea and from its western provinces, Communist forces had severed the land routes between Cambodia and South Vietnam and had developed an indigenous "Liberation Army," the Khmer Rouge, in hopes of overthrowing Lon Nol.[64]

With hindsight, events in the United States seem almost as ominous. For on the very day the incursion ended, the Senate passed the Cooper-Church amendment barring future funding for U.S. forces in Cambodia. It was a portent of things to come. In 1975, Congress would once more exercise its power over the purse to cut off, finally and definitively, all American support for the war.

15

A Change of Direction

In the months following the incursion, even normally optimistic officials tended to agree that progress in the war remained elusive. South Vietnam seemed as dependent as ever on the United States, and the nation's government and military had yet to attract enough capable leaders to compete successfully with the enemy for the loyalty of the common people. Meanwhile, the United States was spending close to $1.5 billion a year just on ammunition for the war, while the Soviet Union and Communist China spent less than 7 percent of that amount on munitions for North Vietnam.[1]

That the war had become a bottomless pit was apparent to many more than just military analysts. The soldier in the field, whether officer or enlisted in rank, and the reporter who followed his work were both well aware of what was happening. The malaise of the spirit that resulted among the members of each group was at first difficult to see because the two sets of individuals followed routine and met their deadlines. It became, nevertheless, a matter of increasing concern to thoughtful observers on both sides as the year progressed.

Signs of wear first appeared in MACV's public affairs program during February 1970, when information officers who should have known better authorized army intelligence agents to pose as journalists. Leaked inevitably to the press, the development set off a storm of protest in the media, where reporters concluded that the army was attempting "to spy out" their sources. Although the agents were keeping watch on a militant antiwar activist rather than the Saigon correspondents, when questions began to arise in Congress, MACV had no choice but to apologize and to reprimand the officer who had made the mistake. On the surface, the episode seemed little more than an example of poor judgment, but, deep down, it was symptomatic of a failure of purpose that was becoming all too familiar among Americans serving in South Vietnam. For in earlier years, all concerned at MACV would have understood that any action with a potential to diminish official credibility in the eyes of the press could also hinder the achievement of American ends in Vietnam.[2]

Institutional fatigue was part of the explanation for what had happened. By mid-1970, the military services were finding it difficult to identify experienced public affairs officers for service in Vietnam. Captains sometimes filled jobs majors and lieutenant colonels would earlier have occupied. In the same way, the system of on-the-job training established early in the war, under which an officer served a year as special assistant for Southeast Asia in Washington before becoming the chief of MACV public affairs, had disappeared in a 1969 Defense Department reorganization. Colonel Cutrona's replacement, Col. Robert Leonard, an officer with broad public affairs experience in Europe but none in Vietnam, thus had no preparation for the job beyond a few weeks spent reading old cables and policy directives at the Pentagon.[3]

Hampered by the fading of institutional memory that these problems entailed, information officers took refuge in the formal rules that governed relations with the press. Meritorious from the standpoint of those who considered the news media an opponent, the approach left little room for the give-and-take that had always been a feature of MACV's relations with reporters. Leonard worked hard to accommodate the press and sometimes bent the rules to preserve official credibility, but the proverbial "book," as Sidle termed it, came more and more to define the limits of what was acceptable in MACV's dealings with the Saigon correspondents.[4]

A case in point occurred in late 1970, when a U.S. Air Force jet crashed in Laos near the South Vietnamese border and American troops moved in to protect the pilot. When reporters asked about the incident, policy dictated that official spokesmen were to indicate that the South Vietnamese had been the ones who violated the border. The officer conducting the session, however, recognized that the press knew everything and answered the question by commenting that if he had been the one to go down he would certainly have wanted his fellow Americans to back him up. The reply satisfied the press, but it upset Leonard, who took the officer to task. A note from Secretary of Defense Laird arrived in Saigon several days later, commending the briefer for his candor and flexibility.[5]

The Saigon correspondents complained bitterly that MACV was unsympathetic to their needs and that repression of the news media was worse than it had ever been. Official spokesmen had stopped arranging briefings from intelligence officers, veteran correspondent Joe Fried avowed, and had even failed to pass on requests for interviews. In addition, they sometimes declined to confirm information already on the record in Washington and refused to respond to questions about their policies on grounds that "the policy has not changed, so there is no point in discussing it."[6]

Although public affairs officers blamed these problems on reductions in personnel within the information office and on the increasing role South Vietnamese spokesmen played in handling the press, changes had, in fact, occurred. Earlier in the war, for example, MACV's intelligence directorate had held off-the-record briefings to keep the press up to date on newsworthy developments. By 1970 that was no longer the case. Unwilling to deal with reporters, the general in charge had ceded the task entirely to public affairs officers, who were viewed by reporters as having something to sell. In the same way, many officers in positions of responsibility, out of anger at press coverage or for reasons of career preservation, sought to avoid reporters and declined to give interviews. A few of the angriest actively discriminated against journalists by cutting off the flow of information to those they disliked.[7]

One public affairs officer, a captain serving in a lieutenant colonel's slot as public affairs adviser to the South Vietnamese Ninth Division in the Mekong delta, decided on his own to reduce the number of reporters visiting his command. To that end, he never revealed that he had access to a helicopter when visiting correspondents requested transportation. He also pushed to have his division's press camp closed so that reporters would have to use far less agreeable South Vietnamese accommodations. By the spring of 1971, as a result, the number of reporters visiting the Ninth Division had fallen from three or four per week to one every two weeks. All of this occurred at a time when Colonel Leonard was trying to interest the media in the progress South Vietnamese forces were making in the delta.[8]

Toleration between the two groups fell so low that, by the beginning of 1972, emotion sometimes took precedence over good sense. When a shoving match, for example, occurred at the Da Nang press center between NBC correspondent James Bennett and the chief of public affairs for XXIV Corps, the U.S. headquarters responsible for the northern portion of South Vietnam, Lt. Col. Perry G. Stevens, the episode led not only to the disaccreditation of the reporter but also to the closing of the center. The reason cited, that the facility was no longer cost-effective, was only an excuse. MACV's inspector general, Col. Robert Cook, and his investigators had, in fact, decided that the reporters there were shiftless freeloaders living off of the beneficence of the military. The press center, with its well-developed facilities for handling correspondents, would be sorely missed a short while later during the Laotian operation.[9]

The situation might have declined further if General Abrams had yielded to instructions from Admiral McCain in October 1970 to reduce MACV's services to the press. With public affairs problems on every side, Abrams cited a 16 percent cut MACV public affairs had already absorbed and deferred all reductions until later.[10]

By that time, the war was becoming a financial drain on many press organizations, and the news media themselves were coming under stress. To save money, bureau chiefs had begun to fill gaps with freelancers when veteran correspondents returned home. Less reliable than staff reporters—who could ill afford to alienate the official sources who provided their bread and butter—the stringers were hard to handle because they often lived day-to-day and for the moment.

Depending on post exchange privileges and inexpensive press camp accommodations for sustenance, a few brokered dollars on the black market or dealt in drugs. Whether involved in vice or not, others were capable of gross distortions of fact, if that was what it took to sell a story.[11]

Although a number of correspondents of long experience remained in South Vietnam, a new kind of reporter had also begun to appear, one who was more attuned to the sentiments of the young in the United States than his predecessors. Sometimes close in age to the draftees fighting the war, these individuals sported the same hairstyles, used the same slang, and, in the case of television correspondents, even played rock and roll as background in their reports. Sympathetic to the antiwar movement at home, some participated in antigovernment political activities. The South Vietnamese disaccredited stringer Michael Morrow in November 1970 for addressing a meeting of anti-Thieu demonstrators. Stringing for CBS News, John Steinbeck IV narrowly escaped the same fate when the local police photographed him participating in a Saigon political rally. A correspondent for the U.S. Conference of the World Council of Churches, Don Luce, was suspected of serving as liaison between antiwar groups in the United States and similar organizations in South Vietnam.[12]

MACV's office of information attempted to eliminate reporters who rarely produced by requiring freelancers to present letters from established news outlets firmly committing those agencies to publish their work. The rules, however, had hardly any effect. Bureau chiefs continued to provide letters of reference to anyone who showed the slightest promise of being able to draft a news dispatch.[13]

There had been problems with the news media in the best of times, but the fatigue and declining morale burdening both MACV and the press gave the controversies that developed during the war's final years a hard edge of confrontation. An example occurred during July 1970, when Don Luce and a congressional aide, Thomas R. Harkin, revealed substandard conditions at a South Vietnamese prison. Alleging that the government was mistreating both civilian inmates and captive Viet Cong sympathizers, the exposé came at the worst possible moment for the United States, at a time when Nixon was preparing two initiatives affecting prisoners of war. The first was an attempt to contrast North Vietnam's ruthless treatment of its American prisoners with humanitarian policies in effect in South Vietnam by repatriating sixty-two sick and disabled North Vietnamese captives. The second involved a clandestine thrust into North Vietnam to rescue dozens of American pilots imprisoned at Son Tay, a village northwest of Hanoi. Whether successful or not, the raid would highlight the concern of the United States for its captive personnel while emphasizing North Vietnam's brutality.[14]

The affair began on 2 July, when Luce, with the connivance of Harkin, accompanied a group of U.S. congressmen on a visit to a prison on Con Son Island, one hundred kilometers off the Mekong delta in the South China Sea. Over the protests of the facility's commandant, Harkin photographed some of the inmates. Then the party chanced upon what were known as "tiger cages," cells topped with iron grills that held between four and five hundred dangerous prisoners, or "tigers" in local parlance. More than half were women. In response to questions, the prisoners claimed that when they were disobedient, the guards sprinkled them from above with powdered lime that burned their flesh and eyes. The commandant avowed that the lime in evidence around the site was used only as whitewash, but the party's U.S. escorts later observed that the substance was visible on top of the grillwork covering the cages.[15]

The U.S. officials who accompanied the group stressed throughout the visit that South Vietnam rather than the United States had responsibility for Con Son and that the nation, appearances notwithstanding, was improving its prisons. Later, someone passed that point to the

One of the tiger cages at Con Son.
(Senator Tom Harkin)

chairman of the delegation, Congressman G. V. "Sonny" Montgomery of Mississippi, who had not been present during the episode. Montgomery promised to do what he could to smooth things over. He was as good as his word. The lengthy report his committee filed on 6 July devoted only a single paragraph to Con Son. It affirmed that the delegation had uncovered problems on the island but that the South Vietnamese government had promised an investigation.[16]

Luce and Harkin were not to be denied. Soon after the report appeared, Luce informed the Saigon correspondents of what had transpired at Con Son. Harkin, meanwhile, resigned his position with Congress to hold a news conference at which he accused Montgomery of accepting military assurances uncritically. Two congressmen who had visited the prison with Harkin also spoke. One claimed that several prisoners had claimed the loss of the use of their legs because of beatings, malnutrition, and forced inactivity. The other termed Con Son a symbol of how the United States continued to cooperate with corruption and torture to keep Thieu in power. The press gave both statements heavy play.[17]

The congressman's allegations notwithstanding, U.S. officials in Saigon had little sympathy for the abuses Harkin and Luce had described. If they confirmed that U.S. advisers had been aware of the cages and had discussed the problem with the South Vietnamese, however, they followed the official line by stressing that the facility was under South Vietnamese control. Conditions in South Vietnam's civil prisons were harsh, they added, but the prisoners were not abused. Whatever the truth of that assertion—American observers visited the facility only once a month and never at night—the Nixon administration saw little value in denying anything. Seeking to play down morality and to make the problem a political issue, it urged the South Vietnamese government to construct a hospital, to build more barracks, to hire additional guards, and to allow more freedom of movement for the prisoners.[18]

Beyond making a play for additional funding, the Thieu regime did little to push the changes the Americans wanted. As General Abrams remarked later in the year when the Red Cross began to criticize conditions at a camp on Phu Quoc Island in the Gulf of Thailand for strictly military prisoners, South Vietnam's leaders found it difficult to understand why they should provide supplies and accommodations for enemy captives that their own troops lacked.[19]

That being the case, the United States could do little more than attempt to limit the damage. The Defense Department prevailed upon the Red Cross to replace the inspector who had raised the questions about Phu Quoc with one more open to the American point of view. It also advised the South Vietnamese to reject a request by CBS News for permission to photograph prisoner-of-war camps. As President Nixon's special consultant on public affairs, former ABC correspondent John Scali, explained at the time, anyone who would allow reporters to photograph those camps would have to be "out of his mind." Whether these efforts had much effect is open to question. At the least, few of the complications that might have occurred as a result of the controversy came to pass. The prisoner-of-war release went ahead as scheduled, making only a modest ripple in the press. As for the raid on Son Tay, it failed to rescue any prisoners, but it nonetheless demonstrated to the families of the men and the world that the president had their best interests at heart.[20]

There the matter might have ended, but for the South Vietnamese government, which moved during October to cancel Luce's press credentials and to expel him from the country. When Ambassador Bunker protested, the Thieu regime extended the reporter's visa but declined to reinstate his credentials to cover the war, in effect forcing MACV to terminate all American assistance to the reporter. Luce did nothing to placate his adversaries. In addition to arguing in favor of allowing Viet Cong representation in the South Vietnamese government on a national television program, he escorted an antiwar congressman, Paul N. McCloskey, Jr., of California, on a visit to a joint U.S.–South Vietnamese prisoner-of-war interrogation center. On 26 April 1971, citing a "special reason," the South Vietnamese Ministry of Foreign Affairs notified the reporter that his visa would expire on 16 May.[21]

Over the days that followed, Luce's supporters in Congress and the press depicted him as a victim of South Vietnamese repression, and Senator Fulbright invited him to Washington to testify on the plight of prisoners in South Vietnam.

U.S. official spokesmen responded by pointing out that the order against Luce was the result of the reporter's political activities, not of his work as a newsman. Most of the 412 correspondents resident in Saigon, they said, had written stories critical of the South Vietnamese. A raft of articles had even appeared on Con Son. No one but Luce had experienced any problems.[22]

On the day before Luce was to testify, in an attempt to upstage the reporter's appearance before Congress, public affairs officers in Saigon planted a question with Maggie Kilgore of UPI for use at that evening's briefing. During that session, Kilgore asked for the "special reason" behind Luce's expulsion. Nguyen Ngoc Huyen, the South Vietnamese spokesman present, responded that the reporter's activities had been inconsistent with the role of a journalist because he had served as an intermediary between antiwar groups in the United States and South Vietnam. Flourishing a handful of papers, Huyen offered to prove the allegation. The documents he presented, however, were mimeographed copies of Viet Cong and North Vietnamese news articles, one of which had originally appeared in the *Washington Post*. During the chaotic give-and-take that followed, Jeff Williams of NBC News pointed out that Luce's apartment had been burglarized two weeks before. Where, he asked, had Huyen obtained his materials? Huyen responded that correspondents never divulged their sources and neither would he.[23]

From that point on, the Con Son "tiger cages" entered into the expanding lore of the Vietnam War, to resurface whenever an antiwar activist sought to portray the alleged injustice of the American cause. In fact, although conditions at Con Son were indeed cruel, the incident probably said as much about the fragmenting American consensus on the war as it did about the conflict itself. For Con Son, or something like it, had long existed in South Vietnam, with neither the U.S. government nor the Saigon correspondents paying much attention. Only with the advent of American withdrawals and the decline in support for the war in Congress and the news media had it begun to matter.

Although important for the military's public image, the controversies surrounding Don Luce were little more than passing irritations to General Abrams and his commanders, who had far bigger problems to consider. For if all the institutions, military and civilian, serving in Vietnam were under stress, hardly anyone was prepared for the situation that developed as 1970 lengthened and the withdrawal of American forces began in earnest.

Reflecting on a tour of duty as commanding general of the central portion of South Vietnam during 1970, Lt. Gen. Arthur S. Collins described what was happening. The U.S. Army in Vietnam had begun to deteriorate badly, he said:

> Bizarre uniforms, shirts and helmets not worn in combat situations that warranted them, the excessive number of accidental shootings—too many of which appeared other than accidental—and the promiscuous throwing of grenades that lent new meaning to the expression *fragging* should leave us all

with an ill-at-ease feeling. . . . When these indicators of lower standards are combined with the number of friendly casualties caused by our own fire . . . [and] other accidents caused by carelessness, it appears to me that we have a serious disciplinary problem which has resulted in operational slippage.[24]

The conditions that Collins described were hardly unique to South Vietnam. By the time the general made his report, grave morale problems were appearing among American forces stationed around the world. Meanwhile, antiwar sentiment had reached such proportions in the United States that a few draft boards had even begun to exempt persons eligible to serve in the army on the basis of simple, unsupported declarations by those individuals that they were conscientious objectors.[25]

It all became a staple for the Saigon correspondents. As in earlier years, the reporters showed considerable respect for the abilities of soldiers who remained in combat. They were nevertheless also quick to point out that cracks were beginning to appear in the army's usually solid facade. Many soldiers, they noted, seemed to consider the conflict "a lifer's war" in which draftees rather than volunteers took the casualties and in which officers pushed their troops to engage the enemy in order to earn medals, promotions, and prestige assignments for themselves. A new kind of soldier had come into being as a result: one who weighed orders carefully and who seemed to believe, as John Saar wrote in *Life*, "that since the U.S. had decided not to . . . win the war, there's no sense in being the last to die." That individual wore his hair long, sported love beads and peace medallions, and clearly sympathized with antiwar protesters at home. "A lot of our buddies got killed here," one soldier told Kevin Buckley, "but they died for nothing."[26]

Military professionals spurned such stories. "The writers reflect their own life style," Lt. Gen. William J. McCaffrey told a friend with disdain. "It makes them more comfortable to define the 'lifers' as eccentrics and the pot-smokers as normal." Although sometimes more sweeping than the situation in South Vietnam required, the reporters' conclusions nonetheless paralleled the views not only of Collins but also of other high-ranking officers. General Westmoreland, for one, was tactful but left no doubts about where he stood. He told Haynes Johnson and George Wilson of the *Washington Post* in a 1971 interview that the conflict had become "a very traumatic experience for us." Gen. Michael S. Davison, the commander in chief, U.S. Army, Europe, was more blunt. "When you look at the attitudes reflected in the country today," he told the two reporters, seconding the soldier who had spoken with Buckley, "it is really hard to say that [the price of Vietnam] has been worth it."[27]

If some officers were willing to acknowledge that serious problems existed, the news media's penchant for stories that depicted the military in the worst possible light was still a source of irritation to most, whatever their stand on the war. Public affairs officers in Saigon and Washington offered a line of defense of sorts, but they could deal only with confirmed facts—often incomplete, late in arriving, or open to interpretation. Following instinct and gathering impressions, reporters could be much more flexible and to the point.

The Saigon correspondents asserted repeatedly, for example, that combat refusals were beginning to occur with frequency. The U.S. command had little choice but to admit that refusals took place, but it refused to concede that they were anything more than a nuisance. Reporters could see for themselves, however, and the stories they filed were always embarrassing. Peter Arnett's report during September 1969 on the brief combat refusal of Company A appears to have sensitized the press to the subject. But few, if any, of the articles that appeared had the immediacy of one by Jack Laurence that played on CBS during April 1970. Laurence had joined Company C, "Charlie Company," of the Second Battalion, Seventh Cavalry, First Cavalry Division (Airmobile), while the unit was operating some eighty kilometers northwest of Saigon near the Cambodian border. Documenting the daily life of an American unit in the field, the reporter had recorded not only such day-to-day events as mail call and meals but also the reaction of the men to the departure of experienced commanders and their hesitant acceptance of the new officers who arrived.[28]

On 6 April, the reporter was nearby when brigade and battalion commanders instructed the company to vacate the area it was occupying as quickly as possible. Since those orders came by radio in an unencoded transmission, the officers issuing them could not reveal that an incoming B-52 strike was behind the move. The company's commander thus had no reason to give his men when he ordered them to head down an unsecured road to a clearing where helicopters could land quickly. With Laurence's camera grinding, the unit's lead platoon took issue with the command on grounds that the move was unsafe because the enemy often mined unsecured roads or laid ambushes along them. After considerable give-and-take, following a second order, the men moved out, but they walked only a short distance before being diverted to a safer pickup zone.[29]

In the report that followed, Laurence emphasized the objections of the enlisted men while disregarding the point of view of their commanders. One soldier called the road "a shooting gallery." A second said, "I don't think [the captain] . . . knows his stuff; he hasn't been a captain but maybe two weeks—maybe three weeks." Laurence termed the incident a "rebellion" but refused to blame the soldiers. Instead, he suggested that the war had lost any meaning for "normally brave and obedient" fighting men who saw in the road a symbol of how some forty thousand of their predecessors had died.[30]

Because the incident occurred on camera, there was nothing for MACV to deny. Instead, public affairs officers informed Laurence of the impending B-52 strike. They also allowed reporters to interview the men of Charlie Company and made officers available who could explain what had happened from a military point of view. The officers took issue with Laurence's use of the word *rebellion* and questioned his suggestion that the incident was symbolic of larger trends in the war. Instead, they said, the men had shown good sense: "There hasn't been a war in which the troops didn't question certain judgments," one observed. "It happens time and again—it's nothing new."[31]

The approach had some effect. Verifying the imminence of the B-52 strike with the Pentagon, CBS toned down Laurence's story before broadcasting it. As time went on, the story nevertheless achieved a momentum of its own, in part because the First Cavalry Division rekindled it by barring Laurence from further visits to Company C. When Walter Cronkite complained on the air that the army had forced CBS to terminate "one of the most productive news assignments of a long war," letters from congressmen and senators to the secretary of defense ensued, expressing concern that the army was attempting to repress the news media.[32]

Over the year that followed, as disillusionment with the war spread, a scattering of real combat refusals occurred, often within view of the press. During March 1971, an exhausted, underequipped, and undermanned armored squadron near Khe Sanh refused to enter enemy territory at night to retrieve documents and equipment aboard an abandoned armored personnel carrier. Aware of the danger and acting on the spur of the moment, the commander of the brigade involved, Brig. Gen. John G. Hill, Jr., relieved the captain in charge for a failure of leadership but declined to take action against the men. The move was controversial, even within the military, because it demolished the career of an officer who had been popular and proficient, but high-level commanders defended it as the product of a need to return the troop to combat effectiveness as quickly as possible.[33]

Conservatives within the news media disagreed. The military analyst for the *Detroit News,* retired Marine Corps Col. Robert D. Heinl, Jr., for one, rebuked the army for its "supine" handling of the incident. In the same way, ABC News anchorman Howard K. Smith charged that "in a non-sequitur rapidly becoming typical in Vietnam, today the commander was replaced, but the Army announced no charges will be filed against the men because 'they're back in the field doing their duty.' "[34]

Such condemnations to the contrary, most within the press attempted to handle combat refusals impartially. During October 1971, for example, when five members of a platoon stationed at Fire Support Base PACE, located northwest of Saigon near the Cambodian border, refused to go on patrol, reporters scrutinized all sides of the event. Relaying the soldiers' objections that the assignment meant virtual suicide and that the operation was offensive when President Nixon had said U.S. forces would assume a defensive role, they also interviewed officers who noted that the so-called mutiny had never occurred. The mission had been canceled, they said, when a South Vietnamese unit had taken it on.[35]

Nicholas Proffitt of *Newsweek* was one of the most perceptive commentators. Using the incident to confront the dilemmas afflicting military-media relations at that moment in the war, he noted that the episode might never have gained any attention at all, except for the actions of Richard Boyle, the stringer who had broken the story. A radically antiwar newsman who had entered South Vietnam illegally from Cambodia after being expelled for participating in an antigovernment demonstration, Boyle had offered to deliver a letter of protest signed by some sixty-six members of the platoon to Senator Edward Kennedy. In the process, Proffitt suggested, the reporter had overstepped his role as a journalist by becoming directly involved in a story he should only have witnessed and reported. Proffitt added that while the incident at PACE was a minor installment in a much larger story, it still bore directly upon a circumstance that had begun to preoccupy both the military and the news media in Vietnam. For soldiers al-

Blacks and whites were united by common needs in the field. (U.S. Army)

ready in fear of death had become burdened by an "even more intolerable thought," that their deaths would be anonymous: "In a time of 'acceptable' casualty figures (the latest weekly U.S. toll was eight dead and 72 wounded), more and more U.S. soldiers serving in Vietnam are understandably concerned that they may be among the last to die in a war everybody else considers over."[36]

The condition of military morale in the field remained a concern for reporters, but with the American role in combat declining, most found their best opportunities in the rear, where by mid-1970 the military services' difficulties with race relations, assaults on officers, and drug abuse had become staples for them. Many of their reports were sympathetic to the military. Wendell Merick of *U.S. News & World Report,* for one, observed in January 1971 that racial confrontations were often difficult to identify as such. "Given beer, whisky or drugs, mixed in with a crowd of blacks and whites, and you can have trouble," he said. "But you never know which came first—the booze, the drugs, or racial disagreements." Other reporters, however, insisted that problems involving race had become so widespread that black enlisted men had attempted to kill their white officers. "In Vietnam," noted Bruce Biossat of the *Washington Daily News* in January 1971, "the practice of 'fragging officers' . . . has evidently become fairly commonplace. What evidence there is . . . points to black soldiers."[37]

A year after Biossat made his report, Eugene Linden of the *Saturday Review* took up the same theme. Interracial tensions continued unabated, the newsman noted. When MPs were called in to quell a riot at Camp Baxter near Danang, he said, they found that both whites and blacks had secreted fragmentation grenades, ammunition, and even several M-60 machine guns. A few days later at a camp near Hue, five soldiers were injured during two days of rioting that followed an altercation in a mess hall. Linden went on to describe the attempted murder by black enlisted men of an officer suspected of discrimination. In an effort to contain the problem, he said, many units had denied their men weapons in rear areas or had set up forums to improve communication between the ranks. Even so, "the Army has had scant success in stemming the lethal fad."[38]

Following an investigation, in January 1972, Colonel Cook dismissed Linden's allegations and others like them. Although the incident at Camp Baxter had indeed occurred, Cook said, the inexperience of company commanders, inadequate attention to the morale of the troops, an indulgent attitude toward drug abuse by junior officers, poor communications, and the lax enforcement of rules and regulations were as much to blame for what happened as racial animosities. Indeed, Cook said, of fifty-two hundred incidents investigated by MACV during 1971, only thirty-three were attributable to racial problems alone.[39]

Cook's estimate to the contrary, newsmen had ample grounds for concern. Commenting on the situation at Baxter, a black chaplain who had served there asserted, "It was death all over the place. . . . At nightfall most of the camp was divided . . . blacks over here, whites over there. [The commander] didn't go out at night. . . . he had his own trailer and he had guards all around it." Admiral Moorer was equally emphatic. Commanders tended to underestimate their problem with race, he told Laird, and some of their subordinates covered up what was happening rather than reveal anything that might harm their careers.[40]

Public affairs officers, for their part, attempted to spread the blame by avowing that if MACV had a problem with race, so did American society as a whole. As for the fragging, so named because fragmentation grenades were often the weapon of choice, they acknowledged that it existed but avowed that it was hard to track because explosions often occurred accidentally in war zones. In an obvious attempt to play down the issue by erasing the term most associated with it, they then suggested that reporters use the phrase *assault with explosives* in place of *fragging* because the more popular term trivialized a serious offense.[41]

If race relations and fragging created problems for MACV, those complications were nothing in comparison with the ones caused by drug abuse. For by 1970 and 1971, reporters could see that experimentation with marijuana, heroin, and barbiturates had reached epidemic proportions among the troops. On one occasion, reporter Peter Arnett remarked, he had driven to Newport, the U.S. Army port on the Saigon River that handled military cargoes. The guard at the gate seemed semiconscious. Everywhere he stepped inside the facility, empty vials that had contained heroin and other drugs crunched underfoot. "I spoke with the captain in charge," Arnett said. "He confirmed that at any one time close to half of his men were stoned on drugs." Similar circumstances prevailed at Camp Baxter during 1971. "All over the place you could find these little vials," one chaplain recalled, "little plastic things laying around all over the place."[42]

At first, officials in Washington claimed that reporters were exaggerating, but drug abuse continued to increase, and the headlines told the tale. "GI Pot Smoking Called 'Epidemic,' " observed the *Washington Daily News.* "G. I.'s Find Marijuana Is Cheap and Plentiful," noted the *New York Times.* "Does Our Army Fight on Drugs?" asked *Look* magazine. A particularly galling report appeared on 13 November 1970, when CBS broadcast a story in which reporter Gary Sheppard attended a "pot party" held by members of the First Cavalry Division (Airmobile) at fire support base Aries, sixty kilometers northeast of Saigon. Observing that marijuana was "as plentiful in Vietnam as C-rations," the reporter asked one of the men, "Aren't you worried about maybe getting attacked?" The soldier responded, "No, nobody usually seems to worry. . . . We're worried—more worried—about lifers. . . . We're constantly on the guard for lifers when we smoke." Sheppard concluded his report by remarking that according to recent surveys, well over 50 percent of the soldiers in Vietnam used marijuana.[43]

Officers immediately charged that Sheppard had staged the event, but an investigation by MACV proved otherwise. Instead, a series of failures in command had occurred. The officer assigned to escort the reporter had passed the duty to another, who had gone off to pursue his own responsibilities. Sheppard had then fallen in with an enlisted man who had invited him to participate in some "live action." He had gone reluctantly, because little else was happening. More inclined to be "buddies" with their men than to lead, the squad leaders responsible for the group had done nothing to interfere with the party. One had even participated. "We have not denied that there is a problem," Defense Department spokesmen told reporters in the end. "We . . . share it with the rest of society."[44]

For a time, officers in the field seemed to pull in upon themselves. While some readily admitted to reporters that drugs were a difficult problem, others attempted to shield themselves from inquiring newsmen. The result was predictable. Stories began to appear in the press charging that some army units were either setting up systems to rate reporters and their coverage or taking steps to put not only television news teams but all arriving journalists under escort.[45]

They made it seem as though the U.S. command was bent on covering up its problems. In fact, while concerned with containing the damage, General Abrams and his public affairs officers were more inclined to take the opposite approach, if only in self-defense. All concerned understood that any attempt to cut off the press would create an impression that the command was overwhelmed and unable to cope. Following that reasoning, on 30 October 1970, MACV issued a communiqué acknowledging that official statistics on the extent of drug abuse in previous years were defective and that the availability of hard drugs was far greater than anyone had realized.[46]

Although Abrams and the Defense Department recognized the value of can-

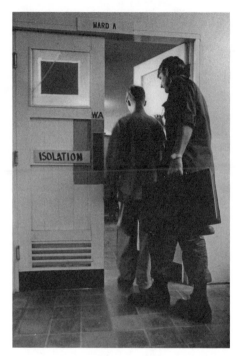

During the last years of the war, more soldiers were evacuated to the United States for drug abuse than for wounds. (U.S. Army)

more drug issues

dor, they were caught between that judgment and the White House, which wanted to put a good face on the war in order to deter those in Congress who might seek to end the conflict at any price. There was also South Vietnam to consider. Its government's morale and good standing before the world were essential if Vietnamization was to succeed, but as reporters were quick to point out, some of its members were clearly involved in selling drugs both to American troops and to their own men.

The attitude of the Nixon administration became apparent in June 1971, when the Defense Department acknowledged publicly that up to 5 percent of the troops in South Vietnam were addicted to heroin. The claim was conservative in comparison with stories appearing in the press, but it sparked anger at the White House. Avowing that the figures provided ammunition to critics of the war, presidential aide Charles Colson instructed John Scali to "please turn Defense Department off!" Within two weeks of that injunction, on grounds that the selective release of statistical data might lead to distortions and misinterpretations, General Abrams forbade the public release—"without my personal approval"—of figures revealing the population of drug detoxification centers, the results of drug tests on soldiers returning home, and the number of individuals evacuated from South Vietnam for drug abuse. The truth, however, was not to be denied. Within three months, MACV had no choice but to reveal that of the more than twenty-five hundred soldiers evacuated from South Vietnam for medical reasons during September 1971, almost 55 percent had been drug abusers.[47]

Drastic in themselves, these figures showed only part of the problem. Interviewing a random sample of soldiers leaving South Vietnam during September 1971, researchers would establish that almost 69 percent had experimented with marijuana. Meanwhile, 45 percent had used unauthorized narcotics, barbiturates, or amphetamines at least once during their tours of duty. Of those, 29 percent said they had used such substances more than weekly, and 20 percent reported that they had been addicted. These figures were far in excess of the 5 percent that tests in the field identified as drug abusers and that official spokesmen often referred to in their dealings with the press.[48]

A 24 January 1971 report by NBC correspondent Phil Brady underscored the problem while shedding considerable light on the contradictions at its root. Describing conditions at Landing Zone English, a base north of Qui Nhon that housed the U.S. 173d Airborne Brigade, Brady played a film showing soldiers purchasing drugs at a house on the base itself. He explained that the army had no control over the situation because both the building and the land on which it stood were the property of a well-connected South Vietnamese citizen. He continued that Vietnamese soldiers stationed at the base also pushed drugs and that their commanders did nothing to stop them. When confronted with evidence of what was happening, in fact, one had complained to his superiors. Not long after, Brady said, the U.S. commander of the base had to write the Vietnamese a letter of apology.[49] Although MACV denied that a letter of the sort had ever been written, it had little choice but to confirm most of Brady's story. American military policemen had requested during November 1970 that the South Vietnamese close the house. Nothing had happened, however, until Brady's report appeared. Then the house was demolished within a week.[50]

American officers tended to make excuses for the South Vietnamese, but neither General Abrams nor Ambassador Bunker was much moved. In a long, detailed talk with Thieu on 3 May, both warned of the danger of continued inaction. With the American press focusing on the heroin traffic and the involvement of high South Vietnamese officials, Bunker said, "I must tell you in all frankness, that no one can assure that . . . the Congress will vote the hundreds of millions required for economic assistance . . . if this situation continues." As it was, he continued, most of the government's efforts appeared to be tokens. After a few arrests and a flare of publicity, the prosecution of culprits slowed to a halt, punishment never occurred, and both cases and culprits disappeared. Meanwhile, military vehicles crossed into South Vietnam from Cambodia without search or check; customs and narcotics officers were often barred from approaching official aircraft and naval vessels arriving from abroad; and black-market money manipulators well known for their service to the narcotics trade flourished everywhere.[51]

Thieu promised to take action and over the weeks that followed replaced his director general of customs and transferred a number of customs officials to less sensitive positions. He also tightened security measures at Tan Son Nhut Airport; replaced all of the police, customs, and military security personnel that had formerly served at the facility; and established a system of tax-free rewards for those who provided information on narcotics trafficking. American officials were encouraged by the effort, but the press was less confident. In August, Mark Gayn of the *Chicago Daily News* charged that profits from the heroin trade permeated the politics of South Vietnam. The next day, Henry Kamm asserted in the *New York*

Times that drugs remained as available as ever in South Vietnam and that Thieu's much-publicized campaign was little more than a gesture. There were also allegations that Thieu and Ky were financing their election campaigns with proceeds from the sale of drugs.[52]

In the end, many of the stories proved only too accurate. As for the allegations about Thieu and Ky, the Nixon administration appears to have made no effort to find out. The political implications would have been "incalculable," Henry Kissinger told Bunker in April 1971, if President Nixon were even to suggest that high-level members of South Vietnam's government were implicated in the sale of drugs to American troops.[53]

In the end, the dilemmas the United States faced as the war wound down would have been painful even if reporters had not been present. That they were only added another layer of complication to an already difficult situation. An exchange of views that occurred in November 1970 between Laird and Bunker exemplifies the complexity of the issue. Bunker complained that the Saigon correspondents had turned to drugs and discipline for stories because, with the American role in combat declining, they had nothing dramatic to write about. Laird could only sympathize. If idle troops meant discipline problems that idle journalists could fasten upon, that was preferable, he said, to the huge number of casualties that would occur if the United States returned to a policy of all-out war.[54]

16

Incursion into Laos

As the end of 1970 approached, the situation in South Vietnam was a cause of concern to both the Defense Department and the White House. Although the South Vietnamese armed forces had performed well in Cambodia and the intensity of enemy operations appeared low, the North Vietnamese were accelerating an effort to shift supplies southward along the Ho Chi Minh Trail in Laos in obvious preparation for a major offensive. Given the long lead times that the enemy needed, analysts reasoned that the attack would probably come early in 1972. With fewer than forty-five thousand American combat troops remaining in South Vietnam by that time and a presidential campaign in full swing in the United States, the enemy was probably thinking that the political uncertainties facing the president would inhibit his ability to respond.[1]

The idea for a series of South Vietnamese attacks into both Cambodia and Laos during 1971 rapidly emerged as the most promising response. If successful, Nixon and Kissinger reasoned, the incursions would buy time for Vietnamization and secure an uneventful American withdrawal. It would also be the last chance the South Vietnamese would ever have to conduct an attack against enemy supply lines while American forces were still strong enough to provide backing. At that time Congress was debating and would shortly pass a law extending the Cooper-Church amendment's provisions on Cambodia to Laos, but the new law contained a loophole. To safeguard the remaining Americans in South Vietnam, it placed no restrictions on the use of American airpower in either country.[2]

On 6 December, Admiral McCain notified Abrams of the president's thinking. Abrams responded the next day with word that Thieu believed the operation should concentrate up to two divisions on the region around the town of Tchepone, located in Laos some fifty kilometers up Highway 9 from the old American base at Khe Sanh. Over the weeks that followed, Abrams devised a two-part campaign that involved an initial attack into Cambodia followed by a

Both the enemy and reporters could see that U.S. forces were moving to the Laotian border. (Department of Defense)

move into Laos. In Cambodia, South Vietnamese forces would operate around a Communist stronghold known as the Chup Plantation, located forty kilometers west of the border near the city of Kompong Cham. The Laotian segment would begin in late January, when an American brigade would secure Highway 9 up to the Laotian border, establish a supply depot at Khe Sanh, and position artillery to support the South Vietnamese force entering Laos. Between 6 and 13 February, Thieu's units supported by B-52 strikes would drive up Highway 9 toward Tchepone while helicopter lifts placed blocking forces north and south of the avenue of attack. When the assault reached its midpoint, a heliborne attack would begin against the airfield at Tchepone. After that, search-and-destroy operations would begin in the region to the town's south, where most of the enemy's supplies were stored. These operations would continue until mid-April, when a withdrawal would start.[3]

General Abrams was cautiously optimistic about the operation, but the CIA's intelligence analysts were wary. They noted quietly that the enemy already knew an attack was coming and that his antiaircraft defenses were so well developed in the region that he could inflict heavy casualties on American air crews assisting the South Vietnamese. Secretary of State Rogers also had doubts. If the attack succeeded, he told the president, it might be worthwhile, but failure seemed more likely. If that occurred, the repercussions might shatter the confidence of the South Vietnamese armed forces and people while raising questions within the American public and Congress.[4]

President Nixon understood that there would be political risks, but he considered them acceptable if the attack could blunt the enemy's ability to damage U.S. forces when their number fell to fewer than one hundred thousand. In response to the warning that the enemy already knew an assault was coming, he and his advisers pointed to the promise of American firepower. If the North Vietnamese stood and fought, they said, so much the better. The result would be devastating to their forces. And if the operation failed, the damage could be contained by packaging the operation as a raid rather than a major invasion and by announcing limited goals. Only when everything was over would anyone "crow" about achievements.[5]

With Nixon so concerned about the image of the operation, military planners decided to handle the press with care. Since the South Vietnamese would be doing most of the fighting, General Abrams insisted that they brief the press on their own activities and coordinate transportation for reporters in the field. Once the operation began, they would also be the ones to fly American reporters into Laos. To preserve military security, all news of the operation would be embargoed until it was safe to make an announcement, but selected journalists would receive briefings at regular intervals in order to cut off speculation.[6]

Admiral McCain, the commander in chief, Pacific, endorsed Abrams's plan but was concerned that open restraints on the press would harm military credibility. He insisted that MACV inform reporters of its plans for handling the press and that it devise a "foolproof" system for lifting whatever restrictions it applied. That would diminish the likelihood of premature disclosures and reduce the chance for misunderstandings. In general, both he and Abrams hoped to keep the incursion secret until 30 January, when the operation would begin, but the logistical effort backing the attack proved to be so enormous that neither the press nor the enemy could ignore it. Abrams therefore decided to invoke the embargo a day early. That would permit reporters to cover everything from the beginning but allow time for perspective to develop.[7]

As Abrams stipulated, on 29 January MACV's spokesmen announced an embargo on all information coming from Military Region 1 (the old I Corps Zone renamed) except for what appeared in official news releases. They promised a background briefing the next evening to describe what was happening and explained that the embargo would end when military security permitted. Requesting cooperation, they added, "This announcement constitutes a part of the embargo and is not for publication." The embargo on the embargo appeared to be an afterthought, but it was in fact essential to Abrams's ends. If there had been none, reporters would have filed stories about a news blackout on the Laotian frontier, eliminating any surprise military security might have achieved.[8]

The press guidance that accompanied the announcement attempted to compromise between Abrams's concern for security and McCain's desire to maintain official credibility. It thus specified that accredited correspondents were to receive billeting, messing, and "all practicable assistance" but also sought to reduce the number of newsmen entering operational areas. To that end, information officers were to discourage travel by single correspondents and to form press pools whenever possible. Groups of reporters in the field were to have official escorts.[9]

Colonel Leonard held the background briefing the next day. Specifying that all information was under embargo, he introduced an intelligence officer who linked the movement of U.S. forces in Military Region 1, code-named Operation Dewey Canyon II, to the threat the enemy's buildup in Laos posed to American withdrawals. A briefer from MACV's Operations Directorate followed with a summary of U.S. and South Vietnamese plans. He avoided any mention of a possible incursion into Laos. By then the reporters were seething. Most saw little reason for secrecy. The movement of huge bodies of troops in Military Region 1, they objected, was obvious to everyone, including the enemy. The reporters wanted to know whether they could speculate on possibilities. Leonard said no.[10]

The situation was nevertheless already out of control. "Speculation is rampant," Moorer was soon telling Abrams, " . . . and high officials are being pressed to comment." Concerned that sensational news reports might foster opposition in Congress and limit the president's options, he suggested that Abrams lift the embargo on at least the movement of U.S. forces into Military Region 1. Abrams declined. "I am convinced," he said, "that as of now the enemy suspects many things but . . . is uncertain as to where, when and in what force allied forces will strike."[11]

Circumstances continued to degenerate the next day. The *New York Times* wire service carried a lead story printed originally in the *London Observer* that speculated brazenly on the information supplied by Leonard's background briefing. It mentioned the embargo and linked it to plans for an invasion of Laos.[12] Unable to link the violation to any individual, Leonard could do little in response. By 1 February, as a result, reports were running in the *Washington Post,* the *Baltimore Sun,* and the *New York Times* on the news blackout in Saigon and the possibility that a strike into Laos was imminent. Meanwhile, senators who had been reassured by the Nixon administration that no U.S. troops would cross into Laos began to speak out publicly to allay the concerns of their constituents, and Soviet Premier Alexei Kosygin went on record to denounce "the outrageous invasion of the southern provinces of Laos." To make matters worse, the deputy assistant secretary of defense for public affairs, Jerry Friedheim, responded to a question from reporters by saying that he would have no comment on matters General Abrams had "embargoed" in Saigon. He added that his "no comment" was itself under embargo.[13]

More disclosures came the next day, many of them based on leaks from U.S. officials seeking either to kill the operation or, more likely, to counteract some of the adverse effects that the embargo appeared to be having on official credibility. Citing anonymous "U.S. officials" in Washington, *New York Times* reporter Terence Smith thus confirmed that a major military operation was under way near Khe Sanh and that Tchepone would be the probable target if an incursion into Laos occurred. CBS diplomatic correspondent Marvin Kalb used "reliable sources" to disclose that twenty-five thousand South Vietnamese and nine thousand American troops were involved. CBS reporter Dan Rather added that "a high ranking administration official who declines to be identified" had told him that a decision one way or another on entering Laos might be made that evening.[14]

General Abrams was unfazed by the revelations and insisted that he would continue the embargo rather than jeopardize the lives of his men, but by 3 February the policy's hours were clearly numbered. That morning, the *Philadelphia Inquirer* complained about the confusion that had resulted from Abrams's no-news policy; a bitter *St. Louis Post-Dispatch* termed the embargo "a disgraceful piece of business"; and the *Chicago Daily News* criticized Nixon for treating the American people like children. By the end of the day, White House media analyst Mort Allen could only conclude that "from a PR standpoint the Indochina situation is very damning."[15]

As the pressure increased, President Nixon decided to act. On 4 February, Admiral Moorer cabled Abrams to inform him of the president's wishes. So much pressure had developed from all sides, he said, that the embargo had to end. Otherwise, it might become "the single factor which prevents us from proceeding with the remainder of the operation." Military spokesmen announced the change a short while later, explaining that the embargo had served its purpose because "our casualties have been at an absolute minimum."[16]

The decision brought with it a chorus of complaints in Congress and the press, but those that came from the Saigon correspondents were by far the angriest. Filing a widely reported protest with MACV, the reporters termed official handling of Dewey Canyon II "incomprehensible." Although public affairs officers had held daily briefings to keep them informed, they charged that MACV had sought to bar them from important news sources and, through its escort policies, to monitor interviews with soldiers in the field. Most damaging of all, they said, was the command's refusal to allow them to make any mention of the embargo, while official sources in Washington had all but acknowledged its existence.[17]

Given U.S. awareness that the attack into Laos had been compromised and the mounting toll the embargo had taken on official credibility, General Abrams's contention that restraints on the press were necessary to preserve American and South Vietnamese lives hardly appears satisfactory on its own. The North Vietnamese had long before decided that an attack into Laos was inevitable and that it would come up Route 9 toward Tchepone. Beginning in October 1970, they had moved their most critical supplies southward, had begun construction of a road to bypass Tchepone, and had prepared an interlocking network of defensive positions along Highway 9. In that light, it seems clear that the embargo served mainly to inflame a situation already fated for controversy by turning it into a confrontation over what the role of the news media in war should be.[18] As Leonard put it:

The press refused to believe there was a military reason for the embargo, while MACV couldn't believe that a few days delay in publication would represent a terrible infringement on the public's right to know. It was a classic confrontation as to which was more important, military security or the public's right. . . . As an old infantryman, my sympathies will always lie with the soldier . . . who always has to fight the war, not [with] the reporter who writes about it. If the embargo saved one life it was worth it.[19]

Whatever the motives behind Abrams's restrictions, within hours of their end President Nixon approved the execution of the drive toward Tchepone along Highway 9. It took until 8 February for the operation itself to begin. When it did, in order to underscore the South Vietnamese role, MACV terminated all references to Dewey Canyon II in its contacts with the press and began to call it by its South Vietnamese name, Lam Son 719.[20]

Prior to the attack, Washington agencies had drafted a plan to ensure that all announcements accompanying the operation created an impression of South Vietnamese competence and American resolution. President Thieu would release first word of the event, take public responsibility for the decision to enter Laos, and affirm South Vietnam's desire to uphold the independence and integrity of its neighbor. The U.S. mission in Saigon was then to announce that no U.S. ground forces or advisers would enter Laos and that American forces would supply only air combat and logistical support. From then on, American spokesmen would keep to the background, supplying information on American portions of the effort but allowing the South Vietnamese to be the primary source for news of what was happening.[21]

The State and Defense Departments encouraged Thieu to state only minimal goals for the attack in his announcement of the operation and to avoid any mention of Tchepone as a target. They also insisted that he substitute the word *disrupt* for *destroy* in his description of what his forces would do. Thieu accepted that advice but balked at a suggestion that he convene a background briefing for the press after his announcement to fill reporters in on what was happening. He would postpone any session of the sort for a day, he said, and would prohibit reporters from accompanying his troops into Laos until all danger of compromise had passed.[22]

Administration spokesmen began a wide-ranging public relations campaign as soon as South Vietnamese forces entered Laos. To put the operation in the best possible light, Charles Colson contacted Howard K. Smith of ABC News, Herbert Klein arranged for a backgrounder on the subject for the AP, Henry Kissinger briefed friendly reporters and columnists, presidential aides started a quiet program to generate letters to the editor praising the president's courage, and efforts went forward to elicit endorsements from labor and other organizations and to evoke favorable comments from friendly congressmen and senators. In each case, administration spokesmen highlighted the success of the previous year's operation in Cambodia, emphasized the bankruptcy of those who criticized administration policy, and asserted that the embargo had saved American lives.[23]

Nixon had insisted that official statements link the operation to the narrowest possible goals, but as the campaign progressed, mistakes occurred. One of MACV's communiqués inadvertently stated that the South Vietnamese were conducting "interdiction operations" in Laos, and Nixon himself stressed during a meeting with congressional leaders that the South Vietnamese were *cutting* the Ho Chi Minh Trail. Both statements fed an impression already prevalent in many quarters that the incursion would choke off the trail, a practical impossibility.[24]

Meanwhile, Secretary Laird exaggerated the ability of the South Vietnamese armed forces to execute major military operations by asserting at a 10 February background briefing that they alone had planned Lam Son 719. As for the operation itself, U.S. forces were providing only air support, more than thirty B-52 and three hundred tactical air and helicopter sorties per day. "I could be wrong," the secretary said, but if everything went well "a very, very dramatic change" would occur in Southeast Asia. General Abrams protested Laird's remarks in a message to Admiral McCain. He said that his command, not the South Vietnamese, had framed the idea for the incursion and had done much of the initial groundwork. As for the statistics on sortie rates, MACV had withheld them from the press on grounds that they were of value to the enemy.[25]

According to Jerry Friedheim, who had helped prepare the backgrounder, Abrams's objections were beside the point. Laird wanted American withdrawals to continue on schedule. He understood that if Lam Son 719 failed, withdrawals would continue or even accelerate, but if it succeeded, Nixon might be tempted to prolong the war. He had thus drafted his remarks very carefully in order to link any victory that occurred in Laos to American withdrawals and to create expectations in the press that would restrain the president rather than allow him the free rein he so clearly desired.[26]

While officials in Washington advanced their agendas, MACV took what steps it could in the field to avoid problems with the press by establishing a special facility at Quang Tri City, where reporters could eat, sleep, and receive briefings. Journalists visiting the troops at Khe Sanh had to request accommodations from the units they visited, but they received them at nominal cost. When they returned to Quang Tri with their stories, MACV provided rapid air transport and telephone and Teletype circuits to move copy and film to Saigon.[27]

Although the arrangements were painstaking, they failed to provide the one thing newsmen wanted most: access to what was happening. Shortly after the operation began, the South Vietnamese commander, Lt. Gen. Hoang Xuan Lam, set up a press center of his own near that of the Americans. He also agreed to provide daily briefings and to transport reporters into the field. These assurances notwithstanding, Lam and his officers—with President Nixon's encouragement—did little to facilitate reporting of the operation. They took three days to

dispatch a public affairs officer to Quang Tri, and they announced almost immediately that forces in the field would be off-limits to the press until the situation
was secure, whenever that would be. Then, when South Vietnamese briefings
finally began at Quang Tri, Lam's spokesmen lied brazenly, telling reporters that
South Vietnamese units had suffered few casualties, even though everyone present had seen helicopters returning continually from the field laden with the bodies of the dead.[28]

The South Vietnamese eased their restrictions on 10 February by allowing a
helicopter to carry newsmen into Laos. To the chagrin of all concerned, the aircraft blundered into an enemy machine gun nest and went down. Larry Burrows
of *Life;* Henri Huet of the AP; Ken Potter of UPI; Keisaburo Shimamoto, stringing for *Newsweek;* and Sgt. Vu Tu, a South Vietnamese army photographer, were
all killed. The South Vietnamese tried again on 13 and 16 February, ferrying seventeen newsmen into the battle zone. Another ten made the trip overland by con-
voy. In all, however, only twenty-seven newsmen entered Laos between 8 and 20
February.[29]

Turning on MACV, the Saigon correspondents complained bitterly about the
command's refusal to allow reporters to ride American helicopters into Laos.
Recognizing that the criticism was tarnishing the image of the effort in Laos, the
Nixon administration suggested that Abrams change the policy, but the general
continued to take a hard line with the press. If MACV allowed reporters to fly
in its helicopters, he said, the newsmen would highlight the role of American air
crews in the operation and even photograph American technicians on the ground
in Laos recovering damaged helicopters. That would detract from the image the
United States sought to convey of a South Vietnam responsible for its own defense.[30]

Fending for themselves, reporters followed their own leads. The news stories
that resulted were often well-founded, but some were unreliable or incomplete. A
number, for example, reported as early as 11 February that the South Vietnamese
had reached Tchepone although those forces had covered only half the distance.
Meanwhile, UPI alleged that at least one hundred Americans had entered Laos
to protect crews retrieving damaged helicopters, and ABC and CBS reported that
U.S. troops, some wearing South Vietnamese uniforms, were fighting with Lam's
forces. The press itself corrected the assertion that the South Vietnamese had
reached Tchepone, but the allegation that U.S. troops were fighting in Laos was so
explosive that General Abrams denied it outright. Although some U.S. units operated so near to Laos that their men probably believed they had crossed the border, he said, South Vietnamese troops alone provided security for crews recovering downed helicopters.[31]

Whatever the anger of the press, however, the response to the incursion both
around the world and in Congress seemed mild in comparison with the outcry
that had accompanied the previous year's incursion into Cambodia. Among
Western nations, only Denmark and France expressed strong opposition. Many of

the rest viewed the attack as a logical extension of earlier cross-border operations and reacted with private expressions of approval. Congressional opinion also appeared subdued. Critics of the war in the Senate opposed the operation and a number of Democrats expressed reservations, but Congress, as a whole, seemed prepared to give the president the benefit of the doubt as long as the incursion enhanced American withdrawals.[32]

The press in the United States was more apprehensive, but its initial comments fit the trend. Editors who had strongly supported administration policy in the past were characteristically approving, while those who had opposed it seemed just as adamant in their opposition. Of the rest, supporters outnumbered opponents by a ratio of 12 to 6, according to the State Department's news analysts, but much of the support was conditional and even grudging. Although the Hearst syndicate swung into line with administration policy, many journals were tentative, approving of the operation only for as long as it did nothing to hamper American withdrawals. So doubtful were some that eight out of twenty-six surveyed by the State Department on 11 February failed to come down either for or against the operation.[33]

The public reaction in the United States also fell flat. Antiwar leaders called for mass demonstrations, but where tens of thousands of Americans had marched in response to the Cambodian incursion, only a relative few attended rallies protesting the Laotian operation. If Americans seemed cool to the antiwar movement's appeals, however, that hardly indicated that they agreed with what was happening. Earlier presidents, for example, had been able to rely on surges in public support when they made difficult decisions, but Nixon saw his own support drop 5 percentage points after he announced the move into Laos. By 31 January 1971, indeed, 73 percent of the Americans interviewed favored an end to all U.S. troop involvement in South Vietnam within the next eleven months, an increase of 18 percent from the previous September. As the editors of the *Omaha World-Herald* remarked at the time, the main difference between those who had supported the war in earlier years and those who had opposed it no longer had to do with whether the conflict was justified. It was all a matter of speed. The hawks wanted out a little more slowly than the doves.[34]

If hardly anyone in the United States was satisfied with what was happening in Laos and the press continued to complain about the official mists obscuring the operation, early news coverage of the operation was nonetheless probably as favorable to the official point of view as it would ever be. On 12 February, Walter Cronkite referred to the helicopters supporting the operation as "sitting ducks" and claimed that twenty-six had been destroyed or damaged during the first five days of the attack rather than the ten MACV had announced. Even so, he repeated claims by President Thieu that the operation was succeeding. The *Washington Star* likewise spent considerable time reporting on helicopter losses, but it also relayed claims that South Vietnamese forces had achieved a 7-to-1 enemy body count. As late as 17 February, a White House news summary cheerfully reported that ABC News had quoted official sources to the effect that the South Vietnamese had cut about half of the enemy's supply routes in Laos and that CBS diplomatic correspondent Marvin Kalb had broadcast the administration's message that "there is great military success so far, leading to greater success in the political sphere." Only David Brinkley of NBC News was particularly negative. He quoted unidentified sources to report that the North Vietnamese had stopped the incursion "dead in its tracks."[35]

Brinkley was right. For by 13 February, the North Vietnamese had launched such a forceful counterattack that the South Vietnamese in Laos were beginning to hold back. Meanwhile, General Lam and his commanders were complaining that Abrams had promised them the support of 130 helicopters, but that after only five days in the field no more than half that number were available.[36] The American commander in the region, Lt. Gen. James W. Sutherland, Jr., reassured Lam that fewer than 130 helicopters were necessary to support the operation, but his assurances carried little weight. The troops invading Laos were not only among South Vietnam's best but also the main backing for the Thieu regime if a coup occurred. Rather than have them destroyed or learn at the last moment that they could not be extracted from Laos because helicopters were lacking, Thieu instructed Lam on 13 February to halt the offensive for the time being at Ban Dong, eighteen kilometers inside Laos and half the distance to Tchepone. General Cao Van Vien, the chief of the South Vietnamese Joint General Staff, assured Abrams that only a three- to five-day delay was involved and that the operation would proceed, but whatever Thieu's intentions, at that moment the South Vietnamese lost the initiative.[37]

The effects of Thieu's decision were immediately apparent to the White House. On 14 February, citing "high-level" interest, Admiral Moorer requested Abrams's opinion on whether the South Vietnamese were attacking aggressively. Without mentioning Thieu's instructions to Lam—the White House would learn of them from Moorer only on 18 March—Abrams responded that the halt at Ban Dong was a temporary adjustment to battlefield conditions. Already tallying a kill ratio of nearly 10 to 1, he said, the troops would resume the attack when circumstances permitted, probably within the week.[38]

Kissinger repeated some of Abrams's reasoning during an informal talk with reporters the next day. "The reason why the ARVN has been moving more slowly than expected," he told the newsmen, "is that as they go, they have to set up fire bases to cover their advance and to hit the still-uncut trails ahead. The North Viets are being forced to turn west with their supplies to do an end-run [around] . . . the ARVN."[39]

Abrams's assurances to the contrary, the situation in Laos began to deteriorate. By 19 February, the enemy had launched a major assault against Lam's northernmost flank, inflicting 326 killed, wounded, and missing upon the Thirty-ninth South Vietnamese Ranger Battalion and forcing it to abandon its position. Watching the battle from afar, the Saigon correspondents received little satisfaction from South Vietnamese briefers, who asserted as late as 21 February that only 23 rangers had been killed and 40 wounded while accounting for 639 enemy dead. Interviewing survivors, returning helicopter pilots, and American officers who kept close touch by radio with the units in the field, reporters nonetheless concluded that a serious setback had occurred and put the word on the wire.[40]

Their initial reports were understandably sketchy. "The first major battle of the twelve-day-old Laotian invasion has broken out," Walter Cronkite noted. "Casualties are . . . heavy." Later reports were much more detailed and critical. One of the best of South Vietnam's fighting units had been driven off a mountaintop, Craig Whitney of the *New York Times* remarked, after heavy enemy fire had downed American helicopters delivering supplies and reinforcements. Although the troops had redeemed themselves by tying down a North Vietnamese regiment, each time medical evacuation helicopters had arrived to remove the wounded, able-bodied soldiers had rushed to board.[41]

Whitney's report and others like it gave a fairly close approximation of what had happened, but General Abrams refused to concede that a defeat had occurred. With the assistance of American air and artillery attacks, he told Moorer, the Rangers had rendered two enemy battalions ineffective before withdrawing with all of their weapons and ammunition. Admiral McCain seconded Abrams. "The impression derived from press articles was totally misleading," he asserted. "The orderly withdrawal of the 39th was omitted, and figures quoted were inflated in favor of the enemy."[42]

President Nixon, for his part, seems to have accepted the military's interpretation, but he was clearly unprepared to tolerate many defeats. The appearance of success in Laos, he told Moorer and Kissinger, was as important as what occurred in the field. He could not allow the South Vietnamese to sustain a serious setback because that might damage President Thieu's coming campaign for reelection and handicap the entire effort to Vietnamize the war.[43]

Admiral Moorer was less concerned about Thieu's reelection than he was about Nixon himself and the effect that rapid, sensational press reporting might have on the president's attitude and that of his staff. Moorer pushed Abrams to begin issuing special "flash" evaluations of unusual incidents that could be used to counter the pessimism press reporting engendered in official circles.[44]

Secretary Laird saw it all differently. Believing that complaints about restrictions on news gathering had tainted many otherwise neutral or favorable press reports, he considered the reestablishment of official credibility the best solution for everyone's concerns. Two steps were necessary, he told Abrams. First, the Saigon correspondents had to become the source for news of the operation rather than reporters in Washington who had access to briefings but little firsthand knowledge of events. To that end, Abrams and his staff would have to hold regular background briefings to explain what was happening. Second, MACV had to remove an important source of friction with the press by allowing newsmen to fly into Laos on American as well as South Vietnamese helicopters.[45]

The U.S. mission in Saigon was already doing much of what Laird wanted. As the situation in Laos had deteriorated, MACV's public affairs officers had continually provided newsmen they considered reliable with material to demonstrate that the operation was succeeding. Meanwhile, both Abrams and his deputy, Gen. Frederick C. Weyand, had held background briefings for influential reporters and bureau chiefs. So had the South Vietnamese, who had also transported a group of reporters representing both the print and the electronic media more than twenty kilometers into Laos to inspect a forward fire base.[46]

Despite these efforts, Abrams promised to do more. At his urging, Thieu's press secretary replaced Lam's briefer at Quang Tri, who spoke only hesitant English, with an officer more fluent in the language. Abrams also dedicated a helicopter to the use of the press and began to transport reporters into Laos on a regular basis. The aircraft made more than one hundred trips over the next thirty days. Official spokesmen likewise began to announce aircraft losses in Laos and on 2 March even revealed that the enemy had launched several surface-to-air missiles in an attempt to repel American air attacks.[47]

Although press reporting became more factual and balanced, the situation was too far gone for the new approach to make much difference. If the incursion had been going well, its success would have shone forth for all to see, but it was faltering, and as it did, contradictions seemed to compound.

Helicopter losses provide a case in point. Reporters continued to complain that MACV was acknowledging as destroyed only aircraft unrecovered from Laos while counting as damaged any it could retrieve, whatever their condition. Public affairs officers held backgrounders to explain the command's damage criteria, but as Colonel Stevens later confirmed, the reporters' suspicions were well-founded. With helicopter losses growing as South Vietnamese fortunes declined, Stevens said, official spokesmen had devised a clever dodge. Rather than lie, they simply allowed bureaucracy to take its course by counting as destroyed only those aircraft that were irretrievable. Those that were unflyable fell into the damaged category until either repaired or rated as total losses. Since heavily damaged aircraft were sometimes carried to repair facilities as far away as the United States, the change in determination could take months. By the time it did, so the reasoning went, reporters would have moved on to other things. As late as mid-March, as a result, official sources were still admitting to the loss of only 50 helicopters, while pilots estimated that 119 had gone down during the first week of the attack alone. At the end of the operation, MACV acknowledged that 103 helicopters had been lost and 500 more damaged, but Walter Cronkite announced that sources available to CBS had revealed that at least 200 of those listed as damaged would never fly again.[48]

Although the policy of hiding helicopter losses fit well with the Nixon administration's desire to depict the South Vietnamese effort as a success, the news stories that followed from it would have led to some compromise on the figures, but for a second concern: the fact that helicopter losses had been so high they had forced MACV to curtail resupply, medical, and combat support missions for the troops in Laos. Indeed, of the 132 gunships programmed to assist the operation, only 33 were flyable on 23 February. While those losses seemed reasonable in light of the heavy volume of sorties flown—thirty-two thousand between 26 February and 4 March alone—that U.S. commanders would confirm them for the enemy was unthinkable.[49]

In general, Bunker, Abrams, and the other Americans involved in the operation appear to have believed that the enormous firepower they could bring to bear in Laos would swing the advantage to their side. They thus pressed Lam to return to the offensive and expressed only optimism in their reports. By 25 February, however, Henry Kissinger was convinced that the incursion had bogged down and that substantial losses were occurring. "I do not understand what Abrams is doing," he told Moorer. "I think the units north of . . . [Highway] 9 are just dug in in a static position. . . . And I don't see anything aggressive [to the] south of . . . 9 either. If we are getting run out of Laos, . . . I promise you the president will collapse on Vietnam. . . . If we are getting our pants beaten off here, we've had it in Vietnam for psychological reasons. . . . I am talking to you as a friend. I have told the president everything is great."[50]

President Nixon, for his part, accepted the assurances he received, but he had no intention of being taken by surprise if the operation failed. He told Moorer and Kissinger that official spokesmen had placed too much emphasis on Tchepone as a goal and that they had exaggerated the success of the South Vietnamese in cutting the Ho Chi Minh Trail. As a hedge in case the unthinkable occurred, all concerned had to reemphasize to the press that the incursion aimed only at disrupting enemy supply lines and that Tchepone was at best a minor station along the way. Thus instructed, General Abrams began to make the points in conversations with newsmen, and Nixon himself repeated them at a 4 March news conference. Reporters perceived the change in rhetoric but accepted it with little question. Over the days that followed, they made disruption of the trail one of the criteria by which they judged the success of the operation.[51]

While the president and his advisers thus succeeded in emphasizing limited goals, they made no effort to temper the optimism that continued to cushion official remarks about the incursion. Instead, Nixon himself avowed at a news conference that General Abrams had assured him "the South Vietnamese by themselves can hack it."[52]

So many problems nevertheless remained in Laos that newsmen had little difficulty confirming their doubts. Conferring with their sources, NBC's correspondents revealed the bitter conclusion of some South Vietnamese that by entering Laos they had become pawns of the United States. Marvin Kalb charged on CBS that U.S. intelligence had seriously underestimated the strength of North Vietnamese artillery and antiaircraft batteries. A whole series of reports arose

François Sully. (Don North)

around a fight that had erupted at a landing zone in Laos known as Hill 31, where Lam's forces were again faltering. Nixon became so enraged at it all that he ordered up another assault on the news media for Agnew to deliver.[53]

By the end of February, pessimism was spreading within the U.S. government itself. On the twenty-fourth, intelligence reports revealed that the enemy had constructed a bypass on the Ho Chi Minh Trail that went around Tchepone, allowing the flow of supplies to the south to continue undeterred. The next day, Lt. Gen. Do Cao Tri, the commander of the incursion's little-noticed Cambodian segment, died in a helicopter crash along with correspondent François Sully. Almost immediately progress in that area slowed because Tri's replacement, Lt. Gen. Nguyen Van Minh, refused to take risks. Then the enemy captured Hill 31 in Laos, along with some 115 South Vietnamese officers and enlisted men. Kissinger was aghast at the equanimity with which Abrams and Moorer seemed to greet each new disaster. "I got a briefing this morning," he told Laird, "and they didn't mention Hill 31, and I pick it up in the newspapers and if someone asks me I don't know what's going on."[54]

The next day, in what appeared a burst of renewed aggressiveness, General Lam announced preparations for an airborne assault on Tchepone and launched a series of moves to consolidate security along Highway 9. The development heartened U.S. commanders, but on the same day Lam refused to reinforce his units in Laos with a third division. Shortly thereafter, alluding vaguely to "politics," he confirmed a decision by Thieu to withdraw the South Vietnamese Airborne Division from Laos within ten days.[55]

Press reports mirrored these uncertainties, with journalists at the end of the month wavering between whether the incursion was going well or poorly. On 27 February, NBC commentator Edwin Newman repeated South Vietnamese claims that Communist forces were running away. But on the same program one of his colleagues, correspondent George Lewis, suggested that South Vietnamese officials were of two minds. Some told reporters that the force in Laos had gone as far as it intended to go, while others said the troops were digging in rather than preparing to pull out. In the same way, the AP repeated official claims that the incursion had disrupted Hanoi's plans for a dry-season offensive but also relayed allegations by unidentified sources that some of Lam's units had abandoned their wounded and "bugged out."[56]

On 6 March the South Vietnamese appeared to settle the question of whether they were going to stay or depart by launching their air assault into Tchepone. The enemy received more than thirty-six hours' advance notice of the attack, but massive air assaults eliminated most of any opposition that waited. When the first troops arrived, they encountered only sporadic gunfire and large numbers of enemy dead. President Nixon was so buoyed by the development that he commended Abrams and Bunker for the excellence of their reporting. Passing the compliment to Bunker, Henry Kissinger noted, "The president made the additional comment that our worst enemy seems to be the press."[57]

17

Saving Face

The assault on Tchepone came at a difficult moment for the U.S. Army in the press. Stories continued on My Lai and its aftermath. More were appearing on allegations that the army had conducted covert surveillance of private citizens in order to anticipate possibly violent antiwar protests. Meanwhile, a stinging documentary criticizing the Defense Department's wide-ranging public affairs program had just aired on CBS. Titled "The Selling of the Pentagon" and broadcast on 23 February 1971, the program claimed that the agency was spending more than the combined annual news budgets of all three television networks on activities extolling the violence of war. The criticism coincided with growing public discontent. Gallup polls during March reported a sharp, 18-point drop in approval for Nixon's handling of the war. Harris polls were even more alarming. They revealed that 42 percent of those surveyed disapproved of the incursion into Laos and that 51 percent would favor a congressional resolution requiring a final U.S. withdrawal from Vietnam by the end of the year.[1]

Secretary Laird attempted to assuage public opinion by hinting broadly during an interview that the president might announce the recall of more than one hundred thousand troops by January 1972. Where "The Selling of the Pentagon" was concerned, however, a more active approach seemed necessary. While conceding that the Defense Department's public affairs had been heavy-handed at times, Daniel Henkin thus declared in a widely reprinted letter to the House Armed Services Committee that CBS had changed the meaning of his remarks on the program by reducing the size of one comment and then inserting two sentences from his response to a different question. He later pointed out that the network's producers had also edited the comments of other speakers to make points the originators had never intended.[2]

Researcher Marvin Barrett would later assert that these "rearrangements" had at most flawed an otherwise admirable piece of journalism. Whether or not that was so, the program attracted fewer than ten million viewers out of an audience of fifty-eight million and would have disappeared quickly from the public eye but for the Laotian incursion. For in the days that followed the seizure of Tchepone, the South Vietnamese force in Laos disintegrated, leading the White House in search of some way to save face. "The Selling of the Pentagon" seemed tailor-made for the purpose, particularly since it had nothing to do with Laos.[3]

As questions rose in the United States, they continued in South Vietnam, where the Saigon correspondents persisted in their complaint that MACV was impeding news coverage of the incursion. Concentrating on sources they themselves had developed rather than the word of official spokesmen, they missed very little.

The American pilots assisting the South Vietnamese remained prominent in their reports. The enemy's gunners were "definitely good," one young warrant officer told Iver Peterson of the *New York Times*. "And they're getting better because of all the practice we've given them." Another complained, "I'd rather hand it out for my own people—all of us would. . . . Now we get blown away for people who don't even like us." The newsmen also watched as the pilots' helicopters bore a steady stream of killed and wounded back from the battlefield. "Sometimes you don't have to go to Laos to see the evidence of South Vietnamese problems on the other side of the border," ABC correspondent Steve Bell commented. "This is just one of many helicopters . . . bringing back . . . wounded and dead. . . . It's the kind of story that often fails to show up in the official releases."[4]

Meanwhile, Craig Whitney of the *New York Times* suggested that MACV's policies had contributed to the death of General Tri. Naming Col. Robert Montague, an important American expert on South Vietnam, as his source, he noted that Tri had usually flown only with reliable American helicopter crews. On the day he died, however, he had chosen to employ less skilled South Vietnamese because Sully was to ride with him, and U.S. policy specified that reporters were not to cross the border in American aircraft. Although tied to a credible source, Whitney's comments about the death of Tri were questionable. Since no one had witnessed the crash, the conclusion that South Vietnamese incompetence was involved was unwarranted.[5]

By that time, Abrams himself appears to have begun to question whether the incursion would end as he wished. Although he was confident on the surface, some of his communications with his military superiors contained an undercurrent of doubt. "Morale and confidence of the ARVN commanders has risen appreciably during the past three or four days," he thus told Admiral Moorer, chairman of the Joint Chiefs, on 8 March. Even so, he added, those commanders "do not concede that there is still much to be done . . . or that there is now the opportunity to exploit initial successes with even more telling results." The observation set off an alarm for General Haig. It provided, he told Kissinger, "ample notice of potential setbacks."[6]

President Nixon confers with Henry Kissinger. (U.S. Army)

Suspicious of Thieu's intentions himself, Kissinger instructed Bunker on 9 March to impress upon the president that, "from our perspective, every week ARVN stays in Laos represents a serious blow to the enemy's offensive capability." Acutely aware that the units in Laos were fatigued but unwilling to reinforce them, Thieu pledged to continue operations once his troops withdrew to rest. Kissinger recognized at once that it was all just a facade and that the South Vietnamese would, as he put it, "bug out in the next ten days." In the same way, when Moorer predicted on 13 March that Thieu's forces would remain in Laos for the full extent of the dry season, the national security adviser could only respond, "Across roads or horsing around?"[7]

Neither Kissinger's nor Abrams's doubts appeared in public. Instead, administration spokesmen continued to speak of success and to concentrate on the enemy's losses. Lam's forces were killing Communists at a very heavy rate, Moorer told Republican leaders on 6 March. While they would never win every battle, they were "doing very well indeed." Optimism also prevailed at MACV. At a backgrounder where candor might have prepared the press for reverses to come, command spokesmen noted instead that enemy casualties were running nine to one in favor of allied forces, that there had been a 50 percent decline in enemy truck activity through the region, and that the enemy had lost vast stores of food and ammunition.[8]

Unconvinced, the Saigon correspondents continued on their own way. Alvin Shuster, for one, challenged the assertion that truck traffic on the Ho Chi Minh Trail had fallen. In fact, he said, his own sources indicated that the flow of supplies had returned almost to preinvasion levels in areas little touched by the fighting. Other reporters picked at MACV'S statistics. "The ARVN claim 90 tanks, you say 50. Why the divergence?" one asked at a Saigon briefing. "Our figures are based on U.S. observations," came the reply, " . . . and the figures you get from the ARVN are based on their observations." Iver Peterson took on Admiral Moorer during ABC's *Issues and Answers*. Administration spokesmen claimed, the reporter said, that the incursion demonstrated the effectiveness of Vietnamization. Yet the South Vietnamese had received the assistance of massive U.S. air support. "How do you call this an indication that Vietnamization is working?" Moorer waved the question aside. The tactic, he said, had "paid off handsomely."[9]

Over the days that followed, enemy pressure against the force in Laos increased. Squabbling broke out among senior South Vietnamese commanders, and problems of all sorts proliferated. By 15 March, the troops were beginning to withdraw. By the eighteenth, a full retreat was in progress, and the story was receiving heavy play in the United States. Jerry Friedheim at the Pentagon declared that everything was proceeding according to plan and that the South Vietnamese were only engaging in airmobile operations against the enemy, but the remarks of Americans in the field were an effective counterpoint. "They can talk about helicopter mobility all they want," one army pilot told the AP, "but from where I'm flying there's only one way to describe it—retreat, and a bad one."[10]

General Sutherland blamed much of what was happening on the press. "Future plans are reported before they happen," he told General Haig, "causing problems for ARVN." Neglecting the enemy's long-standing penetration of South Vietnamese security on the operation, Haig agreed. It seemed to him, he said, that reporters had all along wanted the incursion to fail.[11] Kissinger, however, blamed the South Vietnamese. Their withdrawal would "kill us domestically," he told Moorer on 18 March. "If they had told us a week ago they were . . . [going to do] this we could have said we have our victory. . . . Of course, we control the helicopters." Moorer was startled. "We can't just leave them in there," he responded. "Why not?" asked Kissinger. "We could," said Moorer, "but [that would] make more political problems."[12]

To finish the operation on some sort of face-saving upswing, General Abrams suggested that Thieu mount a surprise raid on an enemy supply point about twenty kilometers to the south of Tchepone near the Laotian town of Muong Nong. Arriving by helicopter after heavy B-52 attacks, the troops would destroy enemy stockpiles but leave before the enemy could respond. That would allow Thieu to declare publicly that his forces retained the ability to strike at will in Laos. Thieu agreed but declined to take action until most of his troops were out of Laos. In the interim, administration spokesmen sought to counter increasing reports of panic in the press. "This was not a rout," Vice President Agnew insisted at a news conference in Boston. "This was an orderly retreat . . . in accordance with plan. They were not forced out."

Reporters dutifully repeated the points, but James McCartney could only observe caustically in the *Philadelphia Inquirer* that "U.S. military men used to criticize the South Vietnamese for a tendency to 'cut and run.' . . . Now, when the South Vietnamese flee, Pentagon spokesmen are inclined to praise their 'mobility.' "[13] McCartney's opinionated comments were hardly more sarcastic than those appearing in some quarters in official circles. Informed, for example, during a 22 March meeting that the enemy had released large quantities of rice wine to his troops to whip them into a suicidal frenzy, Henry Kissinger could only remark, alluding to the South Vietnamese army's increasing problem with drug abuse, that "this ought to be a great battle, one army hopped up on drugs and the other . . . on booze."[14]

General Abrams remained upbeat. At a special backgrounder for the Saigon correspondents on 21 March, he denied that any sort of catastrophe had occurred and concentrated on the supplies Lam's forces had destroyed and the favorable kill ratios they had incurred. He conceded that the enemy had in one case routed a battalion of Airborne troops whose commander had deserted his men, but he still insisted that the members of more successful units would emerge from Laos with greater confidence than they had ever possessed.[15]

Such assurances notwithstanding, strong questioning persisted in the press. "The generals of the ARVN High Command insist the withdrawal is going according to plan," Tom Streithorst of NBC News declared on 23 March, "but . . . we filmed three separate instances of panicked ARVN soldiers who rode on the skids of helicopters in preference to waiting for another helicopter that might not come." Changing subjects, the reporter then noted that as the South Vietnamese left Laos, the American units that had braced the operation from the rear would face increasing danger. Many of those troops, he said, already believed that the U.S. Army had failed to provide them with adequate support, and others seemed so exhausted they were on the verge of rebellion.[16] Streithorst's report galled Kissinger, who had little confidence left in the South Vietnamese but even less in the press. "I just don't see how we can fight a war like this," he told congressional leaders at a White House briefing. "Interviewing GI's is the worst way to find out what's going on. . . . The people in the middle of . . . [a battle] have the least idea of what is happening."[17]

The president's staff fought back by asking administration supporters on Capitol Hill to back Nixon and to do what they could to humble the news media. On 12 March, as a result, Senator Clifford P. Hansen of Wyoming held a two-hour screening of television news segments dealing with the incursion that purported to demonstrate bias on the part of CBS and NBC. Meanwhile, fact sheets on the incursion went to Republican legislators along with instructions on how they could be used in support of the administration's policies.[18]

South Vietnamese soldiers struggle to board a helicopter leaving Laos. (AP/Wide World Photos)

As these efforts proceeded, Vice President Agnew launched a broad attack on CBS News in which he resurrected "The Selling of the Pentagon" as an example of what he said were efforts by CBS to warp facts to fit its own needs. During the days that followed, the president of CBS News, Frank Stanton, responded that his network had done nothing unethical. CBS then rebroadcast the program along with comments by Agnew, Laird, and Congressman F. Edward Hebert. More charges and countercharges followed because CBS had declined to cede editorial judgments to outsiders and had refused to allow Agnew and the others to choose which of their remarks would appear on the program.[19]

At the height of the controversy, during a televised interview with ABC newsman Howard K. Smith on the evening of 22 March, Nixon himself entered the fray. Cautioning that it was too soon to judge whether the incursion was a success or a failure, he emphasized that the impression of panic conveyed by television news films was inaccurate. "What have the pictures shown?" he asked. "They've shown only those men in the four ARVN battalions . . . that were in trouble. They haven't shown people in the other 18 battalions. That is not because it's been deliberate. It's because those make news." Never raising his voice, he went on to score the press for its alarmism and to assert that he had received less support from the news media than any president in the century.[20]

Commentators in the press took as a given the president's claim that the final results of the incursion would become apparent only in the future. They nonetheless questioned a number of his other assertions. Fixing on a remark Nixon had attributed to General Abrams, that the South Vietnamese "by themselves can hack it and they can give a better account of themselves than the North Vietnamese," the *Philadelphia Bulletin,* for one, remarked, "Without our air cover and without 51 battalions of U.S. troops holding the fort . . . one can only guess at how much worse the situation might have been." The *Boston Globe* was equally skeptical. "One does not expect, in this war," its editors said, "the total honesty of the late Gen. Joseph 'Vinegar Joe' Stilwell who declared, after Burma in World War II, 'I claim we got a hell of a beating . . . and it is damned humiliating.' But there is no excuse for concealing . . . facts known only too well in Hanoi."[21]

By 25 March, most of the troops had returned to South Vietnam, and the incursion had all but ended. Instead of diminishing, however, tensions increased in official circles. Concern began to rise in Washington that the enemy might attack Khe Sanh, where he could inflict significant casualties on American forces or lay down a siege similar to the one imposed in 1968. Meanwhile, the South Vietnamese commanders of the incursion continued to fight among themselves, prompting General Sutherland to tell Abrams, "We can take [the South Vietnamese] . . . only so far; beyond that point they must go on their own. . . . Today I am not sure of how much further we can take them."[22]

Whatever the wrangling among the South Vietnamese, there was little possibility that the Nixon administration would relax its efforts to save face both for itself and for them. By official tally, the force in Laos had lost 1,100 men, but the actual number undoubtedly was much larger. If it became clear that those deaths had been in vain and that the incursion had been a devastating defeat, the political implications would be heavy in the United States, and the South Vietnamese people might lose all faith in Thieu and his regime.[23] When AP reporter Tammy Arbuckle alleged in a 25 March dispatch that South Vietnam had suffered nearly 10,000 killed and wounded in Laos and that government casualty figures were less than honest, Secretary Laird thus wasted little time in contacting the reporter's employers. He succeeded in having the story withdrawn on grounds that it was erroneous, but even if Arbuckle's figures were exaggerated, information available to MACV confirmed that dissembling had occurred. For if official tallies for the incursion came to 7,683 killed, wounded, and missing, the actual figure was clearly much higher. Government reports, for example, listed 491 dead for the First South Vietnamese Infantry Division, but the unit's officers confirmed privately in conversations with their American advisers that they had lost at least 775.[24]

Although the American news media paid little attention to official avowals of success, they were intensely interested in the long-term results of the incursion. Besides accepting Nixon's assertion that time alone would tell whether the attack had achieved its ends, a number of commentators adopted themes that could only have pleased the president. Both the *Omaha World-Herald* and the *National Ob-*

server were quick to note, for example, that those who were criticizing the operation had a personal stake in its failure because they had predicted disaster long before it occurred. Meanwhile, the influential financial weekly *Barron's Magazine* scored the "distorted and slanted reporting" that it saw exemplified in "The Selling of the Pentagon" and called on the Federal Communications Commission to revoke CBS's access to the nation's airwaves.[25]

If some commentators sided with the Nixon administration, however, many more criticized the incursion and its results. ABC News, for one, interviewed four of its correspondents in Saigon in an attempt to describe the difficulties newsmen had encountered in covering the operation. Summarizing many of the controversies that had occurred, Jim Giggins, Howard Tuckner, Steve Bell, and Don Farmer complained bitterly that public affairs officers in both South Vietnam and Washington had attempted to mislead the press. An article in the *Christian Science Monitor* by correspondent Daniel Southerland, meanwhile, asserted that North Vietnam's response to the operation cast doubt on the assumptions that formed the basis for American withdrawals. For if the enemy was so strongly motivated that he was willing to lose more than three divisions in a fight for the Ho Chi Minh Trail, it hardly seemed likely that he would withdraw from South Vietnam following a negotiated settlement. *Time* termed the incursion "a costly miscalculation" and noted that barely a battalion of regular reserves remained in the Saigon area. "Quite frankly, it scares me," an American official told the magazine. " . . . I wonder whether the other side realizes just how bare the cupboard is."[26]

Believing that the president had received information that had diverged too often from realities in the field, one of Kissinger's military assistants, Cmdr. Jon Howe, compiled a study that compared what was happening in the field during the incursion with what the White House knew at any given moment. He found that the president had rarely received the timely information he needed. Instead, South Vietnamese commanders had failed to keep their American advisers informed, and General Abrams himself had been slow in reporting developments. As a result, administration spokesmen had time and again taken positions with the press that varied from the facts.[27]

Kissinger took up his misgivings with the president. According to Nixon's chief of staff, H. R. Haldeman, both decided they had been misled by Abrams on what the operation might accomplish and that the drive toward Tchepone had turned out to be "basically a disaster." The two concluded, Haldeman said, "that they should pull Abrams out, but then the P [president] made the point that this is the end of the military operations anyway so what difference does it make."[28]

Although Kissinger believed that the operation had failed, he and his staff continued to put the best face possible on what had happened. By forcing the North Vietnamese to consume supplies that normally would have gone to South Vietnam, they told reporters, the incursion had eliminated any possibility that the enemy would mount sustained attacks in South Vietnam during the rest of 1971. Their assertions, however, told only half the story. For they had all along expected the enemy's main effort to come in 1972, when they believed a North Vietnamese offensive would complicate the president's chances for reelection. From that standpoint little had changed. Ample time remained for the Communists to regroup and resupply.[29]

In the end, the controversy that developed over the incursion was probably inevitable, given the situation in the field and the bad blood that already existed between the military and the news media in Vietnam. If the attack had triumphed, of course, the success would have shone forth in the press, whatever the animosity of reporters. But it turned into a fiasco, and all attempts to paint it otherwise served only to make matters worse. As it was, the anger of the press endured long after the incursion had ended, marring military relations with the news media from then on. Before the attack, reporters and military officers were often at odds, but a measure of forbearance existed between the two groups. Afterward, the level of antimilitary rhetoric in the press began to grow. Leaks to reporters of highly classified documents seemed to occur on a daily basis, and important journals paid earnest attention to disgruntled officers who sought to air complaints about the army and the war. Meanwhile, *New York Times* correspondent Neil Sheehan accused General Westmoreland and other policy makers of complicity in crimes against humanity.

The military, for their part, sought to save face by holding controversial developments as close as possible and by saying no more than necessary on subjects likely to attract adverse press coverage. In the case of Sheehan's charges, for example, when the reporter alleged in the 28 March edition of the *New York Times Book Review* that the violent manner in which the United States had fought the war constituted a war crime, teams of researchers at the Pentagon constructed a wide-ranging rebuttal. In the end, however, the army dropped the matter. Polemics might only aggravate the issue, so the reasoning went, and much of the material that would have to be cited was itself so ambiguous that it could be made to serve either side of the question.[30]

Much the same approach prevailed in the case of Col. David Hackworth, a highly respected veteran with more than five years of experience in Vietnam. Unhappy with the way the United States was fighting the war, the officer decided he had no choice but to go to the press. During a series of interviews with ABC News, he launched into a broad critique of the war that included charges about South Vietnamese corruption, cover-ups of war crimes, and the falsification of official statistics. Seeking to determine whether these charges were valid, General Abrams instituted an investigation. The inspector general rapidly determined that the colonel's material was too amorphous or too old to be verified, but during the course of the effort, one of Hackworth's subordinates came forward with information indicating that the colonel himself had indulged in black-market trading, currency manipulation, drug abuse, and organized prostitution while serving as a commander in South Vietnam. Abrams sought to bring charges against Hackworth, but the army declined to pursue the matter. Laird later explained that the case had fallen apart upon close examination, but since Hackworth confirmed much of it years afterward in a personal memoir, it seems clear that the colonel had benefited from his connections with the press and the army's desire to incur no more self-inflicted wounds than necessary at that late stage in the war.[31]

If the controversies sparked by Sheehan and Hackworth posed problems, they were only symptoms of a deeper malaise by then spreading at the heart of the American effort in Vietnam. For as questions continued to arise in the United States and the various sides in the debate over the war hardened, the codes that had earlier defined the limits of proper conduct for soldiers and civilian officials were breaking down.

During March, April, and May, for example, syndicated columnist Jack Anderson made a number of revelations based on highly classified documents that could only have come from high-level sources. They dealt with long-hidden aspects of the war: U.S. Air Force efforts to increase rainfall along the Ho Chi Minh Trail, Pentagon programs for domestic surveillance, plans for the bombing of the North Vietnamese port at Haiphong, the enemy's advance knowledge of the incursion into Laos, and American efforts to spy on the Saigon regime. At that time, the *New York Times* also began publication of a secret Defense Department history of war-related decision making during the Johnson administration that would shortly become known as *The Pentagon Papers*. With Henry Kissinger about to depart on a secret visit to China to begin the normalization of U.S. relations with that country, the two sets of leaks shook the president. From his point of view, any suggestion that the U.S. government might be incapable of keeping secrets complicated everything.[32]

The president and his advisers moved immediately to block publication of *The Pentagon Papers*. They also attempted to find out who was behind the leaks to Anderson and the *Times*. Over the next several months, they identified Daniel Ellsberg, a former Defense Department analyst, as the one who had released *The Pentagon Papers* and YN1 Charles Radford, a U.S. Navy yeoman on the National Security Council staff, as Anderson's probable source.[33]

Ellsberg's revelations drew most of the attention of the press, but they dealt only with the decisions of the Johnson administration. Radford's disclosures were much more alarming to Nixon because the yeoman had passed stolen White House documents through his military superiors to Admiral Moorer, who apparently so mistrusted the White House that he felt a need for a clandestine source to keep him informed of what the National Security Council might do next. Stricken in conscience by the contents of some of the material involved, the yeoman appears to have turned to Anderson, a fellow member of his church, for advice, and to have ended up slipping part of what he knew to the reporter.[34]

Moorer denied everything, and Radford insisted he had never passed documents to Anderson. Nixon himself, however, appears to have had no doubts. He told his advisers dejectedly (if perhaps disingenuously) that he would have given the admiral any information he wanted, if only he had asked. In the end, as with Hackworth, Nixon declined to take any action against either Radford or his supervisors because the move would have played hard in the press. Even so, he became so distrustful of the military that he briefly questioned the advisability of continuing to employ officers in key positions on the National Security Council staff.[35]

The official inclination to submerge bad news, however, is probably best exemplified by an episode that occurred in March 1971, when the enemy attacked a Twenty-third Infantry American Division fire support base named Mary Ann, located some eighty kilometers south of Da Nang. After firing hundreds of mortar rounds, some sixty enemy sappers penetrated the base, demolished the facility's operations center along with many bunkers, and killed thirty Americans while wounding eighty-two. Since the toll added up to more than one-third of the week's casualties, it was impossible to hide from the press. MACV had little choice but to provide details.[36]

Of the news stories that followed, one of the most thorough was by *Newsweek* reporter Nicholas Proffitt. The situation in the area around Mary Ann had seemed so secure, the reporter said, that the American was in the process of abandoning the base, and the facility's officers had let go to such an extent that they had even failed to send out reconnaissance patrols on the night of the attack. As for the facility's garrison, close to fifty men were serving guard duty that night, but none had detected the enemy's approach. Although allegations that some of the guards might have been smoking marijuana at the time had proved groundless, Proffitt said, the episode's implications were still ominous. For it was clear that despite the recent invasion of Laos, the enemy retained the ability to inflict stunning losses on U.S. forces.[37]

Investigators employed by the American Division corroborated Proffitt's report. They found, for example, that the officers at Mary Ann had failed to post at least one guard at each entrance to the facility's tactical operations center and others at each bunker on its perimeter. In addition, it was doubtful that enough mines, tear gas dispensers, napalm charges, and wire-detonated explosives had been in place where they were needed and that adequate lines of fire had been laid out for the men. Commissioned and noncommissioned officers alike had failed to check the bunker line at least once an hour during the night, a roving guard force had never been assigned to patrol open areas, and searchlights that should have illuminated the base's perimeter were not operating.[38]

With questions rising in Congress and the news media, General Westmoreland pushed Abrams for a final report, but the general demurred. He wanted to investigate the role higher officers had played in the affair and recommended that Westmoreland put off questions for at least a month by making some sort of noncommittal statement.[39]

The report, when it finally came on 5 July, was to the point. The attack had occurred much as originally described. Security had been lax because senior officers at the brigade and division levels, including the Americal's commander, Maj. Gen. James L. Baldwin, had failed to ensure that Mary Ann's troops adhered to proper procedures. In addition, a number of officers had lied under oath when informed by investigators that the bodies of five of the enemy's dead had been burned in the base's trash dump rather than buried as regulations required. The infraction was relatively minor, but the lies were not. Colonel William S. Hathaway, the commander of the 196th Infantry Brigade (Light), had perjured himself, as had division's chief of staff, Col. Alphus R. Clark. Baldwin himself had failed both to report the incident to higher headquarters and to discipline the individuals involved. At a time when the U.S. role in combat was declining and the news media were focusing on American withdrawals, the report's authors concluded, complacency among the troops was growing: "If this type of situation is allowed to prevail, we can expect that in the months to come, there may occur an even greater disaster. Therefore, the hard facts . . . which have been revealed during this investigation must be recognized and acted upon."[40]

General Abrams removed Baldwin from command. The step caused a flurry of comment in the press, but the army was deeply involved in determining how it should discipline Baldwin and his officers and continued to postpone any substantial revelation of the facts. Although the chairmen of both the House and the Senate Armed Services Committee received confidential briefings, anyone else who inquired had to settle for a brief description of the incident that omitted the burned bodies, an avowal that the investigation was taking longer than expected, and an assertion that the release of further details might prejudice the rights of the accused.[41]

Concerned that a news release was nonetheless necessary, Lt. Gen. William J. McCaffrey, the deputy commander of the U.S. Army, Vietnam, suggested on 21 July that MACV reveal the full extent of its finding to the press but hold back the names of the individuals under investigation. Westmoreland declined, noting that a partial news release during July would have to be followed by a complete accounting later. "We would all do better," he said, "to try to condense the story into just one major overall bad story."[42]

In the days that followed, McCaffrey decided to punish all of the officers involved. Baldwin was to receive a reprimand and reduction in rank; Hathaway would be removed from the list for promotion to brigadier general and reprimanded; and there would be reductions in rank for everyone else. At that time, McCaffrey again recommended a press release and Westmoreland again held off, this time on grounds that all avenues of recourse for the accused had yet to be exhausted. Since more news releases would become necessary once those reviews were complete, he said, the communiqué "would not wind up the entire case with a single bad day of publicity as we had hoped. . . . The secretary [of the army] and I want to do our best to reduce the number of self-inflicted wounds which the Army is receiving."[43]

The instruction stood for almost a year, until 21 April 1972, when the secretary of the army at last announced that he had issued a letter of admonition to Baldwin, reprimanded Hathaway and one other officer, and removed Hathaway from the list for promotion to brigadier general. Brief notices followed in many papers, but by then the news media were so preoccupied with the enemy's massive Easter offensive of 1972 that the single day of bad publicity Westmoreland had worked so long to postpone never occurred.[44]

If General Westmoreland and other officials in Washington sought to reduce controversy in the press, some of the officers in South Vietnam were causing it by acting out their animosity toward reporters. During the weeks following the Laotian incursion, for example, the Saigon correspondents began to complain that commanders were attempting to black out reporting of the war by putting journalists who visited their units under leash. They cited as an example an episode involving Morley Safer, who visited South Vietnam briefly during April 1971. In a memorandum that later fell into the hands of the press, a public affairs officer near Pleiku had warned commanders in the area to be cautious because Safer was obviously seeking an exposé. Although Colonel Leonard responded by dispatching a circular message to all commanders that reemphasized MACV'S commitment to cooperation with the press, the *San Francisco Chronicle* could not resist charging that the army was "ringing the leper's bell" everywhere Safer went.[45]

The campaign following the incursion into Laos, Lam Son 720, provided an even stronger example of the mistrust army officers harbored toward the press. A major attack against enemy strongholds in the A Shau Valley by South Vietnamese units and portions of the U.S. 101st Airborne Division, the operation came to involve so many restrictions on reporters that CBS broadcast a special report on the subject. Following a comment by anchorman Walter Cronkite implying that democratic values were at stake, correspondent Ed Rabel claimed that the division's commander had placed guards at the doors of his forward command post to keep newsmen out. The reporter then interviewed a lieutenant who added that reporters had permission to ride helicopters into the field only when an official escort was present, and that he and other officers had been told to "watch what we say" in front of them. Noting that he had served in Vietnam for nineteen months during 1966 and 1967, the officer avowed that he had never seen restrictions on the press as stringent as the ones then in effect. Rides into the field had always been available to newsmen, and soldiers had always been able to speak freely with reporters.[46]

When word of the restrictions arrived in Washington, the director of defense information, Colonel Hill, was aghast. Concluding that commanders had obviously taken it upon themselves to deny the press access to American units in the field, he cabled Leonard to warn that the issue was so explosive, all concerned should keep careful records so that they could document that every step they took was "justifiable." The implied threat had no effect on Leonard. He responded that the officers in charge were well within their rights because the A Shau Valley was a dangerous place. The security of the men, he said, took precedence over the wishes of the press. Leonard never explained how the presence of an escort with reporters riding helicopters contributed to the safety of the troops. That was not, in fact, the issue. "The major complaint [of the press]," he explained years later in a letter, " . . . seemed to revolve around the escort officer 'intimidating' soldiers' responses to reporters' questions. Like it or not, the escort officer could bring balance to some soldiers' remarks."[47]

Confronted by Leonard's unwillingness to push against the growing prejudice of the military toward the press, Hill could do nothing. In the weeks that followed, as a result, the secrecy surrounding the operation received almost as much play in the press as the fighting. Distressed, Daniel Henkin finally instructed General Sidle to travel to Saigon to assess the situation. The general was to arrive with the least possible advance notice in order to cut off any attempt by officers to hide their bad decisions.[48]

Upon arrival, Sidle spoke with trusted contacts among the Saigon correspondents. They told him that if the majority of public affairs officers remained well-intentioned, some of the generals who coordinated official responses to queries from the press had come to dislike reporters with an intensity bordering on hatred. As a result, the time it took official agencies to reply to legitimate queries from the press had increased noticeably between 1970 and 1971, causing reporters time and again to miss deadlines. Meanwhile, there had been no attempt in months to provide selected correspondents with the intelligence briefings they had received in earlier years. Concluding that reliable newsmen had been denied the information they needed to put events into context, Sidle told Henkin that determined leadership at the MACV's office of information might have remedied the problem but that the officers in charge seemed incapable of the strong words and actions circumstances required.[49]

Sidle wanted Leonard replaced, but Abrams demurred. As a substitute, since Leonard was approaching the end of his tour of duty anyway, Henkin decided to restructure the assignment of the next chief of MACV information, Col. Phillip H. Stevens. That officer would go to South Vietnam as planned but would serve initially as deputy to Hill, who would head MACOI for up to six months. Well liked by reporters, Stevens would work to improve relations with the press. A brigadier general by the time he arrived, Hill would push his fellow generals to ease up on the press.[50]

When Hill arrived in South Vietnam toward the end of July, he realized immediately that if the MACV's office of information had changed, so had the press. Although a number of highly experienced correspondents remained among the 335 newsmen accredited to MACV, the television networks were rotating reporters in and out with abandon. Journalists would arrive, stay about three months (just long enough to put the term *war correspondent* on their job résumés), and then rotate to new assignments before learning much of substance about the war. Meanwhile, since American forces were less involved than ever in the fighting, only a few reporters were following combat in the field.[51]

Circumstances were no better on the military side. Hill confirmed that

MACV'S chief of intelligence had long before ended direct intelligence briefings for selected members of the press, and that reporters resented having to receive what word they got on the subject from public affairs officers. Meanwhile, many of the programs he and Sidle had instituted earlier in the war to keep the press informed had ceased. The chief of information had maintained a villa in Saigon where he and his officers could meet informally with reporters and where General Abrams could host quiet dinners for selected correspondents. By 1971, the dinners had ended because Abrams believed they had degenerated into little more than complaint sessions for the press. The house itself was run-down and deserted.[52]

Recognizing that Hill was in South Vietnam to improve military relations with the news media, reporters gave him the benefit of the doubt. Even so, there was little the general could do. Officers with grievances against newsmen remained hostile, and correspondents who had experienced frustration at the hands of the military were not about to forget. Nothing short of a wholesale change of personnel on both sides could have tempered the hostilities that prevailed, and that would take more than a generation because the members of each group were even then passing on their hostilities to the new people moving into their professions. In the end, as with Westmoreland, Hill could do little more than hold the line. Keeping the Pentagon informed of developments, he attempted to head off problems with the press before they developed into full-blown controversies.[53]

The general was more successful in other areas. Under instructions to begin the process of weaning reporters away from their American sources, he put an end to MACV's Sunday evening briefings. Although this development prompted a brief flurry of complaints, most reporters had never had much interest in the sessions and went along with the change. On the side, Hill also drafted a contingency plan for the gradual but orderly elimination of MACV's office of information. The document avoided mentioning dates beyond July 1972, when the office was expected to consist of fewer than seventeen people, but there had to be some sort of plan in place if the program was to end on anything more than a haphazard basis.[54]

Even as Hill and Sidle fought to hold on, however, the ability of American policy makers to control what was happening in South Vietnam was slipping away. The failure of the attempt to save face for the South Vietnamese during the last days of the Laotian incursion, Sheehan's call for war crimes trials, the leaks to Anderson, the Hackworth affair, and Admiral Moorer's use of Yeoman Radford all showed it clearly. So, too, did the attempts by commanders in the field to restrain the Saigon correspondents. Although American involvement in the war would continue for another year, the line was breaking. The war was spinning toward its conclusion with a momentum all its own.

18

The Easter Offensive

Lam Son 719 marked the last time the U.S. Army encountered sustained combat in South Vietnam. From then on, the size of American forces dropped steadily, from a high of 554,000 in April 1969 to fewer than 141,000 in the first months of 1972. The number of reporters covering the war, meanwhile, diminished from 468 to fewer than 200.[1]

The composition of the corps of correspondents also changed. A few old hands remained, but many newcomers were also present. Some of them had settled in quickly. Craig Whitney of the *New York Times,* Holger Jensen of the AP, and Alexander Shimkin of *Newsweek,* to name a few, had produced perceptive reports during and following Lam Son 719. Shimkin was fluent in the Vietnamese language. A number of correspondents were also present who would someday gain prominence—among them, Henry Bradsher of the *Washington Star,* Bob Simon and Phil Jones of CBS, and Peter Osnos of the *Washington Post.* Many of the rest, however, seemed to General Sidle "inexperienced, lazy, trying to make a reputation, or some combination of the three." Sidle added, by way of example, that the long strides the South Vietnamese had made in providing their own logistical support had gone unmentioned in the newcomers' work, as had the successful establishment of a new, first-rate South Vietnamese Third Infantry Division.[2]

The best of the Saigon correspondents, for their part, were willing to concede, as *New York Times* reporter Sydney Schanberg remarked, that some of their colleagues were suffering from "a hardening of viewpoint." Even so, Schanberg said, it was unfair to judge a journalist by one or two reports. A pattern of truth would emerge from a person's work over time, if that individual was honest.[3]

Neither Sidle nor Schanberg was wrong. The situation in South Vietnam was so contradictory by that time that anyone could say almost anything about it and find evidence to support the claim. Sidle's contention, for example, that the Third

Division was a great success was justified in military eyes because the successful equipping of a large combat force was always a massive undertaking. At the very moment the general was making his observations, however, CBS correspondent Phil Jones was visiting the division and seeing only problems. The division's officers were straining to comprehend sophisticated American tactics and equipment, he said. Meanwhile, its logistical systems were faltering, and some of its men had not been paid in two months. Events would bear out Jones rather than the general. When the Third came up against the North Vietnamese in April, it was virtually destroyed.[4]

The need to turn public affairs over to the South Vietnamese as the American role in the war diminished complicated matters. For example, guidelines for the press that the Thieu regime inaugurated in December 1971 bore a superficial resemblance to MACV's, but they were designed, as one spokesman for the high command candidly admitted, to "very much restrict reporting on military operations." Reporters could interview the commanders of regiments and other large units, all of whom were well attuned to political realities, but they had to check with official spokesmen before using material from battalion commanders and below. An offense against the rules might result in a sixty-day disaccreditation, and repeated violations could lead to expulsion from the country.[5]

The system threw the Saigon correspondents even more onto their own resources. As a correspondent for Reuters remarked, the information the South Vietnamese dispensed was so unreliable that reporters had to resort to an "amorphous structure" of untrustworthy government functionaries along with official and semiofficial radio, television, and print media reports for much of the news about South Vietnam they used. Everyone, of course, blamed MACV. "The word has gone down the line in somewhat garbled form," Arthur Higbee said. " . . . it's an all-Vietnamese war now, so don't write about us Americans."[6]

To make matters worse, with negotiations proceeding and the war approaching its climax, even the news that MACV dispensed was becoming less immediate than it had been earlier in the war. Despite the rule that the command would be the principal source of news of the war, the command's spokesmen were sometimes instructed to avoid answering questions on sensitive topics, only to find later that higher-ups, for reasons either of state or of expediency, had released the information themselves in Washington. When that happened, a storm of recriminations inevitably followed from angry correspondents who expected the old rules to apply.[7]

Although sometimes justified in their complaints, enterprising correspondents still received great volumes of information from their private contacts and sympathetic U.S. officials. The imminence of the enemy's offensive also worked to their advantage. Expecting a major attack and recalling the erroneous reporting that had accompanied the Tet offensive of 1968, the Nixon administration did everything it could to prepare reporters for the fight. John Scali thus told Charles Colson on 25 January, "I am personally responsible for two stories by Stu

Hensley of UPI warning of how the North Vietnamese are building up more forces in an effort to undermine the president's China trip; one story by Bill Gill and another by Tom Jarriel, warning of the same; a similar piece by Lou Gulick of AP; several radio reports and a piece by Bob Pierpoint of CBS." During February and early March 1972, when the offensive failed to materialize, unidentified South Vietnamese and American sources likewise took pains to tell reporters that the enemy had merely postponed the attack. Some of the news stories that resulted played the administration's game well by speculating that the enemy intended to use the attack to create damaging headlines in the United States in order to corrupt the American public's will to continue the war.[8]

The assault came on 30 March, when North Vietnamese forces struck across the Demilitarized Zone into Quang Tri, South Vietnam's northernmost province. During the two days that followed, they also launched major attacks on South Vietnamese positions in the hills west of Hue, around Kontum in Military Region 2, and at Loc Ninh and An Loc in Military Region 3. A number of assaults also occurred in Military Region 4, where enemy forces reentered areas they had abandoned under heavy pressure earlier in the war.

As the invasion developed, little went well for the South Vietnamese. The Third Division's commanders had expected an attack from the west out of Laos rather than across the relatively flat and open Demilitarized Zone. Caught unprepared while their troops were on the move, they withdrew from the edge of the Demilitarized Zone to a line slightly to the south behind the Cua Viet and Cam Lo Rivers. There they held, but not without considerable difficulty. On 2 April, members of the Division's Fifty-seventh Regiment panicked and joined a stream of refugees fleeing south along Highway 1. Commanders managed to stem the rout, but by then the unit's Fifty-sixth regiment, located on the division's western flank, was also in trouble. Under heavy attack and lacking effective air and artillery support, the unit's commander needlessly surrendered hundreds of men and the most powerful artillery array in the region. Despite these setbacks, the South Vietnamese still managed to hold their positions south of the Cua Viet until 9 April, when the enemy withdrew temporarily to resupply.[9]

The assault on Kontum opened more slowly but also produced demoralizing defeats. North Vietnamese artillery hit the command post of the Twenty-second South Vietnamese Infantry Division, demolishing the regiment that held the base. During an attack on another base near Dak To, the installation's defenders fled into the surrounding jungle. By 4 May, Kontum itself lay open to attack. To the east in the coastal lowlands, enemy forces cut Highway 1 and gained control of almost all of Binh Dinh Province.[10]

Perhaps the most important enemy attack came in Military Region 3 on 2 April, when North Vietnamese forces launched a major drive in Binh Long Province to capture the cities of An Loc and Loc Ninh. An Loc was important enough and far enough to the south to serve as a credible capital for the Communist regime that Hanoi intended to install in the South when it solidified its gains.

In the end, however, the enemy fell victim to his own inability to resupply quickly. Although Loc Ninh fell within days, he thus delayed his attack on An Loc for almost a week, leaving time for Maj. Gen. James R. Hollingsworth, the senior American adviser in the region, to coordinate a ground defense and to plot B-52 strikes. When the attack came, the general was ready and beat it back.[11]

As the offensive evolved, the White House attempted to shield the president from any misfortunes that occurred by giving the Department of Defense and MACV primary responsibility for press relations on matters involving the situation in the field. White House spokesmen were to blast Hanoi for its aggression and to reassure the public that the president was keeping a close watch on events, but as Kissinger's assistant Les Janka noted, they were to "let the bad news come from elsewhere."[12]

Over the days that followed, editors and commentators in the United States tended to react to events along ideological lines. Words such as *rout* and *disarray* appeared regularly in the reports of those who had long questioned the war, while journalists who supported official policy were more reassuring. Long opposed to the conflict, *Newsweek,* on the one hand, stressed that the "staggering armada" of American ships and aircraft responding to the attack underscored the failure of Vietnamization and the lack of a will to fight on the part of many South Vietnamese soldiers. A more supportive *Washington Daily News,* on the other, observed that not too much could be made of the South Vietnamese failure to hold along the border because bad weather had inhibited allied air strikes. Jerry Greene of the *New York Daily News,* meanwhile, stressed that, "so far as can be determined . . . South Vietnamese troops . . . have withdrawn in an orderly manner."[13]

Reports from the field, for their part, were much less alarmist than they might have been. At the beginning, when South Vietnamese fortunes wavered, the Saigon correspondents were understandably critical. When the situation stabilized, however, they were quick to point out that the enemy's attack had stalled and that the confidence of South Vietnamese forces was increasing. In the end, nonetheless, most correspondents had little choice but to conclude that the overall performance of the South Vietnamese had been mixed. Some described scenes in which demoralized infantrymen attempted to escape the fighting by clinging to the skids of departing helicopters. Others criticized the South Vietnamese armed forces for the indolent manner in which some of their units had responded to the attack. To the chagrin of the Nixon administration, almost all asserted that overwhelming American airpower had made the difference between whether individual enemy attacks succeeded or failed.[14]

The reporters' assessments were little different from those circulating within the U.S. government. Ambassador Bunker and General Abrams believed that the Thieu regime had displayed "a steady hand and remarkable effectiveness" in repelling the attack, but they also agreed that the South Vietnamese performance had been mixed and that "the fabric [of the nation] would not have held without U.S. air power." Secretary Laird, meanwhile, cabled Abrams to assert his own view that press reporting had been "balanced" and that both he and the president had themselves been "disappointed" by some aspects of the South Vietnamese effort.[15]

If news coverage of the offensive had been accurate, friction still sparked between the military and the news media. Almost as soon as the offensive began, despite rules going back to the beginning of the war that troop movements were embargoed until officially announced, UPI reporter Alan Dawson revealed that U.S. helicopter units were moving into Military Region 1. The newsman contended that MACV's guidelines had little application to his report because the troops in question had reinforced a base rather than entered combat, but he was splitting hairs. MACV disaccredited him.[16]

Sometimes, the mere presence of reporters with a unit in the field could cause problems. A case in point occurred shortly after Dawson's disaccreditation, when officers from the Second Battalion, First Infantry, 196th Infantry Brigade (Light), alleged in signed affidavits that newsmen had caused a near mutiny. Learning that a planned airlift had been canceled and that the troops would be moving overland by truck, correspondents at the scene had supposedly passed along rumors to the men that the road they would be traveling was mined or booby-trapped. Turning on the reporters, the commander of the unit declared in a widely reported remark: "All you press are bastards. I blame you for this, and you can quote me on it."[17]

It seems clear that the reporters involved may have been overbearing, but whether any had promoted a combat refusal was difficult to say. Was the newsman who purportedly asked "Do you think it's right that they send you into a booby-trapped area by trucks?" attempting to incite disobedience or aggressively seeking a reaction from a soldier who already knew that any road in South Vietnam could be mined? In addition, few of the officers who complained had been present when the episode occurred, and none had bothered to learn the reporters' names. Under the circumstances, given the inclination of both the military and the news media to believe the worst of one another, the U.S. command issued a stern warning to the Saigon correspondents but declined to take further action.[18]

As the offensive continued, even well-intentioned reports could cause problems. On one occasion, *Newsweek* carried an interview with General Hollingsworth in which the officer remarked that he intended to "kill" all of An Loc's attackers before they got back to Cambodia. Then CBS News played a taped interview with the general in which he said that he had declined to entertain a proposal from the Red Cross to declare a temporary cease-fire in order to treat the wounded. Since it was clear that Hollingsworth considered himself the commander at An Loc even though a South Vietnamese officer was technically in charge, the remark contradicted U.S. assertions that the South Vietnamese were in total control of their own affairs. Soon after the interview appeared, indeed, an angry General Abrams instructed Hollingsworth to shut his mouth.[19]

On the same day that Hollingsworth's comment appeared, the *New York Times* revealed that South Vietnamese policemen manning checkpoints below An Loc were allowing traffic on the road to pass but were barring reporters. Alluding to the Dawson affair, the author of the report alleged that if relations between the press and the Saigon regime had never been smooth, "Now, [some] United States officials . . . confess that they share Saigon's antipathy."[20] The observation was accurate, to a degree, but U.S. officials still recognized that attempts at harassment and lies to the press would be counterproductive. Ambassador Bunker, for one, insisted in a cable to the White House that the casualty statistics released by government spokesmen contrasted so emphatically with the eyewitness accounts of newsmen that they had created a whole new credibility gap for Thieu. The regime had to improve its handling of the news media, he said, or risk losing its legitimacy before the world.[21]

The South Vietnamese government did nothing to remedy the problem, but its lack of interest probably mattered little. Its credibility was already spent. In addition, by mid-April the Saigon correspondents were preoccupied by a new subject because President Nixon had chosen that moment to push the negotiations in Paris off dead center by pounding North Vietnam until it made the concessions he wanted.

From a purely military standpoint, the expedient seemed questionable. Shortly after the president began to draw up plans for the attack, which involved mining Haiphong harbor and bombing targets near Hanoi, Laird noted in a memo to Kissinger that the impact of the strikes on the enemy hardly justified the outcry that would inevitably follow. The mining of Haiphong, in particular, would never block the importation of war-making materiél into North Vietnam without a massive air campaign to seal off both the nation's coastline and its border with China.[22]

General Abrams was also disturbed. When the president decided to postpone any decision on the mining but to go ahead with two massive air attacks on targets near Hanoi and Haiphong during mid-April, the general requested a delay. The raids would cut air support critical to the effort at An Loc, he said, and would also thwart an attempt to solidify South Vietnamese positions around Quang Tri. Twenty-four hours before the attack, the aircraft carriers stationed off the coast of South Vietnam would have to end their operations to move north. Following the strikes, a similar delay would occur while they steamed back and performed necessary maintenance. Even if the weather was good, two or more days would intervene before the carriers' aircraft were back on station. Intent on demonstrating American determination at a time when secret negotiations were beginning on a Soviet-American summit, Nixon denied the request and sent Haig to Saigon to explain why to Abrams. Haig later told Kissinger that the general understood the president's problem completely but that he had a problem of his own: "The only factor which has prevented a major debacle [at An Loc] has been U.S. air, especially B-52's."[23]

The public affairs handling of the raids was forthright. Shortly after the planes returned on 16 April, MACV introduced reporters to pilots who had participated. Then, to counter potential enemy distortions, official spokesmen released preliminary assessments that revealed major damage to antiaircraft, warehouse, transportation, and oil storage facilities. As these efforts continued, the Nixon administration began preparing the ground for a larger program of air attacks. On the day after the raids, in testimony before the Senate Foreign Relations Committee, Secretary Laird declared emphatically that all of North Vietnam would be subject to attack for as long as the offensive continued and that there was even a possibility that the United States might mine or blockade Haiphong.[24]

The raids generated considerable comment in the United States in both Congress and the news media, much of it along ideological lines. In a five-hour Senate debate, the president's supporters called for more bombing, but his opponents asserted vigorously that he was risking endless war in South Vietnam and disruption of newly established relations with China for the sake of a discredited regime of little value to the United States. Editorials in the dovish *New York Times*, meanwhile, termed the bombing "an exercise in folly and futility," but the more hawkish *San Diego Union* considered it "a courageous, non-political act." The *Los Angeles Times* asserted that "B-52's cannot buy victory," but the *Arizona Republic* avowed that "bombs should continue to fall."[25]

The American people, for their part, sided with the president. Although a massive 76 percent wanted U.S. troops home by the end of the year and 60 percent were willing to remove Thieu in return for a cease-fire, a poll by the Sidlinger organization during April revealed that support for the president himself had gone up by 11 points. When asked by pollsters whether they agreed that attacks on military targets in North Vietnam should continue until that country stopped the offensive, 69 percent agreed, 24 percent disagreed, and 7 percent had no opinion.[26]

President Nixon nonetheless understood that poll results could change dramatically in a matter of days. In order to muffle antiwar sentiment in the United States, reassure right-wing Republicans that he was holding fast to his agenda, and retain the leverage he needed to impose maximum military and psychological pressure on Hanoi, he decided to address the nation on 26 April. At that time, in order to shake North Vietnam's confidence in its Communist allies, he intended to play up U.S.-Soviet efforts in search of détente. Then, to bolster public confidence in Vietnamization, he planned to announce a twenty-thousand-man troop withdrawal. In pursuit of those ends, he instructed Haig to ask Abrams for an estimate of the situation in South Vietnam. In passing the request to Abrams, Haig left no doubt about what the president wanted. Adverting to Nixon's use during Lam Son 719 of Abrams's comment that the South Vietnamese could "hack it," he remarked that "perhaps some colorful terminology of this kind would be helpful."[27] In the end, the general provided the assessment the president wanted but declined to include the turns of phrase Haig had sought. The president followed the same low-key approach during the speech. Emphasizing that the South Vietnamese were bearing up well but that hard fighting would continue, he announced the troop withdrawal and then added that he hoped to travel to the Soviet Union within the month in search of détente.[28]

The address seemed "more of the same" to commentators in the news media, but it was, in fact, the first step in a grim attempt by Nixon to jerk North Vietnam toward the sort of peace he wanted in Southeast Asia. Henry Kissinger laid it out shortly before the speech in a talk to his staff. "We are now engaged on a course," he told his associates, "in which the other side has put all the chips into the pot and in which we have put our chips into the pot and . . . we have convinced our opponents that this time, for once, against all probability, we mean business. . . . We have the possibility now, better than at any time in the Administration, . . . of getting perhaps some serious talks started . . . because the president made [the North Vietnamese] . . . believe they might lose everything and because they have adopted a strategy that if they do not win, they will lose everything."[29]

Intent upon those goals, President Nixon told Kissinger on 30 April to inform North Vietnam's negotiators at a 2 May meeting in Paris that "the President has had enough and now you have only one message to give them—Settle or else!" He added that he considered it essential for the United States to add teeth to the warning by launching, within days of the declaration, another major air strike against Hanoi and Haiphong involving all the aircraft Abrams could spare. With the Russian summit approaching and then the Democratic convention, he added, every day's delay diminished his leverage: "Forget the domestic reaction. Now is the best time to hit them."[30]

Nixon's injunction notwithstanding, public relations was never far from the minds of the president and his advisers in the weeks and months that followed. On the same day that he delivered his instructions to Kissinger, for example, he told Laird to instruct Abrams to hold a background briefing for the press to put the situation in the field into perspective. The Saigon correspondents, he said, had dramatized less than inspiring aspects of the South Vietnamese army's performance. The commanders at the scene were the ones best suited to assert the opposite point of view.[31]

Abrams was open to the idea, but by then it was too late. On 28 April, Communist forces renewed their attack in Military Region 1. Over the next two days, General Lam withdrew his troops to the south, and the units guarding Quang Tri panicked and abandoned the city. Joining a swarm of refugees moving south down Highway 1 toward Hue, the fleeing troops provided an inviting target for North Vietnamese gunners, who were already firing at the refugees on the road. Enemy pressure also increased in Military Region 2, where the South Vietnamese guarding Kontum began to buckle and pull back. Although Thieu immediately replaced Lam with Lt. Gen. Ngo Quang Truong, one of the few truly skilled commanders he possessed, Abrams had little choice but to cable Laird that South Vietnam's senior military leadership had "begun to bend and in some cases to break." In that light, he said, a backgrounder on South Vietnamese successes was unthinkable.[32]

There was, indeed, little that Abrams could have said by then that would have made much difference to the Saigon correspondents. They were already in the field and so close to events that some would never make it back to tell their stories. *Newsweek*'s Alexander Shimkin disappeared in a hail of enemy grenades on the outskirts of Quang Tri City, and photographer James D. Gill, stringing for the *London Daily Telegraph,* was captured north of Da Nang, bound hand and foot, and executed. Those who did return had little good to say about the South Vietnamese.[33]

As in the past, many of their accounts drew upon the word of American advisers. In relating the fall of Tan Canh, north of Kontum, for example, a correspondent for *Time* quoted an American officer who survived the disaster. "Tan Canh fell," the adviser said, "because ARVN never got off its ass and fought." Sydney Schanberg described the havoc the enemy had inflicted on the refugees on Highway 1. "Please understand," an American officer had told him, "Quang Tri is not cut off. We're just not going there today." Richard Levine of the *Wall Street Journal* quoted a U.S. Army general who had said of the South Vietnamese soldier, "You can't give a man guts."[34]

South Vietnam's armed forces took most of the blame, but *Newsweek*'s Lloyd Norman focused on the United States. The appearance of heavy enemy artillery and massive numbers of enemy tanks deep in South Vietnam, he said, showed that America's bombing over the years had been in vain. Although the South Vietnamese armed forces outnumbered and outgunned their adversary, he added, "perhaps the fatal flaw" was that the United States had failed to instill in them "the esprit and determination necessary to take on Hanoi's highly motivated and tightly disciplined troops."[35]

Events in the days that followed did little to stem the criticism. As enemy pressure increased, the performance of South Vietnam's armed forces continued to lag. By 4 May, the situation seemed so grave that General Abrams decided to assert his rights as commander in the field and to cancel the massive air strike against Hanoi and Haiphong that the president had ordered. Air support, particularly the B-52, had been "the principal factor," he told Vice President Agnew, maintaining the morale of the South Vietnamese army. With major enemy attacks predicted for Kontum and Hue, he was concerned that any interruption would be reflected in the will and determination of South Vietnam's generals to fight. Only ten of them, he said, were truly reliable and earning their pay.[36]

Nixon had been dissatisfied with Abrams since Lam Son 719. On the evening of 4 May, a few hours after agreeing reluctantly to cancel the strike, he resolved to replace him. In so doing, clearly out of deference to the army, which was sagging under the weight of the war and considered Abrams a hero, he told Haig he would appoint the general to no more than a two-year term as chief of staff of the army. He announced the change one month later, along with his appointment of Abrams's former deputy, Gen. Frederick C. Weyand, as the new U.S. commander in South Vietnam.[37]

In the interim, the president pursued his ends. On 6 May, Henry Kissinger thus notified Ambassador Bunker that Nixon was contemplating a sharp increase in air attacks on North Vietnam and the mining of the country's ports. To justify that move, he wanted to highlight the enemy's abuse of the South Vietnamese people during a speech to the nation. Bunker was to provide statistics on civilian casualties attributable to the enemy. "Do not hesitate to give us ball-park figures," Kissinger said, "and we will not object if they incline towards the high side."[38]

Nixon made the speech on 8 May. Because the enemy had rejected all offers and had abandoned all restraints, he said, he had ordered the mining of North Vietnam's ports and air and naval strikes to cut the country's lines of communication. The mines were timed to activate within three days. They would remain in service, and air and naval attacks would continue until the enemy had returned all American prisoners of war and had agreed to an internationally supervised cease-fire throughout Indochina.[39]

The announcement provoked a broad range of reactions. A flurry of antiwar demonstrations occurred across the United States, but despite some violence, the protests appear to have involved mainly veteran demonstrators rather than new recruits from the public at large. In the same way, many commentators in the press questioned Nixon's good judgment, but the president also had defenders. While Keyes Beech of the *Chicago Daily News* termed the decision to blockade North Vietnam "the act of an angry and desperate man," the *Washington Star* declared its support for the president, and the *Detroit News* praised Nixon's "guts." The American public, for its part, sided with the president. Seventy-six percent of those who responded to Sidlinger and Opinion Research polls backed the mining of North Vietnam's ports. Harris and ABC News polls tallied a more modest 59 percent, but even that figure was heartening to an administration that viewed itself as increasingly under siege.[40]

To take advantage of the public mood while it lasted, President Nixon instructed official spokesmen to play down any possibility that the United States might pull back in some manner. He also wanted to target facilities in North Vietnam, such as power plants, whose destruction might affect the morale of North Vietnam's civilian population. "We have the power to destroy . . . [the enemy's] war making capacity," he told Kissinger. "The only question is whether we have the will to use that power. What distinguishes me from Johnson is that I have the *will* in spades."[41]

During the days that followed, administration spokesmen worked to maintain the president's options by emphasizing that the enemy was receiving the latest weapons through the port at Haiphong, including antiaircraft artillery and heat-seeking missiles. Laird, meanwhile, underscored the administration's willingness to negotiate and the fact that only forty-nine thousand American troops would remain in South Vietnam on 1 July. When the effect of those initiatives began to wear thin, on 28 June, Nixon reinvigorated the campaign by revealing that no more draftees would go to Vietnam, only volunteers.[42]

As the attack on North Vietnam intensified, the military attempted to open what information they could to the press, but they remained cautious about saying anything that would tip their hand to the enemy. The press was undeterred. Combining official news releases with word from unofficial contacts, *Newsweek,* for example, reported on 22 May that the mines in use at Haiphong contained "a variety of sensors to detect a ship's magnetic field, the noise given off by its turbines and screws, the pressure of its displacement or any combination of these. In fact, it is believed that most . . . were programmed to go off only when all three characteristics registered simultaneously in the mines' minicomputers—thus blocking attempts to trigger them with dummy ships." The security violation, if it was one, probably worked to the advantage of the United States by emphasizing the Nixon administration's determination.[43]

In order to counter enemy propaganda, the MACV's office of information sought permission to release general descriptions of bombing targets and damage assessments. The Defense Department held back at first, releasing the information only after a two- to three-day delay, but it relented when reporters began to question the effectiveness of the attacks. It also instructed MACV to accelerate the release of photographs depicting bomb damage. On 5 June, as a result, *U.S. News & World Report* ran pictures showing the consequences of American pinpoint bombing in an article on how television and laser-guided "smart bombs" were "squeezing" the enemy. The air force could have asked for nothing better.[44]

Less advantageous were revelations that surfaced during May and June that between November 1971 and March 1972 armed escorts accompanying U.S. reconnaissance aircraft in North Vietnam had violated U.S. rules of engagement by flying preplanned attacks on petroleum supplies, transportation facilities, and airfields without the required provocation. On instructions from Gen. John Lavelle, the commander of the U.S. Seventh Air Force in South Vietnam, aircrews and debriefing teams had falsified their reports by indicating that the strikes had been necessary to suppress enemy antiaircraft fire.[45]

The attacks came to the attention of Congress in early March, when a young air force sergeant wrote his senator to complain that his superiors had required him to lie. Following an investigation, the air force relieved Lavelle of command, but to avoid embarrassment and to cover up other questionable operations such as the secret bombing of Cambodia, the Defense Department announced only that Lavelle was retiring for reasons of health.[46]

On 24 May, with both the Senate and the House Armed Services Committee planning hearings on the subject and with leaks certain, the attempt to give the episode a low profile began to fall apart. On that date, the AP published a story based on information from Congressman Otis G. Pike of New York to the effect that Lavelle had detected the enemy buildup prior to the Easter offensive and had conducted raids on his own to deter the attack. At Pike's urging, Seymour Hersh then published a story in the *New York Times* suggesting that Lavelle's superiors in Saigon and Washington might have known what was happening. When the general made the same point in secret testimony before the Senate Armed Services Committee, leaks from that session led to speculation in the press that General Abrams was involved. Allegations also began to appear that other officers had taken the war into their own hands and that civilian control of the military in the United States was under threat. Although those allegations were never proved, neither Henkin nor Friedheim had any doubts that the White House at least was involved. Lavelle was too professional an officer, they said, to have gone off on his own without some intimation from higher-ups that the attacks were in the best interests of the nation.[47]

The Lavelle affair was hardly the only issue confronting the United States as the campaign against Hanoi and Haiphong lengthened. By 9 May, the North Vietnamese had begun to claim that American aircraft had deliberately struck civilian targets in their country, particularly the system of dikes that shielded heavily inhabited areas from floods. To prove these allegations, they allowed American correspondents and celebrities known for their antiwar sympathies to travel to Hanoi to see for themselves.[48]

Among the news stories that followed, those of *New York Times* reporter Anthony Lewis took the lead. Asserting that civilian lives and property had indeed been destroyed, Lewis declined to accept North Vietnamese contentions that the damage had been intentional, but he nonetheless questioned whether American policy makers understood the human costs even mistaken attacks involved. Describing damage to the Red River delta town of Phuc Loc, where villagers claimed that more than 120 civilians had been killed or wounded, he remarked, "Death is always less painful in the abstract. . . . But tallying the numbers of bomb craters is not the same as seeing Phuc Loc." Standard fare for the antiwar movement at the time, Lewis's assertions drew far less attention from the White House than claims the reporter passed along from so-called independent sources that the North Vietnamese were clearing the mines in their harbors. What galled the president was the fact that the *Times* played U.S. denials well down in the article's text while introducing the item with a headline that blared the enemy's side: "Communists Report Mines at Haiphong Swept, Ships Sailing."[49]

On the day after the story appeared, Kenneth W. Clawson, the deputy director of White House communications, charged that the *Times* had become a conduit for enemy propaganda. The paper responded with a stinging editorial alleging that the president wanted the news media to suppress statements by the North

Vietnamese as inherently false while accepting anything the U.S. government said as "the beginning and end of truth." In the end, however, as *Newsweek* observed, neither side in the dispute was blameless. If the Nixon administration's record of "miscalculation, lack of candor and self-serving pronouncements on Vietnam" gave credence to the *Times*'s allegations, the magazine's editors remarked, the newspaper itself had much to answer for. Had its treatment of the bombing and mining been either evenhanded or responsible? And when a supposedly objective journalist, however brilliant, was permitted to take sides the way a syndicated columnist could, what happened to his credibility as a reporter? Lewis, for his part, backed away from the story. "Direct evidence" was "extremely difficult to obtain" in North Vietnam, he said, and most observers conceded that the port at Haiphong was closed.

If President Nixon was incensed by Lewis's article, he appears to have been even more upset by another story in the *Times.* Authored by Benjamin Welles, it alleged that the bombing had caused few disruptions in the lives of ordinary North Vietnamese and that Nixon's mines were set to deactivate prior to a planned presidential trip to Moscow on 22 May. In response, General Haig held a "deep background, off the record" briefing for major media outlets. Pointedly excluding the *Times* from the session, he asserted that the Nixon administration was not about to sell South Vietnam short in return for a deal with the Russians. According to the best intelligence, the cutoff of supplies from China had put North Vietnam's entire social system under stress. Radio Hanoi had begun to warn against saboteurs and hooligans; the courts were trying and executing black-marketeers; and increasing inflation was forcing more and more women into prostitution to supplement family incomes.[50]

Haig had some grounds for his claims, but his clumsy handling of the *Times* ensured that the paper would retaliate. It did so the next morning, revealing Haig's role in the interview and throwing his points into question by connecting them to the president's larger agenda. "U.S. Reports of Foe's Distress Called Old, Out of Context," a headline in the *Washington Star* blared the next day. The State Department and MACV responded by releasing details of the interdiction effort that emphasized its effectiveness, but the effort served mainly to keep the issue alive. Although a variety of news stories followed highlighting the success of the bombing, concern also rose in the press that the president's campaign could precipitate a human disaster in North Vietnam by cutting off food, medicine, and other necessities from the innocent.[51]

If Lewis's and Welles's assertions were troublesome, they were at least open to question. North Vietnam's charges about the dikes were more difficult to handle. For while the United States had never sought to destroy the enemy's flood control system, American pilots had, in fact, hit the dikes both by mistake and to silence antiaircraft batteries mounted on them. Since the issue thus contained a grain of truth, the North Vietnamese made heavy use of it, escorting visiting reporters and antiwar celebrities such as actress Jane Fonda, former U.S. attorney general Ramsey Clark, and Nevin Scrimshaw of the Senate Subcommittee on Refugees to sites where attacks had supposedly occurred.[52]

The Defense Department denied that American aircraft had ever followed a policy of systematically targeting dikes, but it was none too forward, at first, in affirming that some dikes had been hit. Instead, the State Department instructed its foreign posts to label North Vietnam's campaign an instance of "the big lie technique," and President Nixon himself avowed at a news conference that "the United States has used great restraint in its bombing policy. . . . I do not intend to allow any orders to go out which would involve civilian casualties if it can be avoided." These efforts had little effect. With reporters resident in Hanoi continuing to claim that U.S. bombers had hit dikes, Secretary Laird finally had no choice but to reveal what had happened. Affirming that dikes had indeed been hit when enemy antiaircraft batteries had been mounted on them, he made the point that American pilots had always had the right to defend themselves by attacking North Vietnamese gun emplacements.[53]

The statement came too late. By the time Laird made it, films by a Swedish television crew purporting to show damaged dikes had played on American television; Agence France Presse had reported that a group of foreign journalists visiting North Vietnam had narrowly escaped death during an attack on a dike; Dr. Kurt Waldheim, the secretary-general of the United Nations, had accused the president of deliberately bombing dams and levees; and Ramsey Clark had claimed to have seen damaged dikes with his own eyes. Taking up Clark's allegation, Senator Edward Kennedy promised an investigation in the Senate.[54]

In hopes of settling the issue once and for all, Defense Department spokesmen revealed that only twelve dikes had been hit instead of the forty North Vietnam claimed, and that none had been in the Hanoi area. They also released photographs showing that the damage from stray bombs had been minor and easily repaired. President Nixon, however, made the most telling rebuttal. Queried on the subject at a 27 July news conference, he highlighted the thousands of innocent civilians in the South whom North Vietnam's offensive had uprooted and then observed that if the United States had wanted to demolish the dikes it could have flattened them in less than a day.[55]

The president's comments laid much of the controversy to rest, but misdirected bombs continued to embarrass the Nixon administration. On 11 October, Radio Hanoi revealed that U.S. naval aircraft had bombed the French legation in downtown Hanoi, killing the chargé d'affaires. Although doubtful that American aircraft were responsible, the State Department took the precaution of conceding that if an accident had occurred the United States was sorry. It was well that it did. An investigation later confirmed that American bombs had indeed done the damage.[56]

Although wrangling over the dikes, questions about the bombing and min-

Enemy tanks burn on the road to Quang Tri. (U.S. Army)

ing, and the Lavelle affair continued to cause problems for President Nixon, the situation in South Vietnam slowly improved. Kontum and An Loc held firm, and General Truong launched a counteroffensive to retake Quang Tri. After a two-month campaign, on 14 September, the city returned to South Vietnamese hands. There were disappointments, particularly at An Loc, where the Twenty-first Infantry Division made hardly any progress in relieving the siege, but by July, North Vietnam's offensive had clearly failed.[57]

If success was welcome, however, no one expected the enemy to abandon the war. As Radio Hanoi crowed in June, virtually paraphrasing American intelligence reports, "Our people can walk, can use torchlights, can eat diluted congee [water rice gruel]. . . . Even if the enemy succeeds in the bomb destruction of our cities and our large industrial installations, they can never paralyze our economy to the point of preventing our survival and our ability to supply the South."[58]

Yet for all Hanoi's boasting, the bombing and mining had increased the price of continuing the war for North Vietnam. Although the nation had hidden oil pipelines coming from China and could rely on imports arriving by road and equipment stored up in earlier years, the mining of Haiphong spelled the end of supply for most of the heavy equipment and antiaircraft missiles the nation received from the Soviet Union. Understanding these vulnerabilities and sensing the grief the North Vietnamese must have felt when the Soviet Union went on with the summit despite the mining and bombing, Nixon urged the air force to redouble its efforts. "In the period ahead," Kissinger informed Bunker on 30 July, "our best hope for success in the negotiations is the maintenance of a steady and effective level of military pressure against the North." On 29 August, Nixon made the same point in public. The bombing would continue without stint, he told a news conference, until substantial progress had occurred in the negotiations.[59]

19

Endgame

By the end of August 1972, Hanoi's leaders seemed prepared to compromise. Although bloodied during the offensive, their units had increased the Communist presence in areas near Saigon, held strong positions in Military Regions 1 and 2, and were well positioned to claim large amounts of additional territory in South Vietnam if a peace agreement left them in place. Meanwhile, opinion polls in the United States showed that Nixon would win reelection by an impressive margin. An immediate deal with the United States thus held more hope for North Vietnam than a policy of delay that could well end with the president stronger politically.[1]

The North Vietnamese made their move on 1 August, dropping a demand they had made for the dissolution of the Thieu regime as a condition for peace. From then on, the negotiations progressed rapidly. By 11 October, the two sides had agreed that the United States could continue to supply South Vietnam with arms and equipment but would withdraw the remainder of its forces from the South and would contribute to the economic reconstruction of the North. Although a National Council of National Reconciliation and Concord with Viet Cong representation would come into being, that body was to have jurisdiction over little more than elections, to which the South Vietnamese government would have to agree. For the rest, the Thieu regime would remain in power, and North Vietnam's forces would hold their ground in the countryside.[2]

Neither Nixon nor Hanoi had any illusions about the arrangement. By allowing North Vietnamese troops to remain in the South, it left Hanoi with a better than even chance for victory. Nixon nevertheless believed that the agreement was the best the United States would get, and he sent Kissinger to Saigon on 18 October to win Thieu's cooperation. If all went well, the bombing would stop on the twenty-first, Kissinger would initial the accord the next day in Hanoi, and a formal signing would occur in Paris on the thirty-first.[3]

Thieu, however, understood that the treaty jeopardized his nation's prospects and refused emphatically to go along. To reassure him, Nixon began Operation Enhance Plus, a massive airlift of materiél designed to give South Vietnam as much equipment as possible before the treaty went into effect. Thieu was not appeased. He insisted that North Vietnam withdraw from the South and that Nixon eliminate the National Council from the settlement. Stymied, Kissinger canceled his trip to Hanoi and went home.[4]

By that time, both *Time* and *Newsweek* were carrying purported drafts of the agreement. Neither was correct, but Nixon understood that if the United States failed to act, the North Vietnamese would reveal the treaty's provisions to the press in hopes of creating a backlash in Congress that would tie his hands. Kissinger informed Bunker of the president's concern. Thieu had to be made to understand, he said, that he could accept what was good in the treaty or remain intransigent and risk a cutoff in funds "through congressional action if not from us." When Thieu remained unmoved, Nixon had no choice but to inform Hanoi that a "brief delay" had become necessary.[5] The next evening, 26 October, the North Vietnamese did as expected and broadcast the terms of the agreement to the world.

Nixon and Kissinger moved immediately to guarantee that their version of what had happened received greater play in the press than that of the enemy. On the morning after the announcement, Kissinger declared on live television that peace was at hand but that minor details remained unresolved. Seizing on the catchphrase "peace is at hand," the news reports that followed sparked a wave of euphoria around the world that lasted until the next day. Then Thieu drowned the mood by repeating his objections in a statement to the press. Hanoi, meanwhile, announced that it would hold no more meetings with Kissinger and that peace could be found only "at the end of a pen." By then, critics of the war were comparing the treaty's provisions with demands the enemy had made at the start of the negotiations. What, they asked, had Nixon achieved in return for the twenty-five thousand Americans killed in the years since?[6] Nixon responded on 2 November with a major televised speech. "We aren't going to allow an election deadline or any other kind of deadline," he said, " . . . force us into an agreement which would be only a temporary truce. . . . We are going to sign the agreement when the agreement is right, not one day before."[7]

Nixon won the next week's election by the very wide margin everyone had expected, but his good fortune did not extend to his party. Although it gained twelve seats in the House of Representatives, it remained more than fifty short of a majority there. Meanwhile, it lost two seats in the Senate, leaving the Democrats in control of that body by fifty-eight to forty-two. Neither development boded well for the future of South Vietnam.

The North Vietnamese saw the opportunity. When the negotiations reconvened on 20 November and Nixon sought to clarify the nongovernmental nature of the National Council and to establish that North Vietnam had no right to intervene in the South, they drew back. Attempting to delay the proceedings in every way possible, they sought instead to renegotiate portions of the treaty that had seemed all but settled before. Meanwhile, intelligence indicated that Communist commanders in the field had begun to tell their troops that the cease-fire would be "very profitable to us."[8]

Well aware that time was short, Nixon wrote Thieu on 15 November to pledge that the United States would meet continued North Vietnamese aggression with "swift and severe retaliatory action." He added ominously, however, that it was "unrealistic" to seek "absolute assurances." If Thieu became an "obstacle to a peace which American public opinion universally desires, I would, with great reluctance, be forced to consider other [unilateral] measures." A week later, with Thieu still holding fast, Nixon tried again by instructing Bunker to inform the president in the strongest terms that the leading supporters of the war in the Senate were "not only unanimous but vehement." If Saigon remained the only block to an agreement, "they will personally lead the fight when the new Congress reconvenes on January 3 to cut off all military and economic assistance." Delays were dangerous. It was time to "fish or cut bait."[9]

With Hanoi's negotiators in Paris continuing to back and fill, Henry Kissinger had no doubt about how Nixon should respond. "We will have to . . . [drastically step up] the bombing," he told the president. " . . . Precisely because we are at a critical juncture we will need a personal address by you to the American people. . . . Your appeal should not be melodramatic and should make clear that . . . the only remaining task is to pursue a firm policy until we get our men back and can disengage with honor."[10]

Nixon was unmoved. It would be unwise for the United States to demand concessions, he told Kissinger. If the talks broke off, the North Vietnamese "must manifestly be the ones to do it." As for a presidential speech, he continued, "I realize that you think that if I go on television . . . I can rally the American people to support an indefinite continuation of the war. . . . But that can wear very thin within a matter of weeks—particularly as the propaganda organs—not only from North Vietnam, but in this country—begin to hammer away at the fact that we had a much better deal in hand, and then because of Saigon's intransigence we were unable to complete it."[11]

The situation reached its climax on 12 December, when Le Duc Tho, North Vietnam's chief negotiator in Paris, announced that he was leaving for Hanoi and that all remaining issues could be resolved by message. Concluding that Hanoi was playing for time in hopes of exploiting the split between Thieu and the United States once Congress reconvened on 3 January, Kissinger and Nixon both favored a bombing campaign as the best response. Nixon, however, doubted that the American people would go along. Whatever the rationalizations, he told Haig, the reality was that the United States rather than Hanoi had backed away from the agreement. In the end, he decided that anything less than a massive bombing campaign would only lead North Vietnam to conclude that the United

B-52 bombing raids did heavy damage to the outskirts of Hanoi. (Department of Defense)

States was no longer willing to assert itself with vigor. He would "take the same heat" before Congress and in the press, he said, whether he chose a carefully measured military campaign or moved abruptly to shock the enemy into making peace.[12]

To avoid any suggestion that he was delivering an ultimatum, Nixon refused to explain his decision in public. Instead, Kissinger held a press conference to blame North Vietnam for the breakdown in the negotiations. He hinted darkly during the session that the president might adopt stern measures in reaction. It was the only official explanation for the bombing even remotely touching the facts that the public would receive until much later.[13]

The attacks began two days later, on 18 December, when waves of B-52s struck a warehouse complex, the Yen Vien rail yard, and a series of airfields near Hanoi. Over the days that followed, more aircraft struck the Thai Nguyen thermal power plant and the Kinh No and Hanoi oil storage areas. The bombers did severe damage to all their targets, but the North Vietnamese also scored, bringing down nine B-52s by the end of the third day of attacks and damaging three more.[14]

The operation slackened over the next five days. On 22 December, Nixon cabled Hanoi to promise a halt to the bombing above the twentieth parallel if North Vietnam would agree to resume the talks in Paris by 3 January 1973. When no response was forthcoming, he launched the heaviest attack to that date. Over a span of only fifteen minutes on 26 December, 120 bombers struck ten targets in Hanoi and Haiphong. Launching a large number of missiles in response, the North Vietnamese brought down only two bombers. Shortly afterward, they informed Nixon that they would be willing to resume negotiating, but they set 8 January as the date. Over the next week, while the two sides jockeyed for position, Communist gunners brought down two more B-52s but then ran out of missiles. On the twenty-eighth, Hanoi signaled that it would return to the negotiating table without further conditions. Nixon stopped the bombing the next day.

Although the president thus achieved his ends, he conducted his attacks in an environment so heavy with secrecy that he left the propaganda initiative to the enemy. Radio Hanoi and the Soviet news agency TASS were thus the first to reveal that an escalation of the bombing had occurred. When they did, the White House responded with an outright fabrication that linked the raids to the possibility of an enemy offensive in the South and to the peace talks. Pentagon spokesmen later denied off the record that an enemy offensive threatened, but they otherwise confirmed little more than that air operations were in progress throughout North Vietnam. MACV was equally uncommunicative. Refusing to confirm at first that attacks on Hanoi and Haiphong had even begun, the command's spokesmen later relented enough to announce the number of aircraft lost. They declined, however, to reveal what reporters wanted most: the targets of the attacks and the damage done to them. The only excuse anyone received came from Laird, who told Pentagon correspondents that further information might put the lives of the airmen involved at risk.[15]

Denied authoritative information on what was happening, reporters and editors came to their own conclusions. The authors of the president's news summary for 19 December paraphrased the result:

> All nets dominated by the renewed heavy U.S. bombing.... "RN took off the kid gloves," said Cronkite in lead.... Technical talks in Paris broken off by North Vietnam to protest raids.... Reasoner, w/a very harsh commentary, accuses RN of breaking HAK's word and breaking faith with the U.S. public.... AP's Freed [sic] leads: "The futility of the private talks has been underlined by RN's decision to use bombs where diplomacy has failed."... AP says even tho HAK talked of a settlement "99% complete," it was clear the missing 1% dealt w/"the central issue of the war"—political control of South Vietnam.[16]

The North Vietnamese took every opportunity to fill the vacuum by capitalizing on errors in the bombing to claim that the United States was hitting civilian targets on purpose. On 21 December, for example, they charged that American bombs had hit the jail in Hanoi that housed most of the American prisoners of war, the so-called Hanoi Hilton. They also used the American singer and antiwar activist Joan Baez to verify that bombs had hit the civilian air terminal at Hanoi's Gia Lam Airport. On the twenty-third, they alleged that B-52s had destroyed the largest medical center in North Vietnam, the Bach Mai Hospital. Among others, they took the former chief prosecutor at the Nuremberg war crimes trials following World War II, the famous jurist Telford Taylor, to view the damage. Taylor and the others then released photographs of what they had seen to the press.

Avowing at a 4 January meeting that "if anyone is punished for hitting that hospital, I'll fire someone," President Nixon was strongly tempted to respond with a propaganda campaign of his own that emphasized Communist depredations in the South. He remained concerned, however, that the North Vietnamese might respond by adopting a hard line in the negotiations. As a result, the State Department kept "studiously silent" where the bombing was concerned, and the White House said little in public.[17]

The Pentagon thus carried most of the burden in dealing with the press and experienced the greatest damage. As the attacks progressed and controversy mounted, Friedheim and the reporters he briefed went into a dance each time questions arose about the bombing. Urged, for example, to comment on reports of heavy damage to civilians in Hanoi, he responded vaguely, "You have to judge the sources of that information." The reporters then asked him to address allegations that the B-52s were "carpet bombing" civilian areas. He responded by sidestepping the issue. "The adjectives you'll have to choose for yourselves," he said. "If the implication of your question is that we are bombing civilian areas, the answer is no." Calling an end to the game, one reporter finally asked, "Is it your position that you don't want to discuss the topic, and that any comment is that the North Vietnamese often use such situations for propaganda purposes?" Friedheim responded affably, "I'll accept that summation."[18]

Shortly after the attacks ended, the Defense Department finally released a list of targets and a preliminary assessment of damage. It nevertheless took the agency until 2 January to acknowledge that the Bach Mai Hospital had sustained "limited, accidental" damage because it stood less than eleven hundred meters from a military base that had been a prime target for the B-52s. The department then attempted to play down the bombers' role in the incident by noting that spent surface-to-air missiles might have been responsible. Given the huge number of missiles the enemy had fired during the raids, the argument had some merit, but it rang false at the time because it had already been used and discredited in the French embassy bombing.[19]

Lacking adequate explanations from the U.S. government, the news media gave North Vietnam's claims far more prominence than they deserved. Since the B-52s had dropped at least twenty thousand tons of explosives—"the equivalent of the Hiroshima bomb"—on targets that abutted civilian areas, the *New York Times* thus avowed, "It requires no horror stories from Hanoi radio to deduce that the destruction and human suffering [in North Vietnam] must be very ex-

Kin No rail yards and storage facilities after the bombing. (U.S. Air Force)

tensive indeed." In the same way, the *Boston Globe* declared that American bombers had turned North Vietnam into an "all but incredible charnel house."[20]

Columnist David Lawrence took up for the Defense Department. Although civilians had presumably suffered, he said, the Pentagon's list of targets was so extensive and the damage so clear that it was obvious the United States had targeted North Vietnam's war-making potential rather than its civilian population. In the absence of an effective campaign to counter the enemy's propaganda, however, the issues were hardly as clear as Lawrence believed. Since the war had already taken a heavy toll of civilians in both the North and the South, photographs and eyewitness accounts of such damage carried heavier weight with the press than uncommunicative official communiqués. The *Philadelphia Inquirer* provides a case in point. Comparing the Pentagon's acknowledgment of limited damage at Bach Mai with Telford Taylor's graphic descriptions of "huge fresh craters" and "buildings . . . shattered by blasts," it headlined its piece, "Why Can't the United States Be Truthful About Bombing?"[21]

In the end, many of the charges that appeared in the press failed to stand up. Taylor, for one, observed after a second trip to Hanoi in January that damage to civilian areas in the city had obviously been an unintentional by-product of attacks on legitimate military targets. During March and April 1973, reporters such as Malcolm Browne and Peter Arnett also traveled to Hanoi. They discovered, as Browne observed, that the city remained "beautiful and bustling," and that the damage to it had been "grossly overstated by North Vietnamese propaganda." The enemy reinforced these conclusions on 4 January by revealing that 1,318 civilians had been killed in Hanoi during the attacks and 1,261 wounded. The numbers were substantial, but far fewer noncombatants had fallen than would have been the case if the United States had pursued a policy of indiscriminate bombing.[22]

On 4 April the Defense Department produced photographs of Hanoi that refuted the charge that the U.S. Air Force had targeted civilians, but by then the American role in the war was over. Accounts of the final peace treaty with North Vietnam, the withdrawal of the last American military units from the South, the return of the prisoners of war, and the unfolding of the Watergate affair took precedence over any attempt at self-correction. The *Washington Post* carried a brief account buried on page 24 of its 5 April edition. The *New York Times* published a heavier story by Drew Middleton but procrastinated until 2 May before printing it. *Newsweek* and *Time* said nothing.[23]

In any event, the heavy reporting of civilian casualties and of the destruction in Hanoi had little effect on American opinion. Earlier in the war, a president could have counted on a surge in public support whenever he made a difficult decision involving the fighting. This time, the opposite occurred. The public, according to Harris polls, opposed the bombing by a margin of 51 to 37 percent. The reaction had little to do with concerns about morality. Fewer than 50 percent of those interviewed agreed that "it was inhuman and immoral for the U.S. to have bombed Hanoi's civilian centers." Instead, 71 percent said they believed "what we did in bombing Hanoi was no worse than what the Communists have done in the Vietnam War." In the end, what turned the public against the raids was American losses, which had received far less coverage in the press than the supposed brutality of the attacks. Unwilling to tolerate further attrition, whether in aircraft or men, a majority agreed, by 55 to 30 percent, that "we lost many American lives and B-52s unnecessarily in the bombing raids."[24]

As Nixon had predicted, in the days preceding the start of the new legislative session, the House Democratic Caucus revealed the direction Congress would take by voting 154 to 74 to cut off funds for further U.S. operations in Indochina as soon as possible. Spurred by that development, the president pressed ahead. On the day after the Democrats met, he warned Thieu that he intended to initial an agreement as soon as negotiators had settled on a final draft of the accord.[25]

By 13 January the document was complete. Among other provisions, the North Vietnamese agreed to drop the term *administrative structure* from the description of the National Council, to respect both sides of the Demilitarized Zone, and to allow for the continuation of almost unrestricted American military

Henry Kissinger initials the treaty. (Indochina Archives)

assistance to the Saigon regime. In return, to Thieu's chagrin, they retained the right to leave their forces in place in South Vietnam.[26]

The next day, with South Vietnam's leaders still refusing to cooperate, Nixon informed Thieu that he was directing the suspension of all bombing and mining in North Vietnam. When that had no effect and Thieu continued to request revisions, Nixon sent a second message to reassure Thieu that the United States would "react vigorously to violations of the agreement." Even so, he said, the time for delay had passed. Rather than suffer a total cutoff of funds for South Vietnam, he would initial the agreement on 23 January and sign it on the twenty-seventh: "We have only one decision before us, whether or not to continue in peacetime the close partnership that has served us so well in war."[27]

In support of the president's warning, apparently at White House suggestion, Senators Barry Goldwater and John Stennis, who in the past had consistently supported the war, went on record in the press with a warning. If Thieu's recalcitrance continued, Goldwater observed, it would imperil any future assistance South Vietnam might obtain from the United States. At that point, on 20 January, with no room left to maneuver, Thieu relented. The agreement would at least guarantee, he said, continued American support for South Vietnam during the struggle that seemed certain to follow. Kissinger initialed the treaty three days later.[28]

Syndicated columnist Marquis Childs broke first word of the development, but the White House declined to confirm the story. Instead, Nixon made a formal announcement that evening in a brief speech to the nation. Under the treaty, he said, all U.S. combat forces would leave South Vietnam and all American prisoners of war would be returned. Even so, bombing would continue in Cambodia and Laos until settlements ended the conflict in those countries, and civilian contractors would continue to provide technical and engineering support to the South Vietnamese.[29]

Over the days that followed, MACV's office of information went out of existence. Although it provided public affairs support for the American team participating in the military commission that was to monitor the start-up of the treaty, it held the final session of the famous "Five O'Clock Follies" on 27 January, the day the accord went into effect. There were over 385 correspondents in South Vietnam at the time. The command continued briefly to coordinate their activities but progressively ceded that responsibility to the South Vietnamese and to the U.S. embassy's Office of the Special Assistant for Press Affairs.[30]

Although American participation in the war ceased with the treaty, incidents continued to occur as all sides pushed to consolidate their positions. By 31 January, enemy forces had cut all major roads in South Vietnam's Military Region 2 and were moving to intersect the country's main north-south road, Highway 1, to the south of Da Nang. Meanwhile, enemy tanks were reported to be moving along the Ho Chi Minh Trail in Laos, American bombing continued in Cambodia, and COSVN proclaimed "a new era of political struggle" to its adherents in the South.[31]

Part of what was happening found its way into the press, along with the efforts of the South Vietnamese armed forces to curb the Saigon correspondents. News of the return of the prisoners of war, however, was what played the most. A few reporters grumbled that MACV and the Defense Department were attempting to retaliate for years of criticism by keeping the news media away from the prisoners, but that was not so. The army had learned from painful experience that former prisoners sometimes had difficulty adapting to normal life. Premature exposure to even the most carefully structured media interviews could harm the men. A different approach might have prevailed in earlier years, when the cooperation of the press had been necessary. But the war was over. There was nothing left to sell. The American military were closing in on themselves.[32]

Jerry Friedheim's first decision upon succeeding Daniel Henkin as assistant secretary of defense for public affairs shortly after the signing of the treaty symbolized the change. Entering his new office for the first time, he noticed a map of Vietnam that had hung prominently on one wall during all the years of the war. Turning to his secretary, he instructed her to have it removed.[33]

Conclusion

What happened between the military and the news media in Vietnam? At the beginning of the war, correspondents such as Neil Sheehan, Malcolm Browne, David Halberstam, and Peter Arnett disagreed at times with official policy, but their reporting never questioned the ends of the war. Instead, placing great confidence in the American soldier, they argued in favor of more effective tactics and less official obfuscation. The military, for their part, reciprocated, rejecting censorship of the press in favor of a system of voluntary guidelines that respected the willingness of reporters to avoid releasing information of value to the enemy.

The policies that evolved from that decision succeeded in preserving both military security and the rights of the press. Although critics would later cite instances in which reporters violated official guidelines, those episodes pale in the context of the tens of thousands of news reports emanating from the war zone that adhered to the rules. In addition, as General Sidle would later attest, despite some notable lapses, most of that reporting was either advantageous to the U.S. government and its policies or, given the errors of fact that often accompany the transmission of fast-breaking news, a reasonably neutral approximation of what was happening. Meanwhile, if the Saigon correspondents complained that official briefings and news releases were at times incomplete, uninformative, or self-serving, hardly any would deny that the system in place in South Vietnam gave them ample means to do their jobs. Reporters "had to be willing to take dawn airplanes, spend a few nights a month with [South Vietnamese] and American troops, tour key districts with veteran U.S. advisers, dine with political specialists, and ask intelligent questions of generals, sergeants and province chiefs," reporter Peter Braestrup observed, but if they did, "there were always knowledgeable U.S.

291

[officials] . . . ready to offer a viewpoint which conflicted with the White House line . . . [and] always truths to be had at battalion level."*

With so much that started out right, what went wrong? The answer goes beyond the relationship between the news media and the military in Vietnam to the conceptions and complexities that underlay the war itself. For the conflict was born in contradiction and grounded in ambiguity.

The many parallels between Lyndon Johnson's approach to the war and that of his successor, Richard Nixon, show what happened. Johnson was convinced that the conflict was necessary but believed that the American public and Congress lacked the will, without careful handling, to carry it through to a successful conclusion. As a result, he sought to increase the American commitment to the war slowly in order to avoid confrontation with the Soviet Union and China and to retain a solid base of support for his domestic policies. Nixon, for his part, also had a larger agenda. Seeking to build a new world order with his own country in the lead, he wanted to extract the United States from the war gradually, without weakening American influence worldwide.

In pursuit of their goals, both Johnson and Nixon sought to enlist the military as spokesmen for their points of view. Johnson had an easier time of it than Nixon. After some reluctance, Westmoreland went along with the president's wishes. Abrams was more grudging. Unable to escape his president's desire for optimism, he still attempted to keep himself and his command clear of politics by making the war speak for itself. In the end, of course, Nixon prevailed. Continuing a process that had begun under Johnson, he concentrated public affairs policy making in Washington, where he and his staff could tune it to the demands of the moment. By 1972, as a result, many substantive news releases emanating from the military command in South Vietnam were drafted in Washington with only perfunctory input from agencies in the field. It was a far cry from the early days of the war, when MACV and the U.S. mission in Saigon had played a major role in the development of guidelines for the press.

In the end, however, neither Johnson nor Nixon succeeded in managing news coverage of the war. Cultivating the appearance that the conflict was going well despite many indications that he had achieved at best a stalemate, Johnson peppered the public record with so many inconsistencies that when the Tet offensive of 1968 occurred, both the press and important officials within the administration itself questioned Westmoreland's avowals that the enemy had suffered a costly setback. Increasingly ambivalent about the war himself, Johnson declined to run again for office and began the effort to achieve a negotiated settlement.

Johnson's decision had major implications for Nixon. For by giving rise to expectations within the American public and Congress that U.S. involvement in the war would soon end, it cut off many of the new president's options. Nixon responded by using public relations campaigns to gain the leverage he believed he

---

*Peter Braestrup, "Covering the Vietnam War," *Nieman Reports,* 23 Jan 70.

needed either to avert an outright South Vietnamese collapse or, failing that, to create a healthy interval between a final American withdrawal and the disintegration of his ally. By 1972, nevertheless, time had run out for him just as it had for Johnson. With the American public and Congress increasingly restive and with South Vietnamese leaders unwilling or unable to accomplish reforms that might have made their government attractive to Congress, Nixon decided it was time to "cut bait." Proclaiming success, he concluded an unfavorable treaty with North Vietnam and withdrew American forces from the war.

"Our worst enemy seems to be the press!" Nixon exclaimed during the 1971 incursion into Laos, but as with Johnson, so many contradictions existed within his approach to the war that the opposition of many within the news media was almost guaranteed. Nixon had no choice, for example, but to reduce the size of the American force in South Vietnam, but he also sought to cultivate an appearance of resolution in hopes of persuading the enemy to negotiate terms favorable to American ends. The disparity between the two approaches set up ambiguities that led inevitably to criticism. How could it be, many in Congress and the press inevitably asked, that the United States was withdrawing from South Vietnam when it was also sponsoring a major escalation in Cambodia? In the same way, Nixon time and again proclaimed the success of his program to turn the war over to the South Vietnamese. Astute observers within the press, however, could see that American advisers and B-52s had more of an effect on the enemy than South Vietnam's sometimes valiant but often inept armed forces.

A vicious circle developed. When Nixon began the process of withdrawal, the American public, Congress, and the news media viewed the event as an indication that their role in the war would end within a reasonable period of time. Hope soared, only to be dashed when the president approved the attack on Cambodia. The news media, with some exceptions, reacted with anger, raising arguments against the attack that mirrored questions arising within the president's own sharply divided government. In the end, the administration's credibility fell, especially in Congress, which moved to restrict the president's power ever again to employ American forces in Cambodia.

In turn, the president and his advisers hardened their own position. Asserting that the incursion had been a thorough success despite indications that less had been achieved than hoped, they continued the American withdrawal in order to shore up public morale but were still disposed, when an opportunity presented itself in Laos, to duplicate what they considered their earlier achievement. When that operation collapsed, more recriminations followed. Under the lash, the president and his advisers drew into a tighter ring and resolved to forge ahead.

Conditions in the field only made matters worse. Instructed to take as few casualties as possible, American commanders spent less and less time conducting combat operations. Instead, the troops fell into make-work routines that had nothing to do with the original purposes of their presence in South Vietnam. Morale declined, drug abuse flourished, interracial tensions multiplied, and the refusal to obey lawful orders became more common than ever in the past. The press chronicled the story, adding touches of commentary that exhibited little sympathy for the majority of soldiers and officers who had maintained their self-respect. As it did, the military responded much as Nixon had, by withdrawing into a shell. When MACV declined to punish reporters who were obviously acting in good faith, a few commanders even took matters into their own hands. Failing to provide routine transportation for reporters in combat areas, delaying the release of information, and declining to provide timely briefings, they demolished what remained of the military's standing with the press. As a result, by the end of 1972 and the commencement of the Christmas bombing, meaningful give-and-take had all but ceased on both sides.

With so many ambiguities, what was real? For some, it may be comforting to think that the news media pierced the mist, threw everything into focus, and brought the war to an end by forcing the American people to confront reality. Yet press coverage of the Vietnam War, while it often conveyed more of the truth than official pronouncements on such significant matters as drug abuse, race relations, the state of military morale, combat operations, and conditions within the South Vietnamese government and armed forces, was highly circumscribed by the nature of journalism as it is practiced in the United States. Reporters and editors, for example, tended to hew to the sources that gave their work the most weight—the president, the vice president, and other high officials of the executive and legislative branches of the government. During the war, the tendency sometimes harmed official credibility. When Nixon announced during the Cambodian incursion that he had targeted COSVN headquarters, the comment had such an effect that the press picked it up and clung to it, despite later efforts by official spokesmen to issue clarifications. More often, however, it worked to the advantage of government. Every presidential and vice presidential speech of any importance, especially when critical of the press, received heavy coverage, even in those segments of the news media that opposed the war. In that way, Vice President Agnew was able to score heavily against the press, using the very news media he was criticizing. The reverse was also true. If the administration sought to play down some aspect of the war, it could eliminate or significantly delay media coverage by keeping silent or, if it had to comment, by moving the story away from Washington. The Defense Department's handling of the My Lai massacre comes to mind. The agency managed to postpone the initial coverage of the event by announcing the trial of Lt. William Calley at a location far from Washington.

The routines reporters followed also tended to dilute news coverage, particularly during the war's later stages. Adhering to deadlines, constrained to write on subjects that producers and editors believed readers and viewers would want, under increasing pressure because of cutbacks, the Saigon correspondents spent considerably less time covering combat after 1968 than they had earlier in the war. Even when they did, there was no guarantee that what they wrote would see print. Sometimes editors preferred to hold back, either to avoid controversy or, as with Wes Gallagher and Peter Arnett's report on the looting of Snoul, to keep from contributing to the chaos that seemed to be descending on all sides.

Yet official manipulation and journalistic failures are relatively superficial aspects of the story. The question is, did either the press coverage or the government's efforts to manipulate public opinion have much effect on the people of the United States? There is evidence that from the beginning of the war, whatever the efforts of the press or the government, the American public went its own way. As early as March 1966, indeed, a carefully balanced survey of public opinion revealed deep ambivalence on the part of many Americans despite the acquiescence of large portions of the press in President Johnson's effort to mold a public consensus in favor of the conflict. Although a majority approved of the president's handling of the war, the bulk of those interviewed were also willing to accept de-escalation and free elections in South Vietnam even if the Viet Cong should win. Both positions were anathema to Johnson at that stage in the war. In the same way, during the Nixon years, many members of the American public supported Vice President Agnew's contention that television presented the news in a biased fashion, but a large majority nonetheless believed that the news media should continue to criticize government. In that case, it was clear that while Americans may at times voice criticism of institutions such as Congress and the press, they appreciate the underlying values those mechanisms represent and are rarely prepared to countenance radical change.

Although Americans almost invariably rallied to the president's side during times of crisis and were clearly unwilling to abandon the conflict without the return of the prisoners of war, their regret that they had ever become involved increased steadily as American losses mounted. Richard Nixon understood what was happening and bought time for his policies to work by curtailing American combat casualties during the final years of the war. Even so, by the beginning of his second term in office he had still lost most of his leverage. Failing to rise to his support, the public rejected his Christmas bombing campaign by a wide margin.

It would be tempting to conclude that distorted news coverage of the attacks in the press had wrought that effect, or that enemy propaganda designed to depict North Vietnam as the victim of an American terror campaign had succeeded. But, in fact, if the news media through its coverage of Communist claims had inevitably highlighted the issues, telling people, in effect, what to think about, Americans continued to follow their own track. By a margin of almost two to one, they rejected the claims of both the Communists and the press, to side instead, very simply, with the proposition that "we lost many American lives and B-52's . . . in the raids." The reaction had nothing to do with softness, moral laxity, lack of will, an inability to face the necessary frustrations of a long war, or enemy propaganda purveyed by a disloyal press. Following their own third course, exercising their own independence of mind, and displaying a substantial measure of contempt for all those in the press and government who had sought to manipulate them over the years, Americans had used their common sense. If more bombing and more killing had earlier proved to be of no avail, and if the South Vietnamese had shown few of the traits necessary for survival, why prolong the struggle? Enough was enough.

In the end, what happened in Vietnam between the military and the news media was symptomatic of what had occurred in the United States as a whole. At the beginning of the conflict, the country had acquiesced as the Johnson administration moved to contain Chinese and Soviet ambitions in Southeast Asia by going to war in South Vietnam. Although professedly suspicious of government as a matter of principle, the American news media both reflected and reinforced the trend, replaying official statements on the value of the war and supporting the soldier in the field, if not always his generals. With time, under the influence of many deaths and contradictions, American society moved to repudiate that earlier decision. Taking its lead from its sources within the increasingly divided American elite, the press followed along, becoming more and more critical of events in South Vietnam as withdrawals continued and the war gradually lost whatever purpose it had held. The military services lacked the ability to do the same. Remaining behind to retrieve what they could of the nation's honor, those of their members most emotionally tied to the failed policy fixed their anger upon the press, the most visible element of the society that appeared to have rejected them. When the press took up the challenge, anger and recrimination on all sides were the inevitable result. Whether time and circumstance will heal the ensuing rift remains to be seen.

Notes

COMMON ABBREVIATIONS USED IN NOTES

AP—Abrams Papers

ARVN—Army of South Vietnam

ASD PA—Assistant Secretary of Defense, Public Affairs

CINCPAC—Commander in Chief, Pacific

CINFO—Chief of Information

CJCS—Chairman, Joint Chiefs of Staff

CMH—U.S. Army Center of Military History, Washington, D.C.

COMUSMACV—Commander, U.S. Military Assistance Command, Vietnam

CONARC—U.S. Continental Army Command

CORDS—Office of Civilian Operations and Revolutionary Development Support, MACV

CP—Clifford Papers

DCSOPS—Deputy Chief of Staff for Operations

DDI—Directorate of Defense Information

FAIM/IR—U.S. Department of State, Foreign Affairs Information Management, Bureau of Intelligence and Research

GVN—Government of (South) Vietnam

HQ—Headquarters

IG—Inspector General

IO—Information Office

JCS—Joint Chiefs of Staff

JCSM—JCS Memo

JUSPAO—Joint U.S. Public Affairs Office, Vietnam

LBJL—Lyndon Baines Johnson Library, Austin, Texas

MAC—U.S. Military Assistance Command, Vietnam

MACCORDS—Military Assistance Command, Office of Civilian Operations and Revolutionary Development Support

MACV—U.S. Military Assistance Command, Vietnam

MCHC—Marine Corps Historical Center, Washington, D.C.

MFR—Memo for the Record

MHI—U.S. Army Military History Institute, Carlisle, Pennsylvania

Msg—Message

NARA—U.S. National Archives Branch, College Park, Maryland

NMCC—National Military Command Center, the Pentagon

NP—Nixon Papers

NVA—North Vietnamese Army

NVN—North Vietnam

OASD PA—Office of the Assistant Secretary of Defense, Public Affairs

OASD SA—Office of the Assistant Secretary of Defense, Systems Analysis

OCO—Office of Civilian Operations, CORDS

ORLL—Operations Report, Lessons Learned

RTDD—Radio-Television-Defense Dialog

RVN—Republic of (South) Vietnam

RVNAF—Republic of (South) Vietnam Armed Forces

SEA—Southeast Asia

SECDEF—Secretary of Defense

SJA—Staff Judge Advocate

US/UK—United States/United Kingdom

USAF—U.S. Air Force

USIA—U.S. Information Agency

USIS—U.S. Information Service

USMC—U.S. Marine Corps

WH—Westmoreland History

WP—Westmoreland Papers

CHAPTER 1. TAKING SIDES

1. See Clarence Wyatt, *Paper Soldiers: The American Press and the Vietnam War* (New York: Norton, 1993).

2. Ibid.

3. See William Prochnau, *Once upon a Distant War: Young Correspondents and the Early Vietnam Battles* (New York: Random House, 1995).

4. Msg, Saigon 726 to State, 5 Feb 63, U.S. Department of State, Foreign Affairs Information Management, Bureau of Intelligence and Research (FAIM/IR). Unless otherwise indicated, all State Department records are from FAIM/IR.

5. David Halberstam, "Curbs in Vietnam Irk U.S. Officers: Americans Under Orders to Withhold News," *New York Times,* 22 Nov 62.

6. HQ, Commander in Chief Pacific (CINCPAC), Record of the Secretary of Defense Conference at Honolulu, 15 Jan 62, pp. 49–50, Directorate of Defense Information (DDI) files. Cited as Honolulu Conference.

7. John Mecklin, *Mission in Torment: An Intimate Account of the U.S. Role in Vietnam* (New York: Doubleday, 1965), pp. 105–6; Roger Hilsman, *To Move a Nation* (Garden City, N.Y.: Doubleday, 1967), pp. 421–22, 150, 349, 508–45; *The Senator Gravel Edition of the Pentagon Papers: The Defense Department History of United States Decision Making on Vietnam* (hereafter cited as *Pentagon Papers*), 4 vols. (Boston: Beacon Press, 1971), pp. 102–227; MFR, MACV Office of Information (MACOI), 9 May 64, sub: Investigation of Captain Shank's Allegations, 69A702, National Archives Branch, College Park, Maryland (NARA); Louis Harris, *The Anguish of Change* (New York: Norton, 1973), pp. 53–54.

8. Msg, State 1006 to Saigon, 21 Feb 62.

9. Memo, Lt. Col. Lee Baker for Arthur Sylvester, 12 Mar 64, sub: Restrictions on Release of Information in RVN; Phil G. Goulding, *Confirm or Deny: Informing the People on National Security* (New York: Harper and Row, 1970), p. 20.

10. HQ, MACV Advisory Group, Final Report of Col. Daniel B. Porter, Jr., 13 Feb 63, CMH.

11. "McNamara Lauds Gains in Vietnam," *New York Times,* 7 Jul 62; "McNamara Hails Gains in Vietnam," *New York Times,* 25 Jul 62.

12. Robert Trumbull, "Vietnamese Rout Red Unit," *New York Times,* 7 Jul 62; Msg, State 562 to Saigon, 30 Nov 62.

13. Jacques Nevard, "Americans Voice Doubt on Vietnam," *New York Times,* 29 Jul 62.

14. David Halberstam, "U.S. Deeply *Involved* in the Uncertain Struggle for Vietnam," *New York Times,* 21 Oct 62.

15. Robert B. Rigg, "The Asian Way," *Army,* July 70, pp. 45–46; Memo, William H. Sullivan for Robert McNamara [Sep 63], sub: Divergent Attitudes in U.S. Official Community, CMH; David Halberstam, *The Making of a Quagmire* (New York: Random House, 1964), pp. 266–69; Ltr, Frederick B. Nolting to Chalmers Wood, 1 Nov 62; Msg, Saigon 252 to State, 27 Aug 63.

16. Msgs, State 1131 to Saigon, 23 Mar 62; Saigon 1231 to State, 27 Mar 62; Saigon 1215 to State, 23 Mar 62; Saigon 1380 to State, 30 Apr 62.

17. Homer Bigart, "Vietnam Victory Remote," *New York Times,* 25 Jul 62; François Sully, "Vietnam, the Unpleasant Truth," *Newsweek,* 20 Aug 62, pp. 40–41.

18. Mecklin, *Mission in Torment,* pp. 132–35.

19. Ibid., p. 134; Msg, Saigon 255 to State, 6 Sep 62.

20. Msg, State 363 to Saigon, 25 Sep 62; Mecklin, *Mission in Torment,* pp. 137–38.

21. Ibid.

22. Ltr, Chalmers Wood to Nolting, 16 Nov 62; Mecklin, *Mission in Torment,* pp. 138–51.

23. Msgs, Saigon 503 to State, 10 Nov 62; State 513 to Saigon, 12 Nov 62; Saigon 536 to State, 21 Nov 62; Ltr, Frederick G. Dutton to Sen. Philip A. Hart, 27 Dec 62, CMH.

24. Msg, State 562 to Saigon, 30 Nov 62.

25. Neil Sheehan, *A Bright Shining Lie: John Paul Vann and America in Vietnam* (New York: Random House, 1988), pp. 204–65.

26. Ibid.

27. Ibid. See also *Pentagon Papers,* 2:134–35.

28. Msgs, Saigon 656 to State, 8 Jan 63; Saigon 726 to State, 5 Feb 63; "Mistakes, Luck Trip Up Vietnam," *Chicago Daily News,* 3 Jan 63.

29. "Vietnamese Humiliated," *Washington Daily News,* 4 Jan 63; "Reds Eluding Pursuit by Vietnamese," *Baltimore Sun,* 9 Jan 63; "The Mess in Vietnam Calls for a Hard Look," *Detroit Free Press,* 5 Jan 63.

30. Msg, Saigon 656 to State, 8 Jan 63; "Duty's Demand on a General," *Detroit Free Press,* 12 Jan 63.

31. Msg, Saigon 726 to State, 5 Feb 63.

32. Jim Fain, "News in Vietnam Tough Chore," *Atlanta Journal,* 22 Mar 71; Interv with Maj Gen Milton B. Adams, USAF, Jul 65, p. 15, CMH.

33. Dennis J. Duncanson, *Government and Revolution in Vietnam* (New York: Oxford University Press, 1968), pp. 327–28.

34. Mecklin, *Mission in Torment,* p. 163.

35. CIA Information Rept, 17 Jun 63, sub: Status of VC Efforts to Exploit Buddhist Situation, CMH.

36. Mecklin, *Mission in Torment,* pp. 153–65; George W. Goodman, "Our Man in Saigon," *Esquire,* Jan 64; Stanley Karnow, "The Newsman's War in Vietnam," *Nieman Reports,* Dec 63, p. 7.

37. "Vietnam's First Lady," *New York Times,* 11 Aug 63; CIA Information Report, 8 Jul 63, sub: Staff Appraisal, Vietnam, CMH.

38. Max Frankel, "U.S. Warns Diem on Buddhist Issue," *New York Times,* 14 Jun 63.

39. CONARC, Orientation on Press Relations for Personnel Destined for Vietnam [June 1964], in Westmoreland History, CMH (hereafter cited as WH).

40. Ibid.

41. David Halberstam, "G.I.'s Told Not to Criticize Vietnam," *New York Times,* 24 Jun 63.

42. David Halberstam, "Vietnamese Reds Gain in Key Areas," *New York Times,* 15 Aug 63.

43. Ibid.

44. "Excerpts from Rusk News Conference," *New York Times,* 15 Aug 63; Marguerite Higgins, "Vietnam, Fact and Fiction," *New York Herald-Tribune,* 28 Aug 63; Wyatt, *Paper Soldiers,* p. 122.

45. Msg, Saigon 261 to State, 19 Aug 63.

46. Rpt, Col F. P. Serong to Harkins, 14 Mar 63, 69A702, NARA.

47. Memo, Col Daniel B. Porter to Harkins, 13 Feb 63, sub: Final Report; Ltr, Harkins to Felt, 12 Aug 63, 69A702, NARA.

48. "The Infamous Mme. Nhu," *Chicago Tribune,* 8 Aug 63; "The Truth About a War Americans Aren't Winning," *U.S. News & World Report,* 5 Aug 63, pp. 47–49.

49. CIA Information Rpt, 24 Aug 63, sub: Maj. Gen. Tran Van Don Details . . . the Plan to Establish Martial Law; CIA Information Rpt, 23 Aug 63, sub: Nhu's Statements on the Government's Actions, FAIM/IR.

50. Msgs, State 225 to Saigon, 21 Aug 63; State 226 to Saigon, 21 Aug 63.

51. Halberstam, *The Making of a Quagmire*, pp. 228–29.

52. [AP,] "Three Newsmen Detained at Saigon Student Rally," *New York Times*, 25 Aug 63; William P. Bundy, Notes on MACV Briefing, 25 Sep 63, CMH; Msgs, CINCPAC to Sec State, 21 Aug 63; Saigon 327 to State, 24 Aug 63; Saigon 288 to State, 21 Aug 63.

53. Interv, author with Col Roger Bankson, 6 Sep 73, CMH.

54. David Halberstam, "Plan Said to Be Nhu's," *New York Times*, 23 Aug 63; "U.S. Problem in Saigon, Attack Called Surprise to Top Officials," *New York Times*, 24 Aug 63.

55. CIA Information Rept, 24 Aug 63, sub: Maj. Gen. Tran Van Don Details the Present Situation.

56. "U.S. Would Hail Ouster of Diem," *New York World-Telegram-Sun*, 22 Aug 63; "U.S. Sees Need for Coup," *Washington Daily News*, 22 Aug 63; *Pentagon Papers*, 2:734.

57. Msg, Saigon 544 to State, for President from Lodge, 19 Sep 63; Msg, Harkins to Gen Maxwell D. Taylor, quoted in *Pentagon Papers*, 2:747.

58. Msg, Saigon 544 to State, for President from Lodge, 19 Sep 63; "The Church Resolution," *New York Times*, 13 Sep 63.

59. Fact Book—Vietnam, Sep 63, CMH.

60. Memo for the President, sub: Report of the McNamara-Taylor Mission to South Vietnam, 2 Oct 63, *Pentagon Papers*, 2:250.

61. *Pentagon Papers*, 2:766–69, 784–87.

62. Memo, McNamara for the President, 21 Dec 63, sub: Vietnam Situation, *Pentagon Papers*, 3:494.

63. For more on this see Montague Kern, Patricia Levering, and Ralph Levering, *The Kennedy Crises: The Press, The Presidency, and Foreign Policy* (Chapel Hill: University of North Carolina Press, 1983).

64. Peter Arnett, "Reflections on Vietnam," *Nieman Reports*, March 1972, p. 8.

CHAPTER 2. MAXIMUM CANDOR

1. *Pentagon Papers*, 2:304, 3:494–96.

2. Louis Harris, "U.S. Handling of Vietnam Issue Has Public Confused, Cautious," *Washington Post*, 30 Mar 64.

3. "The Gallup Poll: Less Than 40% of People Follow Vietnam Events," *Washington Post*, 27 May 64; DOD News Release no. 249-64, 26 Mar 64, sub: Address by Secretary of Defense McNamara, CMH.

4. "Hard-core Viet Cong Is Declared Probably Best Vietnam Fighter," *Washington Post*, 3 Jan 64; "Reds Escape Trap in Vietnam Clash," *New York Times*, 7 Jan 64; quote, "Anti-Red Move Fails in Vietnam," *Baltimore Sun*, 6 Jan 64.

5. *Pentagon Papers*, 2:306 f.; Msg, Harkins MAC J74 0236 to State, 10 Jan 64, WH. Joseph Fried, "Harkins Curbs Yank Beefs on S. Viet Regime," *New York Daily News*, 3 Mar 64; "South Vietnam Gag," *Chicago Sun-Times*, 8 Mar 64.

6. Msg, Saigon 1423 to State, 29 Jan 64.

7. Memo, Carl Rowan for Secretary McNamara, 4 Jun 64, sub: Improvement of Informational-Psychological Program, CMH; "TV's First War," *Newsweek*, 30 Aug 65, p. 32.

8. Rpt, DCSOPS to Chief of Staff, Army, 21 Mar 64, sub: Actions to Improve U.S.-GVN Operations in South Vietnam, CMH; Memo, B. L. Baker for Arthur Sylvester, 12 Mar 64, sub: Restrictions on Release of Information, U.S. Department of Defense, DDI.

9. Memo, Col C. R. Carlson, USAF, Office of Air Force Information, for the Director of Information, 10 Apr 64, sub: Capt. Shank's Letters Home, Air Force Clipping Service files; "A Captain's Last Letters from Vietnam," *U.S. News & World Report,* 4 May 64, p. 46; U.S. Congress, Senate, *Congressional Record,* 88th Cong., 2d sess., 27 Apr 64, p. 8889; "We Fight and Die, But No One Cares," *Life,* 8 May 64, p. 34B.

10. "Pentagon Hits 'Editing' of Dead Pilot's Letters," *Washington Star,* 23 May 64; Ted Lewis, "Capital Stuff: Kin of Dead GI's Pose a Question," *New York Times,* 13 May 64.

11. Memo, Carl Rowan for the President, 26 May 64; Intervs, author with Rodger Bankson, 6 Sep 73, 16 Jun 75, all CMH.

12. Memo, Carl Rowan for Secretary Rusk, 4 Jun 64, sub: Improvement of Informational-Psychological Program in South Vietnam, CMH; MFR, CINCPAC, 1 Jun 64, sub: Special Meeting on Southeast Asia, 68A4023, NARA.

13. Fact Sheet, 5 Jun 64, South Vietnam Action Program, attached to Memo, William H. Sullivan for the Secretary of State, 5 Jun 64, sub: Measures to Strengthen Situation in South Vietnam, CMH.

14. Msg, State 2192 to Saigon, 6 Jun 64.

15. Msg, MACV 2854 to JCS, 8 Jun 64, sub: Reorganization of Information Program, WH, CMH.

16. Msg, Saigon 2622 to State, 27 Jun 64.

17. Ibid.

18. Msg, State 59 to Saigon, 7 Jul 64.

19. Msg, Westmoreland MAC 3653 to Wheeler, 17 Jul 64, Westmoreland Papers (hereafter cited as WP), CMH.

20. Memo, Sylvester for Wheeler, 9 Jul 64, DDI; Ltr, Wheeler to Westmoreland, 17 Sep 64, WH; Memo, E. B. LeBailly for Sylvester, 28 Dec 64, DDI.

21. Memo, Winant Sidle to the author, 7 Nov 84.

22. Memo, Taylor for Deputy Ambassador U. Alexis Johnson et al., 4 Aug 64, sub: Mission Press Relations, WH.

23. JCS Memorandum (hereafter cited as JCSM) 746-64, 26 Aug 64, sub: U.S. Armed Reconnaissance, CMH.

24. Department of State *Bulletin,* 29 Jun 64, p. 994.

25. Msgs, State 1158 to Vientiane, 8 Jun 64; State to Vientiane, 10 Jun 64.

26. Department of State *Bulletin,* 29 Jun 64, p. 995; Douglas Kiker, "White House Blackout on Asian News," *New York Herald-Tribune,* 12 Jun 64; "The Price of Secrecy," *Washington Post,* 17 Jun 64; "The Credibility Gap," *Aviation Week Magazine,* 15 Jun 64.

27. Cir 89, Joint State/Defense/USIA, 6 Jul 64, CMH.

28. *Pentagon Papers,* 3:145, 182; Memo, Taylor for U. Alexis Johnson et al., 4 Aug 64, sub: Mission Press Relations.

29. Msg, Saigon 4014 to State, 2 Jun 65.

30. Memo, Arthur Sylvester for McNamara, 1 Oct 64, DDI.

31. Msg, Westmoreland MAC 3099 to Harris, 19 Jun 64, WP.

32. Msgs, Wheeler JCS 3635 to Westmoreland, 24 Jul 64, WP; State 478 to Saigon, 19 Aug 64; Draft Msg, Joint State/Defense/USIA to Saigon, 29 Dec 64; Memo, Bankson for Sylvester, 23 Dec 64; Memo, Bankson to Brig Gen G. C. Fogle, JCS, 20 Dec 64, all DDI.

33. Quotes from Circular 89, Joint State/Defense/USIA, 6 Jul 64; Beverly Deepe, "N. Viet Troops Cross Border, U.S. Aides Say," *New York Herald-Tribune,* 14 Jul 64; Peter Grose, "Sabotage Raids Confirmed by Saigon Aide," *New York Times,* 23 Jul 64; Msgs,

Saigon 109 to State, 15 Jul 64; Saigon 414 to State, 14 Aug 64, sub: Mission Monthly Report for July 1964.

34. Msgs, Saigon 193 to State, 23 Jul 64; Saigon 232 to State, 27 Jul 64; Interv, author with Barry Zorthian, 10 Dec 75.

35. Msg, Saigon 193 to State, 23 Jul 64.

36. Msgs, Tokyo 5476 to State, 13 Aug 64; State 462 to Saigon, 17 Aug 64; quote, USIA Talking Paper No. 21 to All Principal USIS Posts, CA-339, 4 Aug 64, CMH.

37. Louis Harris, "Public Solidly Behind Johnson on Vietnam," *Los Angeles Times,* 10 Aug 64; Harris, *Anguish of Change,* p. 56; Daniel Hallin, *The Uncensored War: The Media and Vietnam* (New York: Oxford University Press, 1986).

38. *Pentagon Papers,* 2:334; Msg, Saigon 1124 to State, 13 Oct 64, sub: U.S. Mission Report for September 1964.

39. "South Vietnam: First-half Report," *Newsweek,* 10 Aug 64; Peter Grose, "Pace of Fighting Holds in Vietnam," *New York Times,* 20 Aug 64; Kalisher is quoted in "The Viet Beat," *Newsweek,* 7 Sep 64; Stanley Karnow, "This Is Our Enemy," *Saturday Evening Post,* 22 Aug 64.

40. "The Viet Beat."

41. Memo, Barry Zorthian to Ambassador Taylor, 3 Oct 64, sub: Evaluation of Media Coverage, WH; MACV, Monthly Assessment of Military Activity, September 1964, 8 Oct 64, CMH.

42. Harris, *Anguish of Change,* p. 57.

CHAPTER 3. KEEPING THE OPTIONS OPEN

1. Msg, CINCPAC to JCS, CMIN 95041, for Wheeler from Sharp, 26 Feb 64, General Estimates of the Situation, CMH.

2. Richard Harwood, "Lessons from the Pentagon Papers," reprinted in Laura Babb, ed., *Of the Press, by the Press, for the Press (and Others, Too)* (Washington, D.C.: Washington Post Company, 1974), p. 84.

3. Interv, author with Barry Zorthian, 13 Apr 76, CMH.

4. Ibid.

5. "A *Life* Panel: The Lowdown from the Top U.S. Command in Saigon," *Life,* 27 Nov 64, p. 46; Memo, Westmoreland for Ambassador Taylor, 31 Oct 64, sub: The U.S. Posture Toward Emerging GVN, WH.

6. "A *Life* Panel."

7. U.S. Department of State, Bureau of Public Affairs, Vietnam and Related Topics, in American Opinion Summary, 18 and 25 November 64, FAIM/IR; Richard Egan, "Unrest in Saigon Dims Chances of Go North Plan," *National Observer,* 30 Nov 64.

8. American Opinion Summary, 25 Nov 64; *Pentagon Papers,* 3:248–51, 666.

9. *Pentagon Papers,* 3:252–54; Msg, State 1394 to Saigon, undated [Jan 65].

10. Memo, George Ball for the President, 12 Dec 64, sub: Diplomatic Actions Under South Vietnam Program, CMH; Msg, Saigon 1775 to State, 10 Dec 64, WH; Interv, author with Zorthian, 8 May 76.

11. Msg, Saigon 1775 to State, 10 Dec 64.

12. Notes for the President's Daily Summary, William Bundy, 21 Dec 64, sub: Disclosure of Evidence of North Vietnamese Infiltration into South Vietnam, CMH.

13. Msg, Saigon 2230 to State, 22 Jan 65, sub: U.S. Mission Report for December 1964.

14. Msgs, Saigon A-493 to State, 24 Dec 64, sub: Summary of Conversation, Sunday December 20; Saigon 1876 to State, 21 Dec 64; Saigon 1881 to State, 21 Dec 64; Saigon 1896 to State, 22 Dec 64; Beverly Deepe, "Khanh Assails Gen. Taylor," *New York Herald Tribune,* 23 Dec 64.

15. Beverly Deepe, "Taylor Rips Mask off Khanh," *New York Herald-Tribune,* 25 Dec 64.

16. Interv, author with Zorthian, 18 Jun 76; Msg, State 1347 to Saigon, 24 Dec 64; *Pentagon Papers,* 3:262; Msgs, State 1346 to Saigon, 24 Dec 64; State 1347 to Saigon, 24 Dec 64.

17. MACV 003 to National Military Command Center (NMCC), 9 Jan 65, CMH.

18. Msg, Saigon 2016 to State, 2 Jan 65.

19. "Significant Rumblings," *Newsweek,* 18 Jan 65, p. 13.

20. Rowland Evans and Robert Novak, "Vietnam's Continuing Crisis," *Washington Post,* 8 Jan 65; "To LBJ: What Is Our Aim in Vietnam?" *Life,* 8 Jan 65; *Pentagon Papers,* 3:264.

21. George Gallup, "Americans Believe S. Vietnamese Are Losing War to Communists," *Washington Post,* 31 Jan 65.

22. Harold K. Johnson, "The Defense of Freedom in Vietnam," 14 Jan 65, Department of State *Bulletin,* 8 Feb 65, p. 176: Henry Cabot Lodge, "We Can Win in Vietnam," *New York Times Magazine,* 17 Jan 65; Msg, Joint State/Defense 1513 to Saigon, 22 Jan 65.

23. Airgram, Hong Kong A473 to State, 15 Jan 65, sub: Communist Joint Week No 2; Msgs, MACV to NMCC, 5 Jan 65; MACV J312 0686 to CINCPAC, 8 Jan 65, all CMH; Memo, Bundy for Rusk, 6 Jan 65, sub: Notes on South Vietnamese Situation and Alternative, *Pentagon Papers,* 3:684; Msg, Saigon 2052 to State, 6 Jan 65, for President from Ambassador, WH.

24. Msg, State 1419 to Saigon, 8 Jan 65, for Ambassador from President.

25. Memo, MAC J00 for Ambassador Taylor, 8 Feb 65, sub: Weekly Assessment of Military Activity, 31 Jan–7 Feb 65, WH; "United States and South Vietnamese Forces Launch Retaliatory Attacks," Department of State *Bulletin,* 22 Feb 65, p. 238.

26. David Lawrence, "Mounting Crisis in the Vietnam War," *New York Herald-Tribune,* 8 Feb 65. Lerner is quoted in "Sizing Up Vietnam," *Time,* 19 Feb 65.

27. Draft Msg, William Bundy to Taylor, 14 Feb 65; *Pentagon Papers,* 3:330; Department of State *Bulletin,* p. 344.

28. State Department Publication 7839, *Aggression from the North: The Record of North Vietnam's Campaign to Conquer South Vietnam* (Washington, D.C.: U.S. Government Printing Office, 1965).

29. "White Paper on Vietnam," *Washington Daily News,* 1 Mar 65; "Vietnam Basics," *Baltimore Sun,* 25 Feb 65; "Weak Reed to Lean On," *St Louis Post-Dispatch,* 2 Mar 65; "The White Paper," *New Republic,* 13 Mar 65, p. 10; "Flaws in Our Case for Vietnam Support," *Providence Journal,* 28 Feb 65.

30. Chester L. Cooper, *The Last Crusade* (New York: Dodd, Mead, 1970), p. 264; Harris, *Anguish of Change,* p. 58; "The One-Way Street," *New York Times,* 7 Mar 65.

31. USIA, Report of Far East Public Affairs Conference at Baguio, PI, 11–15 January 1965, 70A371, NARA.

32. Memo, ASD PA for SECDEF, 19 Jan 65, sub: News Media Treatment of BARREL ROLL NINE, DDI.

33. Msg, State 596 to Vientiane, 14 Jan 65; Laurence Barrett, "Secrecy in Southeast Asia," *New York Herald-Tribune,* 19 Jan 65; "The Quiet Escalation," *Time,* 22 Jan 65. Westmoreland quotes Monroney in Msg, Westmoreland MAC 309 to Gen George V. Underwood, Chief of Army Information, 21 Jan 65, WP.

34. Msgs, Saigon 2186 to State, 18 Jan 65; State to Saigon, 6 Feb 65; Wheeler JCS 553-65 to Sharp and Westmoreland, 13 Feb 65, WP; Interv, author with Zorthian, 1 Dec 76, CMH.

35. Msgs, Defense 5083 to CINCPAC, 12 Feb 65, DDI; Wheeler JCS 553-65 to Sharp and Westmoreland, 13 Feb 65, WP; Sharp to Westmoreland, 14 Feb 65, WH.

36. Interv, author with Zorthian, 1 Dec 76.

37. Msg, Saigon 2560 to State, 13 Feb 65; Interv, author with Zorthian, 1 Dec 76.

38. Msg, Westmoreland MAC 831 to Wheeler, 17 Feb 65, WP.

39. Msgs, Wheeler JCS 736-65 to Westmoreland, 27 Feb 65, WH; MAC JOO 6394 to CINCPAC, 2 Mar 65; MAC J-3 to JCS, 18 Feb 65; Joint State/Defense 6068 to Saigon 27 Feb 65, all CMH. Westmoreland MAC 1110 to McNamara, 3 Mar 65, WP.

40. Msg, Saigon 2876 to State, 6 Mar 65.

41. Msg, State 1881 to Saigon, 3 Mar 65.

42. Msg, Saigon 2876.

43. Ibid.

44. Memo, James L. Greenfield for Leonard Unger, Deputy Assistant Secretary of State, Far Eastern Affairs, 10 Mar 65, sub: Suggest Steps to Reduce Press Coverage of Air Strikes, DDI; Memo, Adm Francis J. Blouin, to Leonard Unger, 16 Mar 65, sub: BARREL ROLL and the Press, 70A3717, NARA.

45. Msgs, Saigon 2950 to State, 13 Mar 65; Joint State/Defense/USIA 7890 to Saigon, 26 Mar 65; Defense 6826 to CINCPAC, 10 Mar 65, all DDI.

46. [AP], "Vietnam Curbs Hit by Newsmen," *Baltimore Sun,* 18 Mar 65; Richard Starnes, "Pentagon Has Viet Story—But It's Kept Secret," *New York World-Telegram,* 19 Mar 65.

47. "New Restrictions Disavowed by U.S.," *New York Times,* 19 Mar 65.

48. This section is based on ASD PA Report of the Honolulu Information Conference, 10–20 March 65, tabs D and E, DDI (hereafter cited as Honolulu Conference Report).

49. Wheeler CSM-518-65, for ASD PA, 29 Mar 65, sub: Information Policy in Vietnam, DDI.

50. Msg, Saigon 3322 to State, 10 Apr 65.

CHAPTER 4. THE GROUND WAR

1. Msgs, JCS 5147 to CINCPAC, 12 Feb 65, Wheeler for Sharp, CMH; JCS 1008-65 to CINCPAC, 20 Feb 65, Wheeler for Sharp, WP; MACV, Commander's Estimate of the Situation, 25 Mar 65, WH.

2. *Pentagon Papers,* 3:374; Msg, State 2184 to Saigon, 3 Apr 65.

3. Msgs, State 2184 to Saigon, 3 Apr 65; CINCPAC to MACV, 14 Apr 65, WP; MFR, 3 Apr 65, sub: Meeting Between Rusk, Taylor, McGeorge Bundy et al, WH; Msg, Sharp to Westmoreland, 13 Jun 65, WH.

4. Msgs, Saigon 3539 to State, 26 Apr 65; Saigon 3820 to State, 20 May 65.

5. Ibid.

6. Interv, author with Col Ralph Ropp and Lt Col Richard Bryan, 24 Jan 77, CMH.

7. [AP,] untitled, datelined Tokyo, 22 Mar 65; Msg, Saigon 3124 to State, 28 Mar 65, for Greenfield from Zorthian, DDI.

8. Msgs, Saigon 3124 to State, 28 Mar 65; Saigon 3053 to State, 23 Mar 65, DDI; Westmoreland MAC 16878 to Wheeler, 28 Mar 65, WP.

9. "Blackening Our Name," *Washington Post,* 24 Mar 65; "Gas (Non-lethal) in Vietnam," *New York Times,* 24 Mar 65; Federation of American Scientists, News Release, 25 Mar 65, DDI; USIA for the President, 25 Mar 65, sub: Daily Reaction Report, DDI.

10. Philip Geyelin, "Vietnam Vexation: Outcry over Use of Gas Points Up U.S. Aloneness There," *Wall Street Journal,* 26 Mar 65.

11. Msg, MAC J311 to CINCPAC, 9 Sep 65, DDI; quote, Msg, Wheeler JCS 1071 to Westmoreland, 25 Mar 65, WP.

12. Msgs, State 294 to Saigon, 29 Jul 65; State 370 to Saigon, 7 Aug 65.

13. Msgs, State 294 to Saigon, 29 Jul 65; State 370 to Saigon, 7 Aug 65; State 2217 to Saigon, 6 Apr 65; Wheeler JCS 1271-65 to Westmoreland, 10 Apr 65, WP.

14. Quote, Msg, Wheeler JCS 1271-65 to Westmoreland, 10 Apr 65. See also Wheeler JCS 1272 to Westmoreland, 10 Apr 65, WP.

15. First quote, Msg, Westmoreland MAC 1985 to Wheeler, 11 Apr 65; second quote, Msg, CINCPAC to JCS, 10 Apr 65, for Wheeler from Sharp, WP.

16. Memo, Bankson for Philip Goulding, 8 May 65, DDI.

17. Msg, Joint State/Defense/USIA 8876 to All Military Commands, 8 May 65, CMH.

18. *Pentagon Papers,* 3:410; John T. McNauthton, Minutes of the 20 April 1965 Honolulu Meeting, 23 Apr 65, CMH; Msgs, Saigon 3538 to State, 26 Apr 65; State 2451 to Saigon, 28 Apr 65.

19. Msg, Joint State/Defense 2498 to Saigon, 4 May 65.

20. Msg, Defense 1897 to CINCPAC, MACV, 11 May 65, DDI.

21. MFR, Rodger Bankson for Arthur Sylvester, 14 May 65, sub: Background Briefing, DDI.

22. Interv, author with Barry Zorthian, 29 Jun 77, CMH. Msgs, MACV 18608 to OSD PA, 2 Jun 65, WH; Saigon 4058 to State, 5 Jun 65; Saigon 4074 to State, 5 Jun 65. MACV 18896 to OSD PA, 4 Jun 65, sub: Press Trends No. 148-65, FAIM/IR; Saigon 4058 to State, 5 Jun 65.

23. Msg, State 2810 to Saigon, 5 Jun 65.

24. Msg, State 2832 to Saigon, 8 Jun 65.

25. John W. Finney, "U.S. Denies Shift on Troop Policy in Vietnam War," *New York Times,* 10 Jun 65; Circular 2470 to All Diplomatic Posts, 9 Jun 65, FAIM/IR; "Ground War in Washington," *New York Times,* 10 Jun 65; Kenneth Crawford, "On Taking the Heat," *Newsweek,* 21 Jun 65, p. 36.

26. Arthur Krock, "By Any Other Name, It's Still War," *New York Times,* 10 Jun 65.

27. Msgs, MACV 19118 to CINCPAC, 7 Jun 65, FAIM/IR; Westmoreland MAC 3077 to Sharp, 13 Jun 65, WP.

28. Memo, MACV for Westmoreland, 13 Jun 65, sub: Telephone Call from Adm. Sharp, CMH Msgs, Sharp to Westmoreland, 13 Jun 65, WH; Saigon to NMCC, 13 Jun 65.

29. Msg, Saigon to NMCC, 13 Jun 65.

30. Msg, State 2891 to Saigon, 14 Jun 65. This section is based on Msgs, Saigon 4205 to State, 15 Jun 65; and Saigon 4238 to State, 19 Jun 65.

31. Msgs, MACV 20217 to JCS, 15 Jun 65, CMH; State 2933 to Saigon, 16 Jun 65.

32. Ibid.

33. Msgs, Saigon 4240 to State, 17 Jun 65; Saigon 4297 to State, 20 Jun 65; NMCC to CINCPAC, 18 Jun 65, DDI.

34. Ibid. The TV reports are close paraphrases. See Radio-TV Reports, Inc, Dialog: Detailed Broadcast Log, 18 Jun 65, DDI (hereafter cited as RTDD).

35. Msgs, Saigon 4297 to State, 20 Jun 65; MACV 21020 to OASD PA, 19 Jun 65, sub: Press Trends 163A65, FAIM/IR; quote, Msg, MACOI to NMCC, 20 Jun 65; MFR, DDI, 19 Jun 65, sub: Statement by Dept of State; MACV 21538 to CINCPAC, 24 Jun 65; Defense 5597 to CINCPAC, 12 Jul 65, all DDI.

36. Msg, Sharp to Westmoreland, 19 Jun 65, CMH.

37. Msgs, MACV 2138 to CINCPAC, 23 Jun 65, DDI; Wheeler JCS 2330-65 to Sharp, 24 Jun 65, WP; Saigon 4414 to State, 28 Jun 65; Saigon 4372 to State, 25 Jun 65.

38. Msgs, MACV 22042 to CINCPAC, 27 Jun 65, FAIM/IR; Saigon 4414 to State, 28 Jun 65; Saigon 4416 to State, 28 Jun 65; Saigon 4430 to State, 29 Jun 65.

39. Msg, State 40 to Saigon, 3 Jul 65.

40. This section is based on Msg, MACV 24135 to OASD PA, 12 Jul 65, sub: Supplemental Press Trends 186A-65, FAIM/IR.

41. Keyes Beech, "U.S. Considers Tighter Rein on Security," *Chicago Daily News*, 14 Jul 65.

42. Msg, State Circular to All Diplomatic Posts, 13 Jul 65.

43. Memo, Sylvester for the Secretary of Defense, 6 Aug 65, sub: CBS TV Show on Vietnam, 70A3717, NARA.

44. U.S. Dept. of State, Record of the U.S./UK Information Working Group Meeting, London, 20–21 Jul 65, FAIM/IR.

45. Ball is quoted in Mark Lorell and Charles Kelley, Jr., *Casualties, Public Opinion, and Presidential Policy During the Vietnam War* (Santa Monica, Calif.: Rand Corporation, 1985), p. 52.

46. Memo, Harlan Cleveland for Secretary Rusk, 22 Jul 65, sub: Vietnam; Msg, Wheeler JCS 2800-65 to Westmoreland, 28 Jul 65, WP.

47. For more on this see John Mueller, *War, Presidents, and Public Opinion* (New York: Wiley, 1973).

48. Morley Safer, "Television Covers the War," in U.S. Congress, Senate, Committee on Foreign Relations, *News Policies in Vietnam, Hearing, 17 and 31 Aug 66*, 89th Cong., 2d sess., p. 90; Interv, author with Zorthian, 10 Feb 84.

49. Msgs, Saigon 301 to State, 26 Jul 65; Saigon 302 to State, 28 Jul 65; Jack Langguth, "U.S. Silences Aides in Saigon on Missile Site Raid," *New York Times*, 29 Jul 65.

50. Jack Shulimson and Maj. Charles M. Johnson, USMC, *U.S. Marines in Vietnam: The Landing and the Buildup, 1965* (cited hereafter as *The Landing and the Buildup*) (Washington, D.C.: History and Museums Division, USMC, 1978), pp. 50–65; Memo, Counsel for Commandant, U.S. Marine Corps, 3 Sep 65, sub: Cam Ne, 7A22065, History and Museums Division, USMC (hereafter cited as Cam Ne file).

51. Memo, HQ Marine Corps for ASD (PA), 9 Aug 65, sub: Mr. Morley Safer's Report of Marine Attack on the Village of Cam Ne, Cam Ne file.

52. CBS Evening News, 3 Aug 65, RTDD.

53. Transcript, CBS Evening News Broadcast of 5 Aug 65, Cam Ne file.

54. MFR, 9 Aug 65, sub: Leonard F. Chapman conversation with Editor of the *Washington Post,* Cam Ne file. Safer report, RTDD, 7 Aug 65; Shulimson and Johnson, *The Landing and the Buildup,* pp. 50–65.

55. Ltr, Arthur Sylvester to Fred Friendly, 12 Aug 65, Cam Ne file.

56. Ltr, Friendly to Sylvester, 16 Aug 65, Cam Ne file.

57. Ibid.

58. Ltr, Westmoreland to Walt, 14 Aug 65, WH.

59. MACV Directive 525-3, 7 Sep 65, sub: Minimizing Non-Combatant Battle Casualties, DDI.

60. Safer report, RTDD, 18 Aug 65.

61. Msgs, Westmoreland to Throckmorton, 6 Aug 65, WP; Defense 8096 to Secretary of the Army et al., 12 Aug 65, DDI.

62. Interv, author with Charles W. Hinkle, 11 Apr 78.

63. Memo, Joseph Lumen, State Department Office of Public Affairs, for OSD (PA), 24 Aug 65, sub: Hazards of Field Press Censorship, DDI; Msg, MACV 29892 to OSD (PA), 25 Aug 65, DDI.

64. Intervs, author with Rodger Bankson, 28 Aug 75; Charles W. Hinkle, 11 Apr 78; and Maj Gen Winant Sidle, 6 May 73.

65. Ltr, Sylvester to Dixon Donnelly, 6 Aug 66, DDI.

CHAPTER 5. KEEPING A LOW PROFILE

1. Joint U.S. Public Affairs Office (JUSPAO), Breakdown of News Correspondents as of 18 Jan 66, Papers of Barry Zorthian.

2. Msgs, Saigon 595 to State, 24 Aug 65; Saigon 825 to State, 9 Sep 65; Saigon 1908 to State, 27 Nov 65.

3. Memo, Bankson for Sylvester, 22 Nov 65, sub: Backgrounders, DDI.

4. Msgs, Wheeler JCS 3423-65 to Westmoreland, 16 Sep 65; Westmoreland MAC 4647 to Wheeler, 18 Sep 65, WP.

5. Msg, MACV to NMCC, 7 Sep 65, DDI; Shulimson and Johnson, *The Landing and the Buildup,* pp. 90–91.

6. The AP, UPI, and Reuters dispatches were in DDI files.

7. Cir 567, State to All Diplomatic Posts, 7 Oct 65, DDI.

8. Msgs, State 823 to Saigon, 22 Sep 65; Defense 2425 to Westmoreland, 23 Sep 65, DDI; Saigon 1175 to State 5 Oct 65; State 964 to Saigon, 6 Oct 65.

9. John Maffre, "U.S. Publicizes Tear Gas Attack in Vietnam," *Washington Post,* 9 Oct 65; Msgs, Westmoreland MAC 5056 to Sharp, 10 Oct 65; JCS 4207-65 to Westmoreland, 3 Nov 65, CMH.

10. MFR, 26 Aug 65, sub: Points Discussed in the President's Luncheon, 19 Aug 65, FAIM/IR. Msgs, Saigon 484 to State, 14 Aug 65; Saigon 489 to State, 15 Aug 65; Saigon 511 to State, 17 Aug 65; Saigon 670 to State, 28 Aug 65; Saigon 685 to State, 30 Aug 65.

11. Msgs, Wheeler JCS 3377-65 to Sharp, 11 Sep 65; Sharp to Wheeler 14 Sep 65; Westmoreland MAC 4620 to Sharp, 15 Sep 65, CMH.

12. Msgs, Wheeler JCS 3479 to Westmoreland, 18 Sep 65; Westmoreland MAC 4690 to Wheeler, 20 Sep 65, WP.

13. Msg, Sylvester Defense 4109 to MACV IO, 14 Oct 65, DDI; MFR, sub: Public Affairs Policy Committee Meeting of 20 Sep 65, 703717, NARA.

14. Msgs, DA 737529 to All Military Commands, 22 Oct 65, sub: Secretary's 21 October Backgrounder, CMH; CINCPAC to COMUSMACV, 30 Oct 65, DDI.

15. Msg, Saigon 1256 to State, 11 Oct 65.

16. Charles Mohr, "The Siege of Plei Me," *New York Times,* 28 Oct 65.

17. This section is based on Combat After Action Report, U.S. First Cavalry Division (airmobile), Pleiku Campaign, 4 Mar 66, CMH.

18. Westmoreland Diary, vol. 2, CMH.

19. Msgs, MACV 41188 to OSD PA, 20 Nov 65; Saigon 1820 to State, 20 Nov 65, FAIM/IR.

20. Charles Mohr, "War and Misinformation," *New York Times,* 26 Nov 65; Denis Warner, "Army's Word Suspect in Vietnam," *Denver Post,* 7 Dec 65; "Moderation in All," *Newsweek,* 6 Dec 65, p. 42.

21. Eric Sevareid, "The Final Troubled Hours of Adlai Stevenson," *Look,* 30 Nov 65, p. 81.

22. Msgs, State 1697 to Saigon, 17 Dec 65; State 1739 to Saigon, 21 Dec 65.

23. Msg, State 1739 to Saigon, 21 Dec 65; R. W. Apple, Jr., "U.S. to Let Forces Go into Cambodia in Self-Defense," *New York Times,* 21 Dec 65.

24. Msgs, State 391 to Vientiane, 15 Dec 65; Saigon 2257 to State, 16 Dec 65; State 1709 to Saigon, 18 Dec 65; Vientiane 665 to State, 20 Dec 65.

25. Msgs, Vientiane 580 to State, 29 Nov 65; Vientiane 687 to State, 27 Dec 65; State 451 to Vientiane, 7 Jan 66; Vientiane 731 to State, 8 Jan 66; State 455 to Vientiane, 10 Jan 66; Vientiane to State, 11 Jan 66.

26. Memo, Robert McNamara, 9 Dec 65, sub: Telephone Conversations with Members of Congress, FAIM/IR.

27. Msg, MACV 45265 to CINCPAC, 27 Dec 65. For the Rusk message see McNamara Defense 5041 to Wheeler, Sharp, Westmoreland, 29 Dec 65, CMH.

28. "A Bombing Pause," *New York Times,* 27 Dec 65.

29. JCSM 16-66, Wheeler for SECDEF, 8 Jan 66; Msg, Saigon 2399 to State, 5 Jan 66, both FAIM/IR.

30. Msg, MACV 1550 to CINCPAC, 17 Jan 66; Memo, G. Mennen Williams for Rusk, 8 Jan 77, sub: Meeting with the President; State 1907 to Saigon, 6 Jan 66, all FAIM/IR.

31. The report appeared in the *Washington Post* on 25 Jan 66; Harris, *Anguish of Change,* p. 59.

32. Sheldon Appleton, ed., *United States Foreign Policy: An Introduction with Cases* (Boston: Little, Brown, 1968), p. 336.

33. Nelson W. Polesby, "Political Science and the Press: Notes on Coverage of a Public Opinion Survey on the Vietnam War," *Western Political Quarterly* 22 (March 1969): 46.

34. Msgs, Dept of the Army 745350 to All Army commands, 29 Dec 65; Wheeler JCS 460-66 to Westmoreland, 1 Feb 66, CMH.

35. Msgs, Wheeler JCS 457-66 to Sharp, Westmoreland, 31 Jan 66; Westmoreland MACV 885 to Wheeler, 1 Feb 66, CMH.

36. Memo, Sylvester for McNamara, 26 Oct 66, sub: Information Program, DDI; Charles Mohr, "This War—and How We Cover it," *Dateline* 10 (April 1966): 20; Albert R. Kroeger, "Television's Men at War," *Television Magazine,* Jul 65, p. 38.

37. Interv, Maj Robert H. Van Horn with Col Robert J. Coakley, USARV IO, n.d.

(hereafter cited as Coakley interview), CMH; Msgs, Sylvester Defense 4510 to Westmoreland, 22 Nov 65, WP; MACV 44150 to JCS, 17 Dec 65, 69A702, NARA; MACV 4797 to CINCPAC, 15 Feb 66, DDI.

38. Memo, Brig Gen Winant Sidle for Chief of Staff, MACV, 14 Oct 67, sub: Da Nang Press Center, 73A0243, NARA; Ltr, Rodger Bankson to author, 26 Oct 79, CMH.

39. Coakley interview; Transcript, USARV IO Conference, Mar 67, Comments of Col Joseph R. Meacham, 13 Mar 67, 70A748, NARA; Mohr, "This War—and How We Cover It," p. 20.

40. John Maffre, "U.S. Publicizes Tear Gas Attack in Vietnam," *Washington Post*, 9 Oct 65; Msgs, Westmoreland MAC 5056 to Sharp, 10 Oct 65; JCS 4207-65 to Westmoreland, 3 Nov 65, CMH.

41. Ltr, Bankson to the author, 26 Oct 79; Beverly Deepe, "Revised Accreditation Plan Outlined," *Overseas Press Club Bulletin* 20 (18 Nov 65): 3; John Maffre, "Saigon Censors Restore 'Pigeon Post' Popularity," *Washington Post*, 27 Nov 65.

42. Memo, Wheeler CSM 1044-65, 17 Dec 65; Msg, CINCPAC to OSD PA, 28 Dec 65, DDI.

43. Msg, Saigon 1032 to State, 24 Sep 65; U.S. Congress, Senate, Hearings Before the Committee on Foreign Relations, *News Policies in Vietnam,* 89th Cong., 2d sess., p. 68.

44. Msgs, MACV 14147 to CINCPAC, 24 Apr 66; Defense 8911 to MACV et al., 17 Dec 65; MACV 14147 to CINCPAC, 24 Apr 66, DDI.

45. Lawrence Lichty, "Comments on the Influence of Television on Public Opinion," in *Vietnam as History,* ed. Peter Braestrup (Washington, D.C.: Woodrow Wilson International Center for Scholars, 1984), p. 158; Michael Arlen, "The Falklands, Vietnam, and Our Collective Memory," *New Yorker,* 16 Aug 82.

46. Memo, Rodger Bankson for ASD PA, 13 May 66, sub: Personnel Problems, DDI.

47. Memo, Bankson for Chief of Army Information, 18 Apr 68, sub: Briefings, 73A0243, NARA.

48. Memo, Bankson for Chief of Army Information, 18 Apr 68, sub: Briefings, 73A0243, NARA; Ltr, Bankson to Sylvester, 27 Jun 66, DDI.

49. Msg, CINCPAC to OSD PA, 7 May 66; Memo, Col Winant Sidle for Sylvester, 12 May 66, DDI.

50. Msgs, MACV 42527 to CINCPAC, 16 Jul 66; CINCPAC to MACV, 9 Aug 66, DDI.

51. Memo, Sylvester for the SECDEF, 19 Jul 66, sub: Credibility and the Release of Casualty Statistics, DDI.

52. Msg, Defense 8294 to CINCPAC, COMUSMACV, 3 Aug 66, DDI.

53. Memo, Deputy Assistant Secretary of State for Public Affairs for Arthur Sylvester, sub: Public Affairs Handling of U.S. Service Casualties in Laos, DDI.

54. Memo, COMUSMACV for VMAC, 11 May 66, CMH.

CHAPTER 6. THE SOUTH VIETNAMESE DIMENSION

1. Mark Watson, "McNamara and Wheeler Agree to Closed Hearings," *Baltimore Sun,* 5 Feb 66; James Reston, "Ships Passing in the Night," *New York Times,* 9 Feb 66.

2. U.S. Congress, Senate, Committee on Foreign Relations, *Supplemental Foreign Assistance, Fiscal Year 1966,* 89th Cong., 2d sess., pp. 92, 227, 355, 629.

3. Memo, John M. Leddy for Secretary of State, 8 Mar 66, Abortive Effort to Encourage Objective Reporting on Vietnam in France, FAIM/IR.

4. Fact Sheet, Favorable Military Factors, Feb 66, WH.

5. Msg, MACV to SECDEF, 16 Mar 66, III MAF files, Marine Corps Historical Center (MCHC). The Montagnards were hill tribesmen living in South Vietnam's Central Highland region.

6. Ray Herndon [UPI], "Viet Cong Horde Crushes Stand of Green Berets," *Philadelphia Inquirer,* 10 Mar 66; Robin Mannock, "Wave by Wave They Came," *Washington Star,* 11 Mar 66.

7. Jim Lucas, "A Shau Chief Charges Vietnam Treachery," *Washington Daily News,* 14 Mar 66.

8. Msg, NMCC to MACV, 14 Mar 66, Battle for A Shau, 69A729, NARA; Interv with Brig Gen Marion E. Carl, 1969, MCHC.

9. Msgs, State 2653 to Saigon, 9 Mar 66; Saigon 3286 to State, 19 Mar 66; State 2673 to Saigon, 10 Mar 66; Msg, Saigon 3269 to State, 9 Mar 65; Saigon 3288 to State, 10 Mar 66.

10. Jeffrey Clarke, *The U.S. Army in Vietnam: Advice and Support, The Final Years* (Washington, D.C.: Government Printing Office, 1988), ch. 7 (hereafter cited as *The Final Years*); Msgs, State 2862 to Saigon, 29 Mar 66; State 2877 to Saigon, 29 Mar 66; State 2743 to Saigon, 16 Mar 66.

11. "It Happened Before in Saigon," *New York Post,* 17 Mar 66; Neil Sheehan, "7000 in Hue Call for Civilian Rule," *New York Times,* 15 Mar 66; Wesley Pruden, "Viet Regime Fires a General, Kills a Merchant," *National Observer,* 21 Mar 66; Dan Rather, CBS Evening News, 25 Mar 66, RTDD.

12. Msg, Saigon 3483 to State, 24 Mar 66, WH; "Vietnam: War Within War," *New York Times,* 4 Apr 66.

13. Msgs, Saigon 3647 to State, 1 Apr 66; State 2923 to Saigon, 1 Apr 66; State 2945 to Saigon, 2 Apr 66; Jack Foisie, "'Rebel City' Setting Up Defenses," *Washington Post,* 5 Apr 66; Jack Foisie, "Deadly Vietnam Contrast," *New York Journal American,* 4 Apr 66; "The Story Breaks," *Time,* 14 Apr 66.

14. Eric Wentworth, "Viet Fighting Unimpaired, Ball Asserts," *Washington Post,* 11 Apr 66; Max Frankel, "Vietnam Turmoil Now Slows War, Washington Says," *New York Times,* 12 Apr 66; Msgs, Sharp to Westmoreland, 19 Apr 66; Wheeler JCS 1974-66 to Westmoreland, 13 Apr 66, WP; [AP,] "MP's in Saigon Draw Guns on U.S. Newsmen," *Chicago Tribune,* 9 Apr 66.

15. Clarke, *The Final Years,* ch. 7.

16. Msg, Saigon 4401 to State, 6 May 66; Memo, Zorthian for Lodge, 2 May 66, sub: Report of Conversation Between Brig. Gen. John F. Freund and Senior ARVN Officer, WH.

17. Msgs, Wheeler JCS 2644-66 to Westmoreland, 12 May 66; Westmoreland MACV 1529 to Wheeler, 12 May 66, WP; Clarke, *The Final Years,* ch. 7.

18. MFR, 20 Jun 66, sub: MACV Commanders Conference, 5 Jun 66, WH; Msg, Saigon 5147 to State, 31 May 66.

19. Msgs, Wheeler JCS 2844-66 to Westmoreland, 23 May 66, WH; Wheeler JCS 2837-66 to Westmoreland, 20 May 66, WP.

20. Denis Warner, "How Much Power Does Tri Quang Want?" *Reporter,* 5 May 66, p. 11.

21. Msg, Saigon 5830 to State, 29 Jun 66.

22. Ward Just, "Pacifying a Province," *Washington Post,* 6 Nov 66.

23. Richard A. Hunt, *Pacification: The American Struggle for Vietnam's Hearts and Minds* (Boulder, Colo.: Westview Press, 1995), pp. 63–99.

24. Ltr, Westmoreland to All Commanders, 22 Oct 66, sub: Command Emphasis on Revolutionary Development/Civic Action, WH.

25. Wendell Merick, "A Way Out for U.S. in Vietnam War," *U.S. News & World Report,* 17 Jul 67, p. 28.

26. Jonathan Schell, "The Village of Ben Suc," *New Yorker,* 15 Jul 67, p. 28.

27. Statements of Lt Col R. L. Schweitzer [Aug 67], sub: Operation CEDAR FALLS, and sub: Comments Relating to the 15 July *New Yorker* article, "The Village of Ben Suc," CMH.

28. Memo, Director, Region III, OCO, for Province Representative, Binh Duong, 20 Feb 67, sub: After Action Report, Operation CEDAR FALLS, CMH.

29. MFR, 17 Jan 67, sub: Meeting with Gen. Thieu, 13 Jan 67, WH; ORLL, Twenty-fifth Division, Period Ending 31 Oct 67, p. 67; MACCORDS, The Refugee Operation, National Overview, Dec 67, CMH.

30. Peter Arnett, "South Viet Army Lacks Strength, Unity, Morale," *Washington Star,* 21 Apr 67.

31. MFR, 9 Feb 67, sub: MACV Commanders' Conference, 22 Jan 67, WH; MACV Directive 550-3, 23 Jan 67, sub: Public Awareness of RVNAF, DDI.

32. MACV Directive 550-3.

33. Msgs, Wheeler JCS 6105 to Westmoreland, 2 Aug 67; Westmoreland MACV 7180 to Wheeler, 2 Aug 67, WP; Westmoreland MACV 7757 to Frank Bartimo, 18 Aug 67, enclosing OASD PA Fact Sheet [mid-1967], sub: RVNAF Effectiveness, DDI.

34. Msg, Westmoreland MACV 7757 to Frank Bartimo, 18 Aug 67, DDI.

35. Tom Buckley, "The Men of Third Squad, Second Platoon, C Company, Third Battalion," *New York Times Magazine,* 5 Nov 67, p. 32.

36. OASD PA Fact Sheet [mid-1967], sub: RVNAF Effectiveness; David Halberstam, "Return to Vietnam," *Harper's,* December 1967.

37. Douglas Kinnard, *The War Managers* (Hanover, N.H.: University Press of New England, 1977), p. 92; Msgs, Wheeler JCS 6336 to Westmoreland, 8 Aug 67; Wheeler JCS 6305 to Westmoreland, 2 Aug 67, WP.

38. Tran Van Dinh, "A Look at the Vietnamese Armies," *Christian Science Monitor,* 15 Jun 67; "The War: Taking Stock," *Time,* 14 Jul 67, p. 20; "The War in the Delta," *Newsweek,* 14 Aug 67, p. 28.

39. Msg, Westmoreland MAC 7430 to Sharp, 8 Aug 67, WP.

40. Peter Arnett, "South Vietnamese Army Fights Five-and-One-Half-Day Week," *Washington Post,* 17 Sep 67; Everett G. Martin, "Vietnam: Last Chance," *Newsweek,* 25 Sep 67, p. 64; Merton Perry, "Their Lions, Our Rabbits," *Newsweek,* 9 Oct 67, p. 44.

41. Msgs, Saigon 8347 to State, 12 Oct 67; Saigon 7987 to State, 12 Oct 67.

42. Allen Goodman, *Politics in War: The Bases of Political Community in South Vietnam* (Cambridge, Mass.: Harvard University Press, 1973), pp. 40–63; Memo, Walt W. Rostow for the President, 8 Mar 67, Major Themes, National Security Papers, Lyndon Baines Johnson Library, Austin, Texas (LBJL).

43. Msgs, Saigon 3754 to State, 17 Aug 66; Saigon 6414 to State, 21 Sep 66.

44. Msgs, Saigon 2805 to State, 14 Jun 67; Saigon 28493 to State, 21 Jun 67; Saigon 305 to State, 5 Jul 67.

45. Msg, Saigon 2686 to State, 9 Aug 67, for President from Bunker.

46. Msg, State 27494 to Saigon, 26 Aug 67.

47. Howard E. Penniman, *Elections in South Vietnam* (Stanford, Calif.: Hoover Institution on War, Revolution, and Peace—American Enterprise Institute Publications, 1972), pp. 66, 76.

48. Ibid., p. 84.

49. Msg, Walt Rostow to Ambassador Bunker, 27 Sep 67, LBJL

50. Memo, Sidle for Chief of Staff, MACV [Sep 67], sub: Joint State/Defense Msg, 45007, DDI.

CHAPTER 7. CLAIMS OF PROGRESS—AND COUNTERCLAIMS

1. William P. Bundy, Working Paper, 21 Dec 66, sub: 1967 and Beyond, FAIM/IR.

2. Westmoreland Diary, 10 Aug 66, WH; "CBS Reports Ky Gets $15,000 a Week," *Washington Post,* 29 Jul 66.

3. Hugh A. Mulligan, "Saigon's 'PX Alley' Offers Stocks of Glittering GI Goods," *Washington Post,* 16 Nov 66; Msgs, State 85357 to Saigon, 15 Nov 66; Saigon 11056 to State, 16 Nov 66; R. W. Apple, "Vast U.S. Aid Loss in Vietnam Denied," *New York Times,* 18 Nov 66.

4. Msg, Saigon 3218 to State, 5 Mar 66.

5. Westmoreland Briefing, 20 Aug 66, DDI.

6. "Civilian Casualties in Vietnam," *New York Times,* 21 Aug 66; Charles Mohr, "U.S. Acts to Save Vietnam Civilians," *New York Times,* 17 Aug 66.

7. Msg, Wheeler JCS 4484 to Westmoreland, 17 Aug 66, WP.

8. Westmoreland Briefing, 24 Aug 66, DDI.

9. [AP,] "TASS Says Hanoi Parades U.S. Pilot," *Washington Post,* 30 Jun 66; Louis Harris, "Bombing Raises LBJ Popularity," *Washington Post,* 11 Jul 66.

10. Memo, Robert H. Wenzel for Benjamin H. Reid, 3 Mar 67, sub: ROLLING THUNDER Patterns in Late 1966; Msgs, Joint State/Defense 83718 to Saigon, 12 Nov 66; JCS 7735 to CINCPAC, 11 Nov 66, FAIM/IR.

11. Chronology of Government Statements and Comments, December 13, 14, 15, and 16, DDI; Phil G. Goulding, *Confirm or Deny* (New York: Harper and Row, 1970), pp. 52–92.

12. Memo for Secretary of State, 30 Dec 66, sub: Updated Chronology of Public Statements on Air Strikes in the Hanoi Area, FAIM/IR.

13. Ibid.; "Vietnam and the Crisis of Credibility," *Kansas City Star,* 16 Dec 66; "Managed News Again," *Chicago Tribune,* 28 Dec 66; "Huntley-Brinkley Report," NBC-TV, 16 Dec 66, RTDD; Msg, Sharp to Wheeler, 24 Dec 66, WP.

14. Harrison Salisbury, "Visitor to Hanoi Inspects Damage Attributed to American Raids," *New York Times,* 26 Dec 66.

15. Harrison Salisbury, "Raids Leave Blocks Razed, Fail to Cut Lines to Hanoi," *New York Times,* 27 Dec 66; Msg, State 11162 to All Diplomatic Missions, 31 Dec 66, sub: Articles by Harrison Salisbury on North Vietnam, DDI.

16. George Hamilton Coombs, Mutual Radio News, 28 Dec 66; CBS Evening News, 27 Dec 66, RTDD; Max Lerner, "The Bombings," *New York Post,* 28 Dec 66.

17. Neil Sheehan, "U.S. Concedes That Bombs Hit Civilian Areas in North Vietnam," *New York Times,* 27 Dec 66; Richard Fryklund, "Every Care Taken to Spare Civilians, Pentagon Says," *Washington Star,* 28 Dec 66.

18. Msg, State 11162 to All American Diplomatic Posts, 31 Dec 66; Ltr, Salisbury to the author, 30 June 92.

19. "Salisbury 'Casualties' Tally with Viet Reds," *Washington Post,* 1 Jan 67; "The Tragedy of Vietnam," *New York Times,* 2 Jan 67.

20. "U.S. Admits Heavy Damage to North Viet Civilian Areas," *Baltimore Sun,* 22 Jan 67; Goulding, *Confirm or Deny,* pp. 90 ff.

21. Msgs, Wheeler CJCS 15494-67 to Westmoreland, 2 Mar 67; Westmoreland MAC 2344 to Wheeler, 10 Mar 67, WP; quote, Wheeler CJCS 1810-67 to Westmoreland, 9 Mar 67, WP.

22. Msg, Wheeler CJCS 184-67 to Westmoreland, 11 Mar 67, WP.

23. Msg, Westmoreland MAC 2450 to Wheeler, 14 Mar 67, WP.

24. Maj. Gen. Joseph A. McChristian, *The Role of Military Intelligence, 1965–1967* (Washington, D.C.: U.S. Army Center of Military History, 1974), p. 128; Msg, Westmoreland MAC 2715 to Sharp, 22 Mar 67, WP.

25. Interv, author with Rodger Bankson, 13 May 80, CMH.

26. Msg, MACV 7835 to USARV, 7 Mar 67, DDI.

27. Murray Fromson, CBS Evening News, 12 May 67 and 23 May 67, CMH.

28. U.S. Congress, House, Committee on Armed Services, *Hearings Before the Special Subcommittee on the M-16 Rifle Program,* 91st Cong., 1st sess, 1967; *Report of the Special Subcommittee on the M-16 Rifle Program,* no. 26, 19 Oct 67, pp. 530 ff., 537. Interv, author with correspondent Frank Faulkner, 1974.

29. Msg, Lt Gen Bruce Palmer to Maj Gen Hay et al., 8 Feb 68, sub: M16A1 Rifle, WP.

30. Westmoreland, *A Soldier Reports,* p. 225.

31. Andrew J. Glass, "Senators Blast War Widening, Dissent Curbs," *Washington Post,* 26 Apr 67; "Dissent Is Not Treason," *Chicago Daily News,* 27 Apr 67; Walter Lippmann, "The Intervention of the General," *Washington Post,* 27 Apr 67.

32. "Stifling Dissent," *Washington Star,* 27 Apr 67; "Meeting Dissent," *Washington Post,* 27 Apr 67; Joseph R. L. Sterne, "Mansfield Chides Dissenters," *Baltimore Sun,* 27 Apr 66; Richard Lyons, "General Is Cheered on the Hill," *Washington Post,* 29 Apr 67.

33. Interv, author with Maj Gen Winant Sidle, 5 Jun 73.

34. *Pentagon Papers,* 4:7, 154–87.

35. Ibid., 197–204.

36. "Generals Out of Control," *New York Times,* 1 Sep 67.

37. Msgs, Wheeler JCS 6105 to Westmoreland, 2 Aug 67; Sharp to Wheeler, 3 Aug 67, WP.

38. OASD SA, Military Results and Initiative in Vietnam, 17 Oct 67, Thayer Papers, CMH.

39. Fred Green for William Bundy, 22 Sep 67, sub: Indicators of Progress, Thayer Papers, CMH.

40. Memo, Sidle for Westmoreland, 11 Sep 67, sub: MACV Information Program, RG 84, NARA.

41. Ibid.; Peter Braestrup, *Big Story: How the American Press and TV Reported and*

Interpreted the Crisis of Tet in 1968 in Vietnam and Washington, 2 vols. (Boulder, Colo.: Westview Press, 1977), 1:1–51.

42. Interv, author with Sidle, 5 Jun 73, CMH.

43. Ibid.; Memo, Sidle to Westmoreland, 11 Sep 67, sub: MACV Information Program.

44. Msg, Westmoreland MAC 9545 to Harold K. Johnson, 11 Oct 67, WP.

45. Msg, MACV 42962, MACV Judge Advocate General to General Counsel, 27 Dec 67, DDI.

46. See Orville Schell, "Cage for the Innocents," *Atlantic Monthly,* Jan 68, p. 29; Msg, State 10067 to Saigon, 18 Jan 68.

47. Msg, Joint State/Defense 45007 to Saigon, 28 Sep 67, DDI.

48. Msg, Saigon 7867 to State, 7 Oct 67.

49. Memo, McGeorge Bundy for the President, 7 Oct 67, sub: Vietnam—October 1967; State/Defense 75209 to Saigon, 27 Nov 67.

50. Ltr, Zorthian to Otis E. Hayes, Dep Asst Director, USIA, 12 Dec 67, FAIM/IR.

51. Msg, MACV to CG, III MAF, et al., 21 Aug 67; MFR MACCORDS-PP, 16 Oct 67, sub: Reporting and Statistics, CMH.

52. Msg, Westmoreland MAC 10547 to Wheeler, 6 Nov 67, WP; Memo, Richard Fryklund for Wheeler [Nov 67], DDI; Orr Kelly, "Loc Ninh Emerging as a Significant Fight," *Washington Star,* 21 Nov 67.

53. Msg, Westmoreland JCS 10011 to Abrams, 21 Nov 67, WP.

54. Msg, Abrams MAC 11329 to Wheeler, 22 Nov 67, WP.

55. Address by General W. C. Westmoreland, National Press Club, 21 Nov 67, CMH.

56. Ward Just, "Hard Sell on Vietnam," *Washington Post,* 26 Nov 67.

57. James Reston, "Why Westmoreland and Bunker Are Optimistic," *New York Times,* 22 Nov 67.

58. George MacArthur and Horst Faas, "Camp in Cambodia Linked to Viet Cong," *Washington Post,* 20 Nov 67.

59. Msg, State 86286 to Saigon, 18 Dec 67; U. S. Grant Sharp and William C. Westmoreland, *Report on the War in Vietnam (As of 30 June 1968)* (Washington, D.C.: Government Printing Office, 1970), p. 144.

60. Louis Harris, "Johnson Regains Popularity," *Philadelphia Inquirer,* 4 Dec 67; "More Protests, Growing Lawlessness," *U.S. News & World Report,* 18 Dec 67, p. 6; Don Oberdorfer, "Wobble on the War," *New York Times,* 17 Dec 67.

61. ABC News, 2 Dec 67, RTDD; Helen D. Bentley, "Vietnam Critics Scored by Rusk," *Baltimore Sun,* 9 Dec 67; William P. Bundy, "Why the U.S. Is in Vietnam: An Official Explanation," *U.S. News & World Report,* 18 Dec 67, p. 63.

62. MACOI, Komer News Conference, 24 Jan 68, DDI.

CHAPTER 8. THE TET OFFENSIVE

1. Msgs, Wheeler JCS 343 to Westmoreland, 11 Jan 68; Sharp to Wheeler, 15 Jan 68; Westmoreland MAC 547 to Wheeler, 12 Jan 68; Westmoreland MAC 862 to Lt Gen Rossen et al., 19 Jan 68, WP.

2. Westmoreland and Sharp, *Report on the War in Vietnam,* pp. 158 f.

3. Msg, Westmoreland MACV 1449 to Wheeler, 31 Jan 68; Hanson W. Baldwin "Target: Public Opinion," *New York Times,* 1 Feb 68.

4. Col. Hoag Ngoc Lung, *The General Offensives of 1968–1969,* Indochina Mono-graphs (Washington, D.C.: U.S. Army Center of Military History, 1981); Braestrup, *Big Story;* Don Oberdorfer, *Tet!* (Garden City, N.Y.: Doubleday, 1971). The CBS report is in RTDD, 1 Feb 68; Tom Buckley, "Offensive Is Said to Pinpoint Enemy's Strengths," *New York Times,* 2 Feb 68; "More Than Just a Diversion," *New York Times,* 2 Feb 68.

5. Notes for 1 Feb 68, WH; Transcript, 1 Feb 68, sub: Westmoreland Briefing, DDI.

6. Braestrup, *Big Story,* 1:124.

7. Orr Kelly, "U.S. Caught Off Guard by Intensity of Attacks," *Washington Star,* 31 Jan 68; Mike Wallace, CBS News Special Report, 31 Jan 68, RTDD; Jerry Green, "Red Terror," *New York Daily News,* 1 Feb 68; "Bloody Path to Peace," *New York Times,* 1 Feb 68.

8. Tom Wicker, "Viet Cong's Attacks Shock Washington," *New York Times,* 1 Feb 68.

9. MACOI, News Releases 31-68, 1 Feb 68, and 32-68, 1 Feb 68, 334-74-593, NARA.

10. Saigon Briefing by Gen Chaisson, 3 Feb 68, DDI; Saigon Briefing by Brig Gen Davidson, 4 Feb 68, DDI.

11. Transcript of the President's News Conference, *New York Times,* 3 Feb 68.

12. Lee Lescaze, "Allied Figures on Casualties Are Thrown into Question," *Washington Post,* 3 Feb 68; Cynthia Parsons, "Saigon Briefings Puzzle Reporter," *Christian Science Monitor,* 9 Feb 68; "Misled in Every Sense," *New Republic,* 17 Feb 68.

13. Transcript, Westmoreland News Conference, 25 Feb 68, DDI.

14. "Grim and Ghastly Picture," *New York Daily News,* 3 Feb 68; Unidentified AP report, 1 Feb 68, DDI; George A. Bailey and Lawrence W. Lichty, "Rough Justice on a Saigon Street: A Gatekeeper Study of NBC's Tet Execution Film," *Journalism Quarterly* 49 (Summer 1972): 274.

15. *New York Times,* 2 Feb 68, p. 1; "Grim and Ghastly Picture"; "A Strong Stomach Helps," *Chicago Daily News,* 7 Feb 68; "The Protesters Are Silent," *Chicago Tribune,* 8 Feb 68.

16. [AP,] "Viet Cong, Allied Atrocities Reflect Bitterness of War," *Baltimore Sun,* 4 Feb 68.

17. Ltr, Wheeler to Henry S. Reus, 3 Feb 68, DDI; [Agence France Presse,] "U.S. Cautioning Saigon on Captives' Treatment," *New York Times,* 5 Feb 68.

18. Msg, Joint State/Defense 118474 to Saigon, 21 Feb 67; Msg, Joint State/Defense 118474 to Saigon, 21 Feb 68, CMH.

19. Bailey and Lichty, "Rough Justice."

20. Msgs, Saigon 18405 to State, 7 Feb 68, sub: The Situation in Kontum; Saigon 18584 to State, 8 Feb 68, sub: The Delta After the Tet Offensive.

21. Msgs, Westmoreland MAC 1614 to Wheeler, 4 Feb 68, WP; Saigon 18584 to State, 8 Feb 68; Saigon 39547 to State, 5 Oct 68, sub: Final Report on Project Recovery, CMH; Interv with Robert Komer, 7 May 70, (1)-20104-ARPA, CMH.

22. Braestrup, *Big Story,* 1:254; "Survivors Hunt Dead of Ben Tre," *New York Times,* 8 Feb 68; "The War: Picking Up the Pieces," *Time,* 16 Feb 68, p. 34.

23. Ward Just, "Guerrillas Wreck Pacification Plan," *Washington Post,* 4 Feb 68; Lee Lescaze, "U.S. and Vietnam: Test in Battle," *Washington Post,* 11 Feb 68; Charles Mohr, "Pacification Program Is Almost at Standstill," *New York Times,* 14 Feb 68; "The Viet Cong's Week of Terror," *Newsweek,* 12 Feb 68, p. 30.

24. Msg, Komer to Alan Enthoven, ASD (SA), 27 Mar 67, CMH; "Bunker Sees Gains," *New York Times,* 19 Feb 68.

25. Msg, no number, Saigon to State, 24 Feb 68, CMH.

26. Bernard Weintraub, "U.S. Admits Blow to Pacification," *New York Times,* 25 Feb 68; Msg, Komer MAC 12697 to Thomas Thayer, OASD SA, 19 Sep 68; Braestrup, *Big Story,* 1:557–58.

27. MACOI News release 39-68, 8 Feb 68, MACV News Release Files, 534-74-593, NARA.

28. Lung, *The General Offensives of 1968–1969,* p. 85; Braestrup, *Big Story,* 1:317; Msg, PHB 54 to Westmoreland, 23 Feb 68, WP.

29. Braestrup, *Big Story,* 1:280 ff.; "Reds Said to Execute 300 in Hue," *Washington Post,* 12 Feb 68; "Hue's Mayor Says Foe Executed 300," *New York Times,* 12 Feb 68; U.S. Mission Press Release 47-68, 9 Mar 68, DDI.

30. Msgs, Westmoreland MAC 1901 to Sharp, 10 Feb 68; Wheeler to JCS 1147 to Westmoreland, 1 Feb 68; Westmoreland MAC 1586 to Wheeler, WP; Memo, CSM 2941, Wheeler to the President, 3 Feb 68, sub: Khe Sanh, FAIM/IR.

31. Msgs, Wheeler JCS 1272 to Westmoreland, 3 Feb 68; Westmoreland MACV 1586 to Wheeler, 3 Feb 68, WP.

32. "Viet Nukes Requested, McCarthy Says," *Washington Post,* 9 Feb 68; "White House Disputes McCarthy on Atom Arms," *New York Times,* 10 Feb 68.

33. Msg, Sharp to Westmoreland, 12 Feb 68, WP; John W. Finney, "Johnson Denies Atom Use in Vietnam Is Considered," *New York Times,* 17 Feb 68.

34. John A. Cash, "Battle of Lang Vei, 7 February 1968," in *Seven Firefights in Vietnam,* Vietnam Studies (Washington, D.C.: Office of the Chief of Military History, Government Printing Office, 1971), pp. 109–38; Msgs, Cushman to Abrams, 25 Feb 68; Westmoreland MACV 2018 to Wheeler, 12 Feb 68, WP; Robert Pisor, *The End of the Line: The Siege of Khe Sanh* (New York: Norton, 1982), p. 226.

35. Ward Just, "U.S. Voices Confidence Raids Were Expected," *Washington Post,* 1 Feb 68; Huntley-Brinkley Report, 5 Feb 68, RTDD; Charles Mohr, "Khe Sanh and Dien Bien Phu: A Comparison," *New York Times,* 8 Mar 68.

36. Braestrup, *Big Story,* 1:338; Murray Fromson, CBS Evening News, 14 Feb 68, RTDD.

37. Don North, ABC Evening News, 19 Feb 68; George Syvertsen, CBS Evening News, 14 Mar 68, both RTDD; Braestrup, *Big Story,* 1:380–404.

38. "Johnson's Rating on Vietnam Drops," *New York Times,* 14 Feb 68; Max Frankel, "Johnson Confers with Eisenhower," *New York Times,* 19 Feb 68; Memo 68-34 (MC), 14 Feb 68, sub: Mission Council Actions, WH; Press Release 57-68, U.S. Mission, Saigon, 20 Mar 68, sub: Viet Cong Headquarters Assesses Tet Offensive, DDI.

39. Msg, Sharp to Westmoreland, 24 Feb 67, WP.

40. Msgs, MACV 6349 to Secretary of Defense, 4 Mar 68, sub: Control of the Press North of the Hai Van Pass, CMH; ASD PA to Sharp, 6 Mar 68, WP. 41Msg, Wheeler JCS 2721 to Westmoreland, 8 Mar 68, WP.

42. "Wherever We Look, Something's Wrong," *Life,* 23 Feb 68, p. 25; CBS News Special Report on Vietnam, 7 Feb 68, RTDD.

43. Howard K. Smith, "A Columnist's Farewell," *Philadelphia Bulletin,* 18 Feb 68.

44. Hazel Erskine, "The Polls: Is War a Mistake?" *Public Opinion Quarterly* 34 (Spring 1970): 135 f.; Burns Roper, "What Public Opinion Polls Said," in Braestrup, *Big Story,* 1:679 ff.

45. Roper, "What Public Opinion Polls Said," 687.

46. McPherson is quoted in Herbert Y. Schandler, *The Unmaking of a President* (Princeton, N.J.: Princeton University Press, 1977), p. 81.

47. Msg, Harold K. Johnson WDC 3166 to Westmoreland, 1 Mar 68, WP.

48. William Tuohy, "Marine Leadership Under Fire in Vietnam," *Washington Post,* 3 Mar 68.

49. Msgs, Wheeler JCS 2581 to Westmoreland, 5 Mar 68; Westmoreland MAC 1011 to Wheeler, 22 Jan 68, WP; MACV 6587 to OASD PA, 6 Mar 68, sub: COMUSMACV Statement to the Press, DDI.

50. Donald Kirk, "The Army-Marine Feud," *Washington Star,* 14 Mar 68; Memo, Sidle for Westmoreland, 17 Apr 68, sub: George Wilson and UPI Stories About Future Plans, WH; Msg, Westmoreland MACV 5120 to Gen Haines, Acting Chief of Staff, Army, 17 Apr 68, WP.

51. Msgs, Wheeler JCS 1590 to Westmoreland, 9 Feb 68; Westmoreland MAC 2018 to Wheeler, 12 Feb 68, WP; MCSM 91-68, 12 Feb 68, sub: Emergency Reinforcement of COMUSMACV, in *Pentagon Papers,* 4:541.

52. Schandler, *The Unmaking of a President,* p. 101.

53. Memo, Wheeler for the President, 27 Feb 68, sub: Military Situation and Requirements for South Vietnam, NSC files, LBJL.

54. Handwritten Notes of Meeting Involving Rusk, McNamara, Clifford, Rostow, William Bundy, Nicholas Katzenbach, Joseph Califano, and Harry McPherson, 27 Feb 68, NSC files, LBJL.

55. MFR, 4 Mar 68, sub: Note of the President's Meeting with His Senior Foreign Policy Advisers, NSC files, LBJL.

56. Hedrick Smith and Neil Sheehan, "Westmoreland Requests More Men," *New York Times,* 10 Mar 68.

57. "Demand for a Voice," *Time,* 15 Mar 68, p. 14; John W. Finney, "Rusk Tells Panel of A to Z Review of Vietnam War," *New York Times,* 12 Mar 68; Finney, "Rusk Tells Panel, 'We Will Consult on Any Troop Rise,'" *New York Times,* 13 Mar 68.

58. Schandler, *The Unmaking of a President,* p. 231 f.; *Pentagon Papers,* 4:593 f.

59. "Poll of Democrats Finds Many Hawks Backed McCarthy," *New York Times,* 15 Mar 68; Louis Harris, "How the Voters See the Issues," *Newsweek,* 25 Mar 68, p. 26; "69% in Poll Back a Pullout in War," *New York Times,* 13 Mar 68.

60. Westmoreland, *A Soldier Reports,* pp. 357 f.

61. Msg, Wheeler JCS 3561 to Sharp, Westmoreland, 31 Mar 68, WP.

62. Address by President Lyndon Johnson, Department of State *Bulletin,* 15 Apr 68, p. 481.

63. White House Press Release, Statement by North Vietnam, 3 Apr 68, Department of State *Bulletin,* 22 Apr 68, p. 513.

CHAPTER 9. "WAR IN A GOLDFISH BOWL"

1. Leon V. Sigal, *Reporters and Officials* (Lexington, Mass.: D. C. Heath, 1973), p. 124; John Mueller, *War, Presidents, and Public Opinion* (New York: Wiley, 1973).

2. Daniel C. Hallin, "The Media, the War in Vietnam, and Political Support: A Critique of the Thesis of an Oppositional Media," *Journal of Politics* 46 (February 1984): 2–24;

Todd Gitlin quotes Frankel in *The Whole World Is Watching* (Berkeley: University of California Press, 1980), p. 205.

3. George A. Bailey, *The Vietnam War According to Chet, David, Walter, Harry, Peter, Bob, Howard, and Frank: A Content Analysis of Journalistic Performance by the Television Evening News Anchormen* (Ann Arbor, Mich.: University Microfilms, 1973), pp. 369–75.

4. Chalmers Roberts, *The Washington Post: The First 100 Years* (Boston: Houghton Mifflin, 1977), p. 395.

5. Harrison E. Salisbury, *Without Fear or Favor* (New York: Times Books, 1980), p. 93.

6. Interv, author with Maj Gen Winant Sidle, 5 Jun 73; Ltr, Sidle to the author, 5 Sep 91, CMH; Ltr, Bunker to Secretary of State, n.d. [Jun 70].

7. Msg, Wheeler JCS 3965 to Westmoreland, 12 Apr 68, WP.

8. Msgs, Wheeler to Clark Clifford, 16 Apr 68; ASD PA 4079 to MACV, 17 Apr 68, citing Msg, Clifford to Wheeler, 16 Apr 68, WP.

9. Msg, Westmoreland MAC 5344 to Wheeler, 23 Apr 68, WP; Ltr, Sidle to the author, 5 Nov 90, CMH.

10. Msgs, Rossen PHB 561 to Westmoreland, 26 Apr 68, WP; Westmoreland MAC 5536 to Phil Goulding, ASD PA, 26 Apr 69, WP; Zalen Grant, "Alsop Lets His Friends Down," *New Republic,* 18 May 68.

11. "Tough General with a Rough Job," *U.S. News & World Report,* 8 Apr 68, p. 21; quote, Charles Mohr, "Westmoreland Departure Could Spur War Changes," *New York Times,* 24 Mar 68.

12. Msg, Westmoreland MAC 5298 to Cushman, 21 Apr 68, WP; Memo, Wheeler CM-3228-68 for Secretary of Defense, 23 Apr 68, sub: Report of High-Ranking Enemy Defector, DDI; [AP,] "Enemy Colonel Is Said to Defect," *New York Times,* 22 Apr 68.

13. Msg, Saigon 27764 to State, 20 May 68, sub: Assessment of Enemy's Offensive, DDI.

14. Msg, Saigon 25826 to State, 28 Apr 68.

15. Lee Lescaze, "G.I.'s Join Fighting in Saigon," *Washington Post,* 8 Apr 68; "A City of Homeless," *U.S. News & World Report,* 17 Jun 68, p. 14; "The Forgotten War," *Newsweek,* 10 Jun 68, p. 54.

16. Msg, Saigon 28986 to State, 3 Jun 68; quote, Msg, Saigon 27764 to State, 20 May 68, sub: Assessment of Enemy's Offensive.

17. Msg, State 175631 to Paris, Donnelly for Jordan, 4 Jun 68; Karl H. Purnell, "Operation Self-destruction," *Nation,* 26 Aug 68, p. 29.

18. Memo, Charles Sweet for General Edward Lansdale, 12 May 68, in Memo, Lansdale for Bunker, 2 May 68, sub: Popular Reaction; Msg, Wheeler JCS 66117 to Abrams, 4 Jun 68, both Papers of Clark Clifford, LBJL (hereafter cited as CP).

19. Msg, Abrams MAC 7404 to Wheeler, 5 Jun 68, CP.

20. Memo, Clifford for Wheeler, 8 Jun 68, CP.

21. Msg, Abrams MAC 7600 to Wheeler, 9 Jun 68, CP; Msg, Abrams MAC 8249 to Weyand, 22 Jun 68, Abrams Papers, CMH (hereafter cited as AP).

22. Msg, Abrams MAC 7236 to All Commanders, 2 Jun 68, sub: Public Affairs Guidance, AP.

23. Msg, Abrams MACV 7429 to All Commanders, 6 Jun 68, AP.

24. Msg, Abrams MAC 7288 to All Commanders, 3 Jun 68, AP; MACV History, 1968, 2, 968.

25. Msg, Abrams MAC 7288 to all Commanders, 3 Jun 68, AP.

26. Msgs, Abrams MAC 8007 to Wheeler, 17 Jun 68; Abrams MAC 8128 to Sharp, 19 Jun 68; Abrams MAC 8250 to Wheeler, 22 Jun 68, AP; Msg, Saigon 30199 to State, 17 Jun 68, AP.

27. Msg, Abrams MAC 8250 to Wheeler, 22 Jun 68, AP.

28. Msgs, Wheeler JCS 7043 to Abrams, 26 Jun 66; Abrams MAC 8515 to Wheeler, 26 Jun 68; Wheeler JCS 7068 to Abrams, 26 Jun 68, AP.

29. Msg, Goulding Defense 7083 to Abrams, 26 Jun 68, AP.

30. Msg, Wheeler JCS 7094 to Abrams, 27 Jun 68, AP; Talking Paper, ASD PA, 27 Jun 68, sub: Inactivation of the Khe Sanh Combat Base, DDI.

31. Huntley-Brinkley Report, 28 Jun 68, RTDD; S. L. A. Marshall, "Penalizing of Carroll Dissected," *Baltimore Sun,* 29 Jul 68; Lee Lescaze, "Secrecy over Khe Sanh Questioned," *Washington Post,* 29 Jul 68.

32. "Carroll Penalty Stiffest of War," *Baltimore Sun,* 28 Jul 68; James MacNees, "Pentagon Asked to Review Carroll's 6-Month Penalty," *Baltimore Sun,* 30 Jul 68; "U.S. Eases Curb on War Reporter," *New York Times,* 31 Jul 68.

33. Msg, Goulding Defense 9553 to Abrams, 17 Aug 68, AP; Msg, Bunker and Abrams MACV 11243 to Goulding, 20 Aug 68, AP.

34. MACV History, 1968, 1:134.

35. Ibid., 2:970.

36. Beverly Deepe, "Chasing Credibility in Saigon," *Christian Science Monitor,* 13 Sep 68.

37. Memo, Clifford for President Johnson, 19 Jul 68, sub: Trip to South Vietnam, 13–18 July 1968, Memos on Vietnam, CP.

38. Handwritten Note, George Christian, 19 Jul 68, sub: Private Conversation Between Rusk, Clifford, Rostow, Christian, Office files of George Christian, LBJL.

39. "Poll Rates Nixon Best at Handling War," *New York Times,* 25 Aug 68.

40. Msg, State 226256 to Saigon, Secretary to Ambassador, 22 Aug 68; Clifford, Notes for 25 May 68 Meeting, Notes Taken at Meetings, CP.

41. "Survival at the Stockyards," *Time,* 6 Sep 68, p. 14; "56% Defend Police in Chicago Strife," *New York Times,* 18 Sep 68; "The Battle of Chicago," *Newsweek,* 9 Sep 68, p. 29.

42. Msgs, Saigon 37046 to State, 4 Sep 68, sub: Ambassador Bunker's 65th Weekly Message to the President; Saigon 38774 to State, 26 Sep 68.

43. Msgs, Abrams MAC 11819 to Wheeler, 1 Sep 68; Abrams 16889 to McCain, 10 Dec 68; Wheeler JCS 11890 to Abrams, 16 Oct 68, AP.

44. Neil Sheehan, "Johnson Asserts Raids Will Go on Until Hanoi Acts," *New York Times,* 11 Sep 68; Msg, Wheeler JCS 10691 to Abrams, 19 Sep 68, AP; quote, Msg, Abrams MAC 12743 to Wheeler, 20 Sep 68, AP; Msg, Abrams MAC 13100 to Wheeler, 28 Sep 68, AP.

45. This section is based on Johnson, Briefing Paper, 28 Oct 68, CP.

46. Quote, Johnson, Briefing Paper, 28 Oct 68, p. 3; Msg, Saigon 40117 to State, from Bunker and Abrams, 12 Oct 68, Meeting Notes, CP.

47. Johnson, Briefing Paper, 28 Oct 68, p. 3.

48. Msg, Saigon 42770 to State, 15 Nov 68, sub: Vietnamese Attitudes Toward War and Peace and the Paris Peace Talks—32nd Report, CP.

49. Beech is quoted in Memo, Daniel Z. Henkin for Secretary of Defense, 17 Nov 68, Presentation on the Paris Peace Talks, CP.

50. Ibid.; Msg, Saigon 41837 to State, 4 Nov 68, Presentation on Paris Peace Talks, CP.

51. Memo, Henkin for Secretary of Defense, 17 Nov 68.

52. "Harris: Bomb Halt Closed Gap," *New York Post,* 4 Nov 68.

53. Clifford, Handwritten MFR, n.d. [Nov 68]; Msg, Saigon 42377 to State, 12 Nov 68; Press Release 264, Department of State *Bulletin,* 16 Dec 68, p. 621.

54. Msgs, McCain to Wheeler, 4 Dec 68; Wheeler JCS 14235 to Abrams, 4 Dec 68, AP.

55. Msgs, Abrams MAC 1340 to McCain, 13 Oct 68; State 274394 to Moscow, 17 Nov 68, relaying Msg, Abrams to JCS, 17 Nov 68.

CHAPTER 10. "I WILL NOT WARN AGAIN"

1. Interv, author with Jerry Friedheim, Deputy Assistant Secretary of Defense, 1969–73, 3 Oct 86; Interv, author with Daniel Z. Henkin, ASD PA, 1969–73, 10 Oct 86.

2. Ibid.

3. Ltrs, Richard Steadman, Deputy Assistant Secretary of Defense for International Security Affairs, to William P. Bundy, 4 Feb 69; Bundy to Steadman, 26 Feb 69, DDI.

4. Msgs, Abrams MAC 2897 to Ambassador to Laos William H. Sullivan, [Mar 69], AP; State 37093 to Vientiane, 11 Mar 69, sub: Press Guidance.

5. Msg, State 37093 to Vientiane, 11 Mar 69, sub: Press Guidance.

6. U.S. Department of State, American Opinion Summary, 26 Feb–12 Mar 69; 13–27 Mar 69; George Gallup, "Favor Extreme Steps to End the War," *Chicago Sun-Times,* 23 Mar 69; MS, Ann David, Study of U.S. Public Opinion, 1 Jun 83, CMH.

7. National Security Study Memorandum (NSSM) 1, Kissinger for the Secretaries of State and Defense and the Director of Central Intelligence, 21 Jan 69, CMH; Msgs, Wheeler JCS 885 to Nazarro, Abrams, 22 Jan 69; Abrams MAC 1102 to Wheeler, 24 Jan 69, AP.

8. Henry A. Kissinger, *The White House Years* (Boston: Little, Brown, 1979), pp. 239–41, 250; Msgs, CIA 22708 to State, 21 May 64, SEA Memorandum, CP; Abrams MAC 1166 to Nazarro, 29 Jan 69, AP; Bangkok 4992 to State, 19 Mar 69.

9. Msgs, Abrams MAC 1782 to Wheeler, 9 Feb 69; McConnell JCS 1915 to Abrams, n.d. [Feb 69], AP; State 2385 to Saigon, 14 Feb 69.

10. Kissinger, *The White House Years,* pp. 242–45; Msgs, Wheeler JCS 2218 to Abrams, 21 Feb 69; Abrams MAC 2372 to Wheeler, 23 Feb 69; Wheeler JCS 259 to Abrams, 23 Feb 69; Abrams MAC 2836 to Wheeler, 5 Mar 69, sub: Retaliatory Actions, AP.

11. Charles Mohr, "Field Checks in Vietnam Show Allies Understated Foe's Gains," *New York Times,* 13 Mar 69; Jack Walsh, "Communist Offensive Not a 'Grade A Fiasco' After All," 15 Mar 69, DDI.

12. MFRs, 15 Mar 69, sub: Press Release; [untitled], C. H. Freudenthal, Lt Col, USAF, 15 Mar 69, DDI.

13. Kissinger, *The White House Years,* pp. 244–45.

14. Memo, Nixon for Secretaries of State and Defense, 16 Mar 69, sub: March 16 Rocket Attack on Saigon, FAIM/IR; Msgs, Wheeler JCS 3287 to Abrams, 17 Mar 69; Wheeler JCS 3297 to Abrams, 17 Mar 69, AP.

15. "Press Conference with Prince Sihanouk," Phnom Penh Domestic News Service, 29 Mar 69, DDI.

16. Msg, Wheeler JCS 3659 to Abrams, 25 Mar 69, AP.

17. Ibid.; Msg, Abrams MAC 3850 to Wheeler, 26 Mar 69, AP.

18. Msgs, State 2480 to Saigon, 5 Apr 69; Wheeler JCS 3787 to Abrams, 27 Mar 69; Wheeler JCS 4067 to Abrams, 3 Apr 69, AP.

19. Msgs, Corcoran NHT 1089 to Abrams, 4 Apr 69; Abrams MAC 4251 to All Commanders, 4 Apr 69, sub: Public Affairs Guidance and National Policy; Abrams MAC 4334 to All Commanders, 6 Apr 69, sub: Attention to Cambodian Citizens, AP; Saigon 6789 to State, 10 Apr 69, sub: Press Leaks.

20. U.S. Congress, Senate, Committee on Armed Services, *Bombing in Cambodia, Hearings, Jul–Aug 73,* 93d Cong., 1st sess., p. 131.

21. Msg, Wheeler JCS 4818 to McCain et al., 20 Apr 69, sub: Operations BREAKFAST BRAVO, BREAKFAST COCO, and LUNCH, AP.

22. Interv, author with Friedheim, 3 Oct 86.

23. Lt Gen Meyer, JCS/J-3 5706 to Abrams, 9 May 69, AP; [AP,] Cambodia Bombing 270, 9 May 69, DDI; William Beecher, "Raids in Cambodia by U.S. Unprotested," *New York Times,* 9 May 69; Interv, author with Friedheim, 3 Oct 86.

24. MFR, sub: Summary of Responses to NSSM 1, attachment to Memo, Henry A. Kissinger for Members of the NSC Review Group, 14 Mar 69, sub: NSSM 1 Vietnam Questions, CMH.

25. Ibid.

26. Draft Memo, Kissinger for the President, n.d. [Sep 71], sub: Gen. Haig's Trip to Vietnam, Papers of Richard Nixon, Nixon Materials Project, National Archives, College Park, Maryland (hereafter cited as NP).

27. Tom Wicker, "In the Nation: The Old Merry-Go-Round," *New York Times,* 20 Mar 69; Rowland Evans and Robert Novak, "Secret Laird Plan Will Allow Early Troop Pullout," *Washington Post,* 24 Mar 69.

28. Msg, Wheeler JCS 4092 to Abrams, 3 Apr 69, AP.

29. Msg, Abrams MAC 4689 to All Commanders, 13 Apr 69, sub: Hanoi's Strategy, AP.

30. Fact Sheet, Office of the Assistant Secretary of Defense for Systems Analysis, 10 Oct 69, sub: Indicators of Enemy Activity in South Vietnam, CMH. Msg, Abrams MAC 4689 to All Commanders, 13 Apr 69, sub: Hanoi's Strategy.

31. Msg, Wheeler JCS 3939 to McCain, Abrams, 1 Apr 69, AP.

32. Msgs, Wheeler JCS 3805 to Abrams, 28 Mar 69; Ewell MHU 292 to Abrams, 29 Mar 69, AP.

33. Msg, Abrams MAC 4967 to Wheeler, 19 Apr 69, 17 Apr 69, AP.

34. Msg, Wheeler JCS 5988 to Abrams, 16 May 69, AP.

35. Combat After Action Report (AAR), The Battle of Dong Ap Bia, reprinted in U.S. Congress, Senate, *Congressional Record,* 29 December 1970, p. S.21403. See also Samuel Zaffiri, *Hamburger Hill, May 11–20, 1969* (San Francisco: Presidio Press, 1988), p. 272.

36. Jay Sharbutt, "Americans Stained with Blood, Sweat, and Mud—10th Assault on Hill Fails," *Washington Star,* 19 May 69; Richard Threlkeld, CBS Evening News, 23 May 69, RTDD.

37. U.S. Congress, Senate, "Statement of Senator Edward Kennedy," *Congressional Record,* 20 May 69, p. S.13003; U.S. Department of State, American Opinion Summary, 5 Jun 69, p. 6.

38. David Hoffman, "Hamburger Hill: The Army's Rationale," *Washington Post,* 23 May 69.

39. "Martin Agronski's Washington," 23 May 69, RTDD; "The Grim and Inaccurate Casualty Numbers Game," *New York Times,* 1 Jun 69; David Culhane, CBS Evening News, 11 Jun 69, RTDD.

40. Richard Homan, "Pentagon Aides Assail Press," *Washington Post,* 7 Jun 69; Transcript, Background Briefing at the White House with Dr. Henry A. Kissinger, 26 May 69, CMH.

41. Msg, Wheeler JCS 6206 to Abrams, 21 May 69, AP.

42. Msgs, McCain to McConnell, Acting CJCS, 25 May 69; McCain to Abrams, 3 Jun 69, AP.

43. Msgs, Abrams MAC 7512 to McCain, 12 Jun 69; McCain to Abrams, 13 Jun 69, both AP.

44. Talking Paper, n.d. [Jun 69], sub: Redeployment of U.S. Units from Vietnam: Public Affairs Guidance; Fact Sheet, OASD PA, 27 Jun 69, sub: Seattle Parade for 3d Battalion, 60th Infantry, DDI.

45. "Beginning of the End?" *Newsweek,* 21 Jul 69, p. 24; "Returnees Jeered," *Washington Post,* 11 Jul 69; Steven V. Roberts, "Girls, Bands, and Tickertape," *New York Times,* 11 Jul 69; Talking Paper, OASD PA, n.d. [Jul 69], sub: Redeployment of U.S. Units from Vietnam: Public Affairs Guidance, DDI.

46. Msg, Abrams MAC 10252 to Wheeler, 8 Aug 69, sub: Publicizing ARVN Achievements, AP.

47. Arnett's report is in Msg, McConnell JCS 7909 to Abrams, 26 Jun 69, AP. See also Peter Arnett, *Live from the Battlefield, From Vietnam to Baghdad: 35 Years in the World's War Zones* (New York: Simon and Schuster, 1994), pp. 260–62.

48. Memo, OSD PA for Col Robert E. Pursley, USAF, Military Assistant to Secretary Laird, 5 Jul 69, sub: UPI Story, DDI.

49. MFR, NMCC, 27 Jun 69, sub: Operations at Ben Het, DDI; Msg, Corcoran to Abrams, 27 Jun 69, sub: MACOI Query Re Peter Arnett Story, AP; Fact Sheet, OASD PA, n.d. [Jun 69], sub: Ben Het, DDI. See also Arnett, *Live from the Battlefield,* p. 261.

50. Interv, author with Sidle, 21 Nov 90, CMH.

51. Msg, McCain to Abrams, 28 Jun 69, AP.

52. Msgs, Corcoran NHT 1089 to Abrams, 29 Jun 69; Abrams MAC 8347 to McCain, 29 Jun 69, AP. Rossen is quoted in "General Flies to Ben Het and Finds Morale 'High,'" *New York Times,* 30 Jun 69.

53. Msg, CG, III MAF, to COMUSMACV, 7 Aug 69, AP.

54. Msg, Abrams MAC 10176 to Nickerson, CG, III MAF, 6 Aug 69, AP.

55. Ibid.

CHAPTER 11. KEEPING CONTROL

1. Harris, *The Anguish of Change,* p. 69; Louis Harris, "55% Remain Attuned to Nixon But Support on Issues Is Soft," *Chicago Daily News,* 29 Sep 69; Memo, Laird for the President, 4 Sep 69, sub: Vietnamizing the War (NSSM 36), FAIM/IR.

2. Sigal, *Reporters and Officials,* p. 128.

3. Ibid., p. 261.

4. Daniel C. Hallin, *The Uncensored War: The Media and Vietnam* (New York: Oxford University Press, 1986), pp. 174–79.

5. "The Faces of the American Dead in Vietnam: One Week's Toll," *Life,* 27 Jun 69; David Brinkley, NBC Nightly News, 26 Jun 69, quoted in George A. Bailey, *The Vietnam War According to Chet, David, Walter, Harry, Peter, Bob, Howard, and Frank: A Content Analysis of Journalistic Performance by the Television Evening News Anchormen* (Ann Arbor, Mich.: University Microfilms, 1973), p. 352.

6. Bailey, *The Vietnam War According to Chet,* pp. 369–71; Marvin Barrett, ed., *The A. I. du Pont–Columbia University Survey of Broadcast Journalism for 1971–1972: The Politics of Broadcasting* (New York: Thomas Y. Crowell, 1973), pp. 6–7.

7. Walter Lippmann, *Public Opinion* (Glencoe, Ill.: Free Press, 1921); Richard A. Lau, Thad A. Brown, and David O. Sears, "Self-Interest and Civilians' Attitudes Toward the Vietnam War," *Public Opinion Quarterly* 42 (Winter 1978): 464.

8. Transcript, President Nixon's Comments to Chiefs of Mission, Bangkok, 30 July 1969, attachment to Ltr, William P. Rogers to the President, 29 Sep 69.

9. Msg, Saigon 9723 to State, 19 May 69; Memo Henkin for Laird, 12 Jan 70; Talking Paper, OASD SA, 3 Oct 69, sub: U.S. Objectives in Southeast Asia, Thayer Papers, CMH.

10. Memo, Laird for the President, 4 Apr 70, sub: Vietnam, Laird Papers (LP), NARA; Kissinger, *The White House Years,* p. 1480; Msg, Saigon 1514 to State, 31 Jan 70.

11. Memo, Marshall Green, EA, for the Acting Secretary, 12 Aug 69, sub: The President's Trip.

12. Ltr, Richard C. Steadman, DASD ISA, to William P. Bundy, 4 Feb 69, DDI.

13. Msg, Vientiane 7409 to State, 28 Oct 69, sub: Press Story on USAF Strikes in Laos, 334-71A374, NARA; Henry Kamm, "U.S. Runs a Secret Laotian Army," *New York Times,* 26 Oct 69; "Dilemma in Laos," *Newsweek,* 3 Nov 69, p. 43.

14. *Facts on File,* 1969, 29:79.

15. Msgs, Abrams MAC 2040 to McCain, 13 Feb 70, AP; Godley to McCain et al., 19 Feb 70, FAIM/IR; MACV 11093 to All Commands, 7 Mar 70, sub: Public Information Guidance on U.S. Involvement in Laos, DDI.

16. Memo, Melvin Laird for Secretary of the Air Force, 23 Mar 70, sub: U.S. Position in Southeast Asia; Msg, Defense 3156 to MACV, CINCPAC, from ASD PA, 14 Mar 70, sub: Public Affairs Policy—U.S. Casualties in Laos, all DDI; Msg, State 39427 to Vientiane, 18 Mar 70, sub: Press Guidance on President's Laos Statement.

17. Msg, Vientiane 2235 to State, 28 Mar 70, sub: Vientiane Press Corps, DDI.

18. Ibid.

19. Msg, Vientiane 1867 to State, 17 Mar 70.

20. Msg, Vientiane 2235 to State, 28 Mar 70.

21. Memo, Alexander Butterfield for Laird, Kissinger, 10 Jun 69, 330-75-089, LP.

22. Memo, Wheeler CM-4446-69 for Director, Joint Staff, 23 Jul 69, sub: Coordination of Press Treatment of RVNAF and Other Free World Forces; Msg, Wheeler CJCS 9587 to Abrams, 4 Jul 69, sub: Publicizing RVNAF Achievements.

23. Msg, Abrams MAC 10252 to Wheeler, 8 Aug 69, sub: Publicizing ARVN Achievements, AP.

24. Talking Paper, OASD PA, 20 Apr 70, sub: Public Affairs Staffing and Operations, 330-76-076, LP; quotes, Memo, the President for Henry Kissinger, 1 Dec 69, NP.

25. MACOI, Report on MACOI Involvement in Reporting the Vietnam War, 10 Feb 70, DDI.

26. Memo, Daniel Z. Henkin for Brig Gen George S. Blanchard, OSD ISA, 29 Jan 70, 330-76-067, LP; Memo, Henkin for Laird, 12 Jan 70; Peter R. Kann, "A Long, Leisurely Drive Through the Mekong Delta," *Wall Street Journal,* 10 Nov 69; Msg, State 7081 to All Diplomatic Posts, for Chiefs of Mission, 16 Jan 70, sub: *CBS Reports: A Timetable for Vietnam.*

27. Jack Anderson, "American Made Millionaires in Vietnam," *Parade,* 8 Jan 69; Msg, McCain to Abrams, 22 Jul 69, AP.

28. Larry Burrows, "Vietnam: A Degree of Disillusion," *Life,* 19 Sep 69, p. 67; "State of the War: An Intelligence Report," *U.S. News & World Report,* 27 Oct 69; John E. Woodruff, "U.S. Evaluation Shows Saigon Forces Decline in Combat Efficiency," *Baltimore Sun,* 29 Oct 69.

29. Memo, Col Robert E. Pursley for Col Alexander Haig, 3 Oct 69, sub: Presidential Inquiry, 330-75-089, LP.

30. "Vietnam Exodus," *Newsweek,* 23 Jun 69; "Newsweek and Reuters Given Warning by Saigon on Reports," *New York Times,* 24 Jun 69; Msg, Saigon 1514 to State, 31 Jan 70, sub: Discussion with President Thieu, Jan 30, AP.

31. Msg, Paris 9365 to State, 20 Jun 69, AP; MFR, U.S. Department of State, 11 Dec 69, sub: Views of Ambassador Bui Diem on President Thieu and Vietnamization.

32. Msgs, Saigon 20975 to State, 18 Oct 69, sub: Meeting with President Thieu, October 17, AP; Saigon 22753 to State, 13 Nov 69, sub: Improving South Vietnam's Image; Saigon 22754 to State, 13 Nov 69, sub: Improving South Vietnam's Image—the Black Market Problem; quote, Msg, Saigon 1515 to State, 31 Jan 70, sub: Discussion with President Thieu, 30 January—Corruption, AP.

33. Memo, Richard Helms, Director, CIA, for Laird, 22 Sep 69, sub: Corruption Within the Inspectorate, 330-75-089, LP.

34. Msg, Saigon 19453 to State, 26 Sep 69, sub: The Current Mood in Saigon.

35. Ibid.; Msgs, Abrams MAC 12029 to Wheeler, 14 Sep 69; Abrams MAC 12080 to Wheeler, 15 Sep 69; Abrams MAC 12096 to Wheeler, 15 Sep 69, AP.

36. Msgs, Wheeler JCS 11423 to McCain, Abrams, 15 Sep 69, DDI; State 157599 to Saigon, 17 Sep 69.

37. Memo, William P. Rogers for the President, 19 Nov 69, sub: Vietnamese Ambassador's Proposal.

38. Msg, Wheeler JCS 9668 to McCain, Abrams, 6 Aug 69, AP; Memo, the President for Henry Kissinger, 24 Nov 69, NP.

39. Laird, Handwritten note attached to copy of Donald Kirk, "1st Cav Finds Mission Unchanged," *Washington Star,* 3 Nov 69, 330-75-089, LP; "The Pursuit of Peace in Vietnam," Address by President Nixon, 3 Nov 69, Department of State *Bulletin,* 24 Nov 69, p. 437.

40. Jeff Stein, *A Murder in Wartime: The Untold Spy Story That Changed the Course of the Vietnam War* (New York: St. Martin's Press, 1992); John Stevens Berry, *Those Gallant Men: On Trial in Vietnam* (Novato, Calif.: Presidio Press, 1984).

41. Statement by Secretary of the Army Stanley R. Resor, 29 Sep 69, CMH; Office of the Judge Advocate General, MACV, Log Maintained by Col Persons, SJA, USARV, 1 Oct 69, Papers of Lt Gen James W. Sutherland, MHI.

42. Msgs, Palmer, Vice Chief of Staff of the Army (VCSA), DA, WDC 12882 to Abrams, 4 Aug 69; Abrams MAC 1011 to Palmer, 5 Aug 69, sub: *New York Times* query, AP; Memo for Correspondents, 14 Aug 69, CMH.

43. Msg, Abrams MAC 1011 to Palmer, 5 Aug 69, sub: *New York Times* query, AP; quote from Donald Kirk, "Attorney in Beret Case Puts Blame on Abrams," *Washington Star,* 13 Aug 69.

44. Msgs, State 133837 to Saigon, 9 Aug 69; Saigon 16057 to State, 10 Aug 69; [UPI,] "Inquiry Said to Be Suspended in Green Beret Case," *New York Times,* 13 Aug 69; Log Maintained by Col Persons, Staff Judge Advocate (SJA), USARV, 1 Oct 69.

45. Ltr, Peter W. Rodino et al. to Honorable Stanley R. Resor, 9 Sep 69, CMH; Msgs, Guy B. Scott, Attorney for Capt Budge E. Williams, to Secretary Laird, 26 Sep 69, 330-75-089, LP; Resor ARV 2270 to Beal, 22 Aug 69, sub: United States v. Rheault et al.

46. Msg, Resor ARV 2270 to Beal, 22 Aug 69, sub: United States v. Rheault et al.; Memo, L. Niederlehner, Acting General Counsel, for the Secretary of Defense, 22 Sep 69, 330-75-089, Viet 250.4, LP; Record of Chief of Staff Telecon with Gen Palmer, 1010, 3 Sep 69, sub: Green Berets and Stano Slot, WP; Lewis Sorley, *Thunderbolt, From the Battle of the Bulge to Vietnam and Beyond: General Creighton Abrams and the Army of His Times* (New York: Simon and Schuster, 1992), p. 275.

47. Statement of the Honorable Peter W. Rodino, U.S. House of Representatives, Special Order for September 23, 1969, CMH; Memo, Record of Chief of Staff Telecon with Maj Gen Clifton, 1350, 22 Sep 69, sub: Golf and Green Berets, WP; Msg, Resor 16511 to Rosson, Deputy COMUSMACV, 29 Sep 69, AP; Statement by Secretary of the Army Stanley R. Resor to the Press, 29 Sep 69, CMH.

48. "The Shade Is Pulled Down," *Philadelphia Bulletin,* 1 Oct 69; "The Green Beret Case," *New York Times,* 3 Oct 69; Carl T. Rowan, "Green Beret Case Taints Reputations Galore," *Washington Post,* 10 Oct 69; "Shadow on Army," *San Diego Union,* 10 Oct 69.

49. Talking Paper, 6 Oct 69, sub: The Phoenix Program, CMH; Memo, Col Raymond T. Reid, Office of the Secretary of the Army, for Secretary of the General Staff, 24 Nov 69, sub: Fact Sheet on Phoenix, DDI; Talking Paper, 20 Oct 69, "The Anti-infrastructure Campaign in South Vietnam, 330-75-089, LP.

50. Memo, Laird for Wheeler, 29 Nov 69, sub: Evaluation of U.S. Involvement in Provincial Reconnaissance Unit Program in RVN; Memo, Wheeler JCSM-752-69 for Secretary of Defense, 8 Dec 69, sub: U.S. Military Involvement in Provincial Reconnaissance Unit Program in RVN, both 330-75-089, Viet 380 Pacification, LP.

CHAPTER 12. QUESTIONING BEGINS

1. *Gallup Opinion Index,* Jul 69, p. 3; Louis Harris, "College Students Radicalized by Vietnam War," *Philadelphia Inquirer,* 3 Jul 69; "Judging the Fourth Estate: A *Time*–Louis Harris Poll," *Time,* 5 Sep 69, p. 38.

2. Kissinger, *The White House Years,* pp. 284–85, 303–406.

3. *Facts on File,* 1969, 29:658–59.

4. "The Pursuit of Peace in Vietnam," Address by President Nixon, 3 Nov 69, Department of State *Bulletin,* 24 Nov 69, pp. 437–43; Memo, Ray S. Cline for the Secretary of State, 6 Nov 69, sub: Hanoi's Angry Reaction to President Nixon's Speech; "Mr. Nixon's

Plan for Peace," *New York Times,* 4 Nov 69; "Nixon Support Soars in Poll After Speech," *Washington Star,* 14 Nov 69.

5. Louis Harris, "Harris Poll: Viet Protests Gaining with the Public," *New York Post,* 10 Nov 69; "The Big March," *Newsweek,* 24 Nov 69, p. 30.

6. "Newsgram-Tomorrow," *U.S. News & World Report,* 27 Oct 69, p. 22; U.S. Department of State, American Opinion Summary, 4–23 Oct 69; George Gallup, "3-Part Peace Plan Favored," *Philadelphia Inquirer,* 29 Oct 69; George Gallup, "58% Back Nixon War Policy," *Washington Post,* 2 Nov 69.

7. William E. Porter, *Assault on the Media: The Nixon Years* (Ann Arbor: University of Michigan Press, 1976), pp. 39–43; U.S. Congress, House, "Address to the Midwest Regional Republican Committee Meeting," *Congressional Record,* 115:34043–49; Louis Harris, "Comparison Shows Gain of 5 Pct. by Nixon on Viet Policy," clipping, 11 Dec 69, CMH.

8. Barrett, *Columbia University Survey of Broadcast Journalism, 1969–1970,* p. 33; Annotated News Summaries, Dec 69, NP.

9. Interv with General William C. Westmoreland, 6 Dec 89, CMH.

10. Georgie Ann Geyer, "Viet Foe 'Hard to Hate,' Troops Say," *Chicago Daily News,* 16 Jan 69; "Seeds of Dissidence," *Newsweek,* 21 Apr 69, p. 36; Donald Kirk, "Growing GI Disillusion," *Washington Star,* 9 Nov 69; "A New G.I.: For Pot and Peace," *Newsweek,* 2 Feb 70, p. 24.

11. Paul Hathaway, "The Negro at War," *Washington Star,* 6 May 68.

12. Msg, Wheeler JCS 3231 to Abrams, 14 Mar 69, AP. See also Carl Rowan, "Racial Strife at U.S. Military Bases Ominous," *Washington Star,* 27 Aug 69; "Army Seeks Clues to Long Binh Riot," *New York Times,* 1 Sep 68; Zalin B. Grant, "Whites Against Blacks in Vietnam," *New Republic,* 18 Jan 69, p. 15.

13. Bennett's report is summarized in Msg, Wheeler JCS 3231 to Abrams, 14 Mar 69. See also Talking Paper, sub: Racial Tensions and Violence Among the Troops, Annex A to Trip Book, Secretary Laird's Trip to Vietnam, 9–13 February 1970, 330-76-076, LP; Richard O. Hope, *Racial Strife in the U.S. Military* (New York: Praeger Publishers, 1979), pp. 40–41.

14. [UPI,] "Racial Rows Force Curbs at Danang," *Washington Post,* 21 Oct 68. Moskowitz is quoted in George C. Wilson, "Troop Racial Trouble Is Tied to Lull in War," *Washington Post,* 15 Nov 69.

15. Memo, Arthur M. Sussman for Assistant Secretary of the Army (M&RA), 14 Jan 70, sub: Race Relations in the Army, CMH.

16. MACV History, 1969, vol. 3, p. XIV-20; Msg, Abrams MAC 14059 to Cushman, 18 Oct 68, AP; [AP,] "Tensions of Black Power Reach Troops in Vietnam," *New York Times,* 13 Apr 69.

17. Memo, Roger T. Kelly for Secretary Laird, 25 May 70, sub: Report on Southeast Asia Trip-2-20 May 70, 330-76-067, LP; Msg, Lt Gen Davison, HOA 2456 to Lt Gen McCaffrey, DCG, USARV, 25 Oct 70, McCaffrey Papers, CMH. The quote is from Briefing, Lt Col James S. White, Seminar on Racial Tension and Equal Opportunity, attachment to Memo, MACOI-C for Major Commands, 9 Feb 70, 334-74-593, NARA.

18. Memo, Col Alfred J. Mock, USARV IO, for DCG, 6 Oct 70, sub: Press Release About Racial Incidents, 73A6994, USARVIO Papers, WNRC.

19. David Breasted, "MAC Wars on Dope in Services," *New York Daily News,* 15 Feb 68; MACV History, 1968, vol. 2, p. 839, and 1969, vol. 3, p. XIV-4.

20. MACV History, 1968, vol. 2, pp. 839–40.

21. "Drug Use Soars Among Viet GI's," *Washington Daily News,* 15 Feb 68; William Grigg, "Steinbeck's Son Quotes Self as Expert on Drugs, Vietnam," *Washington Star,* 6 Mar 68; Breasted, "MAC Wars on Dope in Services."

22. "Army Lists Marijuana Incidence," *Washington Post,* 25 Apr 69; "Pentagon Reports Dope Use Rise," *San Diego Union,* 8 Mar 69; Talking Paper, sub: Use of Drugs by Servicemen, 12 Mar 69, DDI.

23. "In Vietnam: Mama-san Pushers vs. Psyops," *Newsweek,* 21 Apr 69.

24. Note attached to Query, AVHIO for PIO, 1 Apr 69, 72A4722, Historical Inquiry files, NARA.

25. Drummond Ayres, "U.S. Military Spurs Campaign to Curb Marijuana in Vietnam," *New York Times,* 21 Sep 69; "Marijuana Effects Noted in GI's," *Baltimore Sun,* 13 Oct 69; Query, Susan Smith, *Readers' Digest,* for DDI, 28 Sep 69, DDI.

26. Msgs, Sidle WDC 5562 to Lt Col Johnson, IO USARV, 24 Mar 70; Lt Col Johnson, IO USARV, Long Binh, USARV 900 to Brig Gen Sidle, Chief of Information, U.S. Army, 30 Mar 70, 72A6694, USARVIO Papers, NARA.

27. Msg, Abrams MAC 14114 to Secretary of Defense, 28 Oct 70, DDI; Memo, Jerry E. Bush, OASD/Comptroller, for Comdr Joseph Lorfano, 11 Dec 70, DDI; Msg, Abrams MAC 114089 to McCain, 28 Oct 70, DDI.

28. Fred Farrar, "Army Probes Funds Use in Officer Clubs," *Chicago Tribune,* 13 Aug 69; OASD PA News Release 821-69, 30 Sep 69, CMH; *Facts on File,* 29:696, 822.

29. Msg, CG, III MAF, to COMUSMACV, Lt Gen Nickerson to Abrams, 25 Aug 69, AP; Horst Faas and Peter Arnett, "GI Unit Beats Fear, Rejoins Battle in Viet," *Chicago Tribune,* 26 Aug 69; "Incident in Song Chang Valley," *Time,* 5 Sep 69. See also Memo, Daniel Z. Henkin for Secretary Laird, 12 Jan 70, 330-76-067, LP.

30. Faas and Arnett, "GI Unit Beats Fear."

31. Ibid.

32. Msg, CG, III MAF, to COMUSMACV, Nickerson to Abrams, 25 Aug 69; CBS Evening News, 26 Aug 69, RTDD; "Incident in Song Chang Valley"; "The Alpha Incident," *Newsweek,* 8 Sep 69.

33. "General Gives Views," *New York Times,* 29 Aug 69; "Lt. Eugene Shurtz Interviewed," Huntley-Brinkley Report, 29 Aug 69, RTDD.

34. [AP.] "GI Unit That Faltered in Viet Says Entire Company Balked," *Chicago Tribune,* 30 Aug 69.

35. James P. Sterba, "G.I.'s in Battle Shrug Off the Story of Balky Company A," *New York Times,* 29 Aug 69; Kenley Jones, "Lt. Eugene Shurtz Interviewed," Huntley-Brinkley Report, 29 Aug 69. See also Richard Threlkeld, "A Report from Alpha Company," CBS Evening News, 27 Aug 69, *Radio-TV-Defense Dialog;* James Reston, "A Whiff of Mutiny in Vietnam," *New York Times,* 27 Aug 69; "Alpha Company," *Washington Star,* 30 Aug 69; "Battle of Words," *New York Post,* 26 Aug 69; David Lawrence, "What's Become of 'Voluntary Censorship?'" *U.S. News & World Report,* 8 Sep 69, p. 92.

36. Neil Sheehan, "Letters from Hamburger Hill," *Harper's,* Nov 69.

37. "Fine Work, Sarge," *New York Daily News,* 27 Aug 69; "Keep 'Mutiny' in Perspective," *Detroit News,* 2 Sep 69.

38. Msg, Lt Gen Ewell, CG, II FFV, HOA 3384 to Abrams, 10 Nov 69, AP.

39. Ibid.

CHAPTER 13. MY LAI AND OTHER ATROCITIES

1. Today Show, NBC-TV, 3 Nov 69, RTDD; Msgs, COMUSMACV 67972 to CINCPAC, 10 Dec 69, sub: CBS Allegation of Atrocity, DDI; State 186897 to Saigon, 5 Nov 69, sub: TV Reports of Mistreatment of Prisoners.

2. Quote from Msg, Saigon 22749 to State, 13 Nov 69, sub: TV Reports of Mistreatment of Prisoners in SOUTH VIETNAM, DDI. Also see Msgs, Saigon 22371 to State, 7 Nov 69; COMUSMACV 62900 to OASD PA, 11 Nov 69; COMUSMACV 63204 to OASD PA, 13 Nov 69, DDI; Ltr, Richard S. Salant to Norman T. Hatch, Directorate of Defense Information, 15 Dec 69.

3. Msgs, COMUSMACV 67978 to CINCPAC, 10 Dec 69, sub: NBC Allegation of Mistreatment of PW; COMUSMACV 1168 to DA, 8 Jan 70, sub: CBS Allegation of Mistreatment of PW, DDI; State 203462 to Amconsul Halifax, info Saigon, 6 Dec 69, sub: TV Film of Mistreatment of Prisoners.

4. Seymour M. Hersh, "How I Broke the Mylai 4 Story," *Saturday Review*, 11 Jul 70, p. 46.

5. Record of Chief of Staff Telecon with Mr. Frank Pace, 1400, 26 Nov 69, sub: My Lai, WP. This chapter is based in part on Research Report, Ann David, Press Coverage of the My Lai Massacre [U.S. Army Center of Military History, 1984], CMH.

6. Interv, author with Jerry Friedheim, 3 Oct 86; Interv, author with Daniel Z. Henkin, 10 Oct 86, CMH.

7. Talking Paper, OCINFO, U.S. Army, Early Press Coverage—My Lai, 5 Dec 69, 330-76-067, LP; Seymour M. Hersh, "Officer Charged with Murdering 109 in Viet," *Chicago Sun Times,* 13 Nov 69.

8. Seymour M. Hersh, "The Story Everyone Ignored," *Columbia Journalism Review* 9 (Winter 1969/1970): 55–58; MACOI Memo for the Press, 4 May 68, sub: Enemy Statements on the War, CMH.

9. Msg, Sidle WDC 19932 to Woolnough et al., 15 Nov 69, sub: Public Affairs Guidance, AP; Memo for Correspondents 323-69, 19 Nov 69, 334-71A374, 206.02 MACOI, NARA; Joseph Fried, "Hue Massacre Pinned on Reds," *New York Daily News,* 24 Nov 69; [AP,] "Allies Disagree on Toll in Hamlet," *Baltimore Sun,* 23 Nov 69.

10. Msg, Sidle WDC 19932 to Woolnough et al., 15 Nov 69, sub: Public Affairs Guidance; Peter Braestrup, "Vietnam Probe Widens," *Washington Post,* 22 Nov 69; Msg, Sidle WDC 20080 to Woolnough, 18 Nov 69, sub: Public Affairs Guidance, AP; Msg, Sidle WDC 20442 to Woolnough et al., 22 Nov 69, sub: Public Affairs Guidance; "Official U.S. Report on My Lai Investigation," *U.S. News & World Report,* 8 Dec 69, p. 78.

11. Peter Braestrup and Stephen Klaidman, "Three Vietnam Veterans Tell of Hamlet Slayings," *Washington Post,* 20 Nov 69; [Reuters,] "Ex GI Tells of Partaking in Massacre," *Baltimore Sun,* 25 Nov 69; Jim Lucas, "CBS Admits Paying for Meadlo Interview," *Manchester Union Leader,* 1 Dec 69; "Former G.I. Took Pictures of Dead," *New York Times,* 22 Nov 69; "The Massacre at My Lai," *Life,* 5 Dec 69, pp. 36–45.

12. Msgs, State 3577 to Saigon, 3 Dec 69; Saigon 24034 to State, 3 Dec 69; Saigon 24372 to State, 9 Dec 69.

13. David, Press Coverage of the My Lai Massacre, p. 10; Robert J. Heinl, "Witness for the Prosecution Admits He Exploited 'Massacre' at Mi Lai," *Philadelphia Bulletin,* 22 Nov 70.

14. Kenneth Crawford, "Song My's Shock Wave," *Newsweek,* 15 Dec 69, p. 38; "Atrocities and Policies," *Wall Street Journal,* 1 Dec 69; John T. Wheeler, "Even Vietnamese Children Could Terrorize the GIs," *Washington Star,* 5 Dec 69.

15. "No Pinkville Cover Up," *Chicago Sun-Times,* 21 Nov 69; "An American Nightmare," *New York Times,* 22 Nov 69; Msg, Sidle WDC 20471 to Abrams, 24 Nov 69, sub: My Lai Investigation, AP; James Reston, "Who Will Investigate the Investigators?" *New York Times,* 30 Nov 69; "Painful Questions," *Long Island Newsday,* 1 Dec 69.

16. "Assessing Songmy, Doves Recoil but Hawks Tend to See 'Massacre' as Just a Part of War," *Wall Street Journal,* 1 Dec 69; Louis Harris, "66 Percent Against My Lai Court-Martials," *Philadelphia Inquirer,* 6 Jan 70. The *Minneapolis Tribune* poll is summarized in "Poll Finds Doubters on My Lai," *Washington Post,* 22 Dec 69.

17. Memo, Ronald L. Ziegler for H. R. Haldeman, 5 Dec 69, President's Handwriting, NP.

18. Memo, Herbert Klein for Bob Haldeman, 21 Nov 69; Memo, Klein for John Ehrlichman, 5 Oct 71, Klein, NP; John Ehrlichman, Handwritten Note of Meeting with the President, 23 Nov 69, Ehrlichman, NP.

19. Memo, Klein for Haldeman, 21 Nov 69; Memo, Klein for Haldeman, 5 Oct 71, Klein, NP.

20. Peter Braestrup, "Silence Ordered on Mylai," *Washington Post,* 26 Nov 69; Peter Braestrup, "News Stories on Pinkville Upset Judge," *Washington Post,* 29 Nov 69; "Court Right to Reject Media Ban," *Denver Post,* 4 Dec 69; Ltr, John de J. Pemberton, Jr., Executive Director, ACLU, to Secretary Laird, 10 Dec 69, 330-75-089, LP.

21. Chuck Green, "Medina: My Lai Misreported," *Denver Post,* 8 Aug 70; "The Captain's Nightmare," *Newsweek,* 16 Dec 69, p. 41; [UPI,] "Calley Judge Calls for Inquiry into Five News Organizations," *New York Times,* 16 Dec 69.

22. "The Killings at Song My," *Newsweek,* 8 Dec 69, p. 33; Msgs, Col L. Gordon Hill, SA/SEA OASD PA, Defense 15144 to Col Joseph F. H. Cutrona, 3 Dec 69, DDI; Lt Gen Ewell, CG, IIFFV, HOA 3671 to Abrams, 10 Dec 69, AP; *Facts on File,* 15–21 Jan 70, 30:18.

23. Memo, Laird for the Secretaries of the Army, Navy, and Air Force, 11 Dec 69, sub: Atrocity Allegations, 330-75-089, LP; Msg, Hill Defense 15144 to Cutrona, 3 Dec 69, sub: Incident Near Dong Tam; Memo for Correspondents, 22 Sep 72, CMH.

24. Msg, Ewell HOA 3671 to Abrams, 10 Dec 69, AP.

25. End of Tour Rpt, Lt Gen Julian J. Ewell, 17 Sep 69; HQ, Ninth Infantry Division, AVDE-CG, 16 Jan 69, sub: Awards and Decoration Policy, CMH. The records of the trial are in Docket No. CM424795, Clerk of Court, Army Judiciary.

26. Pacification Studies Group, CORDS, Redeployment Effects of the Ninth U.S. Division from Dinh Tuong and Kien Hoa Provinces, 15 Mar 70, CMH; Msg, Saigon A-368 to State, 18 Jul 69; Kevin Buckley, "Pacification's Deadly Price," *Newsweek,* 19 Jun 72, p. 42; Ltr, Col Phillip H. Stevens to Kevin Buckley, 13 Jan 72, DDI.

27. MFR, A. Terry Rambo, Dale K. Brown, Human Sciences Research, ARPA-AGILE, May 67, sub: Korean Military Behavior Toward Vietnamese Civilians in Phu Yen Province, HSR-RN-671-Aa, 330-76-067, LP.

28. Msgs, Saigon 2303 to State, 16 Feb 70; Saigon 442 to State, 11 Jan 70, sub: Alleged ROK Atrocities; State 4219 to Saigon, 10 Jan 70; Saigon 1368 to State, 29 Jan; Memo, Winthrop G. Brown, EA, for Under Secretary Johnson, 11 Feb 70, sub: Alleged Korean Atrocities, FAIM/IR; Msg, Wheeler JCS 624 to Gen Michaelis, CINC, UN Community Korea, sub: Allegations of Korean Atrocities, AP.

29. Ted Sell, "My Lai Company Faces Earlier Crime Charges," *Los Angeles Times,* 8 Feb 70; Fred Farrar, "Pot Use by GIs in Viet Told," *Chicago Tribune,* 25 Mar 70.

30. "Pentagon Eliminates Drugs Re: My Lai," ABC Evening News, 25 Mar 70, RTDD. Lt. Gen. W. R. Peers, U.S. Army (Ret.), *The My Lai Inquiry* (New York: Norton, 1979), pp. 198, 216.

31. OSD PA News Release, 17 Mar 70, sub: Army Announces Peers-McCrate Inquiry Findings, 330-76-067, LP.

32. "No Army Whitewash," *Detroit News,* 19 Mar 70; Frank Reynolds, ABC Evening News, 17 Mar 70, RTDD.

33. The CBS report is in Barrett, *Columbia University Survey of Broadcast Journalism, 1969–1970,* pp. 141–44. See also Richard Wilson, "CBS Stand in War News Probe Is Questioned," *Washington Star,* 11 May 70.

34. Rpt of Investigation, MAC Provost Marshal, 6 Sep 70, sub: CBS Allegations of Mistreatment and Atrocity Against Enemy PW; Interv, author with Col Robert Cook, U.S. Army (Ret.), 22 May 87; with Maj Gen Winant Sidle, 12 Jun 73, CMH; J. W. Fulbright, *The Pentagon Propaganda Machine* (New York: Liveright, 1970), pp. 104–6.

35. William McGriffin, "Lawmakers Plunge Ahead with Own My Lai Inquiry," *Chicago Daily News,* 3 Jan 70; William Kling, "My Lai Probers Allege Coverup Planned by Army," *Chicago Tribune,* 15 Jul 70; Miriam Ottenburg, "Hill Probers Charge My Lai 'Cover-Up,'" *Washington Star,* 15 Jul 70.

36. CBS Evening News, 18 Oct 69, RTDD. For the Jencks Act, see 18 *United States Code* (USC) 3500 (1958).

37. Douglas Robinson, "Songmy Trial Is Snarled as House Panel Refused to Divulge 4 Men's Testimony," *New York Times,* 16 Oct 70.

38. [AP,] "Gen. Koster Censured in Mylai Incident," *New York Times,* 1 Feb 71.

39. "Army Acts Against Two Generals," CBS Evening News, 19 May 71, RTDD.

40. Peers, *The My Lai Inquiry,* pp. 222–24; Samuel S. Stratton, "The Army and General Koster," *New York Times,* 1 Mar 71.

41. Peers, *The My Lai Inquiry,* p. 225.

42. Louis Harris, "Public Opposes Calley Sentence," *Washington Post,* 5 Apr 71; "Officials, Veterans Groups Ask Clemency for Lt. Calley," *Washington Post,* 1 Apr 71.

43. Charles W. Corddry, "Calley Verdict Looses Flood of Protests on Pentagon," *Baltimore Sun,* 30 Mar 71; Note, Jerry Warren to Ronald Ziegler, 7 Apr 71, Ziegler, NP.

44. Talking Paper, 5 Apr 71, 330-76-207, LP; "How Can Justice Be Impartial with Nixon in Calley's Corner?" *Philadelphia Inquirer,* 6 Apr 71; "A Nation Troubled by the Specter of My Lai," *Washington Star,* 4 Apr 71.

45. Memo, Buchanan for the President, 5 Apr 71, sub: The Calley Situation, Buchanan, NP.

46. Nixon's remarks are summarized in *Facts on File,* 29 Apr 70, 30:330–32.

47. This section is based on *Facts on File* for the years 1972 (vol. 32), 1973 (vol. 33), 1974 (vol. 34), and 1975 (vol. 36).

CHAPTER 14. INCURSION INTO CAMBODIA

1. Msg, State 60703 to All Diplomatic Posts, 22 Apr 70, sub: Viet-Nam Highlights.

2. Msg, Saigon 1121 to State, 24 Jan 70, sub: Estimate of Enemy Strategy in 1970;

Memo, Laird for the President, 4 Apr 70, sub: Vietnam, 330-76-076, LP; MFR, OASD SA, 5 Mar 70, sub: Meeting w. Sec. Laird, Thayer Papers, CMH; "Vietnamization: Will It Work?" *Newsweek,* 9 Feb 70, p. 31.

3. Msg, McCain to Wheeler, 28 Jan 70, sub: Vice President Agnew's Visit, WP.

4. Msg, State 125290 to Paris, 28 Jul 69, sub: Cambodian Revelations of Viet Cong/NVA Presence in Svay Rieng.

5. Msg, McCain to Wheeler, 3 Feb 70, sub: Cambodian Aid to the Viet Cong/NVA.

6. Memo, Theodore L. Eliot, Jr., Exec Sec, for Henry Kissinger, 29 Apr 70, sub: Daily Report on Cambodia No. 33; William Shawcross, *Sideshow* (New York: Simon and Schuster, 1979), pp. 114–22; Department of the Army, Office of the Assistant Chief of Staff for Intelligence, The Role of Cambodia in the North Vietnam/Viet Cong War Effort, 1964–1970, 13 Apr 71, pp. 18, 392, 394.

7. JCS History, 1969–1970, pp. 232–35.

8. Msg, Abrams MAC 4199 to McCain, 30 Mar 70, AP.

9. JCS History, 1969–1970, pp. 232–35.

10. Ibid, p. 239.

11. Glenn Currie, "Censors Hard on Newsmen," *Washington Daily News,* 1 May 70; "Beyond the Checkpoint," *Newsweek,* 15 Jun 70; "A Bad Trip," *Newsweek,* 20 Apr 70; "Cambodian Perils High for Newsmen," *New York Times,* 17 May 70.

12. Msgs, Phnom Penh 423 to State, 4 Apr 70; Phnom Penh 447 to State, 7 Apr 70; JCS History, 1969–1970, p. 243.

13. Msgs, Lt Gen Ewell, CG, IIFFV, HOA 843, to Maj Gen Bantz, CG, 25th Inf Div, 12 Apr 70; Wheeler JCS 5405 to Abrams, 20 Apr 70; Lt Gen Davison, CG, IIFFV, HOA 939, to Abrams, 22 Apr 70, AP Msg, State 60712 to Saigon, 23 Apr 70.

14. Msg, State 61525 to Phnom Penh, 24 Apr 70; MFR, U.S. Department of State, n.d., sub: Chronology, Cambodia, 7/7/70–8/7/70.

15. Msg, Abrams MAC 5493 to Wheeler, McCain, 25 Apr 70, sub: Press Guidance for Operations in Cambodia, AP; CBS Evening News, 17 Apr 70, RTDD.

16. White House News Release, 20 Apr 70, sub: Statement by the President of an Update Report on Vietnam, DDI; Kissinger, *The White House Years,* p. 487; Memo, Westmoreland CM-5063-70 for Secretary of Defense, 21 Apr 70, sub: Courses of Action with Regard to Cambodia, WP.

17. Handwritten Note, H. R. Haldeman, 20 Apr 70, Haldeman Notes, NP (hereafter cited as Haldeman, NP); JCS History, 1969–1970, p. 250; Msgs, Moorer JCS 5623 to McCain, Abrams, 23 Apr 70, sub: Operations in Cambodia; Chief of Naval Operations (CNO) to COMUSMACV, CINCPAC, 25 Apr 70; Moorer JCS 5636 to Abrams, 25 Apr 70, AP.

18. Msg, Abrams MAC 5493 to Wheeler, McCain, 25 Apr 70, sub: Press Guidance for Operations in Cambodia, AP.

19. Msg, Wheeler JCS 5711 to Abrams, 25 Apr 70, AP; Msg, CNO to COMUSMACV, CINCPAC, 25 Apr 70, AP.

20. Haldeman, note of meeting with Kissinger, 27 Apr 70, Haldeman Notes, NP.

21. Handwritten Note, H. R. Haldeman, 27 Apr 70, sub: Meeting Between the President, Rogers, Laird, and Kissinger in the President's Executive Office Building Office, Haldeman Notes, NP.

22. Ibid.; Kissinger, *The White House Years,* pp. 501, 1484.

23. Msg, Wheeler JCS 5835 to McCain, Abrams, 28 Apr 70; ASD PA, Statement on Cambodian Operation, 29 Apr 70, DDI; Msg, Wheeler JCS 5836 to Abrams, 28 Apr 70, sub: Press Guidance for Operations in Cambodia, AP.

24. Msg, OASD PA 7461 to MACV, 29 Apr 70, DDI; Undated note attached to Msg, OASD PA 7461 to MACV, 29 Apr 70, DDI.

25. "Escalation in Indochina," *New York Times,* 30 Apr 70; John W. Finney, "Senators Angry," *New York Times,* 30 Apr 70.

26. Msg, Wheeler JCS 5859 to Abrams, 29 Apr 70, AP.

27. Memo, Herbert Klein for the President, 30 Apr 70, Haldeman, NP.

28. "The Cambodia Strike: Defensive Action for Peace," Address by President Nixon, Department of State *Bulletin,* 18 May 70, p. 617.

29. Statement by Gen John Vogt, Commander, U.S. Pacific Air Forces, 2 May 70, DDI; Robert B. Semple, Jr., "Not an Invasion," *New York Times,* 1 May 70.

30. MFR, William C. Westmoreland, 6 May 70, sub: Meeting of Joint Chiefs of Staff with the President, 1 May 70, WP; Memo, Charles Colson for Lawrence Higby, 30 Apr 70, sub: Report from Timmons on the Leadership Meeting, Haldeman, NP; John W. Finney, "Move Stirs Opposition in Senate," *New York Times,* 30 Apr 70.

31. "Editorial Comments on Move in Cambodia," *New York Times,* 1 May 70; "The President Would Rather Be Right," *Chicago Tribune,* 2 May 70.

32. MACV History, 1970, vol. 3, p. xi–1; Interv, author with Wendell "Bud" Merick, 16 Apr 79, CMH; "Beyond the Checkpoint," *Newsweek,* 15 Jun 70, p. 65.

33. Msgs, Wheeler JCS 5971 to McCain, Abrams, 30 Apr 70, sub: Press Guidance, AP; L. G. Hill Defense 6064 to Col Joseph F. H. Cutrona, 2 May 70, and L. G. Hill Defense 6023 to Cutrona, 1 May 70, DDI.

34. Msgs, Cutrona MAC 5912 to Hill, 2 May 70, DDI; Cutrona MAC 6197 to Hill, 7 May 70; and Abrams MAC 5871 to Wheeler, 1 May 70, AP; Memo, President for Kissinger, 25 May 70, President's Personal file, NP; Msg, Maj Gen Bautz CHU 714 to Lt Gen Davison, 14 May 70, sub: PW-COSVN Signal Unit, AP.

35. Msg, Abrams MAC 5871 to Wheeler, 1 May 70, AP; Frank Reynolds, ABC Evening News, 10 May 70, RTDD.

36. "The Gallup Poll—51 Pct Support Nixon on Cambodia Venture," *Washington Post,* 5 May 70; Harris, *The Anguish of Change,* pp. 71, 217–20; Louis Harris, "52% Condemn Protests But Oppose Ban," *Philadelphia Inquirer,* 1 Jun 70.

37. Memo, Alexander P. Butterfield for Members of the Cabinet, 7 May 70, sub: Briefing Material, LP; "At War with War," *Time,* 18 May 70, pp. 6–10; "Kent State Martyrdom That Shook the Country," *Time,* 18 May 70, p. 13.

38. Msg, Moorer JCS 6037 to McCain, 1 May 70, AP; John W. Finney, "Nixon Promises to Quit Cambodia in 3 to 7 Weeks," *New York Times,* 6 May 70.

39. "Laird Says Thousands Have Already Left Cambodia," *New York Times,* 13 May 70; Msg, Haig 592 to Kissinger, 21 May 70, Haig Special file, NP.

40. Interv, Col Chandler P. Robbins with Lt Gen Arthur S. Collins, Jr., 1982, MHI. See also Msg, McCown CTO 486 to Abrams, 1 May 70, AP; "In Search of an Elusive Foe," *Time,* 18 May 70.

41. Henry Kamm, "Phnompenh Given No Prior Notice," *New York Times,* 2 May 70; Max Frankel, "Rogers and Laird Termed Doubtful," *New York Times,* 6 May 70; John R. Woodruff, "Drive Splits U.S. Embassy," *Baltimore Sun,* 3 May 70.

42. Memos, Patrick Buchanan for the President, n.d. [mid-May], attachment to Memo, Herb Klein for H. R. Haldeman, 18 Jun 70; Mort Allen for Jeb Magruder et al., 11 May 70, sub: Major Stories of Week of May 4th, Haldeman, NP; Record of Chief of Staff Telecon with Henkin, 1515, 7 May 70, sub: Cronkite Interview, WP.

43. James P. Streba, "New U.S. Thrusts in Cambodia Open Two More Fronts," *New York Times*, 7 May 70; "Carrot and Stick," *Newsweek*, 25 May 70.

44. Ltr, Cutrona to David Mason, Bureau Chief, AP, Saigon, n.d., 334-74-593, Bad Guy file, NARA. Also see George Esper Disaccreditation file, 72A821, NARA.

45. Arnett is quoted in "Spiking the Loot," *Newsweek*, 18 May 70, p. 76.

46. Msg, Saigon 7214 to State, J. Lowenstein and R. Moose for Carl Marcy, Senate Foreign Relations Committee, 11 May 70, AP; "The Battle for Snuol: An Instant Editorial," *Washington Post*, 7 May 70.

47. "Spiking the Loot," p. 76; Sigal, *Reporters and Officials*, p. 32; Interv, author with Arnett, 14 Oct 92.

48. Memo, Buchanan for the President, n.d., attachment to Memo, Klein for Haldeman, 18 Jun 70; Memo, the President for Haldeman, 11 May 70, Haldeman, NP; Msg, Wheeler JCS/CJCS 6172 to Abrams, 5 May 70, AP.

49. Memo, Laird for the President, 7 May 70, sub: Cambodian Operations, LP; Memo, the President for Haldeman, 11 May 70, Haldeman, NP.

50. "Cambodia: Now It's 'Operation Buy Time,'" *Time*, 25 May 70, p. 28; Msg, Abrams MAC 6017 to Wheeler, 4 May 70, AP; Msg, Abrams MAC 6264 to Wheeler, 8 May 70, AP.

51. Msg, Abrams MAC 7169 to Wheeler, 26 May 70, WP; Msg, Abrams MAC 7018 to Wheeler, 23 May 70, sub: General Haig Visit, AP; Memo, Maj Matthew P. Caulfield for Comdr Howe, [Jun 70,] DDI; Msg, Wheeler JCS 7115 to Abrams, 21 May 70, AP.

52. Fact Sheet, Impact on the Enemy of Supply Losses in Cambodia, 16 May 70, attachment to Memo, OASD SA for Comdr Howe, sub: Request for Information, DDI; Memo, Haldeman for Klein, 19 May 70, Klein, NP.

53. Orr Kelly, "Red Units Rebelled in Fishhook," *Washington Star*, 12 May 70; Gary Shepard, CBS Morning News, 13 May 70, RTDD.

54. "Cambodia: Now It's 'Operation Buy Time,'" *Time*, 25 May 70, p. 28; Msg, Col. L. Gordon Hill OASDPA 6916 to Col A. Lynn, USAF, CINCPAC PAO, 18 May 70, sub: *Newsweek*, DDI.

55. Msg, Wheeler JCS/CJCS 6172 to Abrams, McCain, 5 May 72; Msg, Cutrona MAC 6794 to Hill, 19 May 70, sub: *Newsweek*, DDI.

56. John E. Woodruff, "Communists Forming Base for Long Cambodia Struggle," *Baltimore Sun*, 29 May 70; "Just How Important Are Those Caches?" *Time*, 1 Jun 70, p. 27; James P. Sterba, "Cambodian Foray After a Month," *New York Times*, 30 May 70.

57. Memo, Buchanan for the President, n.d. [mid-May], attachment to Memo, Klein for Haldeman, 18 Jun 70, Haldeman, NP.

58. Memo, the President for H. R. Haldeman, 11 May 70; Memo, H. R. Haldeman for Klein, 11 Jun 70, Haldeman, NP.

59. Memo, Mort Allen for Jeb Magruder et al., 6 Jul 70, sub: Major Stories of Week of June 29; Memo, Jim Keogh for Bob Haldeman, 24 Jun 70, with attachments; quote, Memo, Mort Allen to Jeb Magruder, et al., 8 Jun 70, sub: Major Stories of Week of June 1, Haldeman, NP.

60. Transcript, n.d., sub: John Laurence Report, attachment to Memo, Haldeman for Klein, 11 Jun 70, Klein, NP.

61. "Vietnamizing Cambodia," *New York Times,* 24 May 70.

62. Safer's report is excerpted in Marvin Barrett, ed., *A. I. du Pont–Columbia University Survey of Broadcast Journalism, 1969–1970: Years of Challenge, Year of Crisis* (New York: Grosset and Dunlap, 1970), p. 145; Interv, author with Gen Joseph F. H. Cutrona, 28 May 87, CMH.

63. Memo, Allen for Magruder et al., 11 May 70, sub: Major Stories of Week of May 4th; James McCartney, "Nixon Using Big Guns to Plug for Cambodia," *Philadelphia Inquirer,* 16 May 70.

64. MFR, OASD SA, 4 Feb 71, sub: The War in Cambodia—An Overview, LP.

CHAPTER 15. A CHANGE OF DIRECTION

1. Memo, Pursley for Laird, 20 May 70, sub: Vietnam Special Studies Group, 330-76-067, LP; Fact Book, 3 Aug 70, sub: JCS Meeting, 330-76-076, LP; Fact Sheet, 19 Oct 71, sub: Ammunition Shipped to Southeast Asia During CY 1970, 330-76-197, LP.

2. [AP,] "2 U.S. Agents in S. Viet Pose as Reporters," *Chicago Tribune,* 29 Jan 70; [AP,] "Reprimand Given in Saigon Incident of False Newsmen," *New York Times,* 7 Feb 70. Msg, Abrams MAC 1319 to Wheeler, 27 Jan 70, sub: Alleged Press Accreditation of Intelligence Agency, WP.

3. Ltr, Leonard to the author, 17 Oct 90; Intervs, author with Comdr Joseph Lorfano, Special Assistant for Southeast Asia, 22 Aug 73; Maj Gen Winant Sidle, 12 Jul 73, 26 Oct 88, CMH.

4. Intervs, author with Lorfano, 22 Aug 73; Sidle, 12 Jul 73.

5. Interv, author with Maj Charles Johnson, USMC, former MACV briefer, 2 Aug 73, CMH.

6. [UPI,] 22 Jan 71, DDI.

7. Ltr, Leonard to the author, 17 Oct 90; Intervs, author with Lorfano, 22 Aug 1973; Sidle, 26 Nov 90; Kinnard, *The War Managers,* pp. 124–35.

8. Interv, author with Maj Michael Davidson, 5 May 81, CMH.

9. Interv, author with Col Robert M. Cook, 22 May 87.

10. Msgs, McCain to Abrams, 13 Oct 70, sub: News Media Accreditation and Support; Abrams MAC 14147 to McCain, 30 Oct 70; Abrams MAC 14914 to McCain, 19 Nov 70, AP.

11. Interv, author with Col Perry Stevens, PAO, MR1, 1970–71, 25 Apr 89.

12. Barry L. Sherman, "The Peabody Collection: Vietnam on Television, Television on Vietnam, 1962–1975," *1987 American Film Institute Video Festival* (Los Angeles: American Film Institute, 1987), pp. 28–31; Msgs, Saigon 19213 to State, 6 Dec 70, sub: Luce and Morrow Cases; Saigon 838 to State, 19 Jan 71, sub: Don Luce; Saigon 6918 to State, 6 May 71, sub: Don Luce.

13. Memo for the Press, Col Joseph F. H. Cutrona, 14 Oct 69, 72A5121, JUSPAO Papers, NARA.

14. Msgs, State 119666 to Saigon, 25 Jul 70, sub: Treatment of Prisoners; Saigon 13816 to State, 9 Jul 69, sub: Discussion of Prisoners in Private Meeting; Memo, G. Warren Nutter, I-25620-70 for Secretary of Defense, 17 Nov 70, sub: PW/MIA-Efforts, DDI; Msg, State TOSEC 186 to Saigon, Acting Secretary to Berger, 8 Jul 70, sub: Con Son, AP; Ltr, Melvin Laird to William P. Rogers, 31 Jan 71, FAIM/IR.

15. MFR, Frank E. Walton, 2 Jul 70, sub: Congressional Visit to Con Son Island, CMH.

16. Msg, Saigon 10622 to State, 4 Jul 70, sub: CODEL Montgomery—Visit to Con Son Prison, AP; *Facts on File,* 9–15 Jul 70, 30:494.

17. George C. Wilson, "Viet Prison Whitewash Charged," *Washington Post,* 7 Jul 70; Msgs, State 107856 to Saigon, 8 Jul 70, sub: Press Reports Re Con Son Island Prison Conditions; State 112530 to Saigon, 15 Jul 70, AP.

18. Kaiser, "U.S. Denies Responsibility for 'Tiger Cages' at Conson"; Msg, State 108819 to Saigon, 9 Jul 70, AP; Memo, Herbert G. Klein for John R. Brown III, 14 Jul 70, sub: Action Memorandum P-483, Action Memos, NP.

19. Msg, Abrams MAC 13649 to McCain, 16 Oct 70, sub: ICRC Inspection of Phu Quoc PW Camp, AP.

20. MFR, Phil Odeen, OASD SA, 19 May 71, sub: Vietnamization Meeting with Secretary Laird, Thayer Papers, CMH.

21. Msgs, Saigon 20296 to State, 29 Dec 70, sub: Don Luce; Saigon 19213 to State, 6 Dec 70, sub: Luce and Morrow Cases; State 53095 to Saigon, 30 Mar 71, sub: Don Luce; Saigon 6518 to State, 29 Apr 71, sub: Alleged Expulsion of Don Luce.

22. Msgs, Saigon 6518 to State, 29 Apr 71, sub: Alleged Expulsion of Don Luce; State 6918 to Saigon, 6 May 71, sub: Don Luce; Saigon 77428 to State, 5 May 71, sub: Don Luce.

23. Msg, Saigon 7348 to State, 12 May 71, sub: Don Luce.

24. Debriefing Rpt (RCS-CSFOR-74), 7 Jan 71, Debriefing Report by Lt. Gen. Arthur S. Collins, 330-76-197, Viet 381 (Feb–Apr) 1971, LP.

25. Msgs, Maj Gen Woolnough, CG, CONARC, MRO 1269 to Westmoreland, 10 Sep 70, and Gen Bruce Palmer, VCSA, WDC 16495 to Westmoreland, 9 Sep 70, both WP.

26. "Who Wants to Be the Last American Killed in Vietnam?" *New York Times,* 19 Sep 71; Kevin Buckley, "'You Can Have Your Own Little Castle,'" *Newsweek,* 11 Jan 71, p. 31; "Defense Report: Draftees Shoulder Burden of Fighting and Dying in Vietnam," *National Journal,* 15 Aug 70; "Of Lifers, Grunts and Morale in This 'Crummy' War," *Philadelphia Inquirer,* 5 Jan 71; John Saar, "You Can't Just Hand Out Orders," *Life,* 23 Oct 70.

27. Msg, McCaffrey ARV 3063 to Kerwin, 29 Oct 70, McCaffrey Papers, CMH; Haynes Johnson and George Wilson, *Army in Anguish* (Washington, D.C.: Washington Post, Pocket Books, 1972), p. 83.

28. Jack Laurence, CBS Evening News, 9 Apr 70, RTDD.

29. Msg, Maj Gen Roberts, CG, 1st Cav Div (Airmobile), FCV 490 to Lt Gen Ewell, CG, IIFFV, 7 Apr 70, AP.

30. Laurence, CBS Evening News, 9 Apr 70.

31. [AP,] "GI's Who Defied Order Praised by the Army," *Washington Star,* 13 Apr 70.

32. Walter Cronkite, CBS Evening News, 24 Apr 70, RTDD; Ltr, Jerry Friedheim to Senator Lowell P. Wicker, 15 Jun 70, 330-76-067, LP.

33. Msg, Lt Gen Sutherland, CG, XXIV Corps, QTR 582 to Abrams, 29 Mar 71, McCaffrey Papers, CMH.

34. Howard K. Smith, ABC Evening News, 22 Mar 71, RTDD; R. D. Heinl, Jr., "Troop B's Mutiny Signals Downfall of Army in Viet," *Detroit News,* 25 Mar 71.

35. Harry Reasoner, ABC Evening News, 11 Oct 71, RTDD; "South Vietnam: A Question of Protection," *Time,* 25 Oct 71; Craig Whitney, "Army Says Some G.I.'s Balked Briefly at Patrol," *New York Times,* 12 Oct 71.

36. Nicholas Proffitt, "Soldiers Who Refuse to Die," *Newsweek,* 25 Oct 71.

37. Wendell Merick, "Sagging Morale in Vietnam," *U.S. News & World Report*, 25 Jan 71; Bruce Biossat, "'Fragging' Officers," *Washington Daily News*, 21 Jan 71.

38. Eugene Linden, "The Demoralization of an Army," *Saturday Review*, 8 Jan 72, p. 12.

39. Memo, Col Robert M. Cook for Chief of Staff, MACV, 31 Jan 72, sub: Result of MACIG Field Inquiry into Alleged Racial Incidents, CMH.

40. Henry F. Ackerman, He Was Always There: The U.S. Army Chaplain Ministry in the Vietnam Conflict [unpublished ms, U.S. Army, Office of the Chief of Chaplains, 1988], p. 311; Memo, T. H. Moorer for Secretary of Defense, 20 Jul 71, sub: Discipline in the Armed Forces, 330-76-201, LP.

41. Biossat, "'Fragging' Officers"; Talking Paper, USARV IO, 31 Dec 70, sub: Reply to AP, 72A6994, USARVIO Papers, NARA.

42. Interv, author with Peter Arnett, 6 Sep 88, CMH; Ackerman, He Was Always There, p. 313.

43. [UPI,] "GI Pot Smoking Called 'Epidemic,'" *Washington Daily News*, 18 Aug 70; James Sterba, "G.I.'s Find Marijuana Is Cheap and Plentiful," *New York Times*, 2 Sep 70; Joel H. Kaplan, MD, with Christopher S. Wren, "Does Our Army Fight on Drugs?" *Look*, 16 Jun 70; Msg, Defense 15220 to Leonard, CINFO MACV, 13 Nov 70, sub: CBS News Story, DDI.

44. Msg, Lt Gen Collins, CG, IFFV, NHT 2228 to McCaffrey, 15 Nov 70, CMH; Msg, Lorfano Defense 15268 to Leonard, 13 Nov 70, sub: Statement Re: Marijuana at Fire Base Aries, DDI.

45. Msg, Leonard MAC 15689 to Lorfano, 9 Dec 70, sub: AP Story on 101st Div "Rating System," DDI.

46. Memo, Col Alfred J. Mock, USARV IO, for DCG, USARV, 22 Aug 70, sub: Response to Press Queries Concerning Drug Usage in USARV, 73A6994, USARVIO Papers, NARA; Fact Sheet, untitled, 30 Oct 70, DDI.

47. Memo, Charles Colson for Bud Krough, 22 Jun 71, Scali, NP; Msg, Abrams MAC 6527 to Gen L. D. Clay, Comdr, Seventh AF, et al., 7 Jul 71, sub: Drug Abuse Counter Offensive, AP; Msg, Lorfano to Col Phillip H. Stevens, MACOI, 28 Oct 71, sub: Release of Statistics on MEDEVAC of Drug Abusers, DDI.

48. Lee N. Robbins, Executive Office of the President, Special Action Office for Drug Abuse Prevention, Final Report, *The Vietnam Drug User Returns* (Washington, D.C.: Government Printing Office, 1973), pp. vii–ix, 29–44.

49. Msg, Lt Gen McCaffrey ARV 261 to Maj Gen Brown, CG, IFFV, 26 Jan 71, McCaffrey Papers, CMH.

50. Msg, Maj Gen Brown, CG, IFFV, NHT 217 to Abrams, 27 Jan 71, sub: NBC News Story, AP.

51. Msg, Saigon 6693 to State, 3 May 71, sub: Specific Problems and Actions to Be Taken to Reduce Smuggling and Traffic in Narcotics.

52. Aerogramme, Saigon A-113 to State, 21 Jul 71, sub: Significant Events and Activities in Vietnamese Efforts to Suppress Drug Traffic, FAIM/IR; Mark Gayn, "Drugs: Sordid Fuel for Kings and Wars," *Chicago Daily News*, 29 Aug 71; Henry Kamm, "Drive Fails to Halt Drug Sale in Vietnam," *New York Times*, 30 Aug 71; Phil Brady, NBC Nightly News, 15 Jul 71, RTDD.

53. Msg, Kissinger WH 1040 to Bunker, 27 Apr 71, Bunker Backchannels, NP.

54. MFR, Phil Odeen, 18 Nov 70, sub: Vietnamization Meeting with Secretary Laird, Thayer Papers, CMH.

CHAPTER 16. INCURSION INTO LAOS

1. MFR, 19 Jan 71, sub: Meeting Between the President, Rogers, Laird, Kissinger . . . et al., 18 Jan 71, Special Operations file, NP.

2. Ibid.; JCS History, 1971–1973, p. 19; Talking Paper, Feb 71, sub: Lam Son 719: February 1971, Haig, NP.

3. Msgs, McCain to Abrams, 6 Dec 70; Abrams MAC 15603 to McCain, 7 Dec 70, both AP; Memo, Haig for Kissinger, 29 Jan 71, sub: Meeting with the Vice President et al., 1 Feb 71, Haig Chron, NP.

4. Memo, Haig for Kissinger, 29 Jan 71, sub: Meeting with the Vice President et al., 1 Feb 71.

5. MFR, 19 Jan 71, sub: Meeting Between the President, Rogers, Laird et al.; Talking Paper, Feb 71, sub: Lam Son 719: February 1971.

6. Msgs, CINCPAC to CJCS, 14 Feb 71, 330-76-207, LP; Abrams MAC 775 to Moorer, 24 Jan 71, sub: Cross Border Operation, AP.

7. Msgs, McCain to Moorer, 26 Jan 71, sub: Cross Border Operations, AP; Abrams to McCain, Moorer, 28 Jan 71, sub: Planning for Laos; Moorer 2394 to McCain, 29 Jan 71; McCain to Moorer, Abrams, 29 Jan 71, sub: Planning for Laos, AP.

8. Msg, Abrams to McCain, 29 Jan 71, sub: Planning for Laos–Lam Son 719, AP; Ltr, Leonard to the author, 17 Oct 90, CMH.

9. Msg, MACOI to CG, 101st Abn, et al., 29 Jan 71, sub: Press Guidance, AP.

10. Msg, MACV to CINCPAC, 30 Jan 71, sub: Press Briefing, AP.

11. Msgs, Moorer JCS 2614 to Abrams, 30 Jan 71, sub: Planning for Laos; Abrams to McCain, Moorer, 30 Jan 71, sub: Planning for Laos, AP.

12. MFR, NMCC, 31 Jan 71, sub: News Media Leak, DDI.

13. "News Blackout Continues in Indochina," *Washington Post,* 1 Feb 71; "Viet Moves Shrouded in Secrecy," *Baltimore Sun,* 1 Feb 71; Tillman Durdin, "Laotians Report No Word of an Incursion by Saigon," *New York Times,* 1 Feb 71; Terence Smith, "U.S. B-52's Strike Foe's Laos Bases Around the Clock," *New York Times,* 1 Feb 71; [AP,] Robert Dobkin [AP], 1 Feb 71; Chalmers Roberts, "Laos Border Activities Still a Secret," *Washington Post,* 2 Feb 71.

14. Terence Smith, "U.S. Officials Say Allied Drive Is on in Area Near Laos," *New York Times,* 2 Feb 71; Marvin Kalb, CBS Radio Broadcast, 8:30 A.M., 2 Feb 71; Dan Rather, CBS Evening News, 2 Feb 71, both NP.

15. Msg, Abrams to McCain, 2 Feb 71, sub: Press Guidance; James McCartney, "Mum's the Word on Secret War in Laos," *Philadelphia Inquirer,* 3 Feb 71; "Concealing the Facts on Laos," *St. Louis Post-Dispatch,* 3 Feb 71; "Blindfolding the Public," *Chicago Daily News,* 3 Feb 71; Memo, Mort Allen for H. R. Haldeman, 3 Feb 71, sub: Notations for Feb. 2–3 News Summaries, Buchanan, NP.

16. Msg, Moorer 3224 to McCain, Abrams, 4 Feb 71, sub: Press Guidance, AP; MACV Advisory, 4 Feb 71, DDI.

17. [UPI,] "Writers Rap U.S. Curb on Viet News," *Chicago Tribune,* 6 Feb 71.

18. Maj. Gen. Nguyen Duy Hinh, *Lam Son 719,* Indochina Monographs (Washington, D.C.: U.S. Army Center of Military History, 1979), p. 82.

19. Ltr, Leonard to the author, 17 Oct 90.

20. Msg, State 19640 to Saigon, 4 Feb 71.

21. Memo, Ron Ziegler for Henry Kissinger, 5 Feb 71, sub: Public Relations Scenario for Phase II, Operations in Laos and Cambodia, NP.

22. Msgs, Saigon 1709 to State, 5 Feb 71; State 20549 to Saigon, 5 Feb 71; State to Saigon, number illegible, 6 Feb 71, CMH.

23. Memo, Charles Colson for H. R. Haldeman, 11 Feb 71, sub: Getting Our Line Out on Laos and Cambodia, Haldeman, NP.

24. MACOI Memo for Correspondents 39-71, 8 Feb 71, 334-74-593, NARA; Memo, Buchanan for the President, 10 Feb 71, sub: Notes from Leadership Meeting, February 9, 1971, Buchanan Chron, NP.

25. Msgs, Defense 3781 to All Commands, 11 Feb 71, sub: Background Briefing by Senior Defense Official, 319-84-051, LP; Abrams to McCain, 14 Feb 71, sub: Backgrounder Briefing, AP.

26. Interv, author with Friedheim, 12 Aug 91, CMH.

27. Memo, Lorfano for Henkin, 12 Feb 71, sub: Press Facilities/Services, DDI.

28. Msg, Sutherland QTR 45 to Abrams, 7 Feb 71, AP; Interv, author with Col Perry Stevens, 25 Apr 89, CMH.

29. Msg, Abrams to McCain, Moorer, 12 Feb 71, sub: Lam Son 719, AP.

30. Msg, McCain to Moorer, Abrams, 14 Feb 71, AP.

31. Msg, Moorer 4057 to McCain, Abrams, 14 Feb 71, sub: Lam Son 719, AP; "Airstrip Being Rebuilt," *New York Times,* 11 Feb 71; [UPI,] "Newsmen Report Seeing U.S. Troops Inside Laos," *Washington Star,* 12 Feb 71; Msg, Abrams to McCain, Moorer, 12 Feb 71, sub: Lam Son 719, AP.

32. Memo, Theodore Eliot for Kissinger, 9 Feb 71, sub: U.S. and Foreign Reactions to Operation LAMSON, FAIM/IR; Max Frankel, "Purpose in Laos: A Shorter War," *New York Times,* 9 Feb 71.

33. U.S. Department of State, Status Reports 1, 4, and 5, for 10, 11, and 12 Feb 71, sub: Status Report on Operations in Laos and Cambodia, NP.

34. Martin Weil, "Antiwar Leaders 'Outraged' over Laos," *Washington Post,* 9 Feb 71; Martin Arnold, "Thousands in U.S. Protest on Laos," *New York Times,* 11 Feb 71; Donald E. Graham, "War Protest Calls On Young," *Washington Post,* 11 Feb 71; George Gallup, "Sentiment Grows Markedly to Quit Vietnam Before '72," *Baltimore Sun,* 31 Jan 71; Michael Wheeler, *Lies, Damn Lies, and Statistics: The Manipulation of Public Opinion in America* (New York: Liveright, 1976), p. 147; "Hawks Still Flying," *Omaha World-Herald,* 18 Feb 71.

35. Walter Cronkite, CBS Evening News, 12 Feb 71, RTDD; "Toll for 5 Days One of Highest Since April '67," *Washington Star,* 12 Feb 71; News Summary, 17 Feb 71, Annotated News Summaries, NP.

36. Msg, Sutherland DNG 443 to Abrams, 14 Feb 7, AP.

37. Msg, Abrams MAC 1554 to Sutherland, 13 Feb 71.

38. Msg, Moorer 4057 to Abrams, 14 Feb 71, sub: Lam Son 719; Memo, Jon Howe for Kissinger, 24 Mar 71, sub (February 8–March 20), Telephone Extracts; Msg, Abrams to Moorer, McCain, 14 Feb 71, AP.

39. Pool Rpt, Air Force One—Homestead to Andrews, 15 Feb 71, DDI.

40. Hinh, *Lam Son 719,* p. 79; Memo, Joe Shergalis for General Haig, 21 Feb 71, sub: Morning Cable Summary for 21 Feb 71; Memo, Dave Clark for Jim Fazio, 21 Feb 71, sub: Afternoon Cable Summary for 21 Feb 71, Situation Room Cable Summaries, NP.

41. Walter Cronkite, CBS Evening News, 19 Feb 71, RTDD; Craig Whitney, "Saigon's Rangers Driven from an Outpost in Laos," *New York Times,* 22 Feb 71.

42. Msg, Abrams to Moorer, McCain, 21 Feb 71, AP; quote from Msg, McCain to Abrams, 23 Feb 71, sub: LAM SON 719, AP.

43. Memo for President's file, Haig, 25 Feb 71, sub: The President's Meeting with Moorer and Kissinger in the Oval Office, Howe Chron, NP.

44. Msg, Moorer JCS 4610 to Abrams, 23 Feb 71, sub: LAM SON 719, AP.

45. Msg, Laird 4539 to Abrams, 22 Feb 71, AP.

46. Msg, Abrams to Secretary of Defense, 23 Feb 71, sub: Public Affairs in Support of RVNAF Operations, AP.

47. Msgs, Bunker Saigon 163 to the White House, 23 Feb 71; Leonard MAC 2310 to Henkin, 4 Mar 71, DDI.

48. Harry Reasoner, "ABC Correspondents Discuss Job of Reporting on the War," ABC News, 2 Apr 71, RTDD; Interv, author with Col Perry Stevens, 25 Apr 89; Cronkite, CBS Evening News, 9 Apr 71, RTDD.

49. Msgs, Sutherland QTR 135 to McCaffrey, 23 Feb 71, AP; McCaffrey, ARV 946 to Lt Gen Williams, 16 Mar 71, McCaffrey Papers, CMH.

50. Backchannel Messages Concerning Outlook for Operation and Future Plans, 21 Mar 71, app. II to Telephone Extracts; Telephone Conversations Between Dr. Kissinger and Defense Department Officers, attachment to Telephone Extracts.

51. Telephone Extracts; Memo, Haig for President's file, 25 Feb 71, sub: The President's Meeting With Moorer and Kissinger . . . (12:05–1:09 P.M.); "Red Tanks Hit So. Viet Post in Laos," *Chicago Tribune,* 26 Feb 71; "Transcript of President Nixon's News Conference," *New York Times,* 5 Mar 71; White House News Summary, 26 Feb 71, NP.

52. Msg, JCS 4851 to Unified and Specified Commands, 25 Feb 71, sub: News Briefing by SECDEF, February 24, 1971, 319-84-051, LP; quotes from "Transcript of President Nixon's News Conference."

53. Memo, Mort Allin for Haldeman, 25 Feb 71, sub: Notations for February 25 News Summary, Buchanan, NP; White House News Summary for 28 Feb 71, NP; Marvin Kalb, CBS Evening News, 26 Feb 71, RTDD; Alvin Shuster, "South Vietnamese Base in Laos Reported Under Heavy Attack," *New York Times,* 26 Feb 71; Handwritten Note on White House News Summary, 28 Feb 71, Annotated News Summaries, NP.

54. Memos, Joe Shergalis for Jim Fazio, 24 Feb 71; McManus for Clark, 25 Feb 71, Situation Room Cable Summaries, NP; quote from Telephone Extracts.

55. Msg, Sutherland QTR 197 to Abrams, 2 Mar 71, AP; quote, Msg, Sutherland QTR 237 to Abrams, 2 Mar 71, AP.

56. White House News Summary, 27 February–6 March, 8 March 71, NP; NBC Saturday Evening News, 27 Feb 71, RTDD; [AP,] "Laos, Cambodia Thrusts Seen Foiling Red Plans," *Washington Star,* 2 Mar 71.

57. Msg, Sutherland QTR 306 to Abrams, 10 Mar 71, AP; Hinh, *Lam Son 719,* pp. 97 f.; quote, Msg, Kissinger WH 1012 to Bunker, 9 Mar 71, Backchannels, Bunker, NP.

CHAPTER 17. SAVING FACE

1. Marvin Barrett, ed., *A. I. du Pont–Columbia University Survey of Broadcast Journalism, 1970–1971: A State of Siege* (New York: Grosset and Dunlap, 1971), pp. 151–71

(hereafter cited as *Survey of Broadcast Journalism*); George Gallup, "The Gallup Poll," *Washington Post,* 7 Mar 71; Louis Harris, "The Harris Survey," *Washington Post,* 8 Mar 71.

2. "Pentagon Aide Says CBS Shifted Words," *Washington Post,* 4 Mar 71.

3. Barrett, *Survey of Broadcast Journalism,* p. 37.

4. Iver Peterson, "U.S. Copter Pilots Question the Risks," *New York Times,* 7 Mar 71; Steve Bell, ABC Evening News, 3 Mar 71, RTDD.

5. Craig R. Whitney, "Saigon's Cambodia Drive in Confusion," *New York Times,* 2 Mar 71.

6. Msg, Abrams to McCain, Moorer, 8 Mar 71; Note, Haig to Kissinger, 8 Mar 71, Haig Chron, NP.

7. Msg, Kissinger to Bunker, 9 Mar 71; MFR, David R. Young, 11 Mar 71, sub: Briefing, Laos and Cambodia Briefings, NP, cited hereafter as Kissinger Briefing Notes; Telecon, Kissinger with Moorer, 13 Mar 71, in Extracts from Telephone Conversations Between Dr. Kissinger and Defense Department Officers, p. 13.

8. Memo, Buchanan for President's file, 9 Mar 71, sub: Notes from GOP Leadership Meeting, Buchanan Chron, NP; MACOI, Background Briefing, 10 Mar 71, DDI.

9. Alvin Shuster, "Enemy Supply Traffic Increases North of Saigon's Drive in Laos," *New York Times,* 5 Mar 71; MACV Backgrounder, 10 Mar 71; Transcript, "Interview with Admiral Moorer," ABC News, "Issues and Answers," 14 Mar 71, DDI.

10. [AP,] "Viet Forces in Laos Said to Retreat," *Washington Post,* 18 Mar 71.

11. Msg, Sutherland QTR 843 to Abrams, 18 Mar 71, AP.

12. Telecon, Kissinger with Moorer, 18 Mar 71, Extracts from Telephone Conversations Between Dr. Kissinger and Defense Department Officers, p. 13.

13. Msg, Haig Saigon 641 to Kissinger, 19 Mar 71, Haig Chron, NP; Murray Marder, "Saigon Starts 'Methodical' Laos Pullout," *Washington Post,* 19 Mar 71; David S. Broder, "Agnew Calls Pullback in Laos 'Orderly Retreat,'" *Washington Post,* 20 Mar 71; James McCartney, "S. Vietnamese 'Succeed' by Backing Away," *Philadelphia Inquirer,* 18 Mar 71.

14. MFR, 22 Mar 71, sub: Briefing of March 22, 1971, Kissinger Briefing Notes.

15. Background Briefing in Saigon, 21 Mar 71, DDI.

16. Tom Streithorst, NBC Nightly News, 22 Mar 71, RTDD.

17. Memo of Conversation, 24 Mar 71, sub: Congressional Briefing, Presidential/ HAK Memcons, NP.

18. Memo, Charles Colson for H. R. Haldeman, 22 Mar 71, White House Action Memos, NP; Barrett, *Survey of Broadcast Journalism,* p. 39.

19. [UPI,] "Agnew Assails CBS for Show on Pentagon," *Philadelphia Bulletin,* 19 Mar 71; [UPI,] "CBS-TV Challenged by Agnew," *Boston Herald-Traveler,* 21 Mar 71.

20. Tad Szulc, "Nixon Says Drive by Saigon Helps Reach Key Goals," *New York Times,* 23 Mar 71. Nixon is quoted in Barrett, *Survey of Broadcast Journalism,* pp. 40–41; Robert B. Semple, Jr., "Nixon Suggests Press Distorts Policy," *New York Times,* 23 Mar 71.

21. "'Hacking' It in Laos," *Philadelphia Bulletin,* 23 Mar 71; "The Withdrawal from Laos," *Boston Globe,* 23 Mar 71.

22. Msg, Sutherland QTR 515 to Abrams, 25 Mar 71, AP.

23. Msg, Sutherland QTR 518 to Abrams, 25 Mar 71, AP.

24. Memo, Haig for the President's files, 26 Mar 71, sub: Meeting with the President, Haig Chron, NP; Msg, Sutherland QTR 567 to Abrams, 28 Mar 71, AP; Hinh, *Lam Son 719,* p. 129.

25. "Laos Jury Still Out," *Omaha World-Herald,* 27 Mar 71; Richard Egan, "A Look

at the Balance Sheet on the Laos Affair," *National Observer,* 29 Mar 71; "Broadcast License: CBS Has Forfeited Access to the Nation's Airwaves," *Barron's Magazine,* 29 Mar 71.

26. ABC Evening News, 1 Apr 71, RTDD; Daniel Southerland, "Laos Shortfall Stirs Sticky Queries," *Christian Science Monitor,* 29 Mar 71; "Assessing the Laos Invasion," *Time,* 5 Apr 71, p. 25.

27. MACV History, 1971, p. E-9; Background Briefing with Dr. Henry A. Kissinger, 7 Apr 71, DDI; Memo, Howe for Kissinger, 24 Mar 71, Telephone Extracts.

28. H. R. Haldeman, *The Haldeman Diaries: Inside the White House* (New York: Putnam, 1994), entry for 23 Mar 71, p. 259.

29. MFR, Jeanne W. Davis, 23 Mar 71, sub: Large Staff Meeting, March 23, Laos-Cambodia Briefings, NP.

30. Neil Sheehan, "Should We Have War Crime Trials?" *New York Times Book Review,* 28 Mar 71, p. 1; Memo, Sidle for Col R. W. Argo, Jr., OCSA, 17 Aug 71, sub: Study Group Report, CMH; Memo, Walter Hermes for Brig Gen James L. Collins, 7 May 71, CMH.

31. Howard Tuckner, ABC Evening News, 22, 23, and 24 Jun 71, RTDD; Transcript, "Issues and Answers," 27 Jun 71, CMH; MACVIG, MIV-67-71, 26 Aug 71, sub: Report of Investigation Concerning Col. David Hackworth, 334-77-0074, NARA; MFR, Phil Odeen, 22 Sep 71, sub: Vietnamization Meeting with Secretary Laird, 330-76-197, LP; David Hackworth and Julie Sherman, *About Face: The Odyssey of an American Warrior* (New York: Simon and Schuster, 1989), pp. 803–4.

32. Rpts of Investigation, 13 Apr 71, 21 Jun 71, sub: Unauthorized Disclosure of Classified Defense Information, Young files, NP; Kissinger, *The White House Years,* pp. 729–30.

33. Ibid.; Memo, Fred Malek for Haldeman, 2 Nov 71, sub: Progress Report on Leaks, Young files, NP.

34. Interv, John Ehrlichman with YN1 Charles Radford, 23 Dec 71, Young Project, NP.

35. Memo, David Young for the President, n.d., sub: Record of Investigation of . . . Jack Anderson Articles, December 14 and 16, 1971, Young files, NP; Stephen Ambrose, *Nixon, The Triumph of a Politician, 1962–1972* (New York: Simon and Schuster, 1989), pp. 486–88.

36. Msgs, Abrams MAC 5611 to Westmoreland, 6 Jun 71, sub: 28 Mar 71 Attack on FSB Mary Ann; Baldwin ACD 483 to Abrams, 7 Apr 71, sub: Interim Report, AP.

37. Nicholas Proffitt, "The Massacre at Fire Base Mary Ann," *Newsweek,* 12 Apr 71.

38. Msg, Baldwin ACD 483 to Abrams, 7 Apr 71, sub: Interim Report.

39. Msgs, Westmoreland WDC 9882 to McCaffrey, Dep CG, USARV, 5 Jun 71; Abrams MAC 5611 to Westmoreland, 6 Jun 71, sub: 28 Mar 71 Attack on FSB Mary Ann, AP.

40. MACVIG, Rpt of Investigation, 5 Jul 71, sub: Attack on FSB Mary Ann, 334-77-0074, NARA.

41. Msgs, McCaffrey ARV 2455 to Westmoreland, 21 Jul 71, 319-81-051, NARA; Westmoreland WDC 12471 to Abrams, 13 Jul 71, sub: Attack on FSB Mary Ann, AP.

42. Msgs, Westmoreland WDC 13090 to McCaffrey, 22 Jul 71; McCaffrey ARV 2479 to Westmoreland, 23 Jul 71, AP.

43. Msg, McCaffrey ARV 2638 to Westmoreland, 5 Aug 71, sub: 28 Mar 71 Attack, 319-81-051, NARA; Msg, Westmoreland WDC 14227 to McCaffrey, 9 Aug 71, WP.

44. "General and Two Other Officers Reprimanded in Vietnam Incident," *Washington Post,* 22 Apr 72 [AP].

45. "Newsmen Say U.S. Reduces Viet Reports," *Baltimore Sun,* 17 Jan 71; Msg, Leonard MAC 3990 to Lorfano, 19 Apr 71, DDI; CBS Evening News, 8 Aug 71, RTDD; "The Army Rings a Leper's Bell," *San Francisco Chronicle,* 9 Apr 71.

46. CBS Evening News, 23 Apr 71, RTDD.

47. Msgs, Defense 4444 to MACV, Hill to IO, 22 Apr 71; Leonard MAC 3990 to Lorfano, 19 Apr 71, DDI; Ltr, Leonard to the author, 17 Oct 90, CMH.

48. Interv, author with Sidle, 15 Sep 89, CMH.

49. Ibid.

50. Msg, Sidle WDC 9874 to Abrams for Henkin, 5 Jun 71, sub: TDY of Col. (P) Gordon Hill and Assignment of Col. Phil Stevens, AP.

51. Intervs, author with Hill, 6 Mar 89, 8 Aug 89, CMH.

52. Ibid.; Ltr, Leonard to the author, 17 Oct 70.

53. Interv, author with Hill, 23 Aug 89.

54. Ibid.; Memo, Sidle for ASD PA, 24 Jan 72, sub: U.S. Public Affairs in SEA, DDI.

CHAPTER 18. THE EASTER OFFENSIVE

1. Ltr, Jerry Friedheim to Honorable Charles S. Gubser, 20 Jun 72, 330-77-0094, LP; [UPI,] Arthur Higbee, "Vietnam News Sources Dry Up as War Wanes," *Editor and Publisher,* 29 Jan 72.

2. Memo, Sidle for ASD PA, 24 Jan 72, sub: Public Affairs in Southeast Asia, DDI.

3. Sydney H. Schanberg, "The Saigon Follies: or Trying to Head Them Off at Credibility Gap," *New York Times Magazine,* 12 Nov 72, p. 38.

4. Phil Jones, CBS Evening News, 14 Jan 72, RTDD; Gen. Ngo Quang Truong, *The Easter Offensive of 1972* (Washington, D.C.: U.S. Army Center of Military History, 1980), pp. 15–41.

5. Quote, [Reuters,] "Saigon Will Tighten Its Rules on Press Coverage of War," *New York Times,* 22 Jul 71; Msg, Saigon 18880 to State, 2 Dec 71, sub: South Vietnam Rules for Press Coverage.

6. Higbee, "Vietnam News Sources Dry Up"; [Reuters,] "Reports, Then Denials, Befog Vietnam News," *New York Times,* 30 Jan 72.

7. Schanberg, "The Saigon Follies," p. 38.

8. Memo, John Scali for Chuck Colson, 25 Jan 72, sub: Your News Summary Attached, Colson Memos, NP; George W. Ashworth, "Hanoi Aim: Damaging Headlines," *Christian Science Monitor,* 21 Jan 72.

9. Lt. Gen. Phillip B. Davidson, U.S.A. (Ret.), *Vietnam at War* (Novato, Calif.: Presidio Press, 1988), pp. 673–713.

10. Ibid.

11. Interv, Dale Andrade with Maj Gen James R. Hollingsworth, U.S.A. (Ret.), 6 Nov 89, CMH.

12. Memo, Les Janka for Haig, 3 Apr 72, sub: Press Handling of Vietnam Offensive; Jon Howe Chron, NP.

13. "The War That Won't Go Away," *Newsweek,* 17 Apr 72, p. 16; "Vietnamization: A

Policy Put to the Test," *Newsweek,* 17 Apr 72, p. 18; "On Hacking It in Vietnam," *Washington Daily News,* 4 Apr 72; Jerry Greene, "Capitol Stuff," *New York Daily News,* 5 Apr 72.

14. Peter Braestrup, *Battle Lines: Report of the Twentieth Century Fund Task Force on the Military and the Media* (New York: Priority Press Publications, 1985); Arthur Higbee, "The ARVN: A Mixed Performance," *Stars and Stripes,* 28 Apr 72; Don Tate, "Frantic ARVNs Dangled from Chopper," *Washington Daily News,* 22 Apr 72.

15. Msg, Bunker Saigon 0061 to Kissinger, 12 Apr 72, sub: Current Situation in South Vietnam, Backchannels, Bunker, NP; Msg, Laird OSD 4215 to Abrams, 30 Apr 72, AP.

16. Msg, Defense 7806 to MACV, 4 Apr 72, sub: Premature Disclosure of News Information, DDI.

17. [AP] "GI Unit Balks," *Washington Star,* 11 Apr 72; "Colonel Assails Newsmen," *New York Times,* 13 Apr 72.

18. Memo, Information Officer, HQ, FRAC, for Chief, IAAD, MACOI, 28 Apr 72, sub: 12 Apr 72 Phu Bai Incident, 334-74-593, Bad Guy List, NARA.

19. Msg, Defense 9791, Friedheim to Stevens, 24 Apr 72, sub: CBS TV Interview, DDI; Interv, Dale Andrade with Hollingsworth, 6 Nov 89, CMH.

20. "Saigon Making Moves to Curb Bad-News Coverage of the War," *New York Times,* 16 Apr 72.

21. Msg, Bunker Saigon 0061 to Kissinger, 12 Apr 72, sub: Current Situation in South Vietnam, NP.

22. Memo, Laird to Assistant for National Security Affairs, 6 Apr 72, sub: Contingency Plans for Operations Against North Vietnam, Howe Chron, NP.

23. Msg, Abrams SPECAT to Moorer and McCain, 14 Apr 71, sub: Freedom Porch, Howe Chron; Msg, Haig Saigon 0064 to Kissinger, 16 Apr 72, Backchannels, Bunker, NP.

24. [UPI-033A,] 17 Apr 72, CMH; [AP] "Hanoi Raid a Success, U.S. Says," *Baltimore Sun,* 23 Apr 72. Laird is quoted in John W. Finney, "Laird Says Raids Can Continue Until Enemy Calls Off Invasion," *New York Times,* 19 Apr 72.

25. Spencer Rich and Mary Russell, "Debate over Bombing Rages on Capitol Hill," *Washington Post,* 20 Apr 72; quotes from "The Bombing Blues," *Time,* 1 May 72.

26. Memo, Alexander P. Butterfield, for Members of the Cabinet, 1 May 72, sub: Americans Strongly Support the President's Vietnam Stand, 330-77-0094, LP.

27. Msg, Haig to Bunker, 23 Apr 72, Haig Chron, NP.

28. Msg, Abrams MAC 3810 to Laird, 26 Apr 72, sub: Personal Assessment, AP; "A Report on the Military Situation in Vietnam . . . An Address by President Nixon," Department of State *Bulletin,* 15 May 72, p. 683.

29. "And the War Goes On," *Newsweek,* 8 May 72, p. 19; Briefing by Dr. Henry Kissinger to Members of White House Staff, 26 Apr 72, Haig files, NP.

30. Memo, the President for Henry Kissinger, 30 Apr 72, NP.

31. Msg, Laird OSD 4215 to Abrams, 30 Apr 72, AP.

32. Msg, Abrams MAC 4021 to Laird, 1 May 72, sub: Personal Assessment, AP.

33. [Reuters-PMS 36,] Photographer, 31 Jul 72, CMH.

34. "Setting in for the Third Indochina War," *Time,* 8 May 72, p. 28; Sydney H. Schanberg, "Convoys to Quangtri Blocked; Refugees Crowd Hue," *New York Times,* 30 Apr 72; Richard J. Levine, "South Vietnam Army Causes Rising Concern for U.S. Military Men," *Wall Street Journal,* 8 May 72.

35. "What Went Wrong in Vietnam: The Fallacies in U.S. Policy," *Newsweek,* 15 May 72, p. 24.

36. Abrams SPECAT to Moorer and McCain, 4 May 72, Howe Chron, NP; Msg, Abrams MAC 4600 to Vice President Agnew, 17 May 72, sub: MEMCON of Meeting, AP.

37. Memo, Haig for Kissinger, 5 May 72, sub: Talking Points for Your Breakfast Meeting with Secretary Laird, Haig Chron, NP.

38. Msg, Kissinger WH 2066 to Bunker, 6 May 72, Backchannels, Bunker, NP.

39. News Release, "Address by the President," 8 May 72, Colson, NP.

40. "Clamor and Caution," *Newsweek,* 22 May 72, p. 24; "Thunder All Around," *Time,* 22 May 72, p. 39; MFR, n.d., sub: The President's Vietnam Initiatives and the Media, Colson, NP; Memo, Bill Rhatican for Chuck Colson, 25 May 72, sub: Commentators, Colson, NP.

41. Memo, Nixon for Henry Kissinger, 9 May 72, President's Office files, NP.

42. Kissinger, *The White House Years,* p. 1305.

43. Msg, CNO to Naval Operations (NAVOP), 9 May 72, sub: Mine and Mine Countermeasures Information, DDI; "How the Mines Work," *Newsweek,* 22 May 72, p. 21.

44. Msg, State 142261 to Saigon, 5 Aug 72, sub: Release of Sanitized Intelligence to Media, DDI; MFR, Jerry Friedheim, 22 May 72, sub: Actions Accomplished per Monday's Discussion, 330-77-0094, LP; "How 'Smart Bombs' Are Squeezing North Vietnam," *U.S. News & World Report,* 5 Jun 72, p. 23.

45. Memo, Laird for the President, 16 Jun 72, sub: Circumstances Surrounding the Replacement of Gen. John D. Lavelle as Commander of 7th Air Force, 330-77-0094, LP.

46. Seymour M. Hersh, *The Price of Power* (New York: Summit Books, 1983), p. 507; MFR, R Adm Daniel J. Murphy, 7 Jun 72, sub: Lavelle, 330-77-0094, LP.

47. Hersh, *The Price of Power,* p. 507; Msg, Laird OSD 6406 to Abrams, 14 Jun 72; "Laird Clears Abrams on Lavelle's Bombing," *Washington Post,* 22 Jun 72; "Was Lavelle Alone?" *Newsweek,* 25 Sep 72; "The Lavelle Case," *Christian Science Monitor,* 16 Jun 72; Intervs, author with Daniel Z. Henkin, 10 Oct 86; Jerry Friedheim, 3 Oct 86, CMH.

48. Craig R. Whitney, "Hanoi Says Raids Struck at Dikes," *New York Times,* 9 May 72.

49. Anthony Lewis, "Death in Phuc Loc," *New York Times,* 22 May 72; Anthony Lewis, "Communists Report Mines at Haiphong Swept, Ships Sailing," *New York Times,* 18 May 72.

50. Benjamin Welles, "Mines Said to Hold Device for Shut Off Before Nixon Trip," *New York Times,* 14 May 72; Memo of Conversation, Haig with Selected Correspondents, 22 May 72, Haig Chron, NP.

51. "White House Aide Says Morale Is Low in Hanoi," *New York Times,* 23 May 72; Henry Bradsher, "U.S. Reports of Foe's Distress Called Old, Out of Context," *Washington Star,* 24 May 72; Memo, Les Janka for Ron Ziegler, 24 May 72, sub: Daily Press Items, Janka Guidance, NP.

52. Memo, Laird for the President, 31 Jul 72, sub: Targeting in North Vietnam.

53. Msg, State Circular 125205 to All Diplomatic Posts, 11 Jul 72, sub: Charges of Bombing North Vietnamese Dikes, DDI.

54. Msg, Belgrade 126 to State, 13 Jul 72, sub: Media on Bombing North Vietnam Dikes; Talking Paper, n.d., sub: Stories Concerning Strikes Against Dikes, DDI.

55. Talking Paper, North Vietnam: The Dike Bombing Issue, covered by Memo, OASD PA for Henkin et al., 28 Jul 72, 330-77-0094, LP; "The President's News Conference

of July 27, 1972," *Public Papers of the Presidents: Richard Nixon, 1972* (Washington, D.C.: Government Printing Office, 1974), p. 752.

56. MACV Statement to the Press, 11 Oct 72, 330-77-094, LP; Memo, Moorer CM-2258-72 for Secretary of Defense, 19 Oct 72, 330-77-0095, LP.

57. Msg, Bunker Saigon 0094 to Kissinger, 19 May 72, sub: Vietnam: Assessment, Howe Chron, NP.

58. Memo, Moorer CM-1951-72 for Secretary of Defense, 15 Jun 72, sub: The Air Campaign in North Vietnam, 330-77-0094, LP; Tad Szulc, "Hanoi Held Able to Fight 2 Years at Present Rate," *New York Times,* 13 Sep 72.

59. Memo, Phil Odeen for Kissinger, 12 Aug 72, sub: CIA Assessment, NP; Msg, Kissinger WH 2093 to Bunker, 30 Jul 72, Backchannels, Bunker, NP; President's News Conference of August 29, 1972, *Public Papers of the Presidents: Nixon,* pp. 827–31.

CHAPTER 19. ENDGAME

1. Memo, Phil Odeen for Dr. Kissinger, 6 Oct 72, sub: Vietnam Trip Report, Gen Haig's SEA Visit NP.

2. Kissinger, *The White House Years,* pp. 1341–59.

3. Ibid.

4. Stephen A. Ambrose, *Nixon: The Triumph of a Politician, 1962–1972* (New York: Simon and Schuster, 1989), pp. 627–35.

5. Msg, Haig WH 29646 to Kissinger, 23 Oct 72, HAK's Saigon Trip, NP; Msg, Kissinger WH 2293 to Bunker, 24 Oct 72; Msg, Haig WH 0081 to Col Guay, Paris, 25 Oct 72, Camp David Cables, NP.

6. Ambrose, *Nixon: The Triumph of a Politician,* pp. 644–45.

7. Excerpt from President Nixon's speech, "A Look to the Future," 2 November 72, Department of State *Bulletin,* 20 Nov 72, p. 605.

8. Msg, Negroponte to Kissinger, 14 Dec 72, sub: Hanoi's Behavior in the Negotiations; quote from Msg, Bunker Saigon 239 to Kissinger, 28 Oct 72, Backchannel Messages, NP.

9. Msg, Kennedy WHP 141 to Haig for Kissinger, 24 Nov 72, Howe Chron, NP; Ltr, Nixon to Thieu, 15 Nov 72; Msg, Kissinger WH 2257 to Bunker, 26 Nov 72, Bunker Papers, FAIM/IR; Memo, Haig for the President, 12 Dec 72, sub: Vietnam Negotiations, Kissinger files, NP.

10. Msg, Kissinger HAKTO 13 to the President, 5 Dec 72; Howe Chron, NP.

11. Msg, the President to Kissinger, TOHAK 71, 6 Dec 72, HAK Paris Trip, NP.

12. Nixon, handwritten comment on Memo, Haig for the President, 12 Dec 72, Memos to Pres, NP; Msg, Haig to Col Guay, 14 Dec 72, Camp David files, NP; quote, Memo, Haig for Kissinger, 13 Dec 72, sub: Items to Discuss with the President's Meeting at 10:00 A.M., December 14, HAK Paris Trip, NP.

13. Kissinger, *The White House Years,* pp. 1448–49; Msg, State 227604 to Saigon, 16 Dec 72, Howe Chron, NP.

14. This section is based on James R. McCarthy and George B. Allison, *Linebacker II: A View from the Rock* (Maxwell Air Force Base, Ala.: Air War College, 1979); and Mark Clodfelter, *The Limits of Air Power* (New York: Free Press, 1989), pp. 184–202.

15. [AP-48 and AP-68,] 18 Dec 72, Howe Chron, NP; Rudy Abramson, "Bombing of

North Resumed by U.S.," *Los Angeles Times,* 19 Dec 72; Joseph Fried, "New Raids on Hanoi Called 'Devastating' by Red Radio," *New York Daily News,* 19 Dec 72; George C. Wilson, "Officials Split on Bombing," *Washington Post,* 21 Dec 72.

16. News Summary, 19 Dec 72, NP.

17. Memo of Conversation, Nixon, Rogers et al., 4 Jan 73, Memcons, NP; Memo, Les Janka for Ronald Ziegler, 22 Dec 72, sub: Janka Guidance for Thursday, Guidance, NP; Memo, Situation Room for Kissinger, 2 Jan 73, HAK's Noon and Evening Notes, NP.

18. Martin F. Herz, *The Prestige Press and the Christmas Bombing* (Washington, D.C.: Ethics and Public Policy Center, 1980), p. 25.

19. Dana Adams Schmidt, "'Terror Raids' by U.S. Denied," *Christian Science Monitor,* 28 Dec 72; [UPI-075 and UPI-076,] 2 Jan 72, CMH.

20. "Terror from the Skies," *New York Times,* 22 Dec 72; "The Slaughter Resumed," *Boston Globe,* 27 Dec 72.

21. "David Lawrence," *Washington Star,* 29 Dec 72; "Why Can't the United States Be Truthful About Bombing?" *Philadelphia Inquirer,* 4 Jan 73.

22. Malcolm Browne, "Hanoi's People Still Curious and Likable," *New York Times,* 31 Mar 73; Memo, Situation Room for Kissinger, 9 Jan 73, HAK's Noon and Evening Notes, NP.

23. Drew Middleton, "Hanoi Films Show No 'Carpet-Bombing,'" *New York Times,* 2 May 72; "Cambodian Peril Is Discounted by Pentagon," *Washington Post,* 5 Apr 72.

24. Harris, *The Anguish of Change,* p. 78.

25. Msg, Kissinger WH 3001 to Bunker relaying a message from the President to Thieu, 4 Jan 73, Backchannel Messages, NP.

26. Msg, WH 3050, Kissinger to Bunker relaying a letter to Thieu, 17 Jan 73, Backchannel Messages, NP; Kissinger, *The White House Years,* p. 1466.

27. Msg, WH 3050, Kissinger to Bunker, 17 Jan 73.

28. Msgs, Kissinger WH 3068 to Bunker, 18 Jan 73, Backchannel Messages NP; Msg, Haig 301 to Kissinger, 19 Dec 72, ToHaig/HaigTo, NP; Kissinger, *The White House Years,* p. 1470.

29. Msg, Scowcroft TOHAK 45 to Kissinger, 23 Jan 73, Camp David Cables, NP.

30. Ltr, Col Robert L. Burke to the author, 27 Jun 90, CMH.

31. Memo, Situation Room for Kissinger, 31 Jan 73, HAK's Noon and Evening Notes, NP.

32. Interv, author with Maj Gen George Hayes, 21 Apr 74, CMH.

33. Interv, author with Jerry Friedheim, 3 Oct 86, CMH.

Index